8/08

WHY THE HUMANITIES MATTER

A Commonsense Approach

FREDERICK LUIS ALDAMA

UNIVERSITY OF TEXAS PRESS

Austin

Requests for permission to reproduce material from
this work should be sent to:
Permissions
University of Texas Press
P.O. Box 7819
Austin, TX 78713-7819
www.utexas.edu/utpress/about/bpermission.html

⊗ The paper used in this book meets the minimum requirements of
ANSI/NISO Z39.48-1992 (R1997) (Permanence of Paper).

Library of Congress Cataloging-in-Publication Data

Aldama, Frederick Luis, 1969–
  Why the humanities matter : a commonsense approach / Frederick
Luis Aldama. — 1st ed.
      p.   cm.
  Includes bibliographical references (p.   ) and index.
  ISBN 978-0-292-71798-5 (cl. : alk. paper)
    1. Postmodernism.   2. Philosophy, Modern—20th century.
3. Philosophy, Modern—21st century.   I. Title.
  B831.2.A43   2008
  001.3--dc22

                                                          2008007807

For those students who keep me on tiptoes,
those oh-so-smart and generous colleagues at OSU,
and to precious Mei-Mei Bruno, Anna, and Corina Isabel.

CONTENTS

INTRODUCTION

A New Humanism

In *Enemies of the Enlightenment* Darrin McMahon details the witch-hunt-like hysteria fanned by eighteenth-century French obscurantist clergy, aristocrats, Sorbonne-censoring *penseurs,* and other representatives of the ancien régime challenged by a progressive generation of thinkers and writers (*les philosophes*) who argued that reason, truth, and knowledge are universal pursuits based on universal human faculties. My intellectual and political interests are not confined within the eighteenth-century French worldview or, more generally, within the European Enlightenment, a fascinating yet veritable mélange of progressive and reactionary figures and outlooks. However, McMahon's scholarly reconstruction of the struggle of obscurantism against scientifically oriented thought in France is timely because that struggle has found new expressions in the academy and society, especially in the past thirty years or so, in America and also in some rather unexpected places.

For me to bear this statement out, I ask for some anecdotal indulgence. Invited to give a lecture on diasporic literature at a university in Switzerland, I suggested that we begin to look past poststructuralist paradigms in our analysis of Latin American, U.S. ethnic, and South Asian postcolonial literature and move forward to the use of tools provided by narratology and cognitive science—not exclusively, though centrally—to explore how authors creatively reframe identities and experiences that are located within postcolonial literary traditions and engage readers belonging not only to those traditions but also to many other, quite different ones. In this context, I suggested too that the study of postcolonial literature would find it conceptually useful (and scientifically interesting) to proceed within a world literature paradigm. I proposed that we keep in mind that literary analysis is as capacious as literature itself in that it may contain all kinds of approaches and evaluations, including, of course, political assessments; but no matter how much meaning and performative theories may be stretched or curtailed on a Procrustean bed, a work of fiction, a book review, or a literary theory dealing with politics can never become the same animal as an organized, actual doing of politics. (For instance, Louis-Ferdinand Céline's or Paul de Man's wartime pro-Nazi and anti-Semitic articles drew their efficaciousness not from themselves but from the social, political, economic, and military barbarism they were supporting as it was spreading and vanquishing along with the deployment of Hitler's, Mussolini's, and Hirohito's troops.) Also, I indicated that the self is not a conceptual construct designed on a blank slate, but a material agency capable of modifying reality and being modified by it in specific circumstances located in time and space. I therefore suggested that the approach I advocate offers interesting means for the advancement of our literary and humanistic endeavors because it is based on hypotheses that are susceptible to empirical verification or refutation and it allows for true research programs. Therefore, I reminded my audience that history is paramount for us. Cosmology, physics, molecular biology, genetics, paleontology, psychology, sociology, economics, history, and most other scientific disciplines deal with time, change, and evolution and are thus in a strict sense historical disciplines. In the case of the human subject and of humanity as a whole, all sciences show that humans are inseparably both the products and the shapers of their bio-social-psychological-historical existence. Following many others before me, I made evident that it is scientifically rewarding to acknowledge the fact that since the ancient division of society into antagonistic social classes (masters and slaves, for instance), the struggle against oppression and exploitation has never ceased.

Today, such a division takes the specifically historical form of a system of class rule based on the private ownership of the main means of production (held by a tiny minority of families) and the exploitation of the vast majority of the planet's inhabitants. Because of the barbarism this system increasingly generates (the gigantic slaughters of two world wars, Hiroshima and Nagasaki, Korea, Vietnam, Cambodia, Yugoslavia, Rwanda, Iraq are but a few of its manifestations), the very survival of the human race is at stake, and humankind must continue the struggle to achieve a classless society, that is, a society in which the world's population is free from oppression and exploitation because all wealth is no longer produced, distributed, exchanged, and consumed according to the ever-insatiable profit-making and capital-accumulation prerequisites of capitalist society. I thus recalled that while all humans share a cognitive and emotive architecture that emerged even before we began our journey as *Homo sapiens sapiens,* each member of our species is unique in the way she uses this universal endowment as well as in how she participates in the transformation of nature and society. There are certainly genetic and psychological factors involved in the love of cruelty and violence by some, but the evidence shows that those proclivities become actions most frequently in social environments that encourage them. I think of today's massive violations of the rights of immigrants, the massive detentions of citizens or aliens—indefinitely, without any due process, right to counsel, or human rights protections—the prescribed use of torture, and the attacks against key constitutional rights, including the right to abortion, the right to vote and to have votes fairly counted, the right to medical care, and the right to a secular and scientific education. Last, I suggested that the approach I advocate is, all in all, beneficial to literary studies and to the humanities in general because it does not require reliance on "gurus" or "master thinkers." I mentioned the findings in the work of Patrick Colm Hogan, David Herman, James Phelan, H. Porter Abbott, Lisa Zunshine, and Kenan Malik, among many others, to show what direction this research is taking today.

This is not the place to enter into particulars. My examples showed, to state it here in its most abstract terms, how postcolonial literature draws its readers into new puzzles—cognitive webs and labyrinths they must negotiate—as well as new forms of personal and social empathy—emotional proximity or distance with respect to the many events, situations, mores, and cultural and individual traits so inadequately summarized by the words *difference* and *other.* Mostly, the talk fell flat. Several scholars in the audience declared the subject and the world socially constructed and indeterminable; others said my approach was tainted by an epistemology of Western essentialism; one acknowledged the importance of a materialist grounding to postcolonial scholarship, attaching to it a "new humanism."

In this book I offer above all a critical view of issues that concern the humanities. And while each chapter deals with specific and delimited questions and problems, making it possible to read them in any order, the book is conceived as a whole. Arguments and findings in one chapter form a chain with discussions in another, and so on. Thus whether a chapter aims to think through the problems of translation, justice, music, literature, or the role of the scholar in society, to name but a few, the result is a prism of analyses and reasons that holds together by the materialist and humanist light shed on each and all.

Disciplinary demarcations are necessary for pedagogical reasons. But they do not mirror reality. Ours is an interconnected and ever-changing world—a supersystem composed of interconnected subsystems of various kinds (physical, cultural, social, and so on) that possess their own peculiar properties and laws. And so, just as nothing in our society is isolated, so these chapters are linked, making up a whole that aims to explore as deeply as possible many of the activities we spin out of ourselves to transform a reality that exists independent of our creating and that in turn shapes us and our subsequent activities. This book keeps centrally in mind, then, not only the fact that in our society nothing is isolated, but also that in our odyssey as *Homo sapiens sapiens* we have been evolving a self able to refine, revise, and create anew all variety of cultural phenomena and a capacity to enjoy them. This book keeps centrally in mind that we are all situated in history. We are all a part of history. We all make history. We are all made by the historical conditions we create.

This book is a formal attempt to move away from the erstwhile free-for-all construction and consumption of notions that see "truth" as "something that must be created" (Friedrich Nietzsche) and the study of the world as "eternal recurrence" (Nietzsche). It is to propose that objectivity and reasoned argument can help to show how arguments used to justify racism, sexism, and class exploitation are specious. As such, my book does not take the position that the material realm is unobservable; that science is de facto bad; that it is the root cause of capitalist enslavement or an appendage to patriarchal power or both. Rather, while science is not perfect in its measurements, it has allowed us to understand more clearly how certain aspects of reality work. We would not get on a plane and fly across the country if this were not so. Not all our ideas about the world are fictions. Indeed, it is because of our building and revising of verifiable facts that we can better understand the earth's history and the evolution of life as well as the economics of capitalism—a system based on profit (surplus value) residing in the use of labor power by the private owners of the means of production.

Indeed, scientific investigation works to eliminate, as Adam Katz remarks, "as many false paths as possible" (24) and to demystify "obscurantist ideological generalities" (25). Our failure to defend a materialist-based politics—instead of pursuing a "politics" of dismantling reason and causality—will result in a loss of any possibility of using science to open "spaces previously closed to scrutiny" (25). If there is no truth—no content and no meaning of subjectivity and only its effects—then, as Katz writes, "experience and interpretations of experience can . . . no longer be seen as either legitimating existing social relations due to their obviousness or naturalness . . . or as providing the kinds of knowledges necessary for emancipatory movements seeking structural transformations" (65). Hence, the general aim of this book is to promote methods and approaches that make a difference and that advance our knowledge of the world.

My book grows out of a restless concern with those who declare that my generation has arrived just as the world is dying: at the end of history, the end of art, ideology, science, the entirety of Western metaphysical thought and philosophy, the end of social classes and class warfare, the end, even, of social reality. To mark this end, scholars of all walks of life— from Latin American, Chicano/Latino, and postcolonial cultural studies scholars, translation theorists, to the high priests of poststructuralism— seem to be dishing out healthy servings of a philosophical Idealism that lead only to endless speculation.

In response, I have written this book, which takes a materialist approach to the self and all the things we spin out of our selves in our transformation of nature—a nature that in turn transforms us. Each chapter treats a subject to enliven critical debate and explore productive new directions of study. Each is an attempt to answer as completely as possible the questions raised by my readings and by students I encounter year after year in my teaching who are hungry to know how the world works. Among the topics the chapters explore are the following: What is music? What is film? What is literature? What are we reading when we read a translation? Is translation nation? How does translation work? What is this thing called modernity? What is language? What is culture? What do cultural phenomenon do in the world? What is the nation? What is the subject? What is justice? What is the role of the scholar/ intellectual in the classroom and in society at large? Each of the fourteen chapters puts one such topic under the microscope to understand it as fully as possible.

Rather than give an overview of each chapter, as is the custom, I ask instead that you imagine the book *in toto* as a Venn diagram composed of a series of sets that overlap and give shape to the individual chapters. The book aims to show clearly to scholars, students, and curious readers alike that there are distinctions that make a difference when we talk about ideas, culture, history, and society; that each matters, but in significantly different ways, in our shaping of the material, cultural, and social conditions that make up present and future reality. In its materialist, humanist, anti-Idealist thrust there is a commitment to clarifying the correspondence between our assertions and reality. The book is committed to upholding the achievements humanity has achieved in its odyssey and to showing that the material and social conditions of the future lie in the labors, struggles, and accomplishments of peoples worldwide. It is also an affirmation of those hardworking, faithful, time-honored, and much-regretted concepts of truth, good, and beauty and of the other concepts and categories, such as time, space, substance, quantity, quality, relation, position, possession, action, and passion.

ONE

SELF, IDENTITY, AND IDEAS

INTRODUCTION

I begin at the beginning: what constitutes the self? Of course, I'm not the first to ask this, nor will I be the last. However, I begin with this seemingly limitless domain of inquiry—approached from so many disciplinary angles, such as history, philosophy, political science, sociology, economics, linguistics, biology, physics, chemistry—because when all is said and done, all of the chapters that make up this book wind back to the many cultural webs we spin out of our selves in the transformation of (our) nature.

In this chapter I will first outline several of the main critical threads that have informed various approaches to the understanding of the self. I will then turn to a discussion of the importance of taking into account the historical and social as well as the biological dimension in the deepening of an understanding of what constitutes the self. I will explore not only the significance of neuro- and cognitive science research on the brain, but also the importance of how the individual, how the higher-minded self (brain + qualia) is always social; from birth to death we are at once biological and social creatures.

From time immemorial, questions of what makes up human consciousness or self-awareness—the uniqueness of the human self—have led to all variety of humanistic and scientific method and approach. We see, for instance, a privileging of the mind (ideas) over the material world (body) whereby mental activities are distinguished from (and set above) physical acts and an objective nature out there (René Descartes). There is a subjectivism whereby transcendental categories, or predetermined mental structures, control experience (Immanuel Kant). There is also the reduction of the world to ideas (George Berkeley) as well as the total denial of any evidence of the existence of the mind (brain) and body or anything beyond direct experience (David Hume).[1] One way or another, such formulations of the self have gravitated around the notion that we are separately bodies (matter) and souls; such formulations consider that in our everyday existence there is a distinction and separation between the executive (brain), an eternal spirit (mind), and the body.

Let me explore briefly a case in point: Descartes's *Meditations*. Here we see an attempt to provide a more solid foundation to the folk-psychology belief in the existence of two ontologically different and in-dependent entities: mind (soul) and body (matter). The grounding of this foundational separation led Descartes (1) to give philosophical expres-sion and logical rigor to a Platonist innatism (or theory of ideas) as well as to legitimate the contemporary dogma of the church; (2) to give philo-sophical expression to a merchant-class worldview (and the new rulers of society) whereby the individual is the self-enclosed center of knowledge and of legal and economic accountability; (3) to give expression to that entity that fills up the space between the mind versus body duality: God. The mind and body are totally separate and totally different in nature; only through the pineal gland (as he called it) do the body and mind interact. He grounds his epistemology in the individual as an atomic, separate, distinct entity, in contact with God, placing the self outside of society; all of society is bracketed, and the self is simply an aggregate of, say, Robinson Crusoes. Descartes's dualistic conception of mind versus body brings together and blesses all at once the church, logic, science, and individualism.[2]

We can add to Descartes's dualism Kant's transcendental argument, which weaves itself into many of the explorations and formulations of the self, even in several of today's research programs, including those within mathematics, linguistics, and the hard sciences generally. There is a relativism at work in Kant's concept of knowledge as determined by subjective experience and sensation and where forms of intuition and a priori truths reside in the mind. If the mind constructs the world, then, as Leonard Jackson sums up, it "makes no sense to talk of a world exist-ing independently of any point of view" (*The Dematerialisation of Karl Marx* 40). We are determined by our subjective perspective of the world. (While the approach and method differ, this ultimately takes us to the kind of relativism of B. F. Skinner's blank slate and the Sapir-Whorf lin-guistic hypothesis whereby culture (among other things) determines everything.)[3]

Whether in opposition or to further entrench, such relativist/subjectivist formulations inform the hypotheses and explorations of the self in many of the research programs of today's physical sciences, mathematics, linguistics, and the humanities generally. Chomsky has been using mathematics and linguistics to identify our innate modular faculty, like a bodily organ, to possess language and to have this language that one possesses grow. Just as we have genes that will propel the formation of the kidney, the heart, and so on, so we have a language organ. However, even here we encounter two problems that connect back to the mind/body split. Chomsky's idea of a language organ fits in with Jerry Fodor's modularity hypothesis that the brain is not like a general computer or any other multipurpose learning device (the reward/punishment system seen in, for instance, the behaviorist approach). It is composed of many kinds of specialized modules—a language module, a math module, an intuitive biology module, a mental map module, and so on—that work individually and also in a unified way; each module has a specific function and at the same time works simultaneously with all the other modules. Even in Chomsky we see a certain Cartesian influence. While he maintains that there are questions we can ask and even find answers to concerning the self, there are questions and problems posed that will forever remain "mysteries" because we as humans are not endowed with the necessary cognitive equipment to explore and find answers to such questions. Chomsky's default position: even if we can understand the chemical/neuronal workings of the brain, we can never know or quantify the sensations and feelings—the qualia of the mind—that are produced by the activity of the brain.

Chomsky follows the Cartesian split of mind from brain (as do others, like Colin McGinn, for instance), but others like Antonio Damasio consider the brain and mind one. In turning to the advances made in mirror neuron systems at work in the brain—that "actual vision perceptions correspond to external objects" ("Minding the Body" 21)—Damasio confirms that the brain is in a constant state of knowledge, so to speak, about the functioning of the body; the brain is constantly registering the body when we feel cold, pain, or tiredness, and all these feelings and sensations can appear as representations—as conscious events—but for the most part, we are not conscious of a whole series of our body's functions. As Damasio argues, the only part of our body whose functioning we don't have a representation of is the brain in its many manifestations; I can see something like a picture and be aware of the fact that my brain is registering, say, the red pigment in the picture, but I don't actually feel the

3

brain working. That is, the brain can have a perception and representation of the body and its functioning at any given moment. I can feel pain and at the same time feel the representation of pain, or grief and the representation of grief. By basing myself on these experiences in my body, I can extrapolate and, say, *read* feelings and thoughts and body functions in other people. I can ascribe to other people the same thoughts, feelings, representations I have experienced. For Damasio, then, there is not a split of mind and brain (body); they exist in a continual loop-back system.

There is always a mixture of the old with the new in discussions about approaches to the self. We see how such mixtures (scientific and mysterian) survive today in the many versions of the Cartesian dualism present in the sciences and humanities. Of course, there are certain technological limits that might not allow us to interpret and give a rational explanation of the self and world today. Aristotle, G. W. F. Hegel, and Karl Marx never doubted that their knowledge was necessarily partial, but partial because of the limitations of their times, not because the world was somehow unknowable. That is to say, we can know better what constitutes the self (mind, body, and brain) if we embrace a materialist ontology and a realist epistemology by avoiding mysterian mind/body splits and a relativism born of a perspectivism and philosophical idealism. Verifiable information and commonsense hypotheses can provide the raw material needed for us to pour a solid foundation for the building of an understanding of what constitutes the self.

As a result of the massive advances in science (biochemistry, genetics, neuro- and cognitive science, linguistics, evolutionary psychology) and the progress made in sociology and history, we can begin to study the self in a way that shuns older and contemporary behavioral and social constructionist (blank slate) paradigms. The self begins ab ovo and ends with death; it depends on the environment (sensory stimulation) and the functional and structural organization of the brain. It is a self that is always at once social and biological. It is our ability, as Bruce E. Wexler writes, "to shape the environment that in turn shapes our brains that has allowed human adaptability and capability to develop at a much faster rate than is possible through alteration of the genetic code itself. This transgenerational shaping of brain function through culture also means that processes that govern the evolution of societies and cultures have a great influence on how our individual brains and minds work" (*Brain and Culture* 3–4).

Let me take a further step back. At first glance, the notion of the self implies the notion of individuality. At the most basic level, this means that the self is a bounded, living organism that envelops billions of bounded cells. At this most basic level, the self is that body which distinguishes between what is *in* and what is *out*. This separate and bounded body is a first level of both sameness (our species' specific, universally shared biological blueprint that maintains a functioning internal state) and difference (me as bounded entity that is different from all that's apart from me).

Though it has yet to map the brain's complex biochemical, neuronal, and affective processes completely, scientific research on the brain can help us refine this initially crude formulation of the self. Its advances have provided a solid, material basis for understanding the self's constitution and function.[4] I think here of the scientifically grounded and testable hypotheses formulated by those scholars included in *The Self from Soul to Brain*. Scholars and scientists such as Antonio Damasio, Giacomo Rizzolatti, Jacek Debiec, V. S. Ramachandran, and Joseph E. LeDoux, for instance, further establish how the brain's total cognitive and affective processes (the neuronal, synaptic, and biochemical activity that allows for the selection, storing, and retrieval of memory and emotion) constitute the self. This and other such research identifies the importance of the brain/body's necessary engagement with objects and organisms other than itself both at the cellular (metabolic regulation and basic learned response mechanisms) and at the more general social level; the self is the result of the complete workings of hardwired activity in the brain and simultaneously the result of engagement with that outside of itself. As Derek Sankey sums up, "Neurologically, we need other selves in order to become truly our 'self.' For this to occur, brains must first interact with one another in interactive and reciprocal dialogue, and second, each brain must have the ability to model the presumed state of the other brain with which it is in communication" ("The neuronal, synaptic self" 176–177). That is to say, the self is always biological and social; theorizing the self is thus not the result of brain processes in isolation from others (other brains). This is why, as I'll develop at various other junctures throughout this book, memory (social and individual), empathy, Theory of Mind capacity (to hypothesize what other minds are thinking and what they are thinking about what you are thinking), and emotions generally (anger, disgust, fear, joy, sadness, and surprise) are so central to a healthy and full constitution of the self.

Our individual brain/body's engagement with the world leads to different behaviors and habits unique to each one of us; this is what we commonly call personality. Morphological and phenotypical variation aside, this is why every person we encounter is different to an infinite degree, as each of us can behave and subscribe to ideas in an infinite number of ways. I don't mean to posit that personality (individual behavior, opinion, and so on) is a phenomenological manifestation of the self, but rather that it results from that cluster of traits (good or bad, and so on) that constitute the self of the person.

Although there are many differences (personality traits) from person to person, there is much that remains stable and the same in the organic blueprint of the self. We are individual, unique, and changing (even at the cellular level), but we are also biologically and socially constant. That we are predictable provides practical everyday advantages. If we were to behave in unpredictable and inconsistent ways, we would face some serious survival problems. Would we risk driving a car if we couldn't predict the behavior of others? So, while we might experience personal epiphanies and transformations of opinion or might change chameleonlike within different social spheres (the way I act at work is not the same as at home) such transformations don't alter fundamentally the blueprint of our biogenetic (cognitive and neural) self. Stability at the social and biochemical level supersedes individually willed self-transformations.

The self experiences constancy in change. In *The Feeling of What Happens* Damasio further elaborates, identifying the interaction between a "core self" that is a "transient entity [that is ceaselessly] re-created for each and every object with which the brain interacts" (17) and the "autobiographical self" that is "a nontransient collection of unique facts and ways of being which characterize a person" (17). In *Homo sapiens sapiens,* both core and autobiographical selves work seamlessly as one self as a result of our higher order-consciousness, which is in turn formed by our engagement with the social; that is, our sense of a coherent narrative unit as both ceaselessly regenerative and bounded as a self-reflexive (acting) agent in a past, present, future world.

For our discussion of the human self (core, autobiographical, and higher consciousness) to mean anything, it must be distinguishable from everything else. Simply identifying it as different doesn't make the self *a self,* so we must make a distinction between the self and that which is not the self that matters. For example, we can distinguish the chemical property of oxygen from that of, say, hydrogen, but we don't refer to oxygen or hydrogen as having a self. That is, in understanding what constitutes the self we must focus on how its difference makes a difference.[5] Thus, we must take into account not just distinctiveness and separation (isolation), but in the case of the human self, the notion of agency and responsibility. The action of, say, bacteria that causes another organism like ours to have a digestive problem is not an action with agency; hence, we never refer to the "self of a bacterium" because while it acts, its actions lack the component of agency and responsibility central to the constitution of the human self. When we do identify an amoeba as a pathological agent for dysentery we use the word in a technical sense that excludes any attribution of moral responsibility: No amoeba will be condemned in a court of law for causing dysentery.

Agency and responsibility are the differences that make a difference in determining the constitution of the human self. In the concluding essay to *The Self from Soul to Brain* Jacek Debiec and Joseph E. LeDoux have identified this central property not only as an adaptive function that arises out of our being social animals but that gives rise to higher-order consciousness that becomes our guide to "authorship of action"— and "authorship of emotion" (309). They elaborate, "The person who feels well for action typically then feels responsibility for that action, and so will also be susceptible to moral emotions such as pride or guilt depending on the action's effects" (309). Our self is biologically constituted and it has agency (responsibility) and the capacity for knowledge of self. So while our organic biochemical makeup differs from other "minded organisms" that regulate life functions in response to the outside world, what makes a difference is how our biological organism develops necessarily within the social.

Yes, our self is grounded in our organism's specific biological, physical, and chemical components. However, the way these elements work together determines the engagement (and sense of belonging) with the material (physical, chemical, biological) and social world. Without appropriate and adequate neural stimulation, gene expression doesn't occur, and so those elements that constitute extended or higher-order conscious selves don't develop. This is why child-rearing practices have much in common cross-culturally: all seek to create social environments that will most effectively trigger cognitive and emotive responses to allow for the healthy development of a sense of higher functioning self (self-reflexive, responsible, and so on). Without stimulus reinforcement and other conditioning responses (at the neuronal level), necessary gene expression would not occur; the growth of synaptic connections necessary for learning, for example, might not develop. When the thirteen-year-old

Genie was discovered naked in a closet hidden away by her mentally disturbed parents, she had been almost completely deprived of language and motor simulation. She never recovered from this deprivation and never acquired motor-driven skills necessary for a healthy life. (See R. Rymer's *Genie: An Abused Child's Flight from Silence*.) Likewise, the self of the person who suffers from chronic depression might experience a diminished will to live; the biochemical and the social interact in such a way as to create a less than vital experience and engagement with the world. (See Louis Cozolino's *The Neuroscience of Human Relationships*.)

Do schizophrenics and people like them, whose biological functions do not allow for a sense of agency and responsibility, lack a self? This is not so much an ethical or ontological question as a question of the presence or not of a higher-consciousness self. Organisms that have a basic "mental *concern* over the organism's own life" (Damasio 25) in their regulation of metabolism and conditioned learning exhibit what Damasio identifies as "core consciousness"; we might identify this as a protean self where the organism is aware of the absolute "now" of itself only in the absolute now of time and space. While this might be the case in schizophrenics (and other nonnormal functioning people), this is not the normal functioning, evolutionarily speaking, of *Homo sapiens sapiens*. Our organism's normal functioning is not that of a "minded organism" (see Damasio), but rather that which includes the full development of cognitive modules such as language, memory, and reason that make up our higher-consciousness self—a self aware of itself in a present, past, and future as well as with an awareness of self-agency within a world beyond its boundaries (our imaginative capacity). It is a self that has developed a capacity for imagining (world making), grammar, memory, empathy (that amplification of feeling for those separate from us), and to create maps of its own maps (as delineated in these pages, even).[6] Our organism's normal functioning self is of a higher order; that those whose biological hardwiring or social development has precluded this possibility doesn't mean a lack of self, simply a lack of this higher-order self. It is this difference that makes a difference between us and other organisms as well as between those selves functioning as per a healthy evolutionary (reproductive) trajectory and those selves that have been left behind in the adaptive order of things.

As discussed, we are both a "basic-minded" (our habitual and "unconscious" biological functions like homeostatic regulation, metabolism, breathing, and so on) and a "higher-minded" organism (self-reflexive, imaginative, responsible, and so on). We have evolved a protean-minded self that regulates and monitors everyday biological functions and that is an emanation of the body much like urine and mucus, as well as a higher-minded self that is the product of our engagement with the material and social world.

I will now turn to a discussion of those differences that make a difference in terms of how our higher-minded self develops in the social.

One way or another, many fashionable formulations of the self (subject/identity) theorize it as boundaryless (disembodied) and/or self-written/written upon; one way or another, they formulate the self as either willed or written into existence and/or as occupying all that exists in the universe. According to the basic principle of discernibility, this leads us nowhere in further refining our understanding of the self. Rather, as I've begun to formulate, the human-minded self is distinguishable from other organic and nonorganic entities, and it is so not just biologically (as discussed above), but because of this important and necessary element of the social. The human self that for one reason or another is unable to have a healthy engagement with the social never develops what I've identified as a higher-minded self. We don't need to look to the example of people with schizophrenia to see this. We know from Jean Piaget's work with children that those who are precluded from healthy social patterning (parenting, reward/punishment systems of learning) fail to develop healthy neurochemical brain functions (memory and language) that in turn allow for the development of a higher-minded self. We saw this in the case of Genie (mentioned above) as well as in that of the earlier Caspar Hauser, who was also raised in complete isolation from the social world and who likewise never developed the necessary motor and symbolic skills that would allow him to develop a higher-minded self.

Of course, the mind/body's development of a higher-minded self begins much earlier in our development. We know from children conceived in countries where there is a shortage of food and basic health care that even before the child is born it has been deprived of the basic nutrients necessary for healthy biological development. It is our species' blueprint that determines that we can exist, develop, and evolve only as organisms intimately tied to other members of our species. Hence, in the case of the fetus developing in conditions of insufficient nourishment, the social has already influenced the biological architecture to such a degree that once the child is born, its development of self has been already marked by such

9

social conditions. So, while it is our organism's evolutionary strategy to develop a higher-minded self, the social conditions do not necessarily guarantee its formation.

Our higher-minded self is the healthy development and interplay between our biological makeup and our social engagement. The social is all that is man-made and all of nature that we transform according to our given needs and concepts of our time. Hence, the configurations of the social change not just from place to place (for example, the poor of Zimbabwe versus the rich of the United States), but also historically. The self is formed in history, beginning with our ancestors' first organization into social units. There is a difference between the self conceived, born, and developed in the twenty-first century and the preagricultural self formed ten centuries ago.[7] The self is not the same when free as it is when enslaved or when it exists in a feudal society. The self developed after the French Revolution swept away all remains of feudalism and the bourgeoisie rose to power is not the same self as that before the revolution. More generally, the self is not the same when living in a capitalist society, where economics of private property determine everyday movement or restrictions of movement.

As we transform the social, as we make history, we in turn transform the self. So, in discussing the self, we must also pay attention to its formation within the class struggle (to protect both one's individual and collective rights as worker and as owner of means of production). For example, the self is not the same today in the United States, where only 10 percent or less of the working class are unionized, as it was in the late nineteenth century. And because the modern self formed within the framework of the modern nation-state that, as a result of the working-class struggle, has had to guarantee rights and protections, to destroy this nation-state would be to destroy this self.[8] The self under the tyrannical dictatorship of an Adolf Hitler, a Francisco Franco, or an Augusto Pinochet, like the defenseless child raised by abusive parents, exists in a state of total subordination. Finally, the self of a person bound to Mexico nationally is not the same as that of an Anglo bound to the United States; nor is it the same for the Mexican crossing borders for gainful employment today as it was for the homebound Mexican of yesteryear.

The understanding of the self requires an understanding of the different ways that society has been organized in time and space. And each of these historical moments is shaped differently because of the different relations established between us in order to survive and develop as we metabolize nature for our survival; since the human being is part of nature, by transforming nature it transforms itself as nature. Moreover, we are unique in that our metabolizing of all of nature takes place necessarily in association with other members of the species: society. It is this metabolizing of nature within the time and place of the social that allows us to establish that the self is constituted biologically and materially (in time and space).

In understanding the self as formed in the social, we must further distinguish between society/culture and the nonhuman world. As a part of nature, we are capable of reflecting on all aspects of nature as well as of modifying all of nature that surrounds us. This transformation is achieved through our labor (work/practical activity) and drive to sustain and perpetuate ourselves to transform all the nature exterior to us: society and culture. Culture is the whole product of man's activities: language, cars, art, and bombs. The distinction between nature and culture is based on what is man-made and not man-made. However, all that is man-made is based on nature because man is a biological organism. This self-generating of man—that is, one part of nature—through his/her work produces what we call society and culture, society being the specific form in which this part of nature can self-generate itself by association with other members of the same self-generating part of nature.

In sum: society is simply the collective formed by individuals—humans—in order to be able to self-generate and self-reproduce. If man were not by necessity and therefore biologically hardwired to be gregarious; if man were an animal that had been hardwired to be isolated from the other animals, there would be no culture, no society, and no man. We can only accomplish our self-generation and reproduction as a species by forming collectives. That which separates man from other animals in the animal kingdom is its specific mode of existence; its specific mode of self-generation and reproduction that leads to the production of what we call culture and society. Just as the spider is inseparable from its web (the mode of existence that allows it to reproduce and eat and continue living) so, too, does man have to spin out culture and society to live. When talking about the self of humankind, then, we are also talking about nature.

That the self is materially (historically, socially, and biologically) constituted means that the very conception of humankind is that it is one fragment of nature. In order to subsist and to maintain our existence evolutionarily speaking, we self-generate and self-reproduce ourselves by producing society and culture. Just as spiders continue existing and reproducing themselves for hundreds of thousands of years by secreting webs, so, too, do humans secrete society and culture to survive.

We have nature and only nature. Within this nature we have differentiation in the way that living organisms perpetuate themselves. If we diagrammed this as a series of sets, nature would be the largest circle and within this circle we would have the circle of the animal kingdom (all living life from microbes to *Homo sapiens sapiens*), and within this smaller circle we would have mammals, and within the circle of mammals we would have humankind. All of these circles are included within the larger set: nature. Within this large set of living nature all living organisms manifest different ways of maintaining their existence (reproducing themselves) over time both individually and as a species. This is to say that the biological self is formed within the social that is a part of this larger set we identify as nature. This is what makes us unique and individual (social beings) as well as what makes us a complete set as individual members that form the same species.

Why talk about all of this? Much of the theoretical formulation of the self fashionable in the humanities today is devoid of a social materialist (historical) purview; many believe that the motor for historical shift is an abstracted movement from one idea to the next; others believe that a performative self can resist oppressive hegemonic master narratives. Rather, the human (higher-minded) self is a self as formed in a society that is itself formed in history, which has been in recent times formed by the class struggle. So even before the self is ethnic or gendered, it is formed in relation to the class struggle (that has guaranteed rights and laws opposite to the interests of a ruling class) within the framework of the modern nation-state. Thus, to understand today's self is to subordinate gender, race, sexuality, and ethnicity to an understanding of it as formed and developed within a capitalist society. It is also to see that capitalism is not a determined element of a natural (biologically determined) human self. It is to see it historically and as arising within these social conditions.

The question of the self and its identities is complex and yet very simple. When we speak of, say, Chicano selves, we identify aspects that make up an individually and socially constituted self. Here, however, when talking of the self and its identities, I want to sidestep formulations of the self as performative and in flux; to get to this point one must necessarily believe that everything that exists in the world is indeterminate.

Of course, as I've already discussed regarding our cellular and atomic constitution, nothing remains fixed and identical in the universe. However, this doesn't mean there isn't coherence and a sense of permanence. Not one single atom that made up my bounded self at the moment of writing this book will exist when it is finally in print, yet we can still identify me as Frederick Luis Aldama constantly. If there weren't a sense of coherence we wouldn't be able to refer to me as Frederick Luis Aldama, nor drive a car, nor study matter (the distinguishing between A and B in biology, physics, chemistry), nor use language and writing to pen a book such as this one. At this most basic level, then, we must be able to identify the difference between A and B not subjectively—as a notion that is invented and that depends on my existence—but objectively. Indeed, as Ramachandran sums up, it is our capacity "to plan open-ended scenarios and try out even improbable scenarios entirely in the mind by juggling images and symbols" (111), and our affiliative ability to holographically imagine ourselves as active agents doing things in the future and/or past that enable us to present ourselves to others as a coherent, predictable self with "certain stable attributes" (111).

Let me clarify further. For the human being to survive and to exchange information with the world (its vital function as a biological organism) it has to develop a sense of self. This development includes the forming of an awareness of the difference between its self and the rest of the world; as this sense of difference develops we also develop a purposeful and intentional sense of acquiring and giving back information directly to the world.[9] This world is constituted by all that exists outside of the human self; that is, if we were to disappear altogether as a species, rocks would still be rocks, and they would still be different from water, which would still be different from fire, and so on. The existence or disappearance of that outside the self doesn't depend on my existence nor on my higher-minded self making distinctions. Even at this most basic level of understanding, we know then that there is a material and objective basis to establishing differences and therefore to identity.

Following this principle, then, we can't assert that, for example, it is biology that determines, say, a Chicano identity. In the mapping of the human genome, we've determined genes for blood group, skin and eye color, and so on, and we've even been able to determine ancestry from such genetic information: the genetic composition of a Native blood type in North America corresponds to that of a group in Asia, and thus we can trace a line of descent for Native North Americans back to Asia. However, such a study doesn't alter the way the human race is characterized by a single genome that singularly characterizes our species and that first came out of Africa thousands of years ago. As Malik sums up in *The Meaning of Race,*

> Geneticists have shown that 85 per cent [of genetic variation] is between local populations or groups within what is considered to be a major race. A further 8 per cent of all genetic variation is between individuals within the same local population. Just 7 per cent of genetic variation is between major races. What this means is that genetic variation between one Englishman and another, or between one Jamaican and another, can be nearly as great as the differences between a 'typical' Englishman and a 'typical' Jamaican. Every population is highly variable and whatever external physical signs there may be—such as skin color—genetic features do not absolutely define one population and distinguish it from another. . . . Race exists only as a statistical correlation, not as an objective fact. The distinction we make between different races is not naturally given but is socially defined. (4–5)

Namely, subordinate to my identification as, say, Chicano (or right-handed with dark hair and of medium build) is my material, biological self as determined by genetic composition as a member of the human race.

Identities matter, of course. How they matter, however, varies greatly depending on whether we are talking about identities that have become socially instituted like ethnicity and gender or talking about the biological. From a nuts-and-bolts bioevolutionary perspective, the identity that makes a difference is sexual. Here, I mean sexual in the sense of sexual reproduction, not sexual preference. Even if my sexual preference might be for those of the same sex, if I choose to reproduce biologically, then I will necessarily have to involve (through in vitro fertilization, say) a member of the opposite sex. So, sexual identity—that which identifies a man as different from a woman in terms of differently evolved and functioning sexual organs—is an identity that makes a difference in the evolutionary scheme. To reproduce the species, we must have the exchange of XX and XY chromosomal information and subsequent mitosis, whether in sexual copulation or by other means. There is no way around this as biological fact; this is how evolution has taken place. It is a material reality that preexists human beings; it preexists society. In this sense, then, the sexual—overtly identified by physical differences that mark every individual member of *Homo sapiens sapiens*—is an elemental identification that, in the case of evolution, matters.

What does sexual (biological) identity mean on an everyday level? As already mentioned, it means that if one desires to be with those of the same sex as well as to reproduce biologically, one must contend with biological fact. It means that to declare, as some are wont to do, sexuality a performative construct neglects the biological material facts. It means that to replace "gender" for "sexuality" in an effort to emancipate women or to "trouble gender" by performing constructs of the feminine, changes little for ordinary people like a farmer in Mexico or a factory worker in the United States. Evolutionarily speaking, my identification as male doesn't matter; what matters is whether or not I function to reproduce the species. From an evolutionary perspective, sexual reproduction is the biological backbone to continued survival and development of the self.

What of identification of the self based on what sex we desire? Again, from an evolutionary point of view, we must strip down desire—the sexual drive—and understand its biological function. Human beings have built-in sexual instincts (sexual drive) like other animals (although ours is perennial and theirs seasonal) that include a corresponding excitation of sexual organs. Evolutionarily speaking, this excitation happens for the purpose of reproduction, and so a sexual drive has evolved that directs an attraction toward those of the opposite sex. Sexual drive, arousal, and this feeling of desire are parts of a very primitive biological mechanism that has evolved since our distant ancestors transcended the unicellular stage of cell reproduction. This doesn't mean that there is anything morally wrong when one desires someone of the same sex. It means simply that desire is not a difference that makes a difference in evolution and therefore in terms of the biologically constituted self.[10]

For human beings everywhere, to exist is to reproduce existence, not just biologically but socially. As already discussed, we exist and in our existence we transform nature, which process in turn transforms us. So while biological reproduction is the minimum condition for survival of the human species, this doesn't mean that how we have sex or who we desire, for example, is evolutionarily predetermined. What is predetermined is the machinery that we need in order to biologically reproduce.

As I've begun to establish, the social and biological are intimately intertwined in the development of the human self. It is for this reason that our feeling of freedom to make conscious choices is always a matter of the biological and the social working hand in hand.

Today we have arrived at a stage in our evolution where we have created social institutions (the census, for example) that identify us as Chicano, Caucasian, African American, Filipino, Native American, and so on. Ethnic identity is the product of our transformation of the social. We see this with the official census forms that determine demographics that in turn determine public and social policy. Within this context, we have established many ways of identifying social differences; some have led to the instituting of racist and homophobic exclusionary practices—one can say that those born in Mexico and their descendants will not have the right to sell their capacity to work, for example—and others that aim to reform such practices; within a capitalist system where exploitation and oppression are the rule, much political organizing and action have helped advance otherwise exploited groups of people. Take, for example, the effects of the working-class-based civil rights movement, which has led to Affirmative Action programs and the founding of scholarships by institutions like the Ford Foundation that award those who historically have suffered as a result of institutional discrimination, such as Alaska Natives, Black/African Americans, Mexican Americans (Chicanos), Puerto Ricans, Native American Indians, and Native Pacific Islanders. It has also opened doors for erstwhile socially discriminated against groups to finally have equal access to education.

Many literary and cultural critics have explored the race/class/gender nexus. And many do base their understanding in material fact. For example, the Chicana lesbian scholar Alicia Gaspar de Alba, sums up, "Sex and race are biologically determined, the genitalia and racial DNA with which we were born" (ix). For Gaspar de Alba, gender and ethnicity are socially constituted and only inflect the biological facts of our differently sexed bodies. As she suggests, we must identify ethnic and sexual preference categories precisely because they've become institutionalized; that is, to fight oppression and exploitation based on these socially instituted categories, we must necessarily make visible such categories.

At an even more basic and necessary level of self-identification, however, we must identify the self as it exists within today's society characterized by an economic system of capitalism: the making dependent of all peoples and all relations on the market for its most basic needs that require the bourgeoisie to maintain social order and conditions favorable for the accumulation of profit by means of exploitation. Class is thus a fundamental identification of self and an identification that makes a difference.

Namely, without identification of class, we can't identify that huge portion of society made dependent on this economic structure, which includes all exploited minorities: working class, women, gays, lesbians, Mexicans, and so on. It's what allowed women and gays, lesbians, and Chicanos historically to struggle effectively against institutionalized exploitation of women in the demand for equal pay, access to health care, and so on. A brief look at women's struggle to gain equal rights—the right to vote, to work, to hold property, to divorce, for example—demonstrates its concrete link to the workers' general movement. In the United States, we have the anarchist Emma Goldman and in Germany the suffragist Clara Zetkin. Women have had to organize themselves within the labor movement to demand not just job security, social security, and equal pay and health benefits, but also basics like day care centers.

Identity politics has become a projection of an expression of a very obscurantist, retrograde, reactionary way of thinking. Instead of isolating myself as a Chicano as per the identity politics formulation, I would do better acknowledging that I am one member of many who make up a collective experience of institutional discrimination and therefore need to organize to form their own political parties to struggle alongside all the other people who have a vested interest in overthrowing capitalism. While identity politics makes visible those who have become targets of institutionalized homophobic and racist policies, for social transformation to take place we must reach beyond our particular experiences to form solidarity with others who experience exploitation and oppression. For real transformation to take place, the struggle needs to be against capitalism. If we isolate our causes from one another, we simply supply capitalists with the weapons to bring about our own destruction. Cesar Chávez knew this when he helped form trade unions to fight to institutionalize equal pay for all members of the working class.

Just as social identification matters because we are a social animal, so too do ideas matter. For instance, whether or not one's boss thinks a person is lazy and/or stupid because he or she is Chicano will not change if one decides to wear a Che Guevara T-shirt to work. They will continue to be exploited until the individual organizes along with other individuals to create the massive material force necessary to transform the capitalist economic system that exploits the working class worldwide. Ideas only really matter when they materialize in the massive unification of millions of people that create the material force necessary for transformation of the policies of the dominant class. When I teach or write about literature and film this *may* encourage people in their struggles, but it cannot be said to cause them or that they determine their outcome. We must keep this in mind when analyzing cultural phenomena and when determining a real politics of social transformation.

Concepts are objective and true when they correspond to reality, in the same way that a map's adequacy is determined by its correspondence to a given territory, even when the features it picks out are selected according to particular purposes or interests. But in its philosophically idealist guise the "territory" has lost all objective existence and the "map" is but an illusion; the world is no longer that which is out there, whether I or the whole human race exist or not, it is what I and the society I live in "make" of it and say it is. It is "that" which is "constructed" by society or "conceived" by language, through language, within the limits of language at a certain time and place. Accordingly, ideas are arbitrary in the sense that their contents are determined not by an independently existing reality but by the kinds of expressions authorized by language and society, which ultimately means that there is no escape from totalitarianism.

CONCLUDING REMARKS

A turn to advances in cognitive- and neuroscience and evolutionary biology in understanding the self is meant to be reductionist to a point. That is, we must keep centrally in mind that everything we do is realized within society—therefore within certain social conditions: We are subjects that transform the world and that are in turn transformed by this changed world; and as such, we have evolved in ways that allow us to overcome our evolutionary heritage. In this sense, a reductionist project that only looks at a particular phenomenon as with the mirror neuron system will likewise only have a limited explanation of the self.

Malik reminds us that "human consciousness is not static or innate but is constantly recreated through changing social and historical circumstances" (224). That is to say, any mechanical formulation of what constitutes the self (human as object through which nature acts) must also see humans as social and historical beings—as humans constantly overcoming obstacles in the world and obstacles of our own evolutionary heritage within specific times and places.[11]

This brings me full circle back to a point that I began to give shape to at the beginning of this chapter: that the advancement of knowledge is *always* necessarily interdisciplinary.[12] From the point of view of episte-mology, each substance requires a cognitive methodology of its own; you will not be able to study the mirror neuron system with the methodology of, say, literary analysis. While each discipline requires its own tools of study, in the long run what we should seek is the knowledge of the whole. Therefore, the approach to the question of the self must look for ways to make these separate distinctive approaches more and more systematic and precise so that we can see more clearly how they are related and how together they shed brighter light on the subject of the self.

TWO

REVISITING DERRIDA, LACAN, AND FOUCAULT

INTRODUCTION

In the last chapter, I discussed briefly how, one way or another, a Cartesian and/or Kantian approach to the self and world leads to idealist and/or relativist epistemological dead-ends. In this chapter, I explore more generally how speculative and idealist formulations of language, knowledge, and the self inform much of the theory circulating in humanities departments today that seeks to identify positions of resistance and reclamation within the straightjacket of a so-called late capitalism. To do so, I discuss Sigmund Freud's metapyschological formulations— *The Ego and the Id* (hydraulic energies of the id, ego, and superego), *Beyond the Pleasure Principle* (the reality and pleasure principles), and *Civilization and its Discontents* (the sex and death drives)—which he never abandons and which find their way into the work of Jacques Derrida, Jacques Lacan, and Michel Foucault. After discussing Derrida, Lacan, and Foucault in detail, I explore how such speculative positions inform the textualist-idealism that suffuses scholarly method and approach in much of the humanities today.

In 1895 Freud wrote a manuscript (unfinished and unpublished) titled, "Project for a Scientific Psychology." In this work Freud began to formulate ideas regarding the foundations for a future neuroscience capable of explaining all major human conscious and unconscious processes by establishing correlates between brain and mind. His stated aim: "to furnish a psychology that shall be a natural science: that is, to represent psychical processes as quantitatively determinate states of specifiable material particles, thus rendering those processes perspicuous and free from contradiction" (87).

"Project for a Scientific Psychology" also contains *in nuce* Freud's "metapsychology"—a set of highly speculative theoretical directions he would in fact follow. It includes the hydraulic vocabulary (energy flows/discharges that can be channeled, diverted, and/or blocked)—that finds expression in *The Ego and the Id*. The basic formulation is as follows: the psyche is conceived of as a mechanistic "hydraulic mind"—a reservoir containing a psychic energy that can flow, be blocked and/or channeled, and that might assume various shapes and experience various transformations.[1] Given that all mental phenomena have their origin in the circulation and distribution of the psychic energy obtained from the instincts that generate it in order to satisfy bodily needs or impulses, it is the blocking of a quantum of energy stored in the body and experienced by the individual as tensions (pain or discomfort) that leads to neurosis. Since all the available psychic energy has an instinctual source, Freud concludes that the action of the instincts builds a sort of mental storage tank or original reservoir (the "id") from which psychic energy is drawn in order to form the two additional basic components ("agencies"): the "ego" and the "superego." The agencies affect one another in a variety of ways, and all possess mechanisms that operate automatically. Together they constitute the energy-distributing "psychical apparatus."[2] The accumulation of psychic energy causes pain or discomfort—its release or discharge produces pleasure—and so the sole function of the id is to divest itself of stimulation or energy and to seek pleasure.

For Freud, the id has no direct contact with the environment, does not recognize anything external to it, is innate, and expands through the mechanism of repression (operated by the ego). The id does not follow laws of reason, logic, or causality, knows no order and succession in time and space, and ignores all values and morality. The id obeys the "pleasure principle," seeking immediate gratification, fulfilling its wishes by imagination, fantasy, hallucinations, and dreams; and it depletes its store of energy if there are no mechanisms to restrain it from immediate discharge in the face of any and all internal or external tensions, excitations, disturbances, or stimulations. As is fairly commonly known, the most important restraining mechanism is the ego—a portion of the id that becomes a separate agency without severing all contact with the id; the ego is in charge of ensuring the survival of the individual and therefore of the species. In Freud's words, "The ego seeks to bring the influence of the external world to bear upon the id and its tendencies, and endeavors to substitute the reality principle for the pleasure principle which reigns unrestrictedly in the id. For the ego, perception plays the part which in the id falls to instinct. The ego represents what may be called reason and common sense, in contrast to the id, which contains the passions" (*The Ego and the Id* 19).[3] The third agency composing the psychic apparatus— the superego—is the last to appear. As Freud explains, it "is in fact the heir to the Oedipus complex and only arises after that complex has been disposed of" (*An Outline of Psycho-Analysis* 95).[4]

An understanding of the mind based on this metapsychological model is certainly creative—but it is also highly speculative.[5] This is odd considering that Freud expressed a deep interest in neuroscience-based research in 1895—an exciting time when such research was already well under way. Already by 1856, the year Freud was born, the German physician Otto Deiters identified dendrites and axons in nerve cells; a few years later, Ernst Brücke, Emile du Bois-Reymond, and Ewald Herring proved that nerves could be stimulated not only electrically, but also chemically. In "Project for a scientific psychology" Freud alludes to this research, stating that "the main substance of these new discoveries is that the nervous system consists of distinct and similarly constructed neurons, which have contact with one another through the medium of a foreign substance" (89). Two years after Freud wrote the "Project for a scientific psychology," the British neurophysiologist Charles Sherrington conducted experiments (for the Spanish historiographer Santiago Ramón y Cajal) to determine how signals traveled from one neuron to another; this led to the conclusion that the neurons were independent cells and did not form, as previously believed, a continuous network. In 1900, Sherrington further demonstrated that certain nerve cells could turn signals on and off.[6] (See Robert H. Biloler et al., *Neuroscience of the Mind on the Centennial of Freud's Project for a Scientific Psychology*, as well as Michael R. Trimble's *The Soul in the Brain*.)

While neuroscience research was certainly in the air, Freud nonetheless ultimately chose a more limited research agenda: to analyze a statistically insignificant number of patients' verbal reports of introspection.[7] He chose to appeal to his own experience as a way to test the reality of his patient's accounts; he chose to shun any measures of objective reality and instead focus on the unconscious mind's blurring of the distinction between fiction and truth: the patient's defensive barrier is not against real trauma in reality, but rather against imagined fantasies constructed in response to an experience of extreme excitation that is irreducible to objective reality. (See *The Complete Letters of Sigmund Freud to Wilhelm Fliess, 1877–1904*.) Moreover, all conscious, partly conscious, and unconscious mental activities become ultimately inaccessible, even in the psychoanalytic method of analyzing verbal reports of introspection.[8]

More and more we see Freud's metapsychology move away from the objective—the analytic as external to the subject—toward something always internal and subjective. In *Beyond the Pleasure Principle* (1920) he complicates his two-pronged psychic mechanism—the principle of reality and the principle of pleasure—by considering how we constantly rub up against and are driven by the principle of death. Given that the pleasure principle has traditionally been considered the main motor of the psychic mechanism, by introducing the death drive—a drive not governed by the pleasure principle and thus not accounted for in psychoanalysis—Freud seeks to account for our compulsion to repeat disagreeable experiences as well as to account for our universal tendency to return to an inorganic state. Despite our resistance to death in life, then, we are ruled by the death instinct. In *Civilization and its Discontents* (1929) he sums up his formulation presented in *Beyond the Pleasure Principle*: "I drew the conclusion that, besides the instinct to preserve living substance and to join it into ever larger units, there must exist another, contrary instinct seeking to dissolve those units and to bring them back to their primeval, inorganic state. That is to say, as well as Eros there was an instinct of death. The phenomena of life could be explained from the concurrent or mutually opposing action of these two instincts" (*Civilization* 77).

Given the massiveness of his domain of inquiry, Freud himself admits that he will never be able to provide objective proof of how the death drive is more of a foundational model than that of the libido when talking of the mind. In *Civilization and its Discontents* he discusses how the death drive expresses itself as aggressiveness and destruction on a planetary scale: "I think, the meaning of evolution of civilization is no longer obscure to us. It must present the struggle between Eros and Death, between the instinct of life and the instinct of destruction, as it works itself out in the human species" (82). Given that the death drive can be, as he states, "pressed into the service of Eros" by destroying that which is not itself (animate or inanimate), then the blockage of the death drive—or aggressiveness—can lead to self-destruction. For Freud, then, civilization "obtains mastery over the individual's dangerous desire for aggression by weakening and disarming it and by setting up an agency within him to watch over it, like a garrison in a conquered city" (84). As civilization develops, an ever-greater repression is necessary to redistribute instinctual energies of aggressiveness in socially beneficial ways. However, this sublimation and control of aggression comes at a price: discontent and neuroses. Freud's formula in a nutshell: Obedience to authority (external and internal) gives way to mounting neuroses and discontent and thus rebellion and destruction; this is then followed by obedience once again. This cyclical to-and-fro motion functions at the level of the individual, family, the nation, and humanity at large. Not only does a healthier functioning society require an outside threat to the individual, family, nation, for this aggressiveness not to be directed inward, but so too does it require the presence of the high priests, the therapists who can reduce to tolerable levels the suppression of instincts. Thus for Freud, "primitive man was better off," for they knew "no restrictions of instinct" (73).

With the problem of society identified as various biological energies clamoring for expression and/or sets of oppositions and instinctive forces, Freud's mechanistic hydraulic metapsychological model ultimately offers a rather pessimistic and tragically deterministic understanding of politics, economics, history, anthropology, and society.[9] (See Martin Wain's *Freud's Answer.*) It is this ad hoc deterministic theorizing (the self as only ever running in circles biting its own tail) and a formulation of the subject as detached from observable and real-world concerns (a fear of the masses and antirevolutionary stance) that one way or another inform the poststructural theories of Derrida, Lacan, and Foucault.

It is certainly the case that Derrida was less interested in employing Freud's metapsychological concepts and more interested in demonstrating their limitations. For example, rather than formulate a mind shaped by an ego, id, and superego, Derrida would rather conceive of the mind as the repetition and deferral of an origin or meaning or truth in language. Likewise, Freud's death and life principles are less energy flows and blockages that we can point to, and more the fact that Freud still aims to identify positively processes of the mind. In "To Speculate—on 'Freud'" Derrida at once affirms Freud's thinking outside a foundational metaphysics and at the same time critiques him for his participation within. For Derrida, there is no foundational ontology, only *différance*. So even Freud's speculations on the death and life drives make the mistake of naming positively what can only ever be, in Derrida's formulation, a trace of a deferral of an unnameable ontological play between presence and absence. Indeed what Freud failed to understand is that he himself exists in deferral between the life drive and death drive as subordinate to the drive toward the "proper name" (560); that psychoanalysis is that "which remains to be done, as the necessary return to the origin of and the condition for such a science"(560). Moreover, Derrida sees the death instinct and the failure of the proper to appropriate itself at work in Freud's writing of *Beyond the Pleasure Principle* while faced with his own mortality (deaths in the family and his own cancer). Derrida writes, "If the guilt is overlapped with the one whose death he lived as his own death, *to wit* the death of the other, of Ernst's younger brother as of his younger brother, Julius, one holds several (only) of the strings in the lace of murderous, mournful, jealous, and guilty identifications which entrap speculation, infinitely. But since the lace constrains speculation, it also constrains it with its rigorous stricture" (564). (See also Derrida's essay, "Freud and the Scene of Writing," collected in *Writing and Difference*.)

In spite of his critical stance, we see in Derrida's ideas an osmosis of Freud's antirationalist and idealist sensibility. On several occasions, he even declares himself to be writing through Freud ("Freud and the Scene of Writing"). For Freud, the mind is governed by instincts and is never clear to itself. We can never know the mind, we can only speculate about its blockages and flows. For Derrida, the mind only ever shows itself as a trace of the unconscious; it is only ever present as a trace of the effect of thought or a trace of the event in our memory after the event. Thus positivist concepts are out, and in their place we have "marks," "undecidables," "unities of simulacrum," and " 'false' verbal properties (nominal or semantic) that can no longer be included within a philosophical (binary) opposition" (*Positions* 43).

When Derrida deconstructs Freud in *The Post Card* and also in *Archive Fever*—the death instinct and failure of the proper become stand-ins for the self-destruction of psychoanalysis—we see yet another shared sensibility. For instance, in *Archive Fever* Derrida's concept of the archive that results from a traumatic breakdown in memory (it no longer has a limit) that can't be named, we see a similar gesture toward a faith in a psychoanalysis to come that Freud expresses in *Civilization and its Discontents*. Accordingly, if the trauma of the Holocaust can't be identified positively, we must simply wait for a future when the condition of the promise of psychoanalysis will disclose its true nature. This is probably why in Derrida's critique there is always a sense of an affirmation of Freud. So while Derrida has Freud sitting squarely within a positivist Western metaphysics, he also reads Freud's move away from scientific method and approach as sitting outside.

The structures of language are central to both Freud's and Derrida's formulation of the mind. For both, just as the unconscious surfaces in the gaps of the patient's verbal records—their texts—so too does the repetition of repressions and exclusions become visible as traces in the gaps of language. In *Speech and Phenomena* Derrida writes of the ego or consciousness as a "relation to nonpresence [that] neither befalls, surrounds, nor conceals the presence of the primordial impression; rather it makes possible its every renewed upsurge and virginity. However, it radically destroys any possibility of a simple self-identity. And this holds in the depth for the constituting flux itself" (66). The ego or consciousness is never transparent—nameable, graspable—it is always "as absolute specter of its own psychic self—to be but a theoretical image and metaphor" (11). Whether theorized as trace or as a patient's verbal record, ontological gaps or the id, condensation or metonymy, both privilege a model of language as that which structures the mind; both formulate language as ultimately deficient along with subjectivism that posits the interminability of the mind. I think here also of Derrida's deliberations on how the dictionary works; for instance, he identifies how any signified (mental image) is also in the position of a signifier (acoustic image). Thus looking up one word always and necessarily implies the previous understanding of another word or words, and so each consultation of an entry implies a previous knowledge of a word ad infinitum. For Derrida, this lexical indexing means necessarily that language as a system of meaning is built on an infinitely regressive series of differences. If there is no ultimate meaning in language, then there is no meaning at all; there's no verifiable subject, no truth, no reason, no science—anywhere—hence his criticism of "logocentrism" and his mocking of the transcendental signifier—the ultimate grounds for meaning. If "meaning" has no foundation, then its construction can be, according to Derrida, infinitely deconstructed—without, of course, naming it as such.

Before moving on to a discussion of Lacan and then Foucault, let me pause and ask, what finally are we to make of such speculations on the subject? What, for instance, do we make of Derrida's "undecidables"? What are we to make of his aim to clear a space for understanding subjectivity based on a nonoppositional, antifoundational "speculative dialectics," a "*pharmakon* [that] is neither remedy nor poison, neither good nor evil, neither the inside nor the outside, neither speech nor writing," a "*hymen* [that] is neither confusion nor distinction, neither identity nor difference, neither consummation nor virginity, neither the veil nor unveiling, neither the inside nor the outside," or an "*incision* [that] is neither the incised integrity of a beginning, or of a simple cutting into, nor simple secondary" (43)? And, aren't these finally concepts, like those of Freud, that ultimately reach toward the demiurgic?

Following from this, I ask, what do we make of the vexed question of Derrida's nonconcept of the "hors-texte"—reality outside the text? When discussing his "principles of reading" Derrida emphasizes the need to use "all the instruments of traditional criticism," for otherwise a critical reading would "risk developing in any direction at all and authorize itself to say almost anything" (*Of Grammatology* 158). He also asserts the opposite—that a text cannot reflect or refer to a preexisting world. For example, he writes, "If reading must not be content with doubling the text, it cannot legitimately transgress the text toward something other than it, toward a referent (a reality that is metaphysical, historical, psycho-biographical, etc.) or toward a signified outside the text whose content could take place, could have taken place outside of language. . . . *There is nothing outside of the text* [there is no outside-text; *il n'y a pas de hors-texte*]" (*Of Grammatology* 158). In *Dissemination* he reaffirms this position, declaring, "There is nothing before the text; there is no pre-text that is not already a text" (328). He continues, "If there is no extra-text, it is because the graphic—graphicity in general—has always already begun, is always implanted in 'prior' writing" (328).

Given that there is no referent, no presence, no meaning, no essence, no *hors-texte,* or transcendental signified, and only "motifs," "marks," "operators of generality," and/or "undecidables" that "ground" the text but do not actually furnish it with a foundation, then there can never be any building of knowledge through processes of verification and refutation. And if meaning of a text is always a context that has no beginning and no end (infinite in time and in its multiplicity) then in actual fact no communication could ever take place: every act of communication in all forms would always necessarily be deferred; every act of communication would always necessarily move back and forth in time and in space within the infinitude of its contexts. As with Freud's speculations, there can only ever be a call to a faith in something to come.

In Derrida we see this turn to a *faith* more explicitly in his essay "Faith and Knowledge: The Two Sources of 'Religion' at the Limits of Reason Alone." In his characteristically labyrinthine way, Derrida argues that faith (the appeal to the faith of the other and the pledge of faith) is the foundation of everything: language, culture, society—even republican democracy. For Derrida, this faith is performative—a "faith without dogma" (*Religion* 18) that, he states, "cannot be contained in any traditional opposition, such as, that between reason and mysticism" (18). It is a faith that is, as he writes, not "identifiable with religion, nor, another point, with theology. All sacredness and all holiness are not necessarily, in the strict sense of the term, if there is one, religious" (8–9). It is a secular faith.

This performative- and secular-identified faith is foundational—like a "desert" (16). For Derrida it is what "makes possible, opens, hollows or infinitizes the other" (16), providing that foundational grounding that precedes "all determinate community, all positive religion, every onto-anthropo-theological horizon" (16). It is the glue that holds together, as he states, "pure singularities prior to any social or political determination, prior to all intersubjectivity, prior even to the opposition between the sacred (or the holy) and the profane" (17). It is the grounding of all originary human activities. It is the container that holds together all of our activities. As he declares,

> No discourse or address of the other without the possibility of an elementary promise. Perjury and broken promises require the same possibility. No promise, therefore, without the promise of a confirmation of the yes. This yes will have implied and will always imply the trustworthiness and fidelity of a faith. (47)

Derrida's faith is belief, credit, the fiduciary or the trustworthiness, trust or confidence in general, fidelity, the promise, the sworn faith, the given word, the testimony (or the testimonial pledge), the experience of witnessing, the expectancy, and the opening toward the future and toward the other. It is "the desert in the desert [that] liberates a universal rationality and the political democracy that cannot be dissociated from it" (19).

From the communication and universal rationality needed to form democracies to what he identifies as "the critical and tele-technoscientific reason" (*Religion* 30) all such human activities are founded on faith; it is based on a faith that Derrida identifies as a "fiduciary experience presupposed by all production of shared knowledge, the testimonial performativity engaged in all technoscientific performance as in the entire capitalistic economy indissociable from it" (44). So, if all our activities are founded on "the promise of keeping one's promise to tell the truth—and to have already told it!—in the very act of promising" (30), then faith is also the great ontological and epistemological democratizer. Religion and reason, then, are seen to develop "in tandem" because they draw from, as he elaborates, "this common resource: the testimonial pledge of every performative, committing it to respond as much *before* the other as *for* the high-performance performativity of technoscience" (28).

Derrida's discussion of the performative act of faith and/or trust—much like Freud's reach toward faith in *Civilization and its Discontents*—leads him to identify today's

> phenomena of ignorance, of irrationality or of 'obscurantism' [as] res-idues, surface effects, the reactive slag of immunitary, indemnificatory or auto-immunitary reactivity [that] mask a deep structure or rather (but also at the same time) a fear of self, a reaction against that with which it is partially linked: the dislocation, expropriation, delocaliza-tion, deracination, disidiomatization and dispossession (in all their dimensions, particularly sexual—*phallic*) that the tele-technoscientific machine does not fail to produce. (45)

Likewise, according to Derrida, critiques of the "tele-technoscientific machine" suppose "trustworthiness" (44) based variously on "an irre-ducible 'faith,'" a "'social bond,'" or "a 'sworn faith'" of a 'testimony' ('I promise to tell you the truth beyond all proof and all theoretical dem-onstration, believe me, etc.') (44). And, finally, Derrida asks us to sign on the dotted line of a faith-based social contractualism, declaring, "It amounts to saying: 'Believe what I say as one believes in a miracle.' Even the slightest testimony concerning the most plausible, ordinary or ev-eryday thing cannot do otherwise: it must still appeal to faith as would a miracle" (*Religion* 63–64).

When all is said and done, Derrida is not much different from Freud. Both consider all modes of inquiry and acts—all our social interactions and activities—as being operated by discursive and/or instinctual forces that are ungraspable and/or invisible; whether a hydraulic metapsychol-ogy or the work of "miracles" at work in "every 'social bond', however ordinary" (*Religion* 64), both lead us away from a real understanding of the self and world.

In his self-proclaimed "return to Freud," Jacques Lacan aims to formu-late a metalinguistic-based psychoanalysis that moves beyond the limi-tations of classical psychoanalysis. (See especially Lacan's Seminar I and his essay "The Freudian Thing.") What actually happens in Lacan is an even greater degree of speculation (bordering on caricature) than that we have seen in Freud's most questionable metapyschological work.

Lacan's work repackages the basic framework in which Freud inserted all his other hypotheses, concepts, and speculations. In this repackaging, Lacan uses several key concepts from the work of Hegel, Nietzsche, Martin Heidegger, and Jean-Paul Sartre as well as Alexandre Kojève, Marcel Mauss, Claude Lévi-Strauss, Henri Wallon, Ferdinand de Saussure, and Roman Jakobson. It is well known, for example, that Lacan rejected the three-pronged psychical apparatus described by Freud and put in its place another ternary structure: "the Real," "the Imaginary," and "the Symbolic." He rejects Freud's biological, instinctual developmental model and replaces it with a linguistic one. Refashioning Saussure's rather basic understanding of language (the notion of the signifier and signified)[10] as well as Jakobson's concept of pronouns as "shifters" (their referents change according to who is speaking), Lacan transformed talk of the ego, id, and superego into formulations of the mind as structured by sets of linguistic oppositions: signifiers and signifieds, metonymy and metaphors, and so on. The mind is structured like language. In *Écrits,* for instance, he thus reformulates the ego as the eternal "stretching forth towards the *desire for something else*—of metonymy" (167). If the mind only ever signifies "*something quite other* than what it says," then we can only know its detours "in the search for the true" (155). Now the symptom "*is* a metaphor" and "desire *is* a metonymy" (175). And for Lacan the aim of the analyst is to be aware of "the appeal of the void, in the ambiguous gap of an attempted seduction of the other" (40); for the patient it is to encounter the misrecognitions (*mésconnaissance*) in one's speech—traces of one's "*manque-à-être,* or lack of being" (40).

Freud surfaces quite visibly in Lacan's 1949 mirror-stage theory. The mirror stage is, as Lacan writes,

> a drama whose internal thrust is precipitated from insufficiency to anticipation—and which manufactures for the subject, caught up in the lure of spatial identification, the succession of phantasies that extends from a fragmented body-image to a form of its totality that I shall call orthopaedic—and, lastly, to the assumption of the armour of an alienating identity, which will mark with its rigid structure the subject's entire mental development. Thus, to break out of the circle of the *Innenwelt* into the *Umwelt* generates the inexhaustible quadrature of the ego's verifications. (*Écrits* 4)

During the mirror stage, there's a moment when the infant (at six to eighteen months) experiences a split between its specular whole as reflected in the mirror and its sense of self (Ideal). This gives rise to the split of the specular I (Imaginary) from the social I (Symbolic). As Lacan writes,

> This jubilant assumption of his specular image by the child at the *infans* stage, still sunk in his motor incapacity and nursling dependence, would seem to exhibit in an exemplary situation the symbolic matrix in which the *I* is precipitated in a primordial form, before it is objectified in the dialectic of identification with the other, and before language restores to it, in the universal, its function as subject. (*Écrits* 2)

In Lacan's return to Freud, then, we see a formulation of an ego split—the infant's "*mésconnaissance*" (6)—before it enters the straightjacketing of the reality principle.

Is Lacan's transposition of structural linguistics (and Lévi-Strauss's structural anthropology) onto the unconscious/conscious workings of the mind really such a break from Freud, or a further slip into the speculative?

In the mirror-stage lecture Lacan's citations already reveal much. At the same time that he cites specifically Lévi-Strauss's *Structural Anthropology* he presents a veritable mélange of theoretical approaches from different centuries and with very different methods and approaches: from Freud and the gestaltist Wolfgang Köhler to the behaviorists James Mark Baldwin and Charlotte Bühler. Lacan's iconoclastic citation becomes even more suspect when one considers his neglect of two prominent scholars working directly in the area that should inform the mirror-stage theory: Wallon's work on specular image development and the child gestalt psychological research of Paul Guillaume. Indeed, Guillaume's research presents conclusions opposite to those of Lacan: namely, that the infant's recognition of the body in the mirror is not instantaneous, but rather a gradual process and that infants derive pleasure in mirror images before a Lacanian jubilance of self-recognition takes place. (See also Michael Billig's "Lacan's Misuse of Psychology: Evidence, Rhetoric and the Mirror Stage.")

In spite of Lacan's claims to the contrary (there is no determinable meaning), we can fault him for not doing his homework. Had Lacan turned to contemporary advances made only in the field of specular development theory (Guillaume's research took place in the mid-1920s), his mirror-stage formulation would not hold up. That others have since taken the mirror-stage formulation at face value is equally disturbing. We know from today's neuroscientific research that visual awareness is not the tip of the iceberg in terms of coming into an awareness of self independent of others (and other things). Those neurons that fire in our brains and that are linked to perceptual processes and awareness (and this is not a simple recognition, but includes perceptual ambiguity and binocular rivalry) are a small minority compared with a vast majority of neuron activity already at work in the infant's higher-minded awareness of self. (See, for instance, the neurobiological research on perception in Nikos K. Logothetis's "Vision: A Window on Consciousness.")

Of course, it is the loose overlaying of structural linguistics with research in gestalt and behaviorist psychology that allows Lacan to declare his model of the mind in, and Freud's out. As Lacan states, "Freud brought within the circle of science the boundary between the object and being that seemed to mark its outer limit" (*Écrits* 175). Lacan's goal: to eliminate a delimiting and parochial positivism (Freud) and instead provide a deep structural (linguistic and mythic anthropological) model of all minds as a foundational ontology; to dispel oppositions and dualities between signifier (concept) and the signified (sound image), between *langue* (language system) and *parole* (individual speech), between phonemic (recognized) levels of speech and abstract systems of signs, between metaphor and metonymy. Symptoms become signifiers, and feelings are assembled along networks of meaning organized in a binary fashion. Centrality of symbolism and language reinforces the centrality of the Imaginary—an *Imaginary* that begins at the mirror phase as the child enters the symbolic order organized through language. Language (spoken) connects the child to the real world through discourse with *Others*. Since much of this discourse is unspoken, it includes fantasy and may be unconscious. Lacan calls this the language of the *id*: it (ça) talks about the other person, it originates in the other person, and it is to be thought of in terms of linguistic structures.

In sum: Lacan's subject is constituted by signs and deferred meanings; it is a discursively fragmented construct; and it exists within chains of signifiers that promise consciousness but forever hold at bay the ultimate realizing of consciousness (the primary signifier, the Phallus).

Freud's nihilism and pessimistic ontology are never, of course, out of the picture. I think readily of Freud lurking in the shadows of Lacan's formulation (albeit more obtuse) of how, say, play in language—"humor, in the malicious grace of the free spirit, symbolizes a truth that does not say its last word" (*Écrits* 60)—annihilates the illusory drive toward meaning (the proper). And, I see Freud clearly visible in Lacan's abstraction of knowledge making not as the result of human activities, but that of a failure of pleasure; recall Freud's reality principle and death drive as the shapers of history. Whether formulated as language structures preceding thought that express an incomplete self or unconscious drives and instincts, in both Lacan and Freud scientific method gives way to mythology and mysticism. It is enough to declare the self and world so organized (our obsessive and illusory chasing of signifiers with momentary pauses when the signifier stuffs the signified, for instance) and driven (Thanatos, for instance). (See Lacan's Seminar XX, in which he talks of this stuffing of the signified.) Whether talking of a verbal record or signifier/signifieds, it is enough to talk of how the unconscious expresses itself in semantic condensations and syntactic displacements in dreams, distortions, breaks, gaps, irregularities, and/or misrecognitions in language. To understand the self it is good enough to state that it is a displacement of the signifier in its acts—"refusals" and "blindness." (See "The Function of Language in Psychoanalysis.") It is good enough to declare the inventing of a new language—Lacan's language—filled with abstruseness and play that will lead to elimination of the repressive components of our existence—and thus will induce social change. It is the declaring, much like Freud, of *faith in* a psychoanalysis to come that will liberate the people.

In a series of intellectual jabs and punches, Freud appears dramatically betwixt and between Derrida and Foucault. In 1963 Derrida delivered the lecture "Cogito and the History of Madness," wherein he critiqued Foucault's formulation of madness in *Folie et déraison* (1961): madness is itself excluded from Western metaphysics because it exists outside discursive practices that have already regulated and constituted the sane subject; thus it is not a stage in the Cartesian cogito, but rather a silent resistance to a rational foundationalist metaphysics. Not surprisingly, Derrida vehemently opposed Foucault's situating of the condition of madness outside Western ontology. For Derrida, there is nothing outside the text, including madness, which has already been inscribed into the Cartesian cogito—the backbone of a rational metaphysics. It is not the thinker thinking (I think, therefore I am) that distances us from madness, but rather, as Derrida writes, it is "the reassurance given against the anguish of being mad [that places us in] greatest proximity to madness" (59). Madness is not only never outside, but its extreme limits identify the contours of the very content of ontology.

After nearly a decade of silence, Foucault reasserts his position on madness in the essay "My Body, This Paper, This Fire" (appended to the 1972 edition of *Folie et déraison*). Foucault makes clear the difference between his approach—"placing discursive practices in the field of transformations where they are carried out" (416)—and that of Derrida—a reduction of discursive practices to "textual traces" wherein lie the "elision of events" and "marks for a reading" (416). Moreover, Foucault calls out Derrida's "invention of voices behind texts [as a way] to avoid having to analyze the modes of implication of the subject in discourses" (416). More poignantly, Foucault declares Derrida's "pedagogy" to be a further authorizing of the "limitless sovereignty" of the hegemonic discourse (416).

Again, after a long period of silence, in 1991 we see Derrida reconcile with a late Foucault. In his lecture "To Do Justice to Freud," Derrida presents a "hospitable" reading of Foucault that seeks to make visible the specter of Freud in Foucault. Foucault's *History of Madness* becomes a "trace" or "marker" of a Freudian epistemology; while Derrida acknowledges that Foucault rejected Freud (psychoanalysis as participating in discourses of pathology and medicine that contain madness), Derrida declares that Freud (the era of psychoanalysis) is already situated centrally in Foucault's thinking. Accordingly, Freud is the "doorman of today, the holder of the keys, of those that open as well as those that close the door, that is, the *huis:* the double figure of the door and the doorkeeper he closes one epoch and opens another" (79). *History of Madness* is thus only ever a Freudian text that repeats with difference. According to Derrida, it is Freud in Foucault's work that allows for the "possibility for reason and unreason to communicate in the danger of a common language, ever ready to break down again and disintegrate into the *inaccessible*" (102). The Freud Derrida is interested in is, as he writes, "the Freud who breaks with psychology, with evolutionism and biologism, the tragic Freud, really, who shows himself *hospitable* to madness (and I risk this word) because he is foreign to the space of the hospital, the tragic Freud who deserves hospitality in the great lineage of mad geniuses, is the Freud who talks it out with death" (104).[11] Foucault, like Freud (and he also mentions Nietzsche in the essay), isn't mad, but rather provides a trace of madness with a difference.

As seen in the works of 1963, 1972, and 1991, then, what begins to materialize is less a critical to-and-fro of disparate formulations and positions, but rather the uniting of Derrida, Foucault, and Freud in their like-spirited rejection of reason, objectivity, meaning, truth, and knowledge. As will become even more clear in the following discussion of Foucault's 1980 lecture, "About the Beginning of the Hermeneutics of the Self" and *History of Sexuality* what we see in actuality is an intellectual quarrel over spilled milk. While for Derrida there is nothing outside the text and for Foucault power archives itself and leaves a text as trace all the while regulating our acts, both ultimately promote a negation of human agency; both promote a philosophical idealism and an ultimate faith in theory as agent of change.

In "About the Beginning of the Hermeneutics of the Self," we see clearly the idealist foundation upon which Foucault builds his approach to mind, language, aesthetics, and logic. For Foucault all of philosophy up till the end of the 1950s had focused exclusively on man-as-subject and thus had considered humanity as the center both of knowledge and of the giving of meaning to things (knowledge and values). Foucault identifies such a Western philosophical tradition (whole and/or splintered) as not only anthropocentric but ultimately destructive. Taking World War II as his proof, he declares that "hermeneutical man"—that entity that gives meaning and value to the world—is based on a faulty epistemological foundation. Hermeneutical man will not lead to knowing the world in ways that will be positive, but rather has only led to the devastations of humanity seen in the irrationality and violent torturing and maiming of peoples apotheosized in World War II.

For Foucault, the "absurdity of wars" (202) along with a long tradition of an "emphasis on the philosophical subject" (202) has led to "two hidden paradoxes" that can no longer be avoided. He identifies them as follows: "The first one was [that] the philosophy of consciousness had failed to found a philosophy of knowledge and especially scientific knowledge, and the second was that this philosophy of meaning paradoxically had failed to take into account the formative mechanisms of signification and the structure of systems of meaning" (202). For Foucault these two theoretical paradoxes are contained in the philosophy based on the subject, especially identified in the work of Plato through Descartes to post-World War II Sartre.

Like Heidegger and then Derrida, Foucault states that all philosophy based on man as the creator of knowledge and values is a philosophy that is obsolete. For Heidegger, it's this long historical development from Plato to the modern era that is characterized by a forgetfulness of Being (universal essence); we've forgotten Being. We have centered all our attention in beings (man) and been dominated by thinking; therefore, the forgetting of Being in what he calls "technical thinking." (All thinking is based on logic, science, and mathematics.) We have been too concentrated on all thinking that is centered on usefulness; on seeing beings only in terms of control and usage and dominion. This has made us forget Being. As for Heidegger so too do we see with Foucault, the idea that we must change our attitudes for Being to come to us. Technical thinking should be challenged and constantly shown to be unstable and not the grounding for anything.

As proven by the devastation of World War II, Foucault declares that any thinking that has been focused on being (man) as the agent capable of rational knowledge and capable of attributing meaning to natural and social reality is bankrupt. For Foucault all philosophy that is centered on man and thus centered on man's capacity for knowledge up till now has failed to give us a rational explanation of consciousness. We still don't know what consciousness is; the Cartesian logic—man as the center of knowledge and attribution of meaning, or what Foucault identifies as the "philosophy of consciousness"—and all knowledge that has been built positively upon this foundation is a house of cards that has collapsed. All logical positivism has failed.

Foucault is aware that Marxism presented itself as an alternative to surmount these theoretical paradoxes. However, for Foucault Marxism failed to give a correct account of knowledge and objectivity. Foucault's proof: Marxism is a humanistic discourse that supported and thus hid the barbaric political reality of Stalinism (202). (Foucault is right in being critical of Stalinism, but he misidentifies and mystifies Marx's work.)

In the period after World War II Foucault identifies the splitting off of two paths that, he states, "led beyond the philosophy of the subject" (202). He identifies the two paths that attempt to move beyond the dead-end Cartesian model as that of (a) logical positivism and in general all philosophies attempting to base themselves directly on science; and (b) structuralist approaches in anthropology (Lévi-Strauss) and Lacanian psychoanalysis that spun out of "a certain school of linguistics" (Saussure). While Foucault identifies these new approaches as attempts at moving beyond the Cartesian subject, they, too, fail. He proposes a third path—*his* path that is indebted to "philosophers who, like Nietzsche, have posed the question of the historicity of the subject" (202). It is a path that gets out of this Cartesian model in the identification of a genealogical method—or, as he states, a "genealogy of this subject, by studying the constitution of the subject" (202).

Foucault's genealogy and/or "archeology" is the name of the method of his third path. Why genealogy? Foucault not only proclaims his debt to Nietzsche but names his method after his famous *Genealogy of Morals*. And, of course, by declaring his debt he also identifies his allegiance to Nietzsche's concept of truth and history.

Let me digress somewhat to clarify this genealogical method. According to Nietzsche there is no truth, there is only "perspectivism": everything is as seen, and since everything is seen according to a perspective (point of view) located in a unique time and space, nobody can say he or she holds the truth. I can't say I hold the truth of the desk I write at because I can only see the topside of it; there might be more to it than I can see.[12] As for Nietzsche's conception of history, it is important to keep in mind that he was trained not as a philosopher but as a philologist and decided not to finish his dissertation but instead, while teaching at the University of Basil, Switzerland, wrote his first book, *The Birth of Tragedy*. It is here that we begin to see Nietzsche developing his genealogical method, applying a highly speculative theory of the Apollonian and Dionysian as the prototypical cultural state of mind that gave rise to the birth of tragedy in Greece in nineteenth-century Europe.

The publication of *The Birth of Tragedy* not only severed all his ties to his fellow philologists (they considered this an act of complete abandonment of history) but marked the beginning of what he would later identify as a genealogical method in his *Genealogy of Morals*. Here again we see a willy-nilly cutting into historical time that the juxtaposing of huge leaps in time glued together by speculative formulations. The genealogical method allowed Nietzsche to make comparisons to things he didn't have to account for in time and space; and, in which he could juxtapose Greek antiquity and nineteenth-century Europe.

In opposition to logical positivism, Marxism, and structuralism, Foucault adapts Nietzsche's genealogy for his third path. Here, rather than study directly how the self developed, he arbitrarily cuts into the time and space of the history of Hellenistic Greece by looking at the stoic philosopher Seneca's conception of the subject, then juxtaposes this with examples from medieval Christian theologians' conception of the self—a conception that is more complex than the stoics and that remains alive and active today.

Already Foucault's concept of the self is situated out of time and place:

the vastly different conceptions of self of the Hellenistic and the medieval Christian historical periods are collapsed into one another. Moreover, we might ask, why begin with Stoics, why not pre-Socratic philosophers, or even before with Buddhism? Why begin with Hellenistic Greece and not another moment in time? More generally we might ask, What does he mean by self? Is this self only referring to that situated in the West?

In adopting Nietzsche's perspectivism on truth, Foucault rejects any possibility of truth; as he is careful to remind his readers constantly, he is neither a philosopher nor a historian. (We see this Nietzschean irrationalism influencing the work of Maurice Blanchot and Georges Bataille, founders of the journal *Critique,* who were both actively anti-Marxist and who sympathized, like Heidegger, with Nazism.) Rather, as he states elsewhere, Foucault self-identifies variously as either a philosopher of science or a historian of science. (We see this also in Gaston Bachelard's self-identification as a philosopher/historian of science; in his books he arbitrarily applies philosophical concepts to questions of space, time, fire, or whatever, without accounting for history.) And, Foucault insists that his third path is not a direct look at the subject as situated in a past, present, and future, but a wedge into disparate times that unearth the archeology of knowledge of technologies, "techniques or technology of the self" (203). Hence he declares, "I'm not trying to measure the objective value of these sciences, nor to know if they can become universally valid. That is the task of an epistemological historian. Rather, I am working on a history of science that is, to some extent, regressive history that seeks to discover the discursive, the institutional, and the social practices from which these sciences arose" (223). That is to say, Foucault is not interested in whether sciences are valid or not. Rather, his aim is to try to see if the institutions and social practices have allowed for the birth of sciences: "technologies" dealing with the subject. Hence, we have his various "histories" of mental illness, of sexuality, of leprosy, and so on.

To defend himself against the arbitrariness of his genealogical method we see in all of his theoretical work the inventing of a whole series of terms like "biopower," "discourse," and "discursive formations." When he defines "discourse," he identifies something very specific: the social and historical conditions that at a certain moment allow the social discussion (talk or inquiry) of, say, mental illness, the surveillance of bodies (the panopticon), and/or leprosy. So a genealogical history of mental illness is an inquiry into the social and historical conditions (discursive formations) that have allowed for the emergence of a knowledge or science concerning mental illness.

Foucault's turn to Hellenistic Greece in this lecture is the same maneuver he makes when theorizing other situations. In none of his research is he interested in finding out whether the nineteenth-century scientific definition of mental illness was empirically grounded—this would be the task of the "epistemological historian" (223). He would rather look at the social and cultural conditions that allowed for, say, the discussion of leprosy, imprisonment, masturbation, the birth of madness. So instead, he is doing an "archeological history" (223)—a third path for understanding the genealogy of the subject. It is this archeology of history that will tell us at what point in time such and such subject matter became a scientific object of inquiry. And because knowledge tends to be organized more or less in chunks and around "forms and norms that are more or less scientific" (223), a study of the discursive formations of, say, physics or psychology can tell us something about the subject. This is also why the study of the discursive formations of confession and repentance—even the appearance of and systematizing of Western concepts such as "know thyself"—can shed light on the genealogy of the subject.[13]

Foucault seeks to move beyond Heidegger—especially with Heidegger's obsession with "*techné*" (science and technical knowledge), which has led to the forgetting about the question of Being. Foucault doesn't reject *techné*, as Heidegger does, but rather seeks to identify how such scientific and technical systems (discourses) give rise to the formation of the subject. Rather than obsess, as Heidegger did, with how *techné* leads to the forgetfulness of Being, Foucault proposes a genealogical/archeological method that will lead one to ask: by what social practices and "technologies" (rules that we follow in our everyday activities) is it possible for the concept of the subject to be born in the West? Since the concept of the subject includes notions of truth and error and freedom and constraint, to know thyself, then, must concern questions of truth and error. It is this dichotomy of freedom and constraint—to know the truth about oneself or to be mistaken about what is the truth about oneself—within various discursive moments that is the essential ingredient to understanding subjectivity. This is both a "theoretical analysis" that has at the "same time a political dimension" (224). That is, Foucault argues that his genealogy is a "critical philosophy" that "seeks the conditions and indefinite possibilities of transforming the subject of transforming ourselves" (224). He promises that if we follow his genealogical method we will open to those conditions that will allow us to transform ourselves.

It is this genealogy of power/discourse/knowledge that informs Foucault's speculations on sexuality and the self. In *The History of Sexuality* Foucault states,

> Sexuality must not be described as a stubborn drive, by nature alien and of necessity disobedient to a power which exhausts itself trying to subdue it and often fails to control it entirely. It appears rather as an especially dense transfer point for relations of power: between men and women, young people and old people, parents and offspring, teachers and students, priest and laity, an administration and a population. (103)

Sexuality is the "dense transfer point" that can both reveal "relations of power" and resist within an omnipresence of power articulations situated in multiple points of resistance. Thus, Foucault writes,

> These points of resistance are present everywhere in the power networks. Hence there is no single locus of great Refusal, no soul of revolt, source of all rebellions, or pure law of the revolutionary. Instead there is a plurality of resistances, each of them a special case: resistances that are possible, necessary, improbable; others that are spontaneous, savage, solitary, concerted, rampant, or violent; still others that are quick to compromise, interests, or sacrificial. (96)

If power circulates in society through discourse—historically inflected ways of speaking, writing, and so on—then resistance to hegemonic power structures is simply the act of decoding the systematic articulation of power through discourse that controls and regulates what is desirable and undesirable.

Namely, for Foucault, because power creates resistance in the instant it exerts force on desiring bodies, power is not simply a top-down, unidirectional force: capitalism's control and regulation of desire—the privileging of bourgeois heterosexuality, for example—de facto leads to its creation of a "reverse discourse" (101). This reverse discourse can and has been located at the site of so-called nonnormative sexual practices. Such a formulation also allows for the simultaneous critique of the discursive power articulations controlling desire—those cultural representations, judicial acts, and so on that prohibit, say, queer desiring—and the use of such controlled desire as a "reverse discourse" to demand its legitimacy and denounce a dominant hegemony.[14]

Foucault's so-called genealogy or "archeological history" (or "critical philosophy"), which seeks to identify the conditions and possibilities of "transforming the subject, of transforming ourselves" (224), remains firmly anchored in the Cartesian model: I think, therefore I exist, I doubt everything but can't doubt my own existence because I'm doubting. Foucault's conception of the self—like Freud's before him—is only ever that of the atomized individual. We see this when Foucault discusses how the self is formed (at what point in time discourse on the self was born) in his conception of the subject as a series of atomized individuals (stoic, monk, leper, and masturbator). This conception of the self gravitates around what one is (monk or masturbator) as well as a faith in unsuspected powers that lie within.

As in Derrida and Lacan—and Freud—we see in Foucault a like idealist formulation of the self (atomized and ahistorical) in the world (discursively constituted); we see in the political dimension of his thought ("critical philosophy") the idealist formulation of power (control and resistance) that operates always within the isolated, ahistorical self.

CONCLUDING REMARKS

In spite of, and arguably because of, the textualist idealism that informs the work of Derrida, Lacan, and Foucault, they continue to exert a strong influence on critical theory today. Indeed, we see various blendings of the three in much of the scholarly abstraction of reality that takes place in supposedly left-oriented, postcolonial, U.S. ethnic, and queer theory. We see this, for instance, in the various identifications of a parodic subject that performs, say, race, sexuality, and gender as a way to radically transform an otherwise oppressive (highly regulated discursively) world.

From this point of view, if one decontextualizes normative race and/or gender identities (discourses) through performance, then one destabilizes oppressive heterosexist ideologies. It means that a theorist like Judith Butler can posit the performative *troubling* of originary and/or "primary" genders in parodic practices of "drag, cross-dressing, and the sexual stylization of butch/femme identities" (*Gender Trouble* 215).[15] In order to make the subject and the world seem coherent and whole, those with power construct signifying systems that pretend wholeness while naturalizing sexual difference. So one can theorize, say, a queer-desiring Chicano subject as performing a multiply desiring, fragmented fiction that exists for itself; as a subject that is both unfixed and fragmented, and because it doesn't lack (Freudian Oedipus and superego as well as Lacan's Phallus) its desire is *full* and productive. Such a subject can be theorized as inhabiting the gaps between signifier and signified, or consciousness and unconsciousness, and so can destabilize the Imaginary where the ego/self is seemingly made to appear unified within dominant signifying systems.

We must ask, however, do such ideas and categories actually help further our understanding of the self and the world?

In real, everyday practical terms, if meaning were infinitely deferrable, then thinkers like Derrida, Lacan, and Foucault would never be able to communicate (even if it is to communicate a tautology) their ideas. Moreover, communication happens everyday, and thus it is clearly not the case that meaning never touches its target; that it never *arrives* or that we are only ever chasing chains of signification. Theories of *différance* or *mésconnaissance* that posit the infinite regress of meaning would render pointless the articulation of "postcolonial," "Chicano/a," and/or "gay," for example. If meaning is this eternal deferral—*différance*—then there is no final meaning, and thus one would have to exhaust the infinite number of words present in the dictionary before being able to understand and communicate the words, say, "postcolonial resistance"—its phonemic sequence would mean absolutely nothing.

Even a cursory look at the facts tells us a different story about how real living, breathing subjects are constituted. So when theorists put forward the fantastical notion that only a performative identity has the strength to make at least a little room for play within the "prison house of language" (a "prison," by the way, of their own theoretical making), and that all a racialized, gendered, and/or sexualized subject can do is to enact a parodic performance within the master narrative structures of power, they uphold a form of philosophical idealism that willfully ignores all sorts of historical and scientific evidence. This allows a scholar like Cindy Patton to declare AIDS research as participating in "narratives of scientific progress [that] help rationalize discriminatory policy and continued pursuit of unwarrantedly narrow research questions" ("Migratory Vices" 19). Scientific procedure (hypothesizing, testing, refuting, and verifying) feeds the interests of an oppressive colonialist/capitalist hegemony, so in its place Patton proposes that we engage in a decoding of "the discursive aspects of the AIDS epidemic [to reveal] a particularly spectacular example of the switching, drifting, *bricoleur* use of supposedly disinvested descriptive frames" that will ultimately shed light on how "medical knowledge is mediated in radically different ways, with compounding ill effects" (34). What does such speculation and idealism actually mean for AIDS research—a real disease that is killing millions of real people across the globe? It would mean we all should simply have faith in a cure to come.

Regardless of the abundance of evidence to the contrary, the mélange of highly speculative concepts of Derrida, Lacan, and Foucault remain *au courant*. Why, for instance, would a scholar like Slavoj Žižek continue to lean so heavily on Lacan when there is so much evidence refuting his work?

Indeed, with the massive advances made in the cognitive and neurosciences—the mirror neuron system found in the frontal lobes of primates and humans that fire when we perform an action or watch another member perform this action—were one to explain to neurobiologists Lacan's mirror stage of development, they would look perplexed. We recognize ourselves in mirrors because we have this mirror neuron system that primes us to imitate the actions and gestures of others, including our self as reflected in the mirror; in terms of a development of self, the evidence strongly suggests that a perceiving of a gestalt (visual) sense of self is of secondary importance to our ability to imitate (action) our mirrored actions—and the actions and gestures of others around us. This is central to our developing of a faculty to read from external gesture interior states of mind (our Theory of Mind capacity).

One way or another Derrida, Lacan, and Foucault allow for scholars to theorize the subject and world as discursively produced and incoherent; consciousness is only ever a fantasy of coherence; it is an illusory chasing down of the infinite chain of signifiers; the search for meaning and truth is pointless.

Rather than continue to perpetuate idealist notions of a resistance everywhere (in the face of rampant exploitation and worldwide oppression of working peoples), or promulgate an anti-Western metaphysics in the gaps, or a perpetual chasing of signifiers, or a miracle to come, perhaps we would do well to leave such textualist-idealism behind.[16]

THREE

DERRIDA GETS MEDIEVAL

It is a matter of marking a place where these messianisms are exceeded by messianicity, that is to say by that waiting without waiting, without horizon for the event to come, the democracy to come with all its contradictions. And I believe we must seek today, very cautiously, to give force and form to this messianicity, without giving in to the old concepts of politics (sovereignism, territorialised nation-state), without giving in to the Churches or the religious powers, theological-political or theocratic of all orders. . . . Messianicity without messianism, that is: independence in respect of religion in general. A faith without religion in some sort.

—JACQUES DERRIDA "FOR A JUSTICE TO COME"

[Faith is] the desert in the desert [that] liberates a universal rationality and the political democracy that cannot be dissociated from it.

—DERRIDA "FAITH AND KNOWLEDGE"

Just as the sense can neither grasp nor perceive the things of the mind, just as representation and shape cannot take in the simple and the shapeless, just as the corporal form cannot lay hold of the intangible and noncorporeal, by the same standard of truth beings are surpassed by the infinity beyond being, intelligence by that oneness which is beyond intelligence . . . nor can any words come up to the inexpressible good, this One, this Source of all unity, this supra-existent Being. Mind beyond mind, word beyond speech, it is gathered up by no discourse, by no intuition, by no name.

—DIONYSIUS OF THE AREOPAGITE (CITED IN COLLEEN
JAURRETCHE'S *THE SENSUAL PHILOSOPHY: JOYCE AND
THE AESTHETICS OF MYSTICISM*)

God should not be said to be ineffable, because when this is said a statement is made. There results a form of verbal strife in that if the ineffable is what cannot be said, then what is called ineffable cannot be ineffable.

—ST. AUGUSTINE

The Matrix is everywhere. It is all around us, even now in this room. You can see it when you look out your window, or when you turn on your television. You can feel it when you go to work, when you go to church, when you pay your taxes. It is the world that has been pulled over your eyes to blind you from the truth . . . a prison that you cannot smell, or taste, or touch.

—MORPHEUS *THE MATRIX*

Being The One is just like being in love . . . You just know it— through and through . . . balls to bone.

—THE ORACLE *THE MATRIX*

The power of The One extends beyond this world.

—THE ORACLE *THE MATRIX*

INTRODUCTION

While teaching a graduate seminar in Michigan and Boulder one se- mester, I realized that behind the grand theoretical posturing—usually a third- or fourth-generation blend of Derrida, Foucault, or Lacan— were students thirsting for a more concrete understanding of buzz con- cepts and formulations. I suggested we detour from the readings on our syllabus and go directly to the source. While I mention concepts formu- lated in other works of Derrida, the chapter is centrally inspired by our reading of two articles that form bookends to Derrida's intellectual ca- reer: "The Ends of Man" (1969) and "For a Justice to Come" (2004).

I offer the quotes above to lay out parallels between Derrida's negative onto-theology and various expressions of a medieval mysticism.[1] Whether it is opening oneself to the "inexpressible good" of a "supra- existent Being,"[2] trusting that Neo (the anagrammatic "One") will save humanity in the year 2199,[3] or a belief in an ever-arriving "messianicity without messianism," all profess a faith in the ineffable and a belief in the existence of the unnameable. They spiritualize reality—and the work that is done to transform this reality.

The professing of a faithless faith, a "messianicity without messianism" and rejection of reason, the material, and the verifiable, as the path that will usher us into a new world of equality and democracy one way or another offers a way for theorists like Derrida and hip filmmakers like the Wachowski brothers to sell us on ideas of a "justice to come."[4]

In *The Matrix* Eastern and Western mystical musings on the mind, body, and an illusory reality lace all parts of its script; its characters don earthy-hemp monastic looking clothes and battle evil with mind games and with shaved heads. The film wears its mysticism literally on its sleeve. This is not entirely remarkable, and several scholars have already pointed this out. For example, in "There is No Spoon: A Buddhist Mirror" Michael Brannigan discusses the mirror motif that runs throughout the film as one of several ways to identify its Buddhist worldview; and Brannigan draws parallels between Neo's journey and the Buddha's eightfold path: meditation, mental concentration, and ultimate liberation.[5] The appearance of glass and mirrors is variously read as moments of Neo's journey toward this awakening to the illusory nature of the self and world; the opening to *maya*. Epic battles in the film are likened to the Buddha's vanquishing of Mara, that force that entraps us in suffering. One scholar, James L. Ford, concludes, "No longer constrained by fear, doubt or ignorance, Neo, like a Buddha, has transcended all dualities, even the ultimate duality of life and death" (140). To others, Neo is the Holy Trinity, and to others a polytheistic bulletproof savior that will lead us to our ultimate salvation. He is, as Gregory Bassham declares, the "second coming of mankind's messiah in an age that needs salvation as desperately as any ever has" (5). For Paul Fontana, Neo offers a "messianic deliverance, restoration and establishment of the Kingdom of God" ("Finding God in the Matrix" 160–161); the film itself offers a way "not to look for God directly, but rather to observe God's presence in the general flow of the film" (177). Other scholars have variously identified how the film reforms our ideas about global capitalism (Baudrillard's "hyperreality" is often quoted here) and how it inspires audiences to revolt against this globalization.[6]

The Matrix is Buddhism. It is the New Testament. It is a political manifesto. It is also a metaphysics. Just as Morpheus welcomes Neo to the unreality of the Matrix—to "the desert of the real itself"—so too does the film (un)speak a Nietzschean nihilism, a Heideggerian Being, a Derridean deconstruction.[7] Reality and the self are discursively constituted—and thus an illusory product of ideology; a prison house of language that we can never escape from; a Baudrillardian "simulacra" that mediates our access to the real. That is, it's a reality governed by master narratives that can be destabilized only if you have the right key—a key that, as Neo announces, will show the people "a world without rules and controls, without borders or boundaries, a world where anything is possible."

Much like Neo, Derrida declares himself to be the bearer of such a key. The key of deconstruction will allow him to show us a "world without rules and controls, without borders or boundaries, a world where anything is possible."

Before discussing in detail Derrida's onto-theological position, already formulated in April 1968 when he first wrote "Ends of Man," let me note that the rhetorical play and neologisms I analyze in chapter 2 follow the formula of the apophatic theologians of the Middle Ages—that brand of Christian mysticism known as negative theology. Derrida's reduction of the whole world to a text has powerful affinities with negative theology. Just as the mystics believed that you cannot name God directly so you name what God is not, so Derrida declares that you cannot name deconstruction directly, so you name what it is not. While this brand of Christian religious thinking—rooted in the work of Plotinus but also seen in Spain with Santa Theresa of Jesus and her mentor, the poet San Juan de la Cruz as well as in Germany with Meister Eckhart—burrowed underground for many a century, it resurfaced in the late nineteenth and early twentieth centuries. It appeared, for instance, in the notable work of Edith Stein and the French Simone Weil.[8] (See John Caputo's *The Mystical Element in Heidegger's Thought*.)

Derrida's general insistence on the indeterminacy of meaning—the ungraspable truth—necessarily must make such an apophatic turn; if you cannot name deconstruction positively because meaning is impossible, then one must simply have faith. As per the medieval mystics, one can only describe what God is not, rather than what God is. God is described only through an absence of attributes: uncreated, infinite (not determined by space), eternal (not determined by time), invisible, incomprehensible, ineffable, and incomparable. Derrida's texts appear always as meaning both one thing and its opposite as well as *neither* one thing *nor* its opposite.

47

In this concept of doubling and indeterminacy Derrida refuses to identify his neologisms as "concepts," but rather refers to them variously as "marks," "motifs," and "operators of generality." For Derrida, then, a key term like "dissemination" can "mean nothing, and cannot be reassembled into a definition" (*Positions* 44). The same applies to arguably one of his most fundamental notions—"the motif of *différance*"—which he characterizes as being "neither a *word* nor a *concept*" (*Speech and Phenomena* 130).[9] On another occasion, he characterizes *différance* as being that which "makes the opposition of presence and absence possible [and thus] produces what it forbids, makes possible the very thing that it makes impossible" (*Of Grammatology* 143). Like the apophatic theological description of God as that which is not (rather than by what God is), so, too, is *différance* described as that which it is not.[10]

The similarities between Derrida's thought and apophatic theology become particularly pointed if we continue to follow his characterization of the motif of *différance*. In *Speech and Phenomena* Derrida begins by stating that the motif of *différance* "cannot be *exposed*" since, as he continues to explain, "we can expose only . . . what can be shown, presented as a present, a being-present in its truth, the truth of a present or the presence of a present" (134). He continues, and I quote here at length:

> However, if difference /is/ (I also cross out the 'is') what makes the presentation of being-present possible, it never presents itself as such. It is never given in the present or to anyone. Holding back and not exposing itself, it goes beyond the order of truth on this specific point and in this determined way, yet is not itself concealed, as if it were something, a mysterious being, in the occult zone of a nonknowing. Any exposition would expose it to disappearing as a disappearance. It would risk appearing, thus disappearing.
>
> Thus, the detours, phrases, and syntax that I shall often have to resort to will resemble (near-indiscernible from) those of negative theology. Already we had to note *that* différance *is not,* does not exist, and is not any sort of being-present (*on*). And we will have to point out everything *that* it *is not* and, consequently, that it has neither existence nor essence. It belongs to no category of being, present or absent. And yet what is thus denoted as difference is not theological, not even in the most negative order of negative theology. The latter, as we know, is always occupied with letting a supraessential reality go beyond the finite categories of essence and existence, that is, of presence, and always hastens to remind us that, if we deny the predicate of existence

to God, it is in order to recognize him as a superior, inconceivable, and ineffable mode of being. Here there is no question of such a move. (*Speech and Phenomena* 134–135)

Indeed, both *dissemination* and *différance*—as well as other "operators of generality," like the quasi-synonymous terms he has used from 1967 on such as "pharmakon," "trace,"[11] "supplement," "hymen," "gram," "incision," and "interval"—function in ways that resemble the classical *modus operandi* of apophatic or negative theology (*Of Grammatology* 47). It is not so surprising, then, that he should conclude that difference is not only "irreducible to every ontological or theological—onto-theological—reappropriation, but also that which opens up the very space in which onto-theology—philosophy—produces its system and its history. It thus encompasses and irrevocably surpasses onto-theology or philosophy" (135).

Already in his 1968 essay "Ends of Man," Derrida concentrates on the ends of means, finalities, purposes—those "teleological" aspects of man. He does so to topple from the mountain all philosophical inquiry, to assert his negative onto-theological position (deconstruction), and to declare himself the One.[12] At the beginning he asks, "Where does France stand with regard to man?" (34) and by the end, he serves himself up as the new philosopher of France and the world.

At the beginning of "Ends of Man" Derrida stresses the fact that he wrote the essay "very precisely" (33) a month before the student demonstrations and worker strikes in France that opposed Vietnam and the French imperialist occupation of Algeria. That he shows his affiliation with the Left is important politically because the essay deals sympathetically with Heidegger's metaphysics, during a period when Heidegger was out of favor among the cognoscenti because of his support of Nazism. Indeed, the bulk of "The Ends of Man" (and I would argue the entirety of Derrida's work) is about his building on, refining, then moving beyond Heidegger.[13] With this political ornamentation completed, Derrida leaves the political behind, writing, "because of its indetermination or its complexity, this political and historical horizon would call for interminable analysis. It is not to be undertaken here. I simply felt obliged to note and date the incertitude and anxiety in which I prepared this paper" (33–34).

To declare himself king of the mountain, Derrida must first topple a number of figures that stand in his way. To do so, he explores, critiques, and ultimately dismisses humanism (also referred to as "onto-theology" or "phenomenological anthropology"), which to varying degrees informs the work of Hegel, Edmund Husserl, Sartre, and even Heidegger—the figure he considered to have come closest to the "destruction of metaphysics or classical ontology" (38). To assert such an undercurrent of humanism, he frames their thinking within the main signature of humanism: Cartesian reason.

Given Sartre's domination of the philosophical scene in France from the mid-1940s through the 1960s, it's not surprising that he begins here. He chooses as his focus of critique Sartre's famous lecture "Existentialism Is Humanism." [14] According to Derrida, Sartre falls flat because he mistakenly bases his lecture on a mistranslation of Heidegger's "Dasein"—a translation that conflates the concept with human reality and thus humanizes ("anthropologizes") the concept. [15] Derrida thus declares, "Not only is existentialism a humanism, but the ground and horizon of what Sartre then called his 'phenomenological ontology' (this is the subtitle of *Being and Nothingness*) remains the unity of human reality. In so far as it describes the structures of human-reality, phenomenological ontology is a philosophical anthropology" (35). But Sartre's misunderstanding of *Dasein* (Heidegger intended it to mean more than human reality) is not the only misstep. According to Derrida, because Sartre's existentialism falls within the degenerative space of humanism ("onto-theology" or "phenomenological anthropology") and because *Being and Nothingness* remains, at the descriptive level, an "onto-theology" and not a phenomenological ontology, Sartre never even came close to getting at the foundations of a fundamental ontology. [16]

As I have suggested, Derrida considered Heidegger the philosopher who came closest to breaking with the anthropologizing of ontology seen in Western philosophy. Now even though he tried to make the break, Heidegger wasn't successful. Derrida writes,

> ordered by the principle of phenomenology, the principle of presence and of the presence within the presence to itself, such as it is manifest to being and in the being which *we* are. It is this presence to itself and this absolute proximity of the questioning being to itself, this proximity to itself of the being which opens itself to the understanding of Being and which intervenes in the determination of the *factum*; it is his proximity to himself of the questioner which motivates the choice

of the exemplary state of being, of the text, of the correct text for the hermeneutics of the sense of Being. (47)

And he concludes of Heidegger: "We see, then, that *Dasein,* if it is *not* man, is *not,* however, *other* than man. It is, as we shall see, a repetition of the essence of man permitting to go back beyond metaphysical concepts of *humanitas.* It is the subtlety and the equivocality of this gesture which have obviously led to all the anthropological deviations in the reading of *Sein und Zeit,* notably in France" (48).

No matter how much Heidegger tried to distance himself from an anthropological metaphysics, according to Derrida, when you determine that the questioner of Being is going to be Dasein, Heidegger necessarily conceives of Dasein as a presence that can be defined (however imperfectly) in a *positive* way; Heidegger's flaw, then, is not only that Dasein characterized a presence, but that it is a presence that is present to itself. No matter how you look at it, Hcidegger's Dasein is not *"other* than man" (48). So even Heidegger posits as a prerequisite the establishment of a complete ontology of Dasein and thus he himself doesn't allow one to know more about Being—the essence of all things in the universe. This is also why many of Derrida's texts ferociously attack any notion of presence—a notion that is systematically denied by deconstruction.[17]

However, Derrida can't completely dismiss the equation set up in Heidegger's *Sein und Zeit;* he has to salvage part of this onto-theology in order to posit (albeit negatively) his own unnamed opening to Being. I quote him at length here:

'Inasmuch as it is this simple, Being remains mysterious, simple proximity (schlicht) of a non-compelling power. This proximity unfolds its essence (west) as language itself. . . . But man is not only a living being who, in addition to other capacities, possesses language. Language is rather the home of Being in which man lives and thus exists, belonging to the truth of Being, whose custody (hütend gehört) he assumes'. This proximity is not ontic proximity, and the characteristically ontological repetition of this thought of the near and the far must be taken into account. The fact remains that Being which is nothing, which is not a being, cannot be said, cannot say itself, except in the ontic metaphor. And the choice of such and such a metaphorics is necessarily significant. It is in the metaphoric emphasis that the interpretation of the sense of being then appears. And if Heidegger radically deconstructed the authority of the *present* over metaphysics, it was in order to lead us to think the presence of the present. But the thought of this presence only metaphorizes, by a profound necessity which cannot be escaped by a simple decision, the language it deconstructs. (52–53)

Derrida is critical of this contradiction in Heidegger's "language is the home of Being"; the finite cannot stand in any relation with the infinite. If, as Heidegger posits, Being has a house and this house is language, then there is an unsolvable contradiction: if man assumes custody of the house of Being, then man is the custodian of Being; yet man (that which is necessarily finite as an entity) cannot exist in any relationship to Being (infinite, ungraspable) as this would make Being an entity. Derrida thus writes, "The fact remains that Being which is nothing, which is not a being, cannot be said, cannot say itself, except in the ontic metaphor?" (53). For Derrida, not only can one not refer to Being, but even when one refers to it indirectly through metaphor, as Heidegger does, then Being becomes an entity—man.

Even Heidegger's mystical conception of Dasein is given a positive presence.[18] For Derrida, Heidegger's ambition to overcome all of metaphysical thought since Plato fails. He remains trapped within "the totality of the discourse of metaphysics" (48). And if Heidegger fails, then all philosophy that attempts to talk about Being with capital B in terms of "*is*" is necessarily a deficient metaphysics. According to Derrida, all descriptions of Being in terms of "is" carry within themselves necessarily the contradiction of talking with a limited vocabulary about something that is, like God, limitless and nothingness. Heidegger fails because his formulation is insufficiently negative.

To overcome this shortcoming, Derrida seeks to use a vocabulary that doesn't positively identify Being; a nonlanguage of Being that expresses a Nothing. This is impossible because this would mean he would have to use a vocabulary that doesn't exist and that would never communicate anything. So Derrida turns to a negative onto-theology to (un)name the never-acknowledged method of deconstruction.

To be coherent with this general position, Derrida can't accept any form of permanence; even a description of this lack of permanence would name—and thus fix—a permanence. This is why in all his work we see an attempt to destroy the notion of presence in all Western philosophy because its language is always already ontic (about things and entities) and not ontological.[19] Therefore, he has to coin neologisms and use synonyms to indicate—but not name—this presence. Thus he can only declare himself channeling deconstruction—something that acts and that has always been acting, and will always act in the future.[20] Since deconstruction always *is*, always has been, and always will be, in the last instance, deconstruction has acted through Derrida.

Derrida and deconstruction will reveal all such metaphysical content of all philosophy—but it must do so without naming it: the nonnaming of deconstruction as the way to get at that which characterizes getting at a deconstruction that is not—that state of nakedness when one opens to the *aletheia* where the Deconstruction that is nothing (nondefined, nonconfined, or nondelimited) discloses itself. It is in action everywhere and in every domain: law, gender, race, sexuality. It's a constant exertion and activity in all domains. Nothing limits it. It is unlimitable and indefinable. Hence, at the conclusion of "Ends of Man," Derrida identifies as both making and unmaking sense in its "attention to system and structure" (55). Here Derrida declares all of "French thought" (55) and metaphysics generally one way or another attending to this "system and structure" (55) in their "*reduction to the sense*" (55)—and this reduction *to* the sense is a process by which you arrive at the essence of something and thus rely on criteria of truth. In contrast, deconstruction's essential goal is "the reduction of the sense" (55). That is, deconstruction deconstructs the usual use of truth and meaning (or sense). So instead of reduction *to* sense, it is a reduction *of* the sense. Instead of having meaning that is governed by criteria like truth or criteria of a reference to the external world, what you have is the delimitation of the circumstances, or the ways in which meaning is possible in such and such a text or such and such phenomena. This is why deconstruction is always on the go; it never starts and never ends. This is also why deconstruction allows one to randomly open a page of, say, Hegel and begin deconstructing; that is, randomly analyzing a series of elements that will allow you to show what makes the text possible—all without any requisite regard for what comes before or after the selected passage.

This reduction of the sense breaks with all anthropologized metaphysics. Hence, as Derrida declares, this "radical displacement can only come from the outside" (56). Deconstruction can only come from outside all philosophical thought and thus it takes place, according to Derrida, "in the violent relationship of *all* of the Occident with its other"(56). Now Derrida offers two options for "setting in motion" (56) this radical changing of philosophical thought: "a) to attempt the sortie and the deconstruction without changing ground, by repeating what is implicit in the founding of concepts and in original problematic, by using against the edifice the instruments or the stones available in the house, which means in language as well" (56). Or, "b) to decide to change ground, in a discontinuous and eruptive manner, by stepping abruptly outside and affirming absolute rupture and difference" (56). Derrida will set deconstruction in motion and make the radical break not by destroying meaning—this would mean necessarily that he would destroy or erase the very sentence he uses to communicate that he's destroying the meaning—but by working within the territory delimited by philosophical thought from Plato to Heidegger and using building materials found already within this territory to demolish the territory.

Put otherwise, he will take language as it is: rather than destroy it outright, he'll use it as a tool to destroy language itself. So while Derrida does say that the outright blasting and destruction of this territory of Western philosophy is attractive, he can't follow this approach because metaphysics is already contained in language. You can't make philosophy out of not talking, communicating, and writing. Deconstruction is thus the use of language to destroy Western thought and assert a negative, apophatic metaphysics. Not surprisingly, then, in a last breath, he celebrates Nietzsche's laughter that "will then break out towards a return which will no longer have the form of the metaphysical repetition of humanism any more than it will undoubtedly take the form, 'beyond' metaphysics, of the memorial or the guard of the sense of the being, or the form of the house and the truth of Being" (57). It is Nietzsche who, Derrida concludes, "will dance, outside the house, this 'aktive Vergeszlichkeit,' this active forgetfulness ('*oubliance*') of Being which would not have had the metaphysical form which Heidegger ascribed to it" (57).

The 2004 interview/essay "For a Justice to Come" is the bookend to decades of Derrida's negative, apophatic onto-theology. This time, however, the political is not presented as mere ornamentation. Our spiral into barbarism—9/11, the U.S. invasion of Iraq, AIDS epidemics in Africa, and so on—forces him to take a position toward justice and inequality. Yet, because of this negative onto-theology that informs all his work, we see even here that he cannot really take a position; he cannot name either justice or inequality positively. Instead, he declares, a "justice to come" in an ever-arriving "messianicity without messianism." And, he continues,

one of the incarnations, one of the implementations of this messianicity, of this messianism without religion, may be found in the alter-globalisation movements. Movements that are still heterogeneous, still somewhat unformed, full of contradictions, but that gather together the weak of the earth, all those who feel themselves crushed by the economic hegemonies, by the liberal market, by sovereignism, etc. I believe it is these weak who will prove to be strongest in the end and who represent the future. (http://www.indymedia.be/news/2004/04/83123.php)

As deconstruction allows for no binaries, Derrida can't positively identify "justice" as opposite to "non-justice." As discussed above, for Derrida Western philosophy's humanist impulse with all its false dichotomies is the equivalent to the original sin and must be avoided at all costs; hence, a preference for justice necessarily would imply participating in a logocentrism and thus the committing of a big metaphysical sin. So, while he mentions justice, he can't state a preference for justice, as this would be declaring it a positive entity opposite to nonjustice; this would be a committing of this original sin. So he enacts his trademark rhetorical maneuver: to use the word "messiah" not as a category or concept, but as a mark simultaneously of something expected to come in the future and of something that is always deferred. To avoid any seeming contradiction in his (non)position of preferring (without preferring) justice, he not only makes sure his readers know that he is not talking about real, actual justice, but of a justice forever to come.

Finally, he can't name positively justice and/or inequality because deconstruction is against representation. To represent is to identify a presence. In all his work, Derrida is against a metaphysics of presence. To accept presence is to accept identity and thus to accept something stable, an essence, a truth—the ultimate sin of Western logocentrism.

For Derrida to talk about politics (justice versus injustice, say) within the context of deconstruction means that he has to follow the same pseudomystical, negative onto-theology formulated in "The Ends of Man."[21] And so we see with "For a Justice to Come" Derrida coming full circle back to a faith in a self-disclosing, unnameable deconstruction that will give us the key—The One—to save humanity. Just as the mystics (medieval and blockbuster avatars) declared the need to relinquish reason to open oneself to the power of alternate spiritual realities, so Derrida dematerializes reality, offering the way for one to get at a "justice to come" and a coming of a "messianicity without messianism".[22]

CONCLUDING REMARKS

Whether in "The Ends of Man" or "For a Justice to Come" Derrida makes certain rhetorical maneuvers to spiritualize reality; a naming that doesn't name; a justice to come; a deconstruction defined by what it isn't. In this nonpositive naming of an ontology (deconstruction) Derrida plucks the self out of history. He can't think outside a tradition—very much embodied in Nietzsche's individualist-driven perspectivism—that atomizes the self and thus is limited by an incapacity to see that an individual (in the modern sense) is the outcome of the historical activity of millions of individuals that came before. That is, Derrida's negative ontology fails to see the world as it really is: that we are all situated in history; we are part of history; and we make history and are made by those historical conditions we create.

That Derrida misses this basic ontological foundation is not surprising. As I mentioned, in asserting a negative onto-theology, he chooses to follow and extend a Heideggerian metaphysics[23] rather than that of Hegel—whom Derrida dismisses early on in "The Ends of Man" for its humanist thrust and an eschatology that has a final terminus in absolute knowledge.[24] While it is true that Hegel's metaphysics contains an implicit theology (the advancement of the supreme being towards self knowledge), Hegel's *telos* importantly conceived of the individual, entity, or substance as always existing *in* history. As this entity overcomes obstacles in this grand odyssey of history that leads to a final knowledge of itself, Hegel posits a mind/self/entity, which is not static but that evolves in time and space. More specifically, Hegel proposes that spirit turns into matter—its opposite—in this odyssey toward self-knowledge; he conceives of spirit and matter as separate entities and as an inseparable entity. Unlike spirit, which is productive, matter is inert; it has no consciousness of itself and is therefore the opposite of spirit. Matter thus has to spiritualize itself without ceasing to be matter. How does it spiritualize itself? It does so through culture. Matter gives birth to cultural and social institutions.

Hegel's aim was to posit not a general theory of history, but rather a conception of how knowledge develops: how the mind acquires knowledge in the transformation of that which is not mind and that allows the mind to transform itself in this process of transforming the world. Here, knowledge accumulates; it isn't the discarded or destroyed. And so the self is always located *within* history, as Hegel's conception of the self is one that must overcome obstacles to reach a point when we are conscious of our history—conscious of how we have made ourselves.

Otherwise interpreted, we were born in some kind of primeval soup that gave birth to organic matter; and through millions of years, these first living organisms evolved into what became *Homo sapiens sapiens.* By suffering, laughing, working, playing, and reflecting, *Homo sapiens sapiens* learned more and more about the world and itself and managed to transform this world and itself.

Otherwise interpreted, we live in our time and we seek to transcend our time—and this is a permanent ambition and aspiration in human beings. This going beyond our time is making projects for the future. In our odyssey we have gathered together to organize ourselves in order to surmount obstacles of exploitation and oppression. And while we exist differently in the world as completely unique and separate entities, today we comprise three billion unique entities inhabiting the same historical period and within a whole world shaped by capitalism.

Finally, it would seem that while the Derridas of the world command high salaries as stars in the academy, and films like *The Matrix* break box office records, not all seek to spiritualize reality. During these times of crisis, not all are turning the clock back to the Middle Ages in their speculative, mystical assertions. There are many who want to see the world as it exists, to learn from our past, to organize, to transform into a better place the world that will be our future. (See Timothy Brennan's *Wars of Position.*) Not everyone wants to follow these "faith healers, purveyors of the occult, spiritual *consiglieri*—the mafioso designation is appropriate—or cunning quacks" (180), as George Steiner aptly calls them.

IMAGINARY EMPIRES, REAL NATIONS

INTRODUCTION

Geopolitics, biopower, biopolitics, subnation, postnation, empire, and a string of other terms slip easily from my graduate students' tongues and off the pages of scholarly tomes lining library bookshelves today. This chapter is in part a response to these terms deployed rapid-fire by my students and often appearing in Left identified scholarship. I seek to clarify and understand better what these buzzwords actually *mean* in the face of our seemingly speedy spiral towards absolute barbarism: sky-rocketing unemployment and homelessness rates, delirious dissipation of basic civil rights, and gaping genocidal wounds worldwide.

The rigors of reasoned method and clear thinking to build knowledge to better understand the world and how we transform it—for better or worse—have given way to obscurantist writing and mystical speculations in the name of Left-wing progressive politics. Think of the so-called Sokal Affair in 1996, when the physicist Alan Sokal revealed just how reactionary so-called Left theory had become. After publishing a deliberately nonsensical piece on physics in *Social Text* (vols. 46/47, 1996), he made public his hoax in *Lingua Franca* (May/June 1996): "Incomprehensibility becomes a virtue, allusions, metaphors, and puns substitute for evidence and logic" ("A Physicist Experiments with Cultural Studies"). Rather then simply playing a game, however, Sokal had a much more serious bone to pick: in the name of Left liberalism, academic theory had rendered meaningless any real knowledge of the real world that might lead to real change.

In spite of this embarrassing episode, facts, reason, and rigors that should be the basis of research in history, sociology, economics, and politics that offer tools for analyzing our objective reality are less in favor than relativist, constructivist, and/or esoteric mystifications. And yet the gurus of Left theory allude to such methods (even while damning them as hegemonic tools of the master) to bolster their speculations. In a recently published interview, for example, Gayatri Spivak tells us that because of the "law of curvature" it would be false to communicate in a clear and "straight line" ("The Politics of the Production of Knowledge" 182). Rather, to write obscurely and "counterintuitively" (182) is not only following a natural law, but is the way for us to resist and intervene in capitalist hegemony and open the possibility for "critical practice" to happen (197). And Judith Butler considers the more obscure and diffi-cult the writing, the more complex the "knowing." Obscure writing dis-arms and takes us to a place of "unknowing" that leads, paradoxically, to a clearer vision of life ("Values of Difficulty" 214). In "The Morality of Form; or, What's 'Bad' About 'Bad Writing,'" David Palumbo-Liu claims that to write badly (to depart from "presumed norms" and use new forms of "linguistic expression" 175) is not only to write from the criminalized and "deviant" margins but to terrorize hegemonic centers in its creat-ing of "an open-ended community-in-the-making" and "non-inclusive critical inquiry into possibilities of knowledge" (178) that threatens "pre-existing ways of thinking" (179). To write badly is to "think differently" (179) and to resist, intervene, and even overturn power structures. And recently Homi Bhabha continued to promote an obscurantist ("partial milieu") writing and local/communal-identified counterintuitive think-ing as a form of resistance to capitalist globalization's "fever of frenetic speeds" and huge appetite for expansion ("On Writing Rights" 172); it is also to attain a "renewed sense of self-recognition that disturbs the language of self and Other, of individual and group, in its search for a discourse of passion in which to inscribe the notion of 'rights'" (172). For Bhabha, to write obscurely is to make visible "emergent, minority cul-tures in multicultural societies" (164); it is to open up to a "wider world of access without a painful 'bending' of freedom" (174); it is to declare the chiasmatic structure of an Adrienne Rich poem a "lateral 'side-by-side' solidarity where differences do not aspire to be represented in sovereign autonomy" (175). It is finally to "protect the 'right to narrate'" and thus "to protect a range of democratic imperatives" (180).

Idealist rhetoric aside, we know from history that writing (obscuran-tist or otherwise) does not a democracy make. Certainly, the writing of laws and constitutions is necessary for the functioning of the nation-state, but it is and always has been the collective will of the people (the "we" of the people) that transforms social and political reality. Indeed, the call for "bad" writing is a Left-identified intellectual elite gift wrapping, then selling a capitalist entrepreneurial spirit in the absolute reification of social ideals. It is, as Rey Chow so aptly identifies, to sell a prepackaged "Otherworldly salvation [that has] little to do with the resistance" (103) and that has become a "potentially gainful means of generating cultural as well as financial capital" (104).

Of course, that this Left-identifying theory juggernaut has not lost steam shouldn't surprise. After all, if by writing badly (destabilizing master narratives and so on) one can change the world for the better, then why bother with organizing workers, unionizing labor, or creating class-based parties—the very entities that have historically proved to best further and maintain true democratic ideals? Symbiotically, those of the so-called Left in the academy can sell an armchair social and political revolution with the full support of a bourgeoisie that seeks such inaction in order to fragment workers and exploit laborers worldwide.[1]

This is perhaps best exemplified in the runaway best-selling success of Michael Hardt's and Antonio Negri's *Empire* (2000). Presented as a powerful new political analysis and critique of global capitalism, this five-hundred-page tome (available now in dozens of other languages and sold worldwide) has been heralded by the Slovenian political philosopher Slavoj Žižek as "nothing less than a rewriting of the 'The Communist Manifesto' for our time." It caught the eye of U.S., Latin American, and European newspapers and was featured on Dutch television. *The New York Times* declared it "a new way of thinking about global politics" (Eakin, "What Is the Next Big Idea?" B7). Its authors have been variously held up to other "progressive" twentieth-century intellectuals such as Derrida, Lacan, Foucault, and Deleuze. Negri has been identified as one of the most "significant figures of current political thought." For many others, *Empire* announced the death of orthodox Marxism in its opening up of new possibilities for resistance in the reclaiming of "Utopia for the multitude," as Nicholas Brown states ("Marxism and Postcolonial Studies Now" 221).

Prima facie, the synthetic historical and intellectual breadth of *Empire* is awe-inspiring. In the pages of this book, we travel from the turn of the twenty-first century back through the history of social, political, and philosophical ideas to imperial Rome. Their central thesis: traditionally structured nation-states have dissolved as a result of globalizing capitalism, and in their place we have a "universal republic" made up of "a network of powers and counterpowers structured in a boundless and inclusive architecture." Within this new economic system "there is no *place* of power—it is both everywhere and nowhere. Empire is an *outopia* or really a *non-place*" (166). With power everywhere and bodies moving through ever-more permeable borders, a so-called biopolitical resistance is no longer working class versus bourgeoisie, but is capitalism now "faced directly with the multitude, without mediation" (237). As there are no "emperors" ruling bounded nation-states (no sites of power), political struggle and activism are now "completely open" (237). Empire is a new world order not based on class struggle, but characterized by a fluid, infinitely expanding and highly organized "supranational organism" that says power is everywhere and therefore resistance can be everywhere: it is where the fight for a true democracy can happen as a simple negation in "the will to be against."

Such a formulation leads at best to a determinism: the erasure of the working-class struggle in a postrevolutionary epoch, a taking out of time and place the growth of capitalism and the nation-state, a formulation of a new political system where resistance is happening everywhere.

To clarify, let me turn to a detailed explication of a more recently published essay, "Globalization and Democracy," that best encapsulates Hardt's and Negri's position. As mentioned above, one of their key terms is "empire"; to describe this ultranation, they take this from the ancient Roman notion of the three classical forms of government: monarchy, aristocracy, democracy. It meets the first criterion because the Pentagon (with its possession of atomic weapons and superior warfare technology) effectively rules the world and because the World Trade Organization, the World Bank, and the International Monetary Fund (IMF) all have a monarchical rule over global economic affairs. It meets the second criterion because the G8, the meetings of the Security Council of the UN, are ruled by a small number of "elite actors" (110) such as France, the United States, Germany, and China, for example. It meets the third criterion because empire is also at the same time democratic to a certain extent, as when the general assembly of the UN meets and makes decisions and NGOs represent segments of the population and work for these segments. Thus for Hardt and Negri, empire possesses simultaneously these three forms and levels of executive power (monarchy, aristocracy, and democracy) and makes for a new supranational "postmodern imperial sovereignty" (110) that stands above the nation-state as the final authority.

Once this definition of "empire" is established, Hardt and Negri discuss issues of accountability and representation (that is, democracy) within this supranational entity. They explode the conception of the nation as sovereign; they do so first by following the traditional understanding of the sovereign nation as identical to the people becoming sovereign. As we know from the U.S. Declaration of Independence and those Declarations in Latin America and Mexico, the nation is sovereign when it is formed by a sovereign population; it is in the name of sovereignty that one can declare the people's independence and thus the nation's independence. However, Hardt and Negri want to dynamite this, so they ask, what or who is the people? They declare that "people is not a natural or empirical entity; one cannot arrive at the identity of the people by summing up or even averaging the entire population. The people rather is a *representation* that creates of the population a unity" (111). Without stating it as such, Hardt's and Negri's destabilizing of the "identity of the people" is semantic; a phrase or noun ("the people") that expresses a type; that is, for Hardt and Negri the people is not a natural or empirical entity because it could be referring to people who are big, young, old, skinny, and so on. According to their argument, the "People" belongs to a large set that includes all sizes, races, and so on; the set can be reduced if you restrict yourself to a particular territory, as happens with the census, for example. But even such a set of "the people" changes every time a new baby is born or every time a person dies. Thus, according to Hardt and Negri, this natural or empirical entity called the people doesn't exist.

Hence, they write, "the people rather is a *representation* that creates of the population a unity" (111). Then they list three crucial elements: "the people is one" as a sovereign identity and in representation; that "the empirical multiplicity of the population is made an identity through mechanisms of representation—and here we should include both the political and the aesthetic connotations of the term representation" (111); and finally, that these "mechanisms of representation are based on a notion and a condition of measure" (111). These three abstract elements of what supposedly defines "the people" (as synonymous with population) ultimately lead to the conclusion that in theory we could know this quantity and thus in theory this population is delimitable. That is, they move from a high level of abstraction—the human being—to say that these human beings can be counted as a unit; that is, as a set (in the technical sense) they are representable and in actual fact they are represented. To further clarify, the people of the United States are the people not only living or counted as existing within a certain territory; they are the people represented as being members of the nation-state called the United States and are represented by a government along with all the institutions of this nation-state. And, as creators of their own state, American citizens are considered to be sovereign, and in theory this is a permanent, eternal sovereignty; in theory the people could decide to change the institutions in place.

All this is asserted in order for them to declare that in the modern period (the late fifteenth and early sixteenth centuries) through to the beginning of postmodernity, the traditional concept of the nation-state had a certain validity; however, beginning in the postmodern epoch (no dates given) the notion of population—the people—is no longer valid because it has been objectively and empirically replaced by the supranational entity called the "multitude," and thus the notion of the nation-state is no longer valid.

To arrive at their concept of empire and multitude—empire as constituting three forms of governance (the monarchy, aristocracy, and democracy) and the people and nation-state as no longer operative—they set up a very elementary and fragile scaffold: that the concept of people is not an empirical concept, so when we talk about people we have to talk about "representation" because this is what gives unification to people; and within the notion of representation is also contained the notion of sovereignty.

They don't say it explicitly, but by this they mean that when I say the "American People" I mean the set of human organisms that are represented by the U.S. government, parliament, and juridical courts, etc. This is what makes the American people different from the "undocumenteds," foreigners, and so on. So what makes the people for Hardt and Negri is the representation. Hardt and Negri declare that with empire the frontiers of the nation-state become increasingly fuzzy: "its definition, national boundaries (although still important) are relativized, and even national imaginaries are destabilized" (112). They don't give this example, but we might see this in Europe, where if there's a law in a European Union (EU) member country that's in contradiction to European legislation, the European legislation will supersede the national rules. And so, as Hardt and Negri write, "As national sovereignty is displaced by the authority of the new supra-national power, empire, political reality loses its measure. In this situation the impossibility of representing the people becomes increasingly clear and thus the concept of the people itself tends to evaporate" (112). Therefore, in today's empire, the identity of the people and the notion of representation are also evaporating. According to Hardt and Negri, empire is spreading all over the world, and the nation-state is shrinking. Thus the people not only feel less and less represented, they *are* less and less represented. Hence, they write, "Political reality loses its measure" (112)—"measure" (in the technical sense) as the set (in the technical sense) of the American citizens as opposed to the set of Mexican citizens. Hence, they replace "people" since they still exist in the world as the "multitude": the set of people created as a set by empire. They ask, "Who is the global people? It seems impossible today to grasp the people as a political subject and moreover to represent it institutionally" (113). They continue, "If we conceive democracy in terms of a sovereign authority that is representative of the people, then democracy in the imperial age is not only unrealized but actually unrealizable" (113). To reinforce this decree of the demise of the people they conjure up Rousseau's social contract (also used by liberal writers like John Rawls) whereby the "people, and capitalism, function in fact to make of the plurality a unity, to make of differences an homologous totality, to make of the wealthy of all the singular live of the population the poverty of some and the power of others. . . . Today, however, the terms have changed" (114).

With the waving of a magic wand, Hardt and Negri decree the nation-state has disappeared. A representational democracy and the people are gone. And this based on a false notion of "the people." Many scholars (not just Marx) have insisted that the idea of a people as a unit is a false idea: you have the working people and on the other hand the bourgeoisie and not as a unit of people with shared interests and shared representation. This is why, for example, the working people of Mexico have more in common with those workers in the United States or Canada than they do with the bourgeoisie within their own country.

You can call it what you like, multitude, empire, or whatever—but nobody in our society is a citizen of empire; that is, nobody is a subject of this entity called empire. It suffices to contrast what Hardt and Negri say above with reality. In the United States, we don't see in any way the boundaries of the nation-state becoming fuzzy; it's exactly the opposite. In the nineteenth century people all over the world who needed to move from one country to another could do so quite easily. I think readily of Albert Einstein's travels to Switzerland to study; Rosa Luxemburg's movements; Fyodor Dostoyevsky's trips to Geneva. Today, there is no blurring of frontiers; indeed, they have never been as clearly and as repressively defined as they are today: we see this in the U.S./Mexico border as well as in the military patrols along borders in all countries in the Middle East. Today in Europe it is much more difficult to enter Europe than before the establishment of the EU; whereas before one might enter through, say, Germany, where the immigration laws might have, say, favored those migrating from the East, now all countries are acting as a unified police.

Hardt's and Negri's idea of borderless empire and resistant multitude doesn't deal with the problem of accountability. If it's the multinational corporations that are deciding more and more what laws are adopted, what people are to be elected to government posts, what is to be nationalized and what is to be privatized, then at the end of the day no one is accountable; neither the transnational corporation, nor its CEOs, nor those elected by the ruling elite to fill government posts are accountable to the populations where they not only conduct their business but impose their law.

In the evaporation of a "contractualism" and "the people" Hardt and Negri assert the disappearance of the class struggle. In so many words, thanks to this disappearance of contractualism, the division of society into classes has disappeared, and thus the class struggle has disappeared. What they are saying, in effect, is that the workers of yesterday were unwilling to use their "monstrous intelligence" (114) and instead have resorted to a cowardly acceptance of things and so could no longer transform society. But fortunately for Hardt and Negri, today things are different because there has been a radical change (without revolution) in the whole of society that has come about in the use of this "monstrous intelligence"; in fact, if it weren't for Hardt and Negri we wouldn't even know that such a radical transformation had taken place.

Last, according to Hardt and Negri, the revolution is behind us, and we are now "a multitude of powerful subjects, a multitude of intelligent monsters" (114). And this multitude or "the flesh of life" (114) is not a unity "as is the people" nor is it the "masses and the mob" (114). The multitude is an "active self-organizing agent" (114); that is, the multitude *is* the multitude because it is not a unity nor the masses and/or mob; and this multitude arrived in silence (seemingly heard only by Hardt and Negri) and without the mobilization of the masses in an overtaking of power and the demolishing of the bourgeois state. It arrived in silence and continues to do its work in silence; it continues to transform society in not making revolutions now or in the future. Now, if the multitude no longer has the ontological properties of a revolutionary-making entity, then Hardt and Negri must also make capitalism disappear. Hence, empire appears—silently and invisibly.

Of course, the economic and political reality today says otherwise: the reinforcement of nation-states in their repressive and counterrevolutionary roles, and at the same time a very deliberate destruction within the nation-states of everything concerning the gains obtained by the workers within the framework of the nation-state.

Nation-state and the emergence of a class consciousness are out, and a "supranational" empire with its abstracted working class ("subjectivity of labor" and/or the "multitude") is in. Power is everywhere and so too is resistance; it follows, then, that if my dog farts, he creates a "biopolitical" resistant act. Namely, power and resistance are nowhere. Indeed, like much other mystical (mystifying) Left theory, that power/resistance is not locatable not only feeds the interests of the bourgeoisie, but more basically, it neglects the facts. As we know from the work of labor historians, for resistance to be effective it must begin with localized organization and with a specific aim (target). Of course, a quick glance at the history of working-class struggles and domination of the bourgeoisie confirms that power is somewhere; state agents and the bourgeoisie assert their power (judicial and/or through violent force) to fragment identifiable sites of resistance like that of labor unions. And a quick glance at today's world events will tell you that where there is no nation-state structure in place (Hardt's and Negri's "supranational organism")—no structure that, even in capitalism, must account for individual rights—Mafia-style barbarous rule of the fist destroys any forms of resistance. (See also Ellen Wood's "A Manifesto for Global Capital?" and other essays included in Gopal Balakrishnan's edited collection, *Debating Empire*.)

"Empire" is an avatar of Negri's erstwhile "autonomism"—a dangerous and destructive anarchism that massively undermined the working-class struggle in Europe in the 1970s. Of course, there is a much longer historical sweep of this type of utopian fantasizing in the name of Left politics. Fifty-plus years ago, intellectuals like Herbert Marcuse had already begun to abstract and erase the people from the face of the earth. Marcuse went so far as to propose that the true revolution would be brought on by the lumpenproletariat, or underworld; others in the Birmingham Cultural Studies group looked to marginal groups like youth subcultures (subway muggers and punk rockers, for example) as the force of social transformation. The list of substitute candidates has increased infinitely since.

Such utopian formulations are not benign. Wittingly or not, in their fragmenting of society (youth vs. whatever) they undermine massively the coalition-building strategies of working-class organizations. Youth subcultures typically rub up against an underworld that is flourishing and that, with payoffs of government officials, more and more directly helps finance the very capitalist economy that neglects youth today—promoting a complacency in the face of the massive destruction of productive forces. Youth subcultures have not checked the lowering of salaries, massive layoffs, and huge out-sourcing of production to undeveloped countries as well as prisons nationally. Youth groups (subway muggers, punks, and so on) have not stopped the massive shutting down of services—schools, hospitals, day care centers, roads, public transportation, energy, water—nor the cuts in Social Security benefits. Wittingly or not, such utopian thinking contributes to the destruction of collective bargaining agreements, statutes, and labor codes. Wittingly or not, it contributes to an economic system that has created the highest levels of speculation ever attained in the finance and money markets, and the highest levels in history attained by the public and the private debts.

So the problem is not at all one of ideas or ideals. It is much deeper than that. But ideas have their place too—albeit a limited one—both in the posing of the problems and in their solution. It's quite amazing how many present-day gurus of Left theory were formed in their youth by the Catholic, the Protestant, or some other church: Mario Tronti, Antonio Negri, Louis Althusser, Michel Foucault, Jacques Lacan, Maurice Blanchot, Georges Bataille, Michel de Certeau, Carl Schmitt, Paul Ricoeur, Félix Guattari, Gilles Deleuze, and, of course, the gurus of all gurus, Friedrich Nietzsche, Hans Georg Gadamer, and Martin Heidegger. Hardt and Negri and the others have a profound aversion to the working class; they are all deeply contemptuous of the many attempts the workers have made the world over since the nineteenth century to build their own organizations as weapons to fight capitalism and overthrow it, and they all blame the proletariat for the defeats it has suffered up to now. Nietzsche's aristocratism; Blanchot's, Gadamer's, Schmitt's, and Heidegger's Naziphilia; Bataille's dark mysticism and fascistic leanings; Guattari's, Deleuze's, and Lacan's loathing of science while saturating their writings with puns, portmanteau words, and neologisms based on scientific terms; Foucault's, Negri's, and Tronti's ultra-Leftism that in fact aspires to a perpetuation of capitalism; and Althusser's striving to defend both the Stalinist bureaucracy and the capitalist regime worldwide—all this and more have been and still are among the most effective ideological weapons that the ruling classes have used to keep one generation after another of young students away from the knowledge that may lead them to join the emancipation struggle of working-class populations. And yet, many intellectuals today (in and out of the academy) believe exactly the opposite: that to further the cause of freedom from exploitation, oppression, and discrimination is to pour forth recklessly these ideas. It's the world upside down.

Of course, the survival of capitalism has been lethal for humankind. Those like Hardt and Negri have blamed (directly and indirectly) the working class for this instead of analyzing the problem rationally. What problems has the working class encountered? Why hasn't the working class been able to build an independent party in the United States and worldwide? What has actually happened with actual people? We have records of what has happened since the nineteenth century; we know about Joe Hill, Emma Goldman, the Wobblies, to speak of the trade unionist and anarchist movement in the United States. Hardt and Negri and other contemporary self-identifying Marxist theorists want the revolution without the revolution. They want to be able to assert that the revolution has already taken place, even though they shout that it is necessary and spend a lifetime looking for a substitute for the class that failed—the proletariat.

Capitalism has survived; it exists still and there hasn't been a revolution to overthrow it. The longer capitalism survives, the more destructive and lethal it has become. The revolution of 1848 in Europe, the Paris commune in 1871, and Russia in 1917 all failed; the latter degenerated into Stalinism. Capitalism continues to survive in the twentieth century and has led to two world wars with millions of soldiers and civilians killed, plus more than a hundred regional wars that have happened on all of the planet's continents, also taking millions of lives. Capitalism has led to the development of the huge famines and epidemics like AIDS as well as the continued exploitation of the majority of the world's population; huge communities still must survive without even basics like water. This is capitalism in its most barbarous form, and not a bio-supranational organism of *no place*—an empire where the revolution has already happened.

The revolution has certainly not been televised—because there hasn't been a revolution. Nor will there be one if we continue to entertain fantasies of biopolitical power and multitudinal resistance based on magical, mystical, deceiving, disjointed, vague, openly mistaken and misguided obscurantist thinking and writing.

Much mopping up of the post-Marxist theory of the Hardt and Negri brand must take place. We must begin by showing how, in the name of Marxism, such alchemists stew up such otherworldly concoctions: that the fight against capitalism and all its monstrous consequences is no longer necessary, because the de facto chaos of capitalism has provided us with a form of communism. We must understand that such brands of Marxist theory include a long list of others who sought to reject programmatic political organization in favor of a rhetoric of anarchy and spontaneity: the council of communism of Europe in the 1930s/1940s, and so-called libertarian communists such as Anton Pannekoek, Karl Korsch, and Otto Ruhle. If we historicize, then we begin to see that the working class has been struggling for more than two hundred years to achieve civil rights (representation, emancipation, and so on) in spite of the massive obstacles put in its way, including today's so-called Marxist theorists, who have one way or another denied them a social/political efficacy.

Much of this mystical speculation arises from a basic misunderstanding of how the individual subject and nation-state are constituted. The subject (and world) is not constructed from language (textual discursivities). To reiterate a central point of chapter 1, as a member of the human species, the subject (from the origins of our species) is both an individual (an indivisible unit) and a social being. That is, while our specific everyday experiences might differ, we all feel pain, grief, happiness, anger, and sadness in the same way. We share a cognitive and emotive architecture that pertains to the species as a whole, at the same time that each member of the species is unique in the way he/she uses this universal endowment as well as in how he/she participates in the transformation of nature and society. The subject is simultaneously human and belongs to a territory controlled by a certain state and a certain church. If you are a subject of the United States, you pledge allegiance to the flag and swear on the Bible; in that sense, subject and citizenship are more or less similar. There is nothing mystical about the subject. We are from birth to death individuals and entities completely subordinate to the state.

The making of the subject is a historical process that begins in prehistory (the Paleolithic era) and is not finished; it's ongoing. If you compare the subject from the time of independence in the United States with U.S. subjects today, you see a huge difference, one that was expressed explicitly by Jefferson: the American subject at the time of independence and the drafting of the Constitution considered that the worst possible evil was to be a subject of any kind of power external to him. People at the time realized that the state could overpower them and that they could maintain rule over the people only through institutions that forbid the state from oppressing them.

In contrast, today you see an uncritical alliance of the people with

U.S. military power, even before 9/11. The 1990s under the Bill Clinton administration—the heyday of liberalism for some—were in the eyes of many critics years of drug war, "race war," and the entrenchment of a domestic police state; years when talk of a post–Cold War peace dividend trembled before the fortification of borders, the militarization of the police, and the policing of social services. Today's hugely inflated military budget, unparalleled in U.S. history, may simply entrench what Dana Priest calls a post–Cold War process of "U.S. leaders . . . turning more and more to the military to solve problems that are often, at their root, political and economic" (11). Even as the borders of the homeland are rigidly policed, the border between foreign and domestic policy is permeable enough to admit $8.5 million for the city of Miami to police the Free Trade Area of the Americas meetings, in the $87 billion bill to fund the war on Iraq.

Thus, the subject is constructed historically and also built and transformed through history by means of the class struggle. The subject is not identical when he/she has no legal traditional guarantees. For instance, those subjects incarcerated today under the Patriot Act and the *desaparecidos* (disappeared-ones) in Argentina differ from those subjects who are "protected" by the civil rights that the class struggle has fought to build from time immemorial. And in a capitalist society, the subject can become a member of a different class: one might be born a worker but end up within the bourgeoisie. Class membership often changes: there are many examples of working-class political or trade leaders adopting/defending the interest of the owning class; and vice versa, those born into the bourgeoisie (Marx or Engels, for instance) fighting for the interest of the working class. From the Great Depression to the Great Bubble of the late 1990s, we have seen owners of the means of production lose everything, and members of the working class fall down into the lumpenproletariat. This, of course, differs from the implicit abstraction of the working class in Hardt and Negri; they negate historical change brought on by the working class and therefore send us back to the Middle Ages, when to be born a serf meant always being a serf.

The working class developed within the confines of the nation-state; its formation is inseparably linked to the emergence of the bourgeoisie and the struggle between these two classes. Through its struggles, the working class imposed on the bourgeoisie a whole series of guarantees and protections under the law; one form or another of social security; and, of course, the right to organize and to exist as a separate class with its own organizations—trade unions and political organizations. In many capitalist countries today, laws to protect the private ownership of the means of production—essential for bourgeoisie to exist—coexist with laws and general agreements that forbid people from working eighteen hours a day, under unhealthy or dangerous conditions, or for no money.

But when the framework of nation-state is destroyed (the real consequence of a theory of a "bio-supranationalism"), the framework that stops the whole community from slipping into barbarism is also destroyed. For instance, today half of Argentina (the southern territory) has envisioned the possibility of becoming independent. This area is where most agriculture, oil, gas, mines, and water sources are located; the policy of American imperialism and the IMF will lead to starvation of the Argentinean people and dislocation of the nation as such. We see this fracturing throughout the world, from the former Yugoslavia to Iraq and Africa. The destruction of the nation-state has been a disaster for the working class because it destroys the fabric of protections and guarantees that are essential to its constitution as a separate working class.

The subject, then, is a member of a class and capable of being active and effective in resisting oppression and exploitation in real life, in actuality—in fact. This is never considered when so-called Marx theorists talk of empowerment; they don't take into account the class struggle and therefore the existence of opposite interests between the classes, and the fact that the people they are talking about—the subjects of their discussion, if you will—belong to one class or another. They disregard actual history and instead provide an imaginary and grandly idealist history made by a series of intellectuals.

To understand the nature of capitalism (as well as the subject, nation-state, and class struggle) is the only way we can combat it. To imagine and bring into existence a true democracy is not to theorize the working-class struggle into oblivion; nor is it to use obscurantist language to ensure basic rights to all. It is also to see that capitalism is not a determined element of human nature. It is to see it historically and arising within specific conditions (agrarian England) and then spreading. It is therefore also to see it as curtailable. Only a more historicized and economic based understanding of capitalism—with its wealth derived from its military, administrative, and juridical practices—allows us to distinguish, unlike Hardt and Negri, Grecian and Roman "empire of property" (which used a land-based system that stimulated unending territorial conquest) from that of Arab, Venetian, and Dutch "empires of commerce" (dedicated to the protection of trade routes and market dominance), the British "empire of capital" (marked by the imposition of market imperatives on conquered territories), and today's "new imperialism"—a globalization that is not to be understood outside history.

CONCLUDING REMARKS

We must move away from a deterministic, reductionist, and mechanical understanding of history and political economy. To do so, we must not only historicize the subject, class, and the nation-state, but also capitalism. Taking into account the historical trajectory that produced the capitalist configuration of classes provides a counterpoint to those Marx theorists who have followed in the tradition of an Althusserian ahistorical, culturalist-based Marxism. It allows us to better account for how capitalism has shaped political issues such as the power to control production and appropriation by segregating them from the political and social sphere and relegating them to the economic arena. Indeed, it allows us to recognize that the nation-state is both the structure that allows for capitalist class domination—its concentration and regulation of power of people through juridical, police, and specialized means.

Capitalism allows for "democracy" only in its most diluted form. Today, most real political activism and progress made by working peoples worldwide have happened as a result of unions, protest movements, and so forth, and not through democratic means; that is to say, democracy today is coming increasingly under the control of capitalists. However, as it has been historically, so it shall be in the future: it is the working people who continue to struggle against capitalist forces that seek to undermine all our civil rights.

This is to confirm what we already know to be a fact: That sites of power must be acknowledged if we are to have any concrete results in preventing our slide into barbarism. Before and during the war in Iraq, people all over the world have participated by the millions in the largest political demonstrations ever seen in history, to condemn the U.S./British military aggression against this country. The demonstrations and the myriad forms of expression of opposition to the war have continued and will certainly persist until the war stops. The war against Iraq is part of the more general war against all working people, their families, and the youth of each country. It is essential to give a more organized expression in each country and internationally to the resistance and opposition of all peoples to the criminal and barbarian political economy of capitalists. If any effective transformation of global capitalism is to take place, we need to look closely at and articulate clearly the historical, political, and social facts. We need to build a solid social base for the kind of political organization necessary to prevent our slipping into a complete state of barbarous Empire-ialism.

FIVE

EDWARD SAID SPACED OUT

INTRODUCTION

Ever since my undergraduate days as an English major at UC Berkeley, when chapters on *Orientalism* were required reading in many upper-division courses, I've been a great admirer of Edward Said. Unlike other *au courant* theorists, Said was refreshing: his accessible erudition and sharp-edged writing style sliced cleanly through a seemingly autochthonous, gelatinous mass of theoretical obscurantism. That he was one of a handful of politically inclined academics in the United States—from the mid-1970s till his death in 2003 he stuck his neck out to defend the Palestinian underdog against a tyrannical Israeli government—made him especially unique and interesting. Said's critical clarity and indefatigable interest in literature also kept me in his grip.

I have revisited his work of late. While Said certainly stands alone as a thinker and writer (postcolonial and otherwise), in my revisiting I've discovered that same thick cord of philosophical idealism that wraps around the work of Derrida, Lacan, and Foucault (see chapter 2) also cinched around Said's scholarly and political formulations. In Said's turn to space and geography as well as in his unrelenting belief in the power of representation as the site of political and social oppression and/or resistance, we see an overarching faith in *Geist* (spirit) that supersedes a materialist understanding of people in and of the world. This idealism informs both the shaping of his scholarly method and approach (especially "Orientalism")[1] as well as his sense of himself as a self-identified "intellectual activist." Of course, he is not alone in this regard; this philosophical idealism has one way or another given shape to much postcolonial theory today.[2] What I found odd is that it was also to be found as a strong current in Said's work—one of the most clearheaded, seemingly materially grounded, and commonsensical of our late twentieth-century intellectuals.

That the scholarly and political are so intimately intertwined isn't entirely surprising. He came into his sense of his "Arab life" while a professor at Columbia University (he was actually on a fellowship at the University of Illinois), telling Mark Edmundson in an interview that he realized there could be "a different kind of life and production for myself" (*Power, Politics, and Culture* 166); that he could take a different tack in his academic career that would include a sense of the political. Realized in the publication of *Orientalism* (1978), Said yoked political and literary (largely) interests in the conceiving of Western systems of texts (from Joseph-Arthur Comte de Gobineau to Jane Austen) that worked ideologically to "control actual populations" (*Power Politics and Culture* 169). Having the key in hand to unlock how nineteenth-century British, French, and American literary, historical, and anthropological texts fix non-Western peoples as Others in Other worlds, he also had the key to unlocking doors that would show the world the humanity of Middle Eastern peoples.

Said considered himself, at least academically, a historian of ideas—a historian of ideology.[3] This feeds directly into his Idealist conception of language, knowledge, and power, and leads him to perceive colonial/anticolonial, imperialist/anti-imperialist in Constructivist (Kuhnean) terms. This is expressed in his "Orientalism" as a spatial, geographical/archeological (Foucaultian) method and approach to cultural phenomena like literature (mostly) that not only "create imperial attitudes towards the rest of the world" (*The Pen and the Sword* 64), but that fix and unfix nations, peoples, lands; it is expressed in his political sense of himself as an intellectual activist driven to destabilize those negative and inhuman representations of Middle Eastern people that would in turn transform for the better their material reality.[4] The following discussion thus takes its cue from Said's worldview: literary analysis and political work are two sides of the same coin.[5]

For the world to be socially constituted, there must be some sense that all perception of reality beyond the mind is filtered; the usual culprit that academics target as the filterer of reality is language. Accordingly, because we can never think outside the prison house of language, then all of reality is formed out of systems of signs. If we can't think outside of language, then the study of language remains beyond our reach. This isn't to say that language is not controllable. Indeed, as Said believes, the ingredients that allow for communication to occur—the "signifier" (acoustic image or phoneme) and the "signified" (the mental image) that point arbitrarily to a sign—are slippery and indeterminate, and thus language is manipulatable; it can be used to shape the world to serve ideological interests. Said uses this notion of the manipulation of sign systems as the foundation of his concepts, such as "Orientalism," which invest texts with the power to create (and contain) peoples, nations, lands.[6]

This language-based, Constructionist theory of reality shares conceptual room with a phenomenological understanding of consciousness and the world we inhabit.[7] We can never get at consciousness; we can never get at reality directly. Consciousness is only ever the mind bracketing off reality and thus has no materiality beyond the mind. One can come close to understanding those building blocks of psychic activity, those purest objects of consciousness, by identifying trace markers of consciousness. We see this phenomenological position in Said's first books, *Joseph Conrad and the Fiction of Autobiography* (1966) and *Beginnings* (1975), in which he uses the "bracketing" methods of literary phenomenologists like George Poulet,[8] Jean Starobinski, and Maurice Merleau-Ponty (and indirectly Roman Ingarden) to discuss the problems of authority in literature. For Said, it is the interplay of the creative and the constrained in, say, Conrad's letters and narrative fictions that bracket off the world and thus provide trace markers of Conrad's consciousness; his "texts" point to his bracketing off (perception) of some parts of reality and not others, directing us to the key to his consciousness.

Now, if for Said language is only ever indeterminate and the shaper of thought, action, and the world beyond the mind, then our phenomenological bracketing off of reality will always already be itself textually ("discursively") constructed; anything beyond consciousness is thus deemed ideologically and/or socially determined.

Accordingly, the positive study of any ingredient that makes up our reality—language, objects, actions, and so on—is fruitless. Thus, rather than ask how strings of signs allow for communication to happen, Said falls back (wittingly or not) on a Derridean indeterminacy of language whereby the signifier/signified/sign relationship to a given referent lacks fixity; thus, for Said, the study is not based on any positive naming of how the syntactic, semantic, and pragmatic mechanisms work, but rather on how signs (words) achieve different rhetorical effects. Thus language becomes a vessel of sorts filled with sign systems (the Arab as terrorist, say) that moves people to think, feel, and act in specific ways that end up shaping the self and our everyday world.[9] In an interview with the editors of *Diacritics* Said states succinctly how writing is "a system of utterances that has all sorts of affiliative, often constricting relationships with the world of nations" ("Beginnings," in *Power, Politics, and Culture* 24). And if the world is mediated through language then it also creates knowledge—a knowledge system like "Orientalism" that can be directed toward the "Orientalizations of the Orient" (*Power, Politics, and Culture* 25). (See also chapters 2 and 8 of this book for more discussions on why the meaning of a given word is not arbitrary, but rather defined within a system of terms.)

If systems of utterances (sign systems, discourse, etc.) create the world, then the deciphering of such systems can uncreate such worlds. Hence, Said's critical study of systems of texts formed by the novels of Jane Austen, Charles Dickens, Joseph Conrad, and documents of Edward Gibbon, Gobineau, and several others, can become sites of articulating countersign systems to clear the way for resistant power structures that will emancipate peoples and nations.[10] A literary critic thus has the power to change the world by casting a critical eye on those textual systems that otherwise dominate and oppress peoples; a critic like Said can now reveal the "institutional and disciplinary presence [that] eliminated, displaced the Oriental as humane and put in his place the Orientalized as specimen" ("In the Shadow of the West," in *Power, Politics, and Culture* 33). It is to unfix and disrupt those sign systems that solidify into "social-cultural-political" (42) forms of oppression and thus "make room for interventions on the part of those represented" (*Power, Politics, and Culture* 42).[11] And, thus "knowledge of the Orient, because generated out of strength, in a sense *creates* the Orient, the Oriental, and his world.... The point is that in each of these cases the Oriental is *contained* and *represented* by dominating frameworks" (40), as Said states in *Orientalism*.

In a world constituted by texts, analysis of aesthetics can carry a certain political cachet; the study of literature can now be meaningful as a rhetorical system directly implicated in the making (and unmaking) of empire. Now it is enough either to analyze or narrate stories (memories and traditions), as they are de facto forms of political resistance and emancipation.[12] The literary critic who destabilizes the sign systems that Otherize people and who unearths from "acres of stereotypes and histories of oppression" (xxxiv), as Moustafa Bayoumi and Andrew Rubin state, becomes the agent of "critical intervention" (*The Edward Said Reader* xxxiii). The better the decoder of sign systems, the better the political activist.[13]

Atop such a nonmaterialist concept of reality and all things in it sits Said's concept of the "secular intellectual." Unlike those of the poststructural priesthood who inhabit "private resorts" (Reith Lectures xiii), as Said states, such a secular intellectual is firmly situated in the world; such a figure understands values, "truth and freedom" (18), and deploys reasoned thinking and clear expression to combat, for example, "corporate thinking, and a sense of class, racial, or gender privilege" (xiii). He or she is the voice of "the poor, the disadvantaged, the voiceless, the unrepresented, the powerless" (Reith Lectures 113). Most important, the secular intellectual uses his or her erudition and rhetorical skill (writing and speaking) "to intervene in language" (20) to represent those counter-knowledge texts (voices, memories, etc.) otherwise Othered and/or erased; it is to give, as he writes in *Representation*, "greater human scope to what a particular race or nation suffered, to associate that experience with the sufferings of others" (44).

But Said doesn't leave us with this rather mystical sense of the intellectual's unfixing of oppressive sign systems (discourse/representations) in his or her clearing of paths to justice, truth, and freedom; he makes a gesture toward a materialist understanding of how the world is shaped. In *Orientalism* he overtly reaches out toward Giambattista Vico's notion that men make history—a sentiment expressed on many other occasions. In an interview with Barbara Harlow, he remarks that his work follows the "premise that human beings, men and women, make their own history" ("The Intellectuals and the War," in *Power, Politics and Culture* 366); and in another interview with Jacqueline Rose he announces, "human beings make history" (in *Edward Said and the Work of the Critic* 18). The responsible analysis of, say, literature is not to forget its place within a history filled with imperialism and conquest nor to be neglectful of its place within moments of human rights progress (see *Power, Politics and Culture*, especially page 216).

Now when Said mentions history he must do so because he can't leave history behind entirely; he claims that his textual decipherings and decodings do change material reality in time and space; that the destabilizing of the Arab as terrorist does lead to the liberation of the people.[14] (See also his discussion of the "historical discipline" in *Power, Politics, and Culture*, especially page 282.) However, he must juggle both a materialist and Constructivist sense of history in order for his argument to hold. That is, on the one hand, history is a marker of material change; we make history in our labors and massive struggles. On the other, it is still a constructed sign system (ideologically, socially), and it can be unmade then remade by the secular intellectual. This way, the labor of the secular intellectual—to represent other texts (histories, images) becomes a form of "intellectual action" (Reith Lectures 20) that will materially alter the lives of the exploited and oppressed. Language is-knowledge-is-power-is-rhetorical-effect, and thus, the truth in history is the truth in representation. And it must be so for Said's method and approach to make sense: the deciphering of, say, sign systems that other the Orient as real, material anticolonial resistance and emancipation; that is, he has to both acknowledge a material reality out there shaped by the struggles of millions of people and at the same time he has to textualize it.

So, history and the social and material reality of the people are out, and space, spirit, and culture are in.[15] Because texts, specifically Western discourse (sign systems), are a "part of the social world, human life, and of course, the historical moments in which they are interpreted" (*The World, the Text, and the Critic* 222), such texts play an "ideological role in constituting collective consciousness" (*Reflections on Exile* 79). This allows him to consider the work he does in, say, *Orientalism* as not only historically but also politically grounded. (He even declares *Orientalism* a "political book," in *Power, Politics, and Culture: Interviews with Edward W. Said* 170–171). It's not that he doesn't consider them imbedded in history, it's that in identifying them as shapers of our material reality, the space in which such texts (and the intellectuals analyzing such texts) circulate become in a *strict sense* the real agents of history. That is, in spatializing material reality, he spiritualizes it. This allows for the side-stepping of any historical accountability—the historical development of capitalism, including its cancerous spread through colonization—as well as for the juggling of all sorts of texts (historical, anthropological, and literary) in any way without having to account for history and what has happened in history.[16]

Finally, in spite of claims to the contrary, Said's secular intellectual is private and cut off from the people. His Reith Lectures reveal as much. Here he envisions the intellectual as "a shipwrecked person who learns how to live in a certain sense with the land, not on it, not like Robinson Crusoe whose goal is to colonize this little island, but more like Marco Polo, whose sense of the marvelous never fails him, and who is always a traveler, a provisional guest, not a freeloader, conqueror, or raider" (59–60). Whether isolated colonizer or quixotic adventurer, Said's conception of the individual remains unmoored from history—isolated from the people and their transformation en masse of the material conditions of the world.[17]

Said's intellectual action—his deciphering of representations as political praxis—has had a certain appeal, especially to literature professors in the United States, Europe, Japan, and India. We see this especially with the success of *Orientalism* (1978); translated into over two dozen languages and cited at nearly every turn in postcolonial scholarly studies, it has arguably become one of the canonical mainstays of English department curricula.

In spite of this, *Orientalism* has had a limited influence beyond U.S. and European English department circles. It's not a text that's taught in history departments; nor has it been picked up by academics in the Middle East—the focus of its argument. (See Gauri Viswanathan's introduction to *Power, Politics, and Culture*.)[18] Of course, we're not to blame Said or the book if it doesn't stretch as far and wide as expected; on a number of occasions Said even acknowledges its distributive shortcomings, especially vis-à-vis its influence in the Arab world. We can make note, however, of the fact that among intellectuals/scholars in the Middle East and other so-called postcolonial countries there has been a reluctance to adopt it. I imagine this might be due to the fact that "Orientalism" doesn't provide the methods, means, values, and worldview particularly suited to exploited and oppressed peoples; that its idealism might in fact invite complacency—there's no need to consider the material basis of the doings of the state and its institutions, for example—and thus feeds into a U.S. imperialist ideology that erodes and destroys worldwide struggles of working peoples. To identify the book as political, then, Said must insist (as he does again and again) that the politics of *Orientalism* is not in its setting forth of a program of action, but in its providing of an analytical method and approach; in the "theoretical framework according to which results are organized" (*Power, Politics, and Culture* 438–439).

This is not, as he attests, a political treatise or a manifesto. But this is precisely where I see one of its weaknesses. While he identifies it as political, the work doesn't do anything really to further the political struggles of the working class (postcolonial or otherwise); it claims to do politics, and yet what it offers is not the kind of work done by other intellectuals, professors, writers, and journalists who have been actively building and supporting the working class in the organizing, translating (*Das Kapital*, say), writing of pamphlets, and fashioning articles for trade union newspapers since before, but especially during, the nineteenth century.[19] So, Said's self-identified political book might never be what it portends precisely because it never shows how we are to move from the private into the public sphere of politics; even as an academic bestseller, it remains restricted to a select few; it doesn't work to generate the material force required for social and political change to take place and thus remains largely a private matter of opinion—even if an opinion shared by a few more academics then just Said.[20] And, as much as people might want to believe otherwise, we know from history (and specifically the work of labor historians) that the personal is never the political.

Said makes a "textualist" (spatial) turn and thus (wittingly or not) does not take a real political stand. He does so, however, without entirely leaving Marx (Marxism) behind. While he considers Marxism to be out of step with current theoretical conceptions of history and the world, he sees a Marxist intellectual-activist figure like Antonio Gramsci as tremendously important. In an interview with Joseph A Buttigieg and Paul A. Bové, Said declares that it was not so much Gramsci's "idea of hegemony and the idea of organic intellectuals" (195) that influenced him most, but the "idea that everything, including civil society to begin with, but really the whole world, is organized according to geography" (195). Unlike a so-identified Marxist figure like Lukács, who, according to Said, works within a Hegelian tradition and thus envisions the transformation of reality within a temporal scheme (*telos*), Said considers Gramsci's geographical, "anti-Hegelian" thinking better suited to understanding a late-capitalist reality shaped by spatial flows and regulations. For Said, *The Prison Notebooks* offers "not a history of modernity" but rather an attempt "to *place* everything, like a military map"(195); for Said, Gramsci's geographical/spatial approach is thus "much more material" (195). Unlike the Hegelian odyssey that conceives of an ultimate resolution to and overcoming of antinomies, Said sees more practical value in Gramsci, who is "really interested in actually working them out as discrepant realities physically, on the ground, where territory is the place that you do it" (195). Said's turn to Gramsci allows him to determine our existence and transformation of reality not in time but in space, location, and geography.[21]

Gramsci was a huge intellect and activist firmly working within the Hegelian tradition; he was arguably the most Hegelian of all the leaders of the Third International.[22] Said's turn to the anti-Hegelian tradition is less a turn to Gramsci than a turn to Foucault's profoundly anti-Hegelian and antihistoricist concept of genealogy and archeology. Indeed, as Patrick Colm Hogan identifies, Said's dissecting of structures of power in *Orientalism* is very much indebted to the work of Foucault. Hogan writes, "In many ways, it is an exemplary instance of Foucaultian discourse analysis" ("The Political and Intellectual Life of Edward Said" 4). Of course, whether identified as Gramscian or not, Said ultimately privileges space over time and geography over history to validate his textualist-based theory of reality. His version of Gramsci is what allows him to privilege space over time in order to justify his decoding of Orientalist texts.[23] Hence, the historical method that requires one to verify assertions and to parse fact from fiction is denied[24] and the geographic, spatial decoding of cultural phenomena privileged.[25] This plays out in *Orientalism* when he randomly cuts into a historical moment to excavate from different strata, but without a full sense of history and chronology (what came before and what followed):[26] the slice into the nineteenth century to excavate the space of a particular moment (like the archeologist's identifying of a geological strata), with little accounting for how the time and the spaces (the layers, say) communicate reciprocally with one another. Reality is conceived of as strata or layers of irreconcilable "paradigms" (Kuhn's term for what Foucault calls "discourse") that don't communicate with one another; where those who inhabit one paradigm don't communicate with those installed in another because of a supposed incommensurability and untranslatability.

This approach goes against historical fact. Let me mention briefly a time/space in the conquest of the Americas; the moment Hernán Cortéz arrived in Mexico (installed in one paradigm/discourse) he encountered the Aztecs (installed in another paradigm/ discourse), and yet, because of a woman called *la malinche* who served as interpreter (she learned Spanish and Nahuatl but was herself Mayan), the two paradigms were able to meet. The incommensurability of paradigms would mean that *la malinche* wouldn't have been able to bridge these paradigms because of how the self and language fixed the boundaries of her worldview; accordingly, then, as a Mayan with her own language and knowledge system (paradigm) she wouldn't have been able to learn Spanish and Nahuatl or relate to either Cortéz or Moctezuma.

In Said's turn to space/geography, people and our knowledge are delimited and deterministic. Knowledge does not develop in our transformation of the world in space and time (progressively or regressively); rather, it is determined by one's spatial/geographic location (Occidental or Oriental, for example); à la Kuhn's Constructivism, Said's sense of knowledge, then, doesn't require adopting criteria such as truth or verifiability, or any kind of ontological commitment about the world out there different from the one posited by the knowledge that's being asserted.

Thus, for Said all knowledge (automatically, immediately, without any mediation) is power—all language dominance—and so the questions concerning the validity of that so-called knowledge or power are completely evacuated, erased, deleted; all epistemological questions in the strict sense of the term are swept aside.

More to the point, Said treats knowledge and power (and their Foucaultian-inspired combination as knowledge/power) as if they were Kantian transcendentals; he treats them as concepts that he doesn't have to justify—or explain or in any way empirically verify—because they are posited as preexisting; they are treated as "primitives" (identified in mathematics and in some branches of philosophy) that preexist all humanity and that are the basis for everything that exists and thus don't have to be proven. Said doesn't have to make any reference to specialists in the philosophical study of knowledge or any reference to any kind of empirically grounded field such as cognitive science; he doesn't have to take a position regarding specific discussions on knowledge and power. He can simply assert. In *Orientalism,* for example, he asserts that the "knowledge of subject races or Orientals is what makes their management easy and profitable; knowledge gives power, more power requires more knowledge, and so on in an increasingly profitable dialectic of information and control" (36). And without reference to any sociological movement or historical event, he can state as a given that

> since the middle of the eighteenth century there had been two principal elements in the relation between East and West. One was a growing systematic knowledge in Europe about the Orient, knowledge reinforced by the colonial encounter as well as by the widespread interest in the alien and unusual, exploited by the developing sciences of ethnology, comparative anatomy, philology, and history; furthermore, to this systematic knowledge was added a sizable body of literature produced by novelists, poets, translators, and gifted travelers. The other feature of Oriental-European relations was that Europe was always in a position of strength, not to say domination. (39–40)

Knowledge and power (knowledge/power) simply *are* constructed. Hence, Said doesn't have to ask whether the botanist who went to the Middle East during this period had in fact discovered a new genus of flower, whether the entomologist had discovered a new insect, or whether the philologist understood Sanskrit or not, because all such endeavors worked to produce "knowledge of the Orient that places things Oriental in class, court, prison, or manual for scrutiny, study, judgment, discipline, or governing" (41).

Perhaps this is also why there's no real interest in positing, say, the Middle East as a fact (as a reality out there); perhaps this is why there's only ever an interest in it as an idea, an Orientalist text. Orientalism is not merely a collection of "lies or myths," but a "created body of theories and practice" (6). It is, Said adds, "a system of knowledge about the Orient, an accepted grid for filtering Orient into Western consciousness" (6). And, Said continues,

> Philosophically, then, the kind of language, thought, and vision that I have been calling Orientalism very generally is a form of radical realism; anyone employing Orientalism, which is the habit for dealing with questions, objects, qualities, and regions deemed Oriental, will designate, name, point to, fix what he is talking or thinking about with a word or phrase, which then is considered either to have acquired, or more simply to be, reality. Rhetorically speaking, Orientalism is absolutely anatomical and enumerative: to use its vocabulary is to engage in the particularizing and dividing of things Oriental into manageable parts. Psychologically, Orientalism is a form of paranoia, knowledge of another kind, say, from ordinary historical knowledge. These are a few of the results, I think, of imaginative geography and of the dramatic boundaries it draws. (72)

In identifying "Orientalism" as a form of "radical realism" (72), thoughts, tropes, dreams, perceptions, representations, and so on, experienced and reproduced by as varied a collection of people as Gobineau (a racist), Ernest Renan (a romantic and a monarchist), and Alexander Von Humboldt (scientist and proponent of freedom) will, as he states, "designate, name, or fix with a word or phrase that which is to be reality" (72).

Just as Said treats knowledge and power as Kantian transcendentals (or "primitives"), so too does "Orientalism" simply exist in some platonic *topos uranus* as an unchanging ideal/idea (*eidos*) that exists out of space and time. All emotional and cultural phenomena of the West produce "a closed system in which objects are what they are *because* they are what they are, for once, for all time, for ontological reasons that no empirical material can either dislodge or alter" (70). The Orient becomes fixed in Said as eternal and unchanging.

There were millions of things studied by those Said identifies as Orientalists, but whether they were all imperialists and/or convinced of the superiority of the European race is not proven at all. Nor, arguably, should it be. Indeed, whatever such scholars believed is as immaterial as their eye color, sexual preference, taste in food, and so on; all these things are completely irrelevant with respect to what is supposedly Said's subject: knowledge. Rather than make a virtue of ad hominem critique, perhaps we'd be better served by asking questions like: Were those scholars studying Sanskrit accurately measuring language, its evolution, vowel placement, genealogy? Were those scholars who studied the language of those in North Africa and those in the Danube correct or not in asserting a common genealogy, an Indo-European genealogy that included Sanskrit?

Epistemology is not concerned with the circumstances of the production of knowledge. It is concerned with the rules and methods of verification, or the refutation of theories and hypotheses concerning facts. That is to say, we're not going to judge the validity of Marx's theory of capitalism against the fact that for quite a few years he suffered from hemorrhoids or that when he wrote *Das Kapital* he was having sex with his maid. Such circumstances should not be used as criteria for judging his hypotheses—such criteria should test the validity of his ideas against the facts.

What we see here is Said's making of ontologically equal scholarly work from all walks of life that devoted time and energy to the study of what they called the Orient. This, according to Said, not only created the concept of the Orient, but a *conceptual* Orient. According to Said, such assigning of a series of characteristics to the Orient coincided with the work done by bureaucrats from Western imperialist states along with the exploitive activities of private companies like the East India Company.

Said's move here is all too clear: To consider the study of Sanskrit or archeological digs as having the same importance (materially and cognitively) as, say, topographic studies used to build forts to violently oppress native peoples (or even the study of caste to better divide and rule), he must erase those differences that make a difference; he must place everything at the same level. Since these fields of scholarly inquiry were extremely diverse and led to radically different outcomes, Said must level all such phenomena to one common denominator: the world as a text. By doing so, he himself creates a category (or classification) of the Orient as a textual product with no distinction made between the different so-called texts. That is, to level the playing field between the nineteenth-century scholarly studies of social and/or natural phenomenon and that of imperialist acts of exploitation and oppression, Said must make all reality a text; and by textualizing all reality, he establishes his divisions— Orient and Occident—as being something real and concrete, something in which there are no differences between its constituent components: They all play the same role as texts.

Said thus divides reality into spaces in an ideological way. In *Orientalism* he writes, "As much as the west itself, the Orient is an idea that has a history and a tradition of thought, imagery, and vocabulary that have given it reality and presence in and for the West" (5). He concludes, "The two geographical entities support and to an extent reflect each other" (5). These two ideological spaces are the Occident and Orient. The net effect: by dividing the world into these two spaces, Said gives authority to what is basically a Stalinist-originated division of the world into first, second, and third worlds. Accordingly, Said's Orientalism would be equivalent to the third world, and the Occident would be equivalent to the first world; this erases the fact that our one world under capitalism is divided—but divided by class conflict worldwide, not by geographic space. The Orient is a conglomeration of peasants and princes/rajas, little kingdoms, and a large proletariat; and there's a huge difference between the Orient of China, India, and Palestine. Yet within the concept of Orientalism they are all are lumped together and are thus devoid of any factual specificity.

With a world so divided, Said can say nothing about, for example, whether Daniel Defoe's *Robinson Crusoe* or even, before, Miguel de Cervantes's *Don Quixote* contributed something culturally valuable beyond the borders of Europe and for humanity as a whole. He can say nothing about the important communication that occurred in the Middle Ages between the Occident and Orient that allowed the survival of Aristotle and Plato; how, for example, to a large extent all the recovered knowledge of Greek civilization that preserved and incorporated the thinking of Aristotle and Plato (and that had a huge impact on the rest of the world) happened through Europe's contact with the Middle East. He can say nothing about how the world is one, a totality, and not split into parts. He can say nothing about how, since we walked out of Africa, the species has been one and the history of the species has been one. He can say nothing of the growing European fear of Islam after Mohammed's death in 632 AD, during the Islamic takeover of Spain, Sicily, and parts of France in the ninth century and its later rule over India, Indonesia, and China in the thirteenth and fourteenth centuries. He can say nothing about what happened after this massive spreading of an Islamic empire. He can say nothing about why capitalism never developed in the

European Islamic world at the end of the Middle Ages; he can say nothing about the significance of capitalism in the conquest of the Americas during the beginning of the Renaissance. With the world fragmented into East and West, Said can say nothing of a global reality shaped by capitalism, and thus his conception of knowledge will necessarily always be distorted; it will be an imaginative history more than an actual history shaped by human labor in space and time.

At base one must ask of *Orientalism* and the scholarly work that follows, Do Said's theoretical tools work to understand what has happened to the world? Since Said abandons and even rejects any concrete study of historical phenomena of the development of capitalism (how it develops and spreads all over the world), he can resort only to an idealist position that declares, it's not material reality that we need to be focused on, but rather the development of ideas and the effects of ideas on reality. In Said's work, then, material reality is transformed not by people situated in and actively shaping history, but simply ideas that are the motor of the transformation itself.

As I mentioned at the very beginning of this chapter, Said's scholarly and political worldview are one. This is not unintentional. Said mentions that he translated Yassir Arafat's speech into English during his visit to the United States in 1974—a moment when his scholarly work (what would become *Orientalism*) and his politics "were joined" (*Power, Politics, Culture* 210). This mid-1970s period, he continues, "married the two things I was most interested in: literature and culture, on the one hand, and studies and analyses of power, on the other" (210).[27] As Eqbal Ahmad sums up, Said's politics resides in his "preoccupation with memory" along with "narratives of the oppressed" and his placing alongside the "dominant myth" (texts/discourse) its marginal, silenced "counterpoint" myth/text/discourse (33).

Everything in Said's political life and in his political positions is marked by an Idealist conception of history and society.[28] With his understanding of U.S. society and erudition along with social rank as an Ivy League professor, he considered his role as that of an Arabic emissary of sorts, best suited for the job of lobbying those with power on Capitol Hill; the best suited to change the minds of D.C. liberals, UN representatives, and the like, regarding foreign (especially U.S.) policy toward the Israeli/Palestinian conflict. As with his idealist vision of destabilizing representations (discourse/texts/sign systems) to bring social change, so, too do we see a like conception of exposing the Middle Eastern problem (with the Palestinian struggle at its core) as the way to change the minds of U.S. policymakers and U.S. society as a whole. Said's political (and scholarly) worldview stripped down can be characterized as follows: the main problem faced by the Palestinians is representation/visibility, so for social and political change to happen, one must expose, unfix, then refix with "counterpoint" myths, sign systems, representations.

Of course, Said's worldview doesn't come out of thin air. In response to the Israeli army's brutal and bloody occupation of Palestinian territories in 1967, Said began to formulate a political position: First, to reveal the complicity of American academics either through their silence or through their lack of will to study and understand the Israel/Palestine problem. Second, to stand up to the injustices in the Middle East when others were afraid to denounce the Israeli occupation. Third, to convince his fellow academics and others that the Palestinian problem was real and worthy of attention. Finally, to alter stereotypical preconceptions (unfix representations) of the Middle Eastern/Palestinian peoples. Bundled together, these impulses led him to declare a singular aim to restore justice. In a 1987 interview with Matthew Stevenson, he identifies the means to this goal by going "beyond the matter of returning land" and pushing for a politics "that involves moral restitution" (319); equality in the Israeli/Palestinian conflict will be brought about by challenging "political perceptions and processes in a fairly massive way" (341–342) and instilling a system of "mutual recognition" ("An Exile's Exile" 319).

The problem with this position is clear: instead of putting his energies into helping the Palestinians form an independent party with its own political force to succeed in their struggle for equality, Said opts for a top-down model of change. The problem doesn't lie with Said alone. Indeed, the Palestinian Liberation Organization (PLO) (of which he was an unofficial member until the signing of the Oslo Accords in 1992), with Arafat at its head, was a parliament-like inner bureaucracy that discussed and submitted proposals regarding the Palestinians; however, the PLO never had a direct mandate from the Palestinian people. It was simply the bureaucracy formed by the then-guerrilla fighter Arafat to defend the Palestinians; in this defense, the PLO with Arafat at its head wrote up a charter that contained two articles: (1) that the Palestinians didn't recognize the Israeli state and that they would never recognize it; for them the situation that had to be reestablished was the recognition of one state for all. The PLO's original charter demanded also the "right of return" for Arabs to villages, lands, and all other places that they were forcefully driven out of during the Zionist colonization.[29]

As a member of the Palestinian National Congress (PNC)—the entity that served as a parliament-like structure of the PLO wherein policy was discussed and voted on—Said was necessarily an important functionary of the PLO. Said sought to play the role of the Palestinian representative in Washington; he was never officially acknowledged as such. When Arafat signed the Oslo Accords renouncing the main demands cited above in defense of the Palestinian people, Said broke with Arafat.[30] Said also arguably broke with Arafat because it became clear that under his leadership Said wouldn't be appointed to represent the PLO in the United States.[31] It became crystal clear that Said had reached a point where he no longer believed his ideas and opinion would modify or influence politically the course of the PLO. He realized (1) that Arafat would never appoint him as the spokesperson for the PLO in the United States; here Said believed that his role in the United States would be to assert his influence as an intellectual, lobby, and change public opinion; that is, to use ideas to transform the world; and (2) that after Arafat signed the Oslo treaty (his authorizing of the making of a separate Palestinian state) he had betrayed the central charter of the PLO: to establish one secular state in the whole Palestinian territory in which its two components (Jewish and Arabic) would exist in harmony and where all would have equal rights and obligations.

Said believed in the power of the individual to enact massive social and political change. And until his self-excision from the PLO, Said believed sincerely in the power of Arafat as the leader who would unify all forces within the PLO, speak to the aspirations of the people, and ultimately liberate them from oppression and exploitation. In many ways, Said revered Arafat, considering him the figure who woke the Palestinians from their stupor and galvanized them into a force to fight for their repatriation.[32] In this spirit, he supported Arafat's first and second *intifadas;* he also therefore turned a blind eye to Arafat's dependence on the Soviet bureaucracies. (Recall that the Oslo Accords followed on the heels of the fall of the Soviet bureaucracy and thus at the moment when Arafat needed most to secure himself and the PLO by establishing relations with another superpower: the United States.)

This is simply to point out that when one believes in saviors, one doesn't have to believe in the class struggle, and thus one doesn't have to believe in the absolute necessity of building an independent organization of workers who do not depend on whether their decisions will gratify whoever happens to be, say, in the White House.

Having rejected Marx as an intellectual guide for his political activity, Said was blind to the realities of the Middle East. He didn't see, for example, that for over half a century the Middle East has been a powder keg ready to explode precisely because the Palestinian question was never properly solved by imperialism. The Israeli bureaucracy, backed by the United States, didn't manage to exterminate all the Palestinians, so they kicked them out of their homeland. This only meant transferring the problem to other territories. Thus the imperialists only managed to increase and multiply the problem. Added to this was the fact that the Palestinian people didn't accept their extermination.[33] Rather than resign themselves to being exterminated, they fought back. In fact, the whole of politics in the Middle East is powerfully marked by the resistance of the Palestinians. Even with the help of Arafat, who finally gave in to U.S. imperialism, the Palestinian spirit of rebellion has not been squashed. Indeed, if the Palestinians have not progressed, it's because their leaders, like those of Israel, have systematically aligned themselves with the policy of U.S. imperialism.

When Arafat signed the Oslo Accords, he effectively authorized the creation of a South African model of Bantu-stans (small territories given to "Coloreds" and surrounded by those under total White rule), as seen in the West Bank and Gaza Strip, which are surrounded by Israel. If the Palestinians survive and continue to make progress in establishing civil rights, it is not because of an individual's actions—Said's destabilizing of representations and/or Arafat's signing of legislative acts—but because of the continued struggle of the Palestinian people.

CONCLUDING REMARKS

Exhibiting a pessimistic vision of the future of the Palestinian peoples, Said, in an interview with Joseph A. Buttigieg and Paul A. Bové, stated that "in my lifetime or in several lifetimes to come, there's no hope that we can win an essentially military or military-based kind of battle with the Israelis, because it's not in the cards, any more than their winning is" ("Culture and Imperialism" 203)—it's not surprising that Said embraces a philosophical idealism in both his literary and political work. It's not surprising that in the interview with Buttigieg and Bové he identifies how the destabilizing of discourses that "control the destiny" (194) of Middle Eastern peoples in the analysis of texts (literary or otherwise) will clear a path not only to "new lines of investigation" (205), but also to social, cultural, and political change. (See also his interview with Nirmala Lakshman "The Road Less Traveled," in *Power, Politics and Culture*.)

As already mentioned, Said's philosophical idealism manifests itself in a variety of ways: a setting aside of chronology and causality in favor of a spatialization of reality that bends more toward social constructionism and relativism than a sociohistorical-based materialism. Patrick Colm Hogan gets straight to the point, asking, "When multiculturalists urge greater curricular breadth, with Europeans reading literature by non-Europeans, they are urging the acquisition of knowledge about Africa. Are they thereby urging the actual acquisition of Africa by Europeans? Are the true anti-imperialists the Americans who refuse to read literature by non-Europeans?" (14).

When all is said and done, it is relativism and identity politics that are finally served up in Said's work. The claim that scholars—European-American Indologists—who have interpreted myths, scripture, rituals, and so on from the outside have served to create an exclusionary Hindu identity conservative nationalist agenda; it has had the same effect in contemporary China and other countries where an identity-based constructivism is used as a nationalist political agenda to violently repress the people as well as censor thought and expression. (See Hogan's "The Political and Intellectual Legacy.") Undressed, Said's constructivist and relativist position vis-à-vis reality is irrational and reactionary; it serves an identity politics that if put into practice globally would lead to the most irrational, totalitarian state of affairs. It would spell the end of Salman Rushdie, Arundhati Roy, Amitav Ghosh, Uma Krishnaswami, and many other authors of Indian and Pakistani descent who write about most anything. It would spell the end of scientific research and the total fragmentation of political collectives.

Said's method and approach grow from a poststructuralist conception of power, as everywhere; they grow from the idea of an all-encompassing discourse (Orientalist) that acts as a physical force, and within this there can arise an individual resistant discourse. As stated in chapter 4, if power is everywhere, then you can speak about the presence of power in music, literature, the way one dresses, the study of exotic languages; it means that you can disregard the study of physical actions and objects like how many rifles, how many men, how many ships, and how many cannons attacked and occupied Middle Eastern territories; it means that you don't have to account for the constant struggle of the people to defend themselves with arms; it means that colonization can be studied directly in its cultural manifestations and intellectual activities as an embodiment of power.[34] Said can find in cultural phenomena directly or indirectly some relationship of power with respect to the Other; this means he can find in a syllogistic manner the Othering of that text, and that Other that is the product of the Othering will always be a subaltern and will be reflected as a subaltern.

This approach allows one to conceive of the labor of cultural decipher-ing as the same work as the organization and struggle of the working class. Thus, such an approach not only eliminates all the inconveniences of the Marxist analysis of political and historical situation, but also fails to account fully for the concrete case of the creation of, say, the state of Israel on the basis of the expulsion of the Palestinians; and therefore it fails to account for the colonization of the Palestinian land by Jewish people coming from Europe and other parts of the world.

Said's heart was in the right place. He was genuinely concerned and had many honorable intentions regarding the Palestinian people. He was angered and frustrated by his fellow academics in the United States and throughout the world who turned a blind eye to the Palestinian strug-gle; many didn't take a public stand for fear of being called out as anti-Semitic. Said showed tremendous courage when others didn't.

This said, we must also consider the problems posed in the spatial-izing of reality (and its division into parts) and the locating of social and political agency only in the individual act. We must keep in mind that to emancipate the subaltern subject there must be an organizing en masse and internationally to topple the oppressive and exploitive condi-tions faced by many under the rule of worldwide capitalism. We must keep centrally in mind that the internal development of global capital-ism touches on all of the world's subjects. We must keep in mind that social and political change will not happen through the unfixing of signs or spaces, but, as history has shown, through the organized struggle of millions of working people worldwide in their massive push to change reality.

If we hold up a balance sheet to Said's ideas and actions, then, what we discover is not so much a research program that formulates a se-ries of hypotheses that are then measured against reality, but rather a textualist-idealism that ultimately provides artillery for the defense of the most reactionary kinds of acts.[35]

SIX

MODERNITY, WHAT?

Modernity this, modernity that, the cup runneth over with modernity. It's seemingly everywhere I turn: in the books I read, conferences I attend, dissertations filed[1]—and in many a graduate student exhalation. Yet, I'm still not sure what exactly it defines or identifies.

The *Oxford English Dictionary* dates the first appearance of the word *modernity* to 1635, when it was used to describe the condition of being modern (in character or style); and dates another appearance of the word to the turn of the twentieth century, when it was used to describe the "intellectual tendency or social perspective characterized by a departure from or repudiation of traditional ideas, doctrines, and cultural values in favour of contemporary or radical values and beliefs (chiefly those of scientific rationalism and liberalism)." It would seem that *modernity* in today's academic parlance is a style, values, and beliefs—and then some. Indeed, in an area of study that I'm particularly focused on in this chapter, postcolonial Latin American literary criticism and analysis, scholars conjure up modernity to periodize history, periodize literary genres and canons, even as a mode of knowing and being.[2]

In this chapter I explore the pros and cons of using the category modernity. I examine whether or not it is useful as a rubric for both distinguishing and making bridges between different literary historical periods and national literary canons; if it is useful as a historical category to distinguish colonial from postcolonial; if it is useful as an economic category to define Western capitalism vs. non-Western noncapitalism;[3] finally, if it is useful as a way of knowing the world that threads in and out of concepts like developmentalism, dependency theory, cosmopolitanism, and a host of other related issues.

To see where this road takes us, I'll begin by providing a lay of the land, by detailing several routes carved out by postcolonial theorists, especially Latin American ones, and where they lead us.

The turn to modernity has been taken by scholars of late as a way to build a postcolonial frame around their studies of literary periods of time past.[4] For example, Ananya Jahanara Kabir and Deanne Williams identify a "post-Enlightenment modernity" in the nineteenth century whereby the scholarly obsession with the Middle Ages is theorized as an act of Orientalist colonization; they consider the scholarly control and containment of the Middle Ages a colonization of "a distant continent" (*Postcolonial Approaches to the European Middle Ages* 1). Hence they can declare "as postcolonial scholars have sought to dismantle the notions of modernity upon which colonialism was predicated, medievalists have, in turn, challenged the binaries of medieval and modern (or early modern) that bracket off the Middle Ages, and keep it as exotic and foreign— and also as domitable—as any orientalist fantasy" (1–2). Others take the opportunity to apply European modernity to identify a variety of shadowed Others to study through the lens of postcolonial theory a whole variety of literary periods. In a special issue of *Modern Language Quarterly* (September 2004), John Dagenais similarly asserts that if in our scholarship of the medieval period we refuse to identify it as Europe's dark Other—like Europe's "similarly cast spatial colonies" (491)—we will "refuse complicity with some of the dire designs of modernity" (491).[5] In this same issue, Barbara Fuchs and David J. Baker decenter and unmoor modernity from its traditionally Anglophone dominance and show its appearance in "other cultures and periods are largely ignored" (337) in order to identify an uneven European coloniality and to turn upside down "historically discrete notions of race and nation states" ("Postcolonial Pasts" 339). And also in this issue, Mary Louise Pratt discusses how "modernity by 1900 had become a European identity discourse that performed" (444) a universal, narcissistic subject; and it is a postcolonial *contramodernidad* approach to the study of Latin American literature that can critically uncover the continued spreading (albeit in a decrepit form) of this "Western modernity" (445).[6]

Then there are the scholars who are arguably more ambitious; in their work we see modernity used not so much as a way to provide scholars with a postcolonial critical means in their study of literature from a variety of different epochs, but as a philosophy of capitalist (colonialist and imperialist) world systems. In *Local Histories/Global Designs,* Walter Mignolo writes of a "monotopic epistemology of modernity" that creates a delimiting "territorial thinking" (67); conversely, it is the local subaltern knowledge "located outside the parameters of modern conceptions of reason and rationality" (67) that can destabilize and resist such an oppressive global modernity. In like spirit, for Santiago Castro-Gómez modernity is defined as "an alterity-generating machine that, in the name of reason and humanism, excludes from its imaginary the hybridity, multiplicity, ambiguity, and contingency of different forms of life ("The Social Sciences, Epistemic Violence, and the Problem of the 'Invention of the Other'" 269). For Marzena Grzegorczyk modernity is a "mechanism of power" (*Private Topographies* 134) that at once produces difference and absorbs difference; it is embodied in colonial fantasies that produce hierarchies of difference (creole vs. indigenous) but that also becomes this difference in time: a *créolité* that morphed into a *mestizaje* and thus into its Other. Such a modernity-producing machine can be resisted in the uncovering of such "conflictive political identities" (136) within scholarly articulations of "postcolonial transitional projects" (136).

For yet others, modernity identifies why the anticolonial revolutionary impulse failed. In Martín Hopenhayn's *No Apocalypse, No Integration* a Western-identified modernity has led to anticolonial "conflict in our peripheral societies" (152) and has destroyed "the will towards utopian constructs" (152); it was the integration of modernity within anticolonial "social projects" (152) in Latin America that ultimately led to their crisis and the ultimate failure of various revolutions.[7] Because of its ties to a masculinist-identified, Western liberal modernity, María Josefina Saldaña-Portillo similarly conceives of the failure of revolution in her *The Revolutionary Imagination in the Americas and the Age of Development*. A figure like Che Guevara falls into this trap; his anticolonial resistance and revolutionary "imagination" fail because he ultimately buys into a modernist, masculinist, liberalist, and developmentalist worldview. Those that present a truly resistant revolutionary imagination are figures like Rigoberta Menchú and Subcomandante Marcos, who at once occupy a "particularity of Indian identity" and a "universality of abstract citizenship" that allow them to most successfully challenge the "developmentalist paradigms" (224). As political and social agents of change aware of and fully anchored in the "particularity" of their class as well as within a nonromanticized ethnicity formed already in "the colonial encounter with imperial reason and modernity" (261), they sidestep a premodern to modern teleology with its "'universal' model of full humanity" (260) as the big payoff. Hence, rather than retreat into nationalist, indigenous, and masculinist discourses of separation from Western colonialism and modernity, these "indigenous subalterns instead assert their place *within* a revolutionary developmentalism" (261). Such figures, Saldaña-Portillo writes, "insist on negotiating the terms of revolutionary subjection in order that the revolutionary imagination in the Americas may incorporate their living and modern difference" (261). That is, in their articulation of "an alternative modernity" (256) that is both nativist and universalist, premodern and modern, local and global they offer a truly revolutionary imagination.

Gareth Williams takes us to a similar place in *The Other Side of the Popular* whereby a global modernity has entered a phase of the "post-national" (11) in Latin America and where it is a "postrevolutionary" subalternity with its "language of postnational belonging" (213) that will exceed modernity's epistemological limits (213); it is the denizens of an insane asylum in Santiago, Chile, that in their "abject, impoverished, speechless, yet dignified commonalties ground in subaltern affect, challenge and undermine the notion of intellectual work and, indeed, make such a notion withdraw before its uncomfortable relation to abject love against all odds and without apparent reason" (294–295). Such subaltern figures' "alternative imaginations" (303) resist modernity's packaging of the Latin American as "tamed" for the tourist's gaze.

Modernity is, for David Scott, a "complex structure of social, economic, juridical, and political relations of knowledge and power" (*Conscripts of Modernity* 112). And like several of the scholars already mentioned, he conceives of it as intimately woven into anticolonial revolutionary ideologies. That is, modernity as the "story of innovation within adaptation" (113) has splintered and produced "different results" (113). And this happened not by choice on the part of the colonized, but by obligation.[8] Such conscripts of modernity include Toussaint Louverture: "a new kind of individual, the modern colonial intellectual" (20); and such conscripts change depending on who is telling the story. For example, Scott identifies a Romance and a Tragic mode of telling in the respective 1938 and 1963 editions of C. L. R. James's *Black Jacobins,* in which historical circumstances (pre-World War II and "*after* Bandung," the 1956 conference that launched the nonaligned movement)[9] have shifted the "mode of emplotting the story of the relation between our pasts, our presents, and our possible futures" (210–211).[10] For Scott, then, modernity is multiple and expresses itself in: the Romance genre (the 1938 edition) that is shaped by a "redemptic mythology" where suffering is the price "paid for the promise of a later emancipation" (134); and in the Tragic genre present in the latter edition as "a literary-philosophical genre [that] offers the most searching reflection on human action, intentions, and chance" (12). He favors the latter because it acknowledges "the contingent, the ambiguous, the paradoxical, and the unyielding in human affairs in such a way as to complicate our most cherished notions about the relation between identity and difference, reason and unreason, blindness and insight, action and responsibility, guilt and innocence" (13). Now this Tragic story of the Haitian revolts could be written only "*after* Bandung"—that is, after the anticolonial revolutions in Africa, Asia, and Latin America failed. Given the bleak prospects of "dead-ended modernities constructed by the postcolonial state" after-*Bandung* and today, the solution for the world's ills, finally, is for us "to be less enthusiastic about the heroic story embodied in the alternative modernities thesis and more concerned to inquire into the modern concepts and institutions upon which these resisting projects themselves depended" (115).

More could be said, of course, about each scholarly work. However, for the purposes of this chapter, I want to begin to identify the potholes in these various routes. One way or another those scholars who formulate various philosophies of modernity (alternative or otherwise) in their discussion of anticolonial movements and/or postcolonial/subaltern subjectivities intersect with economic theories. Scott places a massive emphasis on the failure of the Bandung's "New Nation" project; all the anticolonial efforts to build liberated postcolonial nations have led to a "virtual dead end" (57). And here, rather than look at why such anticolonial governments failed, Scott sees an opportunity to embrace a Tragic, pessimistic, and/or deterministic outlook. That is, rather than uncover capitalist strategies that led to the murder of those like Patrice Lumumba (the Congo) who proclaimed the building of a New Nation governed by the working people, Scott would have us see this as an opportunity to adopt the following position: if one is never optimistic about the future, then you'll never be disappointed. That is, to tell all those in Africa that are dying, "You've got it wrong, if you want to understand, abandon all hope." An analysis of "after Bandung" at the very least would have to consider how all those representatives of the nonallied states that met at Bandung adopted what was identified as a political and economic "third way"—a developmentalist blueprint that ensured the continued exploitation and oppression of the working people in all postcolonial countries.

To mention a few facts that need to be included in any discussion of Bandung: how it became a forum for dictators like Mobutu Sese Seko and Idi Amin (a.k.a. Big Daddy) to justify in the name of developmentalism some of the most barbarous acts of the late twentieth-century; and how it supported dictators like Sukarno and Jawaharlal Nehru in India (both central organizers of the Bandung conference) and Idi Amin's expulsion of forty thousand to eighty thousand Indians and Pakistanis from Uganda.[11]

This leads to another related point. In the identification of modernities pre- and post-Bandung follow the type of division of the world into pieces that we see in Walt Whitman Rostow's booklet *The Stages of Economic Growth* (1960): a country's full economic growth would be achieved only by taking specific economic steps toward realizing the goals and ambitions of capitalism.[12] To clarify, let me turn from Scott back to Saldaña-Portillo's work.[13] For Saldaña-Portillo, whether one is a truly resistant (revolutionary imaginary) subject or not depends on one's worldview: Che Guevara's sense of lifting his people out of a primitivist premodernity into a universalist/masculinist modernity, for example; that is, a revolutionary figure's resistance or not depends on where one stands, she writes, "*within a* racialized and gendered developmentalism" (7). Thus, narratives of figures like Che and Malcolm X reveal an "ethical subject of development typified by Rostow" (263). Specifically, their choice to leave behind their "clan, caste, tribe, or extended family" (263) indicates that they have chosen to "leave behind a prodigal life in favor of a productive one" (263). Finally, their choice to lift the "underdeveloped subject" (263) out of the past (premodern) into the future (modern, transcendental) exemplifies a developmentalist paradigm that sees the "fully developed subjectivity" as masculinist, that privileges "unitary, self-determining consciousness and agency," and that regards the underdeveloped subjectivity as "emasculated" (263–264). In contrast, Menchú and Subcomandante Marcos exceed, Saldaña-Portillo writes, "the terms of the revolution/development dialectic [by] rejecting developmentalist notions that interpret their indigenous and peasant subject positions as premodern" (12). Unlike Che, a figure like Menchú presents a model of "revolutionary subjectivity and theory . . . from an indigenous and peasant subject position simultaneously produced by modernity and in reaction to its developmentalism" (12).

Of course, Saldaña-Portillo is fully aware of Rostow's reactionary, anti-Marxist position. She is also careful to identify those dependency theories introduced to Latin America in the 1940s by the UN's Economic Commission for Latin America (ECLA) that "challenged the essence of liberal development theories by asserting that the underdeveloped and the developed, the periphery and the center, are not mutually exclusive categories" (49–50). This economic model considered the traditional and the modern as "economically, and epistemologically intertwined conditions" (50). She gives the example of the Mexican anthropologist Rodolfo

Stavenhagen, who "interprets modernization in the Third World as a process that begins in the fifteenth century with the expansion of Europe and the integration of rural economies to the urban centers within and beyond the regional colonies" (51).

Like Scott and the others mentioned above, Saldaña-Portillo divides up the world in ways that don't reflect reality and that will not lead to the kind of social and political emancipation she seeks. She does so by aligning the good revolutionary with what she calls a "radical developmentalism" and a bad revolutionary with a Rostow-identified developmentalism; she does so by superimposing economic models over life narratives, asserting on occasion that both the developmentalist model and the revolutionary movement resemble "regimes of subjection" as they ultimately "make men ready either for development or for revolution" (31). Situated in Menchú's and Marcos's revolutionary imaginary, Saldaña-Portillo is effectively asking the Latin American workers to do nothing: to sit back, be patient, and wait for the revolution to happen.[14]

If the world is divided up in the postcolonial recuperation of modernities, one necessarily runs into dead ends that leave only an Idealist path out. Aijaz Ahmad understands this well. *In Theory* is critical of those scholars (postcolonial or otherwise) who one way or another divide the world into: a world defined by its economic structure (capitalist); a social world defined by its economic structure (socialist); and a third world defined by noneconomic criteria (cultural and ethnic identity). Not only is this classification of one, two, three worlds in and of itself incoherent, but it doesn't correspond to yesterday's or today's reality. For Ahmad, such subjective divisions lead to the irrational invention of categories like the Other, the subaltern, and a lot of other terms and concepts posited as either philosophical conclusions, as psychological empirical facts, or as ontological categories. This leads to a skewed vision of reality: that geographic spaces and nation-states can be mutually exclusive.[15]

But it doesn't require Ahmad for us to see this. For example, Stalinism was a huge disaster for working peoples worldwide, yet I've never seen such concepts as the Other or subaltern used to describe the relationship between the Stalinist Soviet Union and its imposition of brutal counterrevolutionary tactics toward the so-called Second and Third Worlds.[16] I think readily of the squashing of worker uprisings in Berlin in 1953, in Hungary and Poland in 1956, and in the Czech Republic in 1968; nor have I seen this self/other used to theorize the "after Bandung" worker defeats organized by the Stalinist bureaucracy in Asia and Africa. And what of Latin America, which has, so to speak, itself Othered or transformed into the Other its own people, as in a Cuba controlled by Stalinist bureaucracy. According to those who divide up the world into First and Third Worlds and invent classifications like subaltern, the peoples of Asia, Africa, and Latin America were never Otherized by the so-called Second World (the Soviet Union and the countries of Eastern Europe).

If one uses categories like modern and premodern that divide up the world into pieces, then there can be no rational or scientific explanation of what, say, the Stalinist bureaucracy was because such categories can't account for how this bureaucracy is an outgrowth of capitalism and imperialism. They can't see what is happening at present in China (and also what is happening in the Soviet Union today): the more the country rebuilds and develops its industry (the more it appropriates capitalism), the more dependent it becomes economically on the main imperialist countries and thus the more vulnerable it is to the economic and political pressure exerted by the imperialist countries (essentially the United States). As a result, their politics necessarily become more reactionary.

This is the reason it's impossible to build socialism in only the postcolonies, or the Third World. If the leadership of the country that has expropriated capital doesn't have a policy of helping workers in the rest of the world to succeed but instead expropriates capital, they will be metabolized by the imperialist countries until the imperialist countries regain their hold over capital; it happened in the Soviet Union and other East European countries, and it will happen in China and Cuba. Not even right wing Democrats or Republicans in the United States consider China's or Cuba's Communist party in any way a revolutionary menace.

The dividing up of the world into parts and oppositions finally plays into the hands of dependency and/or developmentalist theories and thus ultimately distracts people from seeing a one-world system under capitalism. Capitalism, since its inception, has always been global, and thus the transformation of this one-world system must also happen among workers within and between countries globally in the building of their own organizations that will represent exclusively their own interests.

The various assertions of alternative modernities, revolutionary imaginations, and so on divide up the world in ways that at best disguise a decrepit and decayed reality under a globalizing capitalism; and that at worst feed into developmentalist and/or dependency theory models that promise a better future under capitalism. While such theories certainly are aware of today's "downward leveling of living conditions on a world-wide scale—which has brought in its wake heightened instability and political conflict," as Neil Lazarus succinctly states (19), they slip into these developmentalist teleologies and thus turn potential insight into scholarly fantasy.

For Timothy Brennan such postcolonial rhetoric generally fails to do what it intends: to grasp the "complex cultural puzzle of modernity" (Brennan 665); such a subaltern, diasporic "Cosmo-theory" approach doesn't account for the historical and the social.[17] Hence, one can fantasize about how denizens of an insane asylum represent a "postrevolutionary" subalternity with their "language of postnational belonging" (213), as Gareth Williams does.[18] If one doesn't account for our present and past material reality under capitalism by dividing the world into colonial and postcolonial, modern and postmodern, then one risks spiritualizing reality in ways that in fact promote capitalism in the name of "unprejudiced striving, world travel, supple open-mindedness, broad international norms of civic equality, a politics of treaty and understanding rather than conquest" (Brennan 659). As Brennan succinctly comments, such cosmo-theorists one way or another promote a reified identity politics that ultimately lets "power have its way" (Brennan 676).

By the term "Cosmo-theory" Brennan situates this type of ahistorical, aspatial theorizing within an intellectual genealogy that goes back to a mid-nineteenth-century cosmopolitanism. I think it's worth stretching this a little further back. Even since the Renaissance, ideals of the cosmopolitan were in the air, expressed in the nascent desire of scientists and humanists to share ideas. So even though Latin was still the lingua franca for these thinkers, and they were more confined to specific territories because traveling was much harder and the means for distributing work limited, there was a momentum pushing toward the forming of secular humanism across Europe. Think of figures like Rabelais, Cervantes, Shakespeare, and Newton (and before him, Galileo) as well as Bruno, Descartes, and Leibniz, to name a few. Whether one was thinking or writing in Sweden or Spain or Italy, there was a strong commitment to the sharing of ideas as members of a united republic of letters. As I mention elsewhere in this book, this was more an ideal than an actuality, as they didn't have the means to realize this potential at the time. Cosmopolitanism was realized in the late eighteenth- and early nineteenth-centuries by figures like Goethe, Kant, Hegel, Shelley, and Byron, to name a few; this avatar of cosmopolitanism had become a global reality in the massive dispersal and cross-pollination of culture. For the first time, people like Byron could read the work of writers in

Asia, Africa, the Middle East, Turkey, and elsewhere. Some, like Byron, also considered this cosmopolitanism to have a political dimension; he even fought for the independence of Greece from the Turks. During these periods cosmopolitanism already contained an unbounded sense of cultural exchange—and for some, even a political commitment to the enlightenment of humanity.

By the middle of the nineteenth century, however, cosmopolitanism took a radical shift. This was a time of crisis for the bourgeoisie and petite bourgeoisie (liberals); for the first time in history, the workers started building workers' organizations (trade unions and political parties) in European countries with the broader ambition of establishing a world workers' political party; what we know today as the First International. Rather than talk about internationalism, the bourgeoisie began to talk about cosmopolitanism and to circulate reified ideas of being "citizens of the world." This is the seed that has grown into today's cosmo-theory. In this brand of cosmopolitanism we see the spiritualizing of reality and the massive circulation of ideas that have absolutely no practical consequence. This is the brand that threads its way through the thinking and writing of early twentieth-century figures like Thomas Mann, Alfonso Reyes, Roland Rolan, and liberals more generally, who one way or another promoted a spiritualist cosmopolitanism; we see this variously in ideas like the establishing of an international language (Esperanto), the establishing of a "world passport" for themselves as "world citizens," the turning back of the cultural clock to Greek antiquity. This idealist brand of cosmopolitanism was more and more an intellectual pose for certain brands of liberalism that ignored the material reality of the world.

The brand of spiritualist cosmopolitanism went underground after World War II but resurfaced in the late 1960s, when once again the bourgeoisie worldwide was threatened by worker and student movements. This was a moment when the capitalist system was about to blow up, so for capitalism to survive, it had to assert its will against the working class by violent and extreme measures. Richard Nixon's delinking of gold from the dollar in 1971 was one such measure; and there was of course the privatizing of health care, transportation, education, the secular state, and so on aimed at destroying all that had been won by the workers. This is arguably why French theorists, who were the first to systematically justify the spiritualization of reality, were so readily and swiftly picked up by U.S. scholars.

Every time the class struggle becomes a serious threat to capitalism, one sees intellectuals reacting in two ways: Those who spread ideas that claim to be against capitalism but that in actual fact support and sustain globalization politics; and those who one way or another say that we must destroy the very state (recall Williams's "postnation") that has provided the frame within which workers have made significant political gains in the fight for equal rights and representation as well as for collective bargaining and collective agreements. So when theorists today like Mignolo, Williams, Saldaña-Portillo, Scott, and Hopenhayn, to name a few, all favor one way or another the elimination of the state, the destabilizing of modernity, and the promotion of a radical subalternity in the likes of the insane, they participate in a cosmopolitanism that has long worked to undermine—even destroy—the working-class struggle. Those who are hostile to the nation-state, as Brennan identifies in another of his essays, reveal

> an irrepressible ultra-modernism [that] is given an almost aesthetic accent in which *mobility* as an ontological condition is portrayed as the exciting play of an infinite self-fashioning. The cast is "perverse" because in accordance with such a logic one is forced to revile contemptuously, even while resonating with, a specific and conjunctural national-statist project (that of the United States) which in a vigorously broadcast system of images and slogans, embraces the same hybridity, modernity, and mobility as globalization theory. ("Postcolonial Studies and Globalization Theory" 138)

That is, while such theorists are critical of modernity and globalization, they end up spoon-feeding us theories that serve the interests of capitalist globalization.

CONCLUDING REMARKS

In closing, I want to return to the concept of modernity (alternative or otherwise) and its use to periodize history, and geographic space and/or to create canonical cultural clusters. Is modernity a useful category to periodize a specific moment in history? As several scholars have suggested (Kabir, Williams, and Pratt, for example), modernity could refer to the literature of ancient Greece, the Middle Ages, or the Enlightenment, as each could be marked off as a historical shift from one socioeconomic system to another: hunter-gatherer to slavery to feudalism, in this case. Of course, we know that even these categories don't reflect reality. The shift from slavery to feudalism didn't happen overnight; capitalism, growing within the entrails of feudalism, took several centuries to develop. When Dante was writing his *Divina Commedia* merchants and artisans were already present in European cities; urbanizing impulses that moved away from agricultural production to a merchant and artisan economy likewise began to break away from a former isolation during this period. This was also a period, as seen with the likes of Dante, that pushed forward the use of the vernacular languages in creative work; others in the translation of the Bible; in this sense it was progressive, as such moves sought to loosen the grip of that great feudalist appendage, the Catholic church.

The so-called modernity of Europe that came with the conquest of the Americas was another bundle of contradictions: massively exploitative (indigenous genocides and enslavement of Africans to work mines and plantations, for example) and explosive culturally (arts and science) within and outside Europe's borders. This was a period that fueled the rise of the bourgeoisie in Europe and that led to the domination of the world colonized or dominated by this system called capitalism. With the next big creative explosion, known as the Enlightenment, we have both progressive and reactionary philosophers, thinkers, and writers as well as the big growth spurt of the middle class and female readers in Britain; this created a clash in literature between the telling of stories that adhered to facts (historical novel) and that injected a moralism (novel of manners); later this clash would express itself in the battle between lowbrow and highbrow literature, between beauty (domesticated) and the sublime (overpowering). And, of course, within this period a series of writers like Denis Diderot bridge the two. His novel *Jacques le Fataliste* both exalts subjectivity and uncontrolled emotions and unfolds as a series of digressions. If we jump forward in literary history to that period identified as modern, we see a similar mélange of impulses, including Charles Baudelaire's naturalist poems about gritty urban life, written in a technically very experimentalist manner.

Wherever we want to cut into this pie of modernity, then, we begin to see how the category itself might not be that useful. If we pay slight attention to the different times and spaces of these particular historical, literary, geographic periods, we see how modernity becomes an arbitrary assigning of qualities to a great variety of geographic spaces (Europe, say), or historical periods (the conquest of the Americas or the colonization of the Middle East, Africa, and/or India during the Enlightenment)— assignments that are as subjective as a taste for, say, chocolate ice cream.

Moreover, the cutting up of the world into slices leads us back to that problem we faced earlier: an idealist view of reality that neglects the work done to shape this reality today and tomorrow.

Neither modernity nor its affiliative categories discussed above ("Tragic," "discontinuous alterities," "radical revolutionary," "post-national," to name a few) make the distinctions that make a difference; they don't tell us anything because they don't account for our transformation of the world and its transformation of us in time and space. Finally, I think of the ultimate destructiveness of those scholars who refer to counter-modernity as a way to assert some form of "justice to come" and thus promote patience and faith as a path to our salvation.

SEVEN

TEACHERS, SCHOLARS, AND THE HUMANITIES TODAY

INTRODUCTION

I begin this chapter with questions that are very much on the tip of people's tongues, people who are interested in the humanities and the role of the scholar in society. In my classes, students ask, Why become a professor—especially of literature? Why devote years and years of study to a profession that, in the best of cases, will land you a job somewhere you least expect (with little pay) and that seemingly has little consequence on the progressive shaping of an already decrepit reality? My students are not alone here. In the Modern Language Association's 2006 publication of its journal, *Profession,* four scholar/intellectuals run the gamut of responses to the question, What is the "role of the intellectual in the twenty-first century." For Julia Kristeva, rationalist humanism has failed, so we must embrace a secular antifoundational irrationalism and tune into the unconscious;[1] for others, like Ratna Kapur, there's a faith in the power of metaphysical critique as practice; and for Ngugi wa Thiong'o it is to "breathe life" into words and give a tellurian grounding to critical inquiry so as to challenge those that carry "death and devastation" ("For Peace, Justice, and Culture" 39). The responses don't entirely satisfy, so I will explore more deeply in this chapter the question, What is our role as scholar and teacher in the academy?

Of course, many academics and intellectuals are looking for ways to right wrongs in our ever-faster headlong tumble toward barbarism at home and abroad: The U.S.-led occupation of Iraq, the apartheid and Bantu-izing imposed on the Palestinians, the near complete destruction of the African continent, the relentless attacks against the American working people on all fronts, including the decimation of salaries, health care, health insurance, social security, employment, debt and bankruptcy, elementary, lower, and higher education, as well as road and rail maintenance and expansion; a world marked by the unabated polluting of our biosphere, the reduction and/or suppression of civil rights, the limitation of the right to abortion, the strong-armed implementation of religious-based science teaching and research, the infringement of constitutional separation of powers (executive, legislative, judicial), and the near disappearance of a free press.

Oddly, it is within this state of social decrepitude that we see many scholars turning off to reality and turning on to various forms of idealist decodings. We see a turn from research and scholarship with empirical aims and commonsense hypotheses that attempt to see this world more clearly and critically to a retreat into obscurantism and/or a seeking after spiritualized reality. As I've begun to show in earlier chapters, it is good enough to decode domains of culture and assert various formulations of symbolic ("textualist") resistance to effect social and political change.

Many academics have turned (wittingly or not) to rather esoteric formulations of resistance. Ringing loud from academic halls during the oppressive 1980s under Reagan one saw the formulation of a "radical multiculturalism" that could shake up the military-industrial complex.[2] Today there are clarion calls for a "cosmopolitical resistant performativity" and a "symbolic reterritorializing" with an even greater degree of speculation. The trick is always the same: the magician plays only variations on the illusion-effect. It consists of obscure, prophetic-sounding assertions to lead the audience to surrender his or her disbelief and to accept the alchemic transmutation of reality into an omnipresent, omnipowerful, omnieffective *Text*.

In this chapter, I'm particularly interested in scholarship concerned with issues of social equality and that works in fields such as postcolonialism, U.S. ethnic, feminist, and queer studies. All such fields branch out from the early civil rights work of scholars in the late 1960s/1970s academy. Of course, the impulse to actively work to push for equality—across race, class, and gender/sexual orientation lines—is absolutely necessary. That there are scholars committed to this is more than important. Such intellectual work in and out of the classroom can provide the tools for us and others to engage with and actively shape our material world. However, as scholars like the late African Americanist Barbara Christian (I think of her seminal essay "The Race for Theory") have warned, when such work obscures rather than disentangles simpleminded thinking, when its esoteric razzle-dazzle transmutes basely material realities into Logos, then it does not provide the tools necessary for the interrogating of received ideas and for the active shaping of our world.[3] What we see instead are many scholars staking a claim on progressive thinking, but who ultimately are undermining political acts and struggles.

In the wake of 9/11, as George W. Bush was putting the United States in a quasi-state of martial law (with his Patriot Act) and jump-starting his spin machine to justify the illegal invasion of Iraq, a friend studying for her doctorate in English at Harvard told me that classes had been canceled for a week. Professor Homi Bhabha would be participating in the World Economic Forum (WEF), taking place in New York City instead of Davos. At first this didn't surprise me. Academics, after all, are specialists and so can offer some useful information to those outside the academy; we read in the newspaper daily how this or that academic corroborates or not a given story. Like any expert in the field, academics are tapped by media and government agencies, courtrooms, and the like to give expert testimony.[4] However, what surprised me was that a so-called Left postcolonial scholar had been invited.

Then in early 2004, I read that Bhabha had been invited yet again to participate in the WEF in Davos, Switzerland. Along with several novelists (mostly those with exotic sounding last names), Bhabha rubbed elbows with the high priests of capitalism, including Bill Clinton and Jack Straw.[5] He was there to do political work: to workshop concepts of remembering and forgetting as a way to clear a space for humanistic inquiry within the domain of capitalist exploitation. This was for Bhabha his politics in action, remarking that to be an intellectual "is not a little cultural add-on," but to be "engaged" (Cowell 3). The idea of using the proverbial master's tools to rebuild the master's house is commonplace among academics. Perhaps, however, this form of being politically *engagé* was serving another purpose. Perhaps it was a pause: like the clown act at the circus or a magician's performance, Bhabha's session could have functioned as a momentary reprieve after, as fellow invitee Kazuo Ishiguro remarks with a certain sardonic clarity, "a hard day listening to people talking about terrorism or banking" (3). Perhaps, too, the WEF was throwing money at a well-known intellectual figure self-identified as Left in order for him to advertise how global capitalism cares greatly for humanity. Perhaps, finally, it was also self-serving on the part of Bhabha, visibly making good on claims of postcolonial theory's political efficacy in the performing of what he has called elsewhere a "sly-mimicry" in action.

There's more to this, of course, than an academic like Bhabha being complicit with an imperialist agenda such as the one favored by the WEF. It speaks to a larger trend in the academy of cultural studies scholars who are selling—and seemingly well—a new brand of political activ-ism: a "revolutionism" without revolution.

Rather than underscore the important role of the working-class strug-gle historically, these scholars teach how to fancifully decode "vernacu-lar" acts—like an author's use of slang or Urdu or the representation of hybrid cultural objects and characters—to show their "cosmopolitical" identity (see Bishnupriay Ghosh). In doctoral courses, too, the nation-state is theorized as that which territorializes imagined peoples and is itself an imagined identity; as guest editors Sheldon Pollock, Homi K. Bhabha, Carol A. Breckenridge, and Dipesh Chakravarty of *Public Cul-ture* (2000) announce, such an approach satisfies "something of our need to ground our sense of mutuality in conditions of mutability, and to learn to live tenaciously in terrains of historic and cultural transition" ("Cos-mopolitanisms" 580). Formulations regarding the role of the academic-intellectual identify "new forms of struggle and solidarity in places we never thought to look" (233–234), as Michael Denning writes. Such forms are everywhere and are a result of, as Michel Bérubé states, "power rela-tions that shape the most intimate and/or quotidian details of our lives" (40). For Grant Farred, political intervention is "beyond the scope of the party, the trade union, and the 'traditional bourgeoisie'" (*What's My Name* 4); social and political transformation happens by identifying pub-lic figures like Bob Marley, Eartha Kitt, Angela Davis, and Grace Jones as "producers, articulators, and disseminators of cultural knowledge" (5); in their "Vernacularity" (3) they produce a resistant popular culture "as a primary site of politics" (3);[6] political resistance resides in C. L. R. James's critique of a cricket match, and Muhammad Ali's "fistic armory" (8).

When the African Americanist Cornel West was reprimanded by the president at Harvard for spending more time making a rap album than teaching and producing scholarly work, he took offense that his intellec-tual work had not been recognized; he moved from Harvard to Prince-ton and published a book, *Democracy Matters,* that formally declared his version of a *doing* of politics. In *Democracy Matters,* for example, West identifies the loss of "dialogue" as central to the U.S. turn toward author-itarianism today, so the "challenge is mustering the courage to scrutinize *all* forms of dogmatic policing of dialogue and to shatter *all* authoritar-ian strategies of silencing voices" (7). To restore democracy in the United States and worldwide we must "engage in a respectful and candid dia-logue" (10–11), and we must embrace "moral commitments and visions and fortifications of the soul that empower and inspire a democratic way of living in the world" (15). That is, we must look to those "great public intellectuals" (15) like Socrates, Walt Whitman, Herman Melville, Ralph Waldo Emerson, Martin Luther King, Jr., Toni Morrison, James Baldwin, and rap artists, who created forums for dialogue, and we must also "stare painful truths in the face and persevere without cynicism or pessimism" (21). Thus West sees himself as a cultural worker who identifies a "tragicomic hope" (21) directed toward a future—a future he envisions not as a "U.S.-led corporate globalization" but rather as a "democratic globalization" (22). In so doing, he seeks to provide us with a

> Socratic-driven, prophetic-centered, tragicomic-tempered, blues-inflected, jazz-saturated vision that posits America as a confident yet humble democratic experiment that should shore up international law and multilateral institutions that preclude imperial arrangements and colonial invasions; that should also promote wealth-sharing and wealth-producing activities among rich and poor nations abroad; and that should facilitate the principled transfer of wealth from well-to-do to working and poor people by massive investments in health care, education and employment and the preservation of our environment. (62)[7]

According to the abovementioned scholars (a mere sample) knowledge is power, and power is everywhere in society. So knowledge is perforce everywhere too, and to subvert dominant paradigms such as patriarchy, capitalism, neocolonialism, and so on, one only need reveal the constructedness of culture, society, and the relationships of power to discursive structures of knowledge (see chapters 2, 3). One's work in the classroom—and at venues like the World Economic Forum—thus becomes intellectual work that subverts through the decoding of culture and/or the producing of cultural objects. It is a politics that is an identity politics in which the personal is political, and vice versa. It is good-bye and good riddance to the separation of the private and the public; it is the total subsuming of the private to the public. It's the welcoming of Big Brother and the Iron Heel.

Such localized, cultural work appears in different shapes and sizes. Peter Redfield, for example, describes Médecins sans frontières (MSF) as a socially progressive form of "minimalist biopolitics" ("Doctors, Borders, and Life in Crisis" 329). This form of localized cultural work expresses biopolitics in its ability to operate "in the shadow of disaster" while promoting an "ethic of engaged refusal" (329). So while MSF receives a large proportion of its monies from private and corporate entities—in 2002–2003 it received over 80 percent of its funds from private sources and had an estimated income of over 360 million euros that year alone—its efforts "to effect the government of health" (330) and to preserve life negate its imperialist/corporate ties and interests.

In several essays and interviews Gayatri Spivak has rightfully identified NGOs like Doctors without Borders (Médecins sans frontières) as having direct ties to global capitalists, and she has described its beneficent paternalist attitude as an appendage to imperialism. (See *positions: east asia cultures critique*, 2004, and also her essay "Righting Wrongs" in *Human Rights, Human Wrongs: The Oxford Amnesty Lectures 2001*.) We should be wary of those who, like Redfield, celebrate MFS as a localized form of "transnational activism" (349). First, MFS is an NGO tightly strung to the imperialist directives (in Algeria and Somalia, for example) of the former French president François Maurice Mitterrand. Its poster boy was the dashingly good-looking Dr. Bernard Kouchner, who also happened to be the minister of health care—a government entity that nearly wiped out the national health care system in France. (MFS's Website has some short film clips advertising its humanitarian aid; one shows Dr. Kouchner arriving on a beach in Somalia à la D-Day with bags of rice to save the children. Notably, Dr. Kouchner was recently appointed foreign minister in France.) What we see more clearly than Redfield is that in the name of independence and humanitarianism, these so-called antistatist, locally resistant NGOs like MFS (and now they number in the thousands) are not only financed by governments and corporations, but function as social cushions to dissipate social discontent.[8] In effect, NGOs, in their promotion of local power over nation-state power, work more like temporary job agencies: they provide short-term (if that) "relief" to systemic problems caused by the ruling class's destruction of labor legislation, health care, education, transportation, and so on.

Whether NGO, workshops in Davos paid by the World Economic Forum, or theories on how to become a "cultural worker," as long as we're ethically minded and have an eye to cultural difference, all will be well. But this is not the reality. This all has material consequences. When one proposes that students learn to decode culture as a way to effect social and political change, this makes for an ineffective politics that plays into the hands of corporate capitalists. With political activism everywhere—hybrid gaps, rap music, and/or "visions and fortifications of the soul"—then it is nowhere. What better place would capitalists like a Left intellectual to reside than in this space of political nonactivism? What better place than the WEF to invite those intellectuals who sell buzzwords as acts of resistance?

It would seem that the Left academic today has become a member of the "bought priesthood" (*Chomsky on Democracy* 30), washing the dirty laundry of capitalists by keeping the "public at an extremely low cultural and intellectual level, subordinated to power and blind obedience to authority" (*Chomsky on Democracy* 99). Indeed, what better way to make an academic Left complacent than to reward and fatten those who preach acts that have absolutely no practical political effect other than steering students away from the struggle to help workers organize and build their own independent party? What we see increasingly with the creating of an academic star system in the United States is a reciprocating need between capitalist and scholar: the scholar hungers for a spot in the limelight, and the capitalist bureaucrat is eager to have on his/her side a Left-identifying intellectual talking head.[9]

That capitalists need such a high priesthood is not new. The university has served as a main site for the manufacturing of "mandarins" (see Chomsky)—technocrats, administrators, ambassadors, media pundits, those proverbial stenographers of power (journalists), academics, and so on—who one way or another do the business of selling and/or maintaining the ideology of capitalism. Like the mandarins of yesteryear's Chinese dynasties who helped administer China's wide swath of territory, those like Bhabha, West, and others mentioned above extend this lineage. And it is usually during moments of great crisis and economic instability—today's invasion of Iraq and global economic instability, yesterday's invasion of Vietnam, and so on—that such mandarins and their work become most necessary.

Historically, the university has had a twofold function: As a space for independent inquiry (individual and collective), self-analysis, and critical analysis of all aspects that constitute the world. And as a space for the training of and manufacturing of mandarins—those figures that put a human face on capitalist exploitation and oppression. When Bhabha attends the WEF to workshop memory and forgetting within global capitalism, he participates in the functioning of global capitalism as a mandarin.

I turn now to a moment when this Right versus Left battle became front-page news: the 1980s culture wars. The role of the academic and/or self-identifying public intellectual was the topic du jour, especially regarding the literary canon. On the one hand, there were those who deemed it imperative that an Alice Walker or an Adrienne Rich appear on classroom syllabi to reflect more truthfully the tectonic shifts in college student demographics; because of affirmative action programs, more and more students of color and women were admitted to places like Stanford and Berkeley, for example. At the center of such debates and coming from the African American corner of the ring we had Henry Louis Gates (and Jesse Jackson, Cornel West, and so on), who demanded that universities question the Eurocentric assumptions that traditionally give shape to the canon, proposing a multicultural makeover. (See his *Loose Canons*.) On the other side of the academic/public intellectual ring we had those big names such as Secretary of Education E. D. Hirsch as well as big-name professors Harold and Allan Bloom (not related) that declared such makeovers a threat to all of Western civilization. In *History in Literature* Herbert Lindenberger sums up how the move to makeover the canon (literature, philosophy, science, and political theory) was interpreted by such conservative figures "as a sign that the ethnical minorities and feminists who had achieved political consciousness since the 1960s had not merely succeeded in taking over the universities, but that their influence on the curriculum threatened the cultural values articulated by Hirsch and Bloom and also the social stability that some felt had been achieved during the past decade" (150).

Academics on the Left and Right professed oppositional aims but ended up in the same spot. As Walter Benn Michaels succinctly writes, "As long as the left continues to worry about diversity, the right won't have to worry about inequality" (13). As Frank Ferudi sums up in *Where Have All the Intellectuals Gone?* taking sides on either the so-called Left or Right in the so-called culture war, where all is turned into a form of Nietzschean perspectivism either in its "philistinism" or its "unhealthy instrumentalism" (20), is not the answer. This was not just a question of what would be gained or lost when revising the canon or how one would agree upon which books to include to reflect accurately a multiethnic and positively gendered United States.

That such fanfare greeted this issue on both sides of the Left-Right divide reveals a deeper issue. That is, was this culture war between a so-called Left and Right that pitted highly educated academics against each other actually deflecting attention from an increasingly unpleasant real everyday life for women, people of color, and the working class and poor under the Reagan administration?

To focus on what is taught at the university is important. I know this firsthand as the beneficiary of the, say, opening up of the canon. I get paid to teach Chicano/a and postcolonial literature, after all. Another fact, however, is that in a post-culture-war era, the shape of the canon has changed very little. Most of Harold Bloom's "geniuses" seem to be holding up just fine. And rather than spend time rehearsing the culture wars gains and losses we need to look deeper here at the function of the university and how and by what means it is supposed to achieve this function. The locating of politics within debates about culture also points us to a necessary discussion of the role of the intellectual-scholar formed by and working within the university.

First, why was there a decline in support of disciplines like English—even the federally funded National Endowment for the Humanities saw a huge drop in funding—during this period? It would seem that this would be a good place to put money to produce those aforementioned mandarins. Indeed, after years of declining support and interest in the social sciences and concomitant support for disciplines like English in the humanities, just prior to and especially during the Reagan era there was a reversal: the so-called soft sciences were given more support. This isn't so surprising. While much of the so-called soft sciences have been useful, the method of study is not the same as that of hard science and arguably promotes opinion and ideology; that is, the research methods used in the soft sciences (sociology, etc.) lend themselves more readily to speculation. (See Alvin Kernan's *What's Happened to the Humanities?*)

What about the humanities? There was a time, of course, when universities nationwide were allocated huge budgets to build and promote English and ethnic studies departments. This was during the cold war period, when the European grip on Asia and Africa was loosening as a result of the massive efforts of colonized peoples struggling and winning independence and with the simultaneous need of U.S. capitalists to expand markets. What better way to administer new territories than through the production of culture "specialists" who could speak for and humanize the expansion of capitalist interests?

This institutionalizing of liberal arts education and the offering of Western civilization courses in the United States to produce mandarins first began with the instituting of the War Issues course in 1917 at Columbia University; it was a course aimed at educating its students in the culture and heritage of Europe so as to prepare better soldiers during World War I. In *History in Literature* Lindenberger discusses similar courses being offered later at the University of Chicago. After the war, such courses continued to manufacture a newly emerging middle class of educated immigrants who reproduced the "words uttered by the great men of the West" (153) and thus provided comfort to conservatives feeling nervous about their place in a United States with a rapidly changing class and race demographic. For Lindenberger, the institutionalizing of Western civilization courses became the glue that would ultimately bind a newly forming U.S. culture together. According to Lindenberger, the culture wars of the 1980s was enacting something of a reversal of this pattern: stressing a non-European U.S. heritage in its embracing of the "non-Western" (158) that reflected the "waning of America's earlier power" (162).

As I've already suggested, we can link the university's expansion of the humanities to capitalist interests in European markets (World War I and World War II) and then Asian, African, and Latin American markets. The shifts in university curricula during these periods, however, weren't aimed only at "cultivating" conscripted soldiers (as Lindenberger discusses vis-à-vis World War I), but also at the manufacturing of ambassadors, technocrats, and media pundits. Later when the GI Bill was instituted and more working-class soldiers were able to get funding for university—only after serving their terms in the armed services, of course—we would see the increased production of successive generations of mandarins that could oversee the business of U.S. capitalists in their global expansion.

The expansion of U.S. capitalism into other territories happens on many different levels. One way, of course, is the declaration of war and the subsequent invasion. However, given that people generally are pacifist by nature, a massive machine needs to be set in motion to mobilize a nation of people to support war. Whether we look to the facts that led us to war in Europe or later Vietnam—even the more recent invasion of Iraq—we see that an elemental cog in this machine is that of the mandarin—the making of a "bought priesthood." To win public opinion and to gain the necessary support of the people, this group of mandarins humanizes the ideology of the capitalist class.

Let's revisit Lindenberger's discussion of the offering of the War Issues courses at Columbia in 1917. This was a time of great economic unease among capitalists in the United States and Europe. The working-class struggle had shown the world another economic system following the Bolshevik party's seizure of power in Russia. It introduced new laws that would destabilize repressive laws created to exploit the worker. It had the capitalist class worldwide scurrying for stable ground. So this was a moment in history when U.S. capitalism had to assert itself: to save Europe from communism was to save the world from a noncapitalist economic system. Thus, its universities needed to produce intellectuals, politicians, ambassadors, economic representatives, councilors, journalists, and so on who had a better understanding of European traditions and history and customs and who would transmit capitalist ideology.

The American university has certainly existed within and even supported directly the functioning of a capitalist agenda. (Each capitalist nation has its own changing needs and hence its own curricular shifts.)[10] However, the function of the academy varies depending on the different political and economic positions the United States holds in the world. For example, in World War II the United States tasted sweet victory, but it had also stretched itself thin militarily: from Japan and the Philippines to Germany and Spain. This was a time when the country enjoyed unprecedented power, but that also meant a massive stretching of its resources. And we see this overextension again when the United States decided to extend its power to Africa by dislodging the power of the French, Belgians, Germans, and Italians in places like Somalia and Ethiopia. On each occasion, capitalists realized that their presence all over the world required the forming of American language and culture specialists.

Seen in this light, the curriculum changes and university admissions policies that took place within the university during the 1970s and 1980s and increased the presence of scholars of color had as much to do with civil rights acts as with the need for the U.S. administration to produce academics of color; contemporary examples include Colin Powell and Condoleezza Rice, of course. As a result of the U.S. expansion into Mexico (and other Latin American countries) we can now see a steady current of presidents formed by U.S. universities who have been shaped by capitalist conglomerates: the former president of Mexico Vicente Fox, who was CEO of Coca-Cola in Mexico before his election, is a case in point. Others, like former president of Panama Manuel Noriega had been trained in U.S. military academies as well as by the CIA. In less obvious ways, the United States has created mandarins out of prominent cultural figures. The author Carlos Fuentes has become one of the "bought priesthood" that quite overtly supports U.S. imperialist policy. Indeed, as Frances Stonor Saunders studies at length in *Who Paid the Piper? The CIA and the Cultural Cold War,* over $200 million has been spent by the CIA to subsidize academic conferences and journals such as *Partisan Review, Encounter,* and *Der Monat* as well as individual scholars, writers, and intellectuals—all in the name of promoting freedom and democratic values.

The United States needs mandarins to sell such destructive methods as necessary for the establishment of "democracy". Here, I'm reminded once again of Bhabha's attendance at the WEF and more explicitly of the work of Powell and Rice. I think also of the tremendous swelling of university coffers after 9/11, with funds directed to promoting the study of Middle Eastern languages, culture, and history. One of the Bush administration's greatest concerns after 9/11 was the country's lack of knowledge of Iraq, Afghanistan, Pakistan, and the Asian parts of the Soviet Union. Fellowships and university courses directed at Middle Eastern studies seemed to blossom overnight. As in the case of the mandarins of yesteryear, when Chomsky wrote *American Power and the New Mandarins* (1969), we continue to see the university producing figures who one way or another serve the interests of the dominant class.

Let me further refine and clarify Chomsky's "mandarin" here. Our society is divided into the private sector (multinationals, corporations, banks, distribution enterprises) and all those who do not own the means of production or distribution who have to sell their capacity to work. Because the latter's livelihood—life even—depends completely on being able to sell the capacity to work, there's a pressure to adapt and conform to the will of the ruling class. (Along with this economic compulsion, those institutions gathered collectively under the state—the executive, legislative, and judicial power, which are supported by the army and police forces—also keep the people in line; we know this from Bush Jr.'s sending of the National Guard to Oakland to break the dockworkers' strike and, more distant in our history, from the National Guard being sent to Kent State to quash student protests and to kill students.) The capacity to work also entails the acquisition of this capacity through practice, experience, and theory. The latter entails a social transmission of knowledge via universities, trade schools, research institutes, and so on. In many ways, today's Scholastic Aptitude Test is equivalent to the imperial examination taken by those who wanted to become bureaucrats in imperial China; and as in imperial China, where anyone could take this exam and thus move up the social ladder, so in our world today universities function as a way up for those not of the manner born. And, as in imperialist China, so in the modern United States capitalism needs to train a population of workers—from doctors and lawyers to nurses, teachers, and the managers of a General Motors plant—to manage (and in some cases insure the good health of) a larger population of workers. (See Frank Donoghue's *The Last Professors: The Twilight of the Humanities in the Corporate University*.)

Teachers are necessary for this social transmission of knowledge. So, whether in a conscious or unconscious way or simply because one has assimilated the ideology of the bourgeoisie, whatever you teach you will do in accordance with the needs of the bourgeoisie. Today's capitalist system is decaying rapidly; we live in a society where the ruling class is making a lot of noise trying to convince the world that it is strong and confident; that tomorrow will be even better from the point of view of the capitalist system. But this is all show business. Indeed, all the brouhaha over the Terry Schiavo case and the absurd attacks against stem cell research and against the teaching of evolution reveal a ruling class that is no longer confident, robust, strong, and optimistic. It's a ruling class that's decrepit, old, and wizened and that favors newspeak spin and delusion.

Today, what we see is a forming of civil servants, managers, teachers, lawyers—the workforce *grosso modo*—by teachers who are themselves decrepit and who don't *really* have any confidence in the future; a great proportion of teachers in the humanities, for example, denounce truth and reason—even a material reality. This is not the same ruling class of Chomsky's day nor that of, say, the eighteenth century, when a figure like Diderot could spend twenty years of his life or more researching (going out into the world), writing, and editing the *Encyclopedia*. Such a figure is discarded by the new mandarins in today's humanities, who are as decrepit as the masters they are serving. So, we see a rejection of methods and approaches to clarify and advance our understanding of the world and the embrace of a medieval mysticism. It is the rejection of people like Diderot and the turning into demigods of literally sick people like Nietzsche or reactionaries like Heidegger. It means that highly educated people aren't reacting at all to the current offensive against science by a reactionary administration, but are instead wasting energy arguing about the social merits of teaching X and not Y in the classroom.

Today we're in a much worse situation than when Chomsky denounced the intelligentsia's complacent support of the Vietnam War. What we are seeing today is an increasing number of obscurantists and spiritualists who support a dying and decrepit ruling class.

This doesn't mean that there aren't independent thinkers in the academy who choose to follow a different path. But many such scholars one way or another don't take into account the class struggle. As I've said elsewhere in this book, at the same time that we have to defend all that humanity has achieved in its struggle, we also have to keep squarely in mind that our future and the changes required to make this future a better place lie not in the oppositional segment of the bourgeoisie but in the hands of the working class.

I want to return briefly to several points made above. While the university has historically proven—and continues to prove today—subject to the fluctuating needs of capitalists to extend markets, this doesn't mean that we should denounce wholesale, say, the institutionalizing of ethnic studies or Middle Eastern studies. No matter what the curriculum might be, the course of study offered, and so on, even if we know that the course was originally set up to create mandarins in order to secure at all costs the increased wealth of the ruling class—any critique of such disciplines and courses would ultimately prove to be an attack against learning. As academics committed to independent thinking and to the secular advancement of knowledge, we must resist systematically any opposition that might threaten to dismantle the university.

As already outlined, there are several types of scholar-intellectuals who respond in different ways to living in an unstable political situation: those who increasingly attach (wittingly or not) their scholarship and classroom work to a capitalist agenda; those who promote a social/political reading of textual production that claims for itself the capacity to replace real political action by its textual ersatz; and those who continue to be independent thinkers (intellectuals, scholars, students, and so on) who do not have any ambition to secure their position by becoming a member of the bought priesthood.

Now, we all exist within the unitary world of capitalism; it isn't that by choosing to be an independent scholar-intellectual you magically stand outside this world. What, then, is the answer? First, it is to encourage thoughtful and critical thinking. As a scholar and teacher, I consider the classroom a space to impart knowledge and tools that we can use to understand the world better. I like Robert Scholes's idea of imparting tools to his students so they can become "crafty readers" of literature; it's one that I apply in my classroom. And I am absolutely rigid in my opinion that the approach to teaching and research should be secular, rational, and systematic. However, I differ slightly as to the methods and approaches of Scholes and others who one way or another consider the role of the scholar-intellectual to be driven by a moral and/or ethical responsibility. For Scholes, to make "crafty readers" is to combat a "natural enemy that is at large in our world and working powerfully to change that world in ways that are hostile to literature as we know it and to our political freedoms, as we have known them. This enemy of crafty reading is fundamentalist literalism, of whatever kind, and wherever found" (*The Crafty Reader* 216). We see this position also in Bob Brecher's "Do Intellectuals Have a Social Public Responsibility?" Again, I agree with Brecher's identification of the scholar-intellectual's role in society in the commitment "to the pursuit of truth" (36) and to "finding, testing and re-testing reasons; in developing and changing one's views accordingly; and in communicating these processes and their results to others. That is to say, one's job is to think, to be critical" (36). However, Brecher considers finally the scholar-intellectual's responsibility to be that "of trying to make the world a better place, as Plato long ago recognized in his association of truth and goodness" (37–38).

Making the world a better place will not happen only through the efforts of isolated entities (thinkers, teachers, scholars) either in or out of the classroom. And usually a profession of a sense of some moral responsibility to society appeals to a sense of morality (and immorality) outside time and space. We know from Karl Marx and later Leon Trotsky (see his *Their Morals and Ours [1938]*) that notions of morality are shaped by the state and structure of a particular society and its dominant class. That is, morality has a context and a class character. To profess an abstract morality that exists outside of the history of the class struggle ultimately benefits those in power, who seek to preserve the status quo. That is, we must see our actions and our role not as intellectuals isolated from the world and as somehow special, but rather as people among a working people worldwide and living within specific material conditions in a specific social context of class struggle within global capitalism. It is our choice either to transform society in "the alteration of men on a mass scale," as Marx and Friedrich Engels state in "The German Ideology," or to sit back and watch humanity spin to its barbarous destruction. It is not whether I have the right or wrong ideas or ideals that will act as agent of social and political change, but rather the material conditions in which I exist and in which all other workers exist that propel us to fight for working-class interests.

CONCLUDING REMARKS

In closing, let me recount briefly two events that happened while I was teaching at the University of Colorado, Boulder: the walkouts held in

April 2003 to protest the invasion of Iraq and the walkouts conducted to protect freedom of speech that flared up around the so-called Ward Churchill Affair in February 2005.

In the first event, I offered my students the option of walking out or of holding an open forum to debate the U.S. invasion of Iraq. They wanted to discuss the war. The talk went back and forth between those students who thought it an act of U.S. imperialism, those who believed it was the bringing of democracy to those that had most suffered at the hands of Saddam Hussein, and those who supported it because a family member was about to be deployed. Then the students turned to me for advice. I made it clear that I would only be expressing an opinion—just as they were expressing opinions. First, no reason is a good reason to go to war. Second, we need to be careful of the media's spinning of newspeak and to look to the facts. I mentioned a couple of examples: destruction is called construction, oppression is termed freedom, starvation calls for humanitarian feeding, and in the bombing of Baghdad and many other places most of the victims were civilian men, women, and children. Third, I mentioned that in my opinion the Bush administration's invasion of Iraq only deepened the destruction brought on by the Clinton administration, with its imposition of an embargo and its years of dropping bombs, which had already caused massive starvation, deprivation, suffering, and death among Iraqi women, men, and children. Fourth, I discussed with the students the upholding of rights; that whenever they see any action to remove our civil rights—the Bush administration's post-9/11 Patriot Act, for example—no matter what side of the partisan line one stood on, one must stand against this. If we didn't stand against the war, any democratic gains that the working-class movement has made in the last couple of centuries would ever more quickly erode.

Of the second event, I again offered my students the choice: to walk out or debate whether or not Professor Ward Churchill should be fired for writing that the technocrats working in the World Trade Center were like "little Eichmanns." After the students debated and mostly agreed that one should protect freedom of intellectual inquiry even if one didn't necessarily agree with Churchill's opinion (a majority in Colorado wanted him fired, saying that it was their tax dollars paying his salary). I introduced the fact that Churchill had written several responses to 9/11 and that most people who were up in arms hadn't bothered to read any of the versions. For example, in his original essay "Some People Push Back" (published in *Pockets of Resistance,* issue 11, in November 27, 2001) he does not mention "little Eichmanns." He adds this to the revised version published as a chapter in his book *On the Justice of Roosting Chickens* (2003), where we see the "little Eichmanns" comment as a critique more generally of the "cadre of faceless bureaucrats and technical experts" (19) who work as appendages to U.S. imperialist policy. Whether we agree or disagree with Churchill, we would do well to at least read him carefully.

But my position wasn't so much a critique of the irresponsible responses by people who had failed to do a minimum amount of research on Churchill's statement, but rather of the torrent of antirights rhetoric the affair unleashed. For most this was a moment not to defend the right to freedom of speech and thought, but rather to decide how an administration should punish those who speak out in the wrong context: the university. I called attention to the fact that the "little Eichmann" issue was dropped, and that a clamor was raised that Churchill, the Native American who, on the state's dime, sounded "a call to arms" in his classrooms, should be fired. Freedom of speech is no longer an absolute right, but a right to be conditioned by institutional context. I brought up the fact that people were now talking about Churchill's falsified credentials; I asked my students if Churchill's passing of a blood quantum litmus test really has anything to with how well he teaches, studies, and writes about Native Americans. I asked my students if this not-on-the-state's-dime argument wasn't a thinly disguised defense of increased state control and authoritarian rule. I asked them to also think of this debate in light of the big push nationally to erase the line between church and state—a line that has traditionally protected the secular space of the classroom. More and more school boards across the land now require the teaching of creationism (intelligent design) alongside science in the classroom. If the administration bows to the governor's pressure to fire Churchill, I asked them, wouldn't this give the state more authority to impose indoctrination of any kind in any school? Wouldn't this help the state further divest the people—the working people—of their civil rights? Oddly, even though several years had passed since the first walkout, the conclusions seemed the same. For professors, students, and workers generally, the call to defend civil rights against forms of totalitarianism couldn't be more urgent.

As intellectuals and university-trained scholars, we must know well what our job is in the classroom, and we must know well what we can do outside the classroom as citizens and activists. While we can impart knowledge and participate in its shaping in order to help us know the world beyond the classroom better, it is not the same thing to propose that our scholarship and classroom work is political work. Moreover, we need to be mindful of our roles, especially when those who appear to be the heralds of progressive politics in the academy are very often the ones who are promoting inactivity, either in theories and/or in their cultural work for such entities as the World Economic Forum. We need to be mindful of those who feed and support an anti-intellectualism and an antilearning that ultimately feed corporate interests.

EIGHT

TRANSLATION MATTERS

INTRODUCTION

In classes I've taught in Latin American literature in English translation, I am inevitably asked, "Is the meaning of the translation different
from that of the original?" or, "Are we reading Gabriel García Márquez's
One Hundred Years of Solitude or someone else's version?" My answers
seemed too simple: the content is the same but the form is different;
you're reading Márquez's content and the translator Gregory Rabassa's
form. This just raised more questions about form and content—their
separability or inseparability.

My ideas on translation especially seemed to fall short after I received
an invitation a couple of years ago to apply for a postdoctoral fellowship
to work on translation at Cornell's Society for the Humanities. The bro-
chure asked, how can translation enable and complicate "our notions of
languages and cultures and their relations to one another?" It referred to
translation as the movement of bodies, genders, races, and the like across
spaces. Translation seemed to apply equally to all aspects of our "whole
way of life."[1] My ideas on translation at the time seemed incomplete.

In this chapter, then, I seek to map the application of the concept
of translation to today's postcolonial and ethnic literary studies to determine what theories work—or don't—in deepening our knowledge
of literary translation. I follow this with the establishment of a solidly
grounded hypothesis built on Chomskyean linguistics and the firsthand
experiences of literary translators. I do this not only to shed light on
what translation can and cannot do in the world, but also to understand
its crucial importance in the shaping of world literature. Thus I also
consider not only material constraints on the circulation of translations
but also how translations have historically allowed authors and readers

(monolingual or otherwise) worldwide to invent, imagine, and vicariously experience other world authors' fictional landscapes.

Put bluntly, theories of translation circulating in the humanities no longer refer to the transfer of information from one language (A) to another language (B). "Translation" now reaches to the stars and back, touching on all aspects of our everyday existence: self, identity, ethics, society, the nation, and capitalist globalization.[2] Today's translation turn informs all aspects of literary and cultural studies, including the establishment of translation studies as a field of inquiry in the university (as opposed, say, to its place within specialized schools that train translators and interpreters for international organizations). Here, we often see theorized the decoding of translation and/or the making of a "rough" translation with a counterhegemonic power. The 1990s saw a flurry of such publications. I think readily of Susan Bassnett's and André Lefevere's *Translation, History and Culture* (1990); Lawrence Venuti's edited volume *Rethinking Translation* (1993) as well as his *The Translator's Invisibility* (1995), followed by *The Scandals of Translation* (1998). While each book presents a varied lineup of scholars who focus on an array of topics, they share much common ground. Taking their lead from Derrida's notion of language as indeterminable (the concept of *différance* discussed in chapters 2, 3), because there is no singular meaning and no ultimate truth, the translator (a marginal subject vis-à-vis the author) has the power to either conform to and/or destabilize those constructed hierarchies that privilege the original and denigrate the translation. The type of "assemblage, structuration, and fabrication" that informs the translation thus participates "in the powerful acts that create knowledge and shape culture" (*Translation and Power* xxi), as Edwin Gentzler and Maria Tymoczko propose, for example. According to such theorists, then, the translator has the power to determine the shape not only of culture, but also of the systems of discourse that construct nation.

For this new wave of translation scholars, counterhegemonic and/or conformist ideologies stick hard to translators and their translations. As such, it can be an act of manipulation that naturalizes as normal, say, a patriarchal ideology (see Bassnett and Lefevere's *Translation, History and Culture*) and thus serves as handmaiden to oppressive powers of the nation-state. Or, if done correctly (the right assemblage and structuration of the right texts), it can be affirming both culturally and politically. As Gentzler suggests, it can be "a process of gathering and creating *new information* that can be turned to powerful political ends, including resistance, self-determination, and rebellion" ("Translation, Poststructuralism, and Power" 216).

According to such approaches, translation and the role of the translator *grosso modo* are directly implicated in machinations of oppressive discourses of power: either in their service and/or in resistance to them. It follows that if the translated text circulates within networks of signs (ever deferred) that can either manipulate and/or create linguistic (imagined) communities (nation-states or subcultures) that conform to and/or resist master narratives (capitalist, patriarchal, colonial, imperial), then such a translated text and translating subject can now be sites for decoding the social construction—and potential reconstruction—of feminist, queer, and postcolonial identities.

Spinning out of this notion of gaps in language and a sense of the indeterminate meaning in speech acts, there have been also those who identify a space in language that allows for the emergence of alternative voices: traditionally suppressed experiences and identities that rupture patriarchal master narratives. Thus, to destabilize the translation (act/object) is to make visible oppressive social constructions. This can happen in two ways: in the decoding of texts and/or in the act of translating through a feminist lens as seen with the oft-cited examples, Hélène Cixous and Luce Irigaray. The literary translator Diana Bellessi (translator of Adrienne Rich and Lucille Clifton, among others) discusses her deliberate move to translate those whom she considers "extremely talented and at the same time outlaws" (27). She considers her translation of such outlawed writers a form of feminist activism; it is one act of many that helps build a "gallery of mirrors in which to see ourselves, or in which to see reflected certain peculiar features of our way of looking at the world" (28). Bellessi's feminist turn points to the more general trend that identifies the translator's shaping of canons as a shaper of social constructions of women. Therefore, if the canon is shaped differently (translations of women writers), then one extends the range of possible feminist images and identities circulating in the world outside the literary canon. And it usually follows that once this feminist translation is circulating among other discursive networks it can reveal how master narratives naturalize as normal gender inequality.

In like spirit, Susanne de Lotbinière-Harwood identifies a feminist translation as a "quadraphonic site" that reveals and destabilizes constructions of Male (Self) vs. Female (Other) simultaneously in two languages. For other scholars, the feminist translation also reveals how patriarchal society invests men with privileged originality and the "secondariness of women in society" (N. Kamala 40). Others identify how women have survived patriarchal oppression by self-consciously translating and "multiply enunciating" patriarchal worldviews in order to deflect objectification. And others simply claim that to uplift the marginal status of translation is akin to the uplifting of women socially.

Just as certain performances of translation can destabilize imbalances in gendered relationships, for another cadre of scholars it can reveal and potentially alter the relationship between colonizer and colonized. Considering that issues of languages such as the dominance of English over Hindi or Urdu in India and Spanish over Nahuatl or English over Spanish during various moments of British and U.S. empire building, it is not surprising that translation has entered full force into postcolonial and U.S. ethnic theory. For example, in what has become known in Chicano studies as border theory, the intermixing of Spanish *caló* (slang) with Nahuatl and English, for example, has been identified as a border writing that resists translating the Chicano/a subject for easy mainstream consumption. The performance art of Guillermo Gómez-Peña and Coco Fusco, for example, is revealed to be sites of incomplete translation that resist and intervene in monolingual narratives that deploy standardized vocabularies to naturalize uniform images of a nation as white, hetero-male.

Accordingly, the translation can conspire "either to domesticate the foreign text or otherwise to ameliorate its disruptive potential" (172), as Peter Hitchcock writes in *Dialogics of the Oppressed*. This can occur in several ways. First, in the translator's selection of primary text, as in the case of Gayatri Spivak's deliberate choice to translate the native Bengali writer Mahasweta Devi. Second, the way in which such a text is translated: either to cover over and obscure the original voice and/or to perform a translation that allows the palimpsestic presence of both original voice and that of translator. The type of translation will make for a text that either resists and/or uncritically repeats a colonial-colonized paradigm: the translator as European ethnographer (subject) who erases and objectifies the voice of the native.[3]

The translation can also critique and resist such colonial and neocolonial power relations, as we see, for example, in Spivak's claim of her multiply enunciating and hybrid translation of Devi. (Spivak proposes that we must earn the right to translate in our intimate reading and connection with such fictions as Devi's, yet in *Outside the Teaching Machine* she mentions that even while we attend to the source text's "staging of language" (405) and respect its cultural specificities, we will never know the text of the Other because meaning in language is forever contingent and deferred; the translating subject will never grasp the subaltern Other that exists in the "spacey emptiness between two named historical languages" (398).[4] The translator can only ever capture briefly "the disruptive rhetoricity that breaks the surface" (398) and that ultimately unthreads or "frays" ("frayages," she writes) into the ungraspable.[5]

For other "translational" (if I may borrow one such term) postcolonial scholars, because the translation circulates within text systems (pamphlets, laws, political treatise, historical records, and a variety of other cultural texts that include works of fiction) that have traditionally repressed ex-centric voices and texts in the "inventing" and "imagining" of "pure" nations (e.g., pure Englishness and impure Indianness in the naturalizing of British colonial rule), then how one translates determines whether or not one, as Prem Poddar writes, "draws attention to the contortions, occlusions and distortions involved in cultural transmission— the violence within and between nations—while also raising the prospect of transnational narratives or articulations which might recognize—and even celebrate—the multiple and different voices within and across modern communities" ("Introduction: Violent Civilities" 8).[6] So, if the nation is constructed via a system of discourses, then if the postcolonial translator self-reflexively performs "mixture" or "hybridity" this will reveal how such "nations as narrations" are ideological constructs that can be dismantled; thus the texturing of the Other's voice, say, in a performative English translation of a Bengali author reimagines and rewrites a more inclusive nation.[7] Moreover, as Sukanta Chaudhuri discusses, the postcolonial hybrid space of translated language can bring to the fore alternative "possibilities that his own language would not admit but that are instilled in the new text by the structures of the target (or, as I would prefer to call it, 'host') language" (*Translation and Understanding* 2). And, as Susi Tharu and K. Lalita propose, such postcolonial translations can demand "of the reader to do a translation of herself into another sociohistorical ethos" (*Women Writing in India* xx).

Other formulations of translation focus on more abstract concepts of bodies and subjectivities: the space of the migrant, diasporic writer as a translated body writing from a place of displacement and thus enacting constantly the translation process in the forming of a hybrid self within a new host country, for example. Such translational bodies are considered textual constructs (localized ontologies) that come to exist in the gaps of languages and that resist the dominant master narratives of colonialism and/or capitalism. In "The Third Space" Homi Bhabha formulates just such a resistant "translational culture" and hybrid ontology that moves across national boundaries and thus physically distorts and symbolically reconfigures the territories of imagined nations. Translation, for Bhabha and those who follow in his footsteps, then, affirms a diasporic ontology that enacts "a process of alienation and of secondariness *in relation to itself*". (210)[8]

Whether from a feminist, postcolonial, or U.S. ethnic approach, translation has become a ubiquitous term used to talk about the self, power, knowledge, and the world. It is also used to promote a kind of reading and interpreting of literature. In *Translating Orients* (2004) Timothy Weiss identifies the act of identifying those texts and authors that have moved across borders (Salman Rushdie, Kazuo Ishiguro, Paul Bowles, for example) as an act of translation, revealing how such authors embody in movement and writing strategy a type of translated resistance to the "imposition of ideologies, packaged meanings and messages . . . in a society of the spectacle" (204). For Weiss, then, the movement of translation clears a space where the reader can discover new identities and realities and see more clearly "false truths" (204). And, for Andrea Opitz translation becomes an interpretive model for her approach to Native American literature; a way to "turn into its foreignness" otherwise held beyond the Western reader's grasp. As a self-described translator, she aims to make visible how the foreignness of the Native American novel disrupts the self versus other binary configuration and that thus asks the reader-as-translator to be "continuously conscious of our own marginal status" (19).

The translation turn in one way or another promises scholars a better, more correct, more ethical way of approaching texts, language, the self, and the nation. The good translator (not necessarily in quality, but in approach) makes the right choices to not translate too much Otherness, to not make the translation easy and transparent for the consuming audience; the good translator destabilizes scripts of self and nation and becomes an agent of local and global social and political change. And in raising questions about local and global, nation and the so-called postnation, this ethics of translation produces, as Sandra Bermann writes, "a more thoroughgoing interdisciplinarity, as well as a geo-linguistic decentering of major proportions, and intense self-reflection" ("Introduction" 7).[9]

Thus conceived, translation identifies practices of reading and decoding discourse systems of dominance as well as the postcolonial recuperation of erstwhile colonized cultures, knowledge, and peoples. However, what begins to emerge here is not only the making of a vastly amorphous category—translation as a "whole way of life"—but also a series of tautologies. Perhaps this is most clearly exemplified when Sukanta Chaudhuri writes of reading translation as

> making an intellectual construct, the original text that we do not and very likely cannot read directly and literally. We are reading a reality that threatens to burst the confines of the language incorporating it. Finally, we are reading the act of reading and beyond that the act of writing, the construction and deconstruction of texts, the unpredictable courses taken by two interactive semiotic systems both operating, in different ways, outside their usual verbal and cultural orbits. (43)

As seen here and in the others I discuss, we begin to see a paradoxical bind: translations can disrupt socially constructed (culturalist) hierarchies of difference and yet language and thus translation are indeterminate: hence the need for a scholar like Spivak to declare translation a frayed thread that is ultimately ungraspable. It's a way of having one's proverbial cake and eating it too.

Of course, not all "politicized" translation scholarship should be discounted out of hand. Some of it makes sense. When a translator chooses to translate, say, Rich this necessarily means that time and energy will not be spent translating, say, Jeanette Winterson. And we know from the study of literature generally that particulars of history, economics, gender, race, and class relations can and do *inflect* the narrative, and when we talk about literary translation, so, too, must they inflect the translated text. Indeed, the Cuban émigré author Cristina García reflects on the art of the translator as that which labors to capture the "web of cultural context" of the original (48). The translator can choose to acculturate (make more identifiable) cultural practices that might otherwise be difficult to understand. We know too that translator/authors like Jorge Luis Borges might choose to impose greater degrees of their own will over the original text, even rewriting books in the act of so-called translating. And it's possible that a translator's worldview (religious or otherwise) can lead to other types of losses in the translation process. Milan Kundera's experience with the various translations of his novel *The Joke* is a case in point. In *The Art of the Novel,* he writes,

> In France, the translator rewrote the novel by ornamenting my style. In England, the publisher cut out all the reflective passages, elimi-

nated the musicological chapters, changed the order of the parts, re-composed the novel. Another country: I meet my translator, a man who knows not a word of Czech. "Then how did you translate it?" "With my heart." And he pulls a photo of me from his wallet. He was so congenial that I almost believed it was actually possible to translate by some telepathy of the heart. Of course, it turned out to be much simpler: he had worked from the French rewrite, as had the translator in Argentina. (121)

Certainly, languages are anchored within boundaries of the nation-state. So when we discuss broadly the role of language during moments of colonization and conquest, we see how language enables (for better or worse) communication between members of a group (necessary for survival and even organizing against the oppressor); the prominence of a language worldwide, like that of English today, can also indicate a given nation's power over other nations. (For more on this, see Ngugi wa Thiong'O's, insightful essay "Imperialism of Language.") Such an imbalance of nation and its language became the center of discussion and debate in Latin America with the *modernistas* and their declaration of the need to establish the voice of Latin America to hold back the dominance of North America and English as the lingua franca. Such moves, of course, spin out of a long legacy of colonialism (European) and capitalist imperialism (United States). For many of the *modernistas* the abundance of translations into Spanish of North American writers—and the lack of translations flowing in the opposite direction—was certainly looked on with a suspicious eye.

Translated works are also bound to the operations of the capitalist-driven publishing marketplace. In *The Communist Manifesto,* Karl Marx predicted that a side effect of the development and worldwide spread of capitalism would be a transformation of modes of cultural production and consumption:

In place of old and national seclusion and self-sufficiency, we have intercourse in every direction, universal interdependence of nations. And as in material, so also in intellectual production. The intellectual creations of individual nations become common property. National one-sidedness and narrow-mindedness become more and more impossible, and from numerous national and local literatures there arises a world literature. (84)

131

The worldwide production and circulation of translated literature (South Asian, Latin American, and so on) are examples of this globalization of the cultural phenomenon of literature. And, of course, this capitalist economic dynamic is also deeply contradictory. On the one hand, more than at any other time in the history of literary distribution, translations of literature from all over the world are reaching readers worldwide. This allows more readers to come into contact with other cultural histories. This is not an example of the benign nature of capitalism, but rather evidence of its increasingly sophisticated means of determining what will sell and of the manufacturing of markets that allow for a faster turnover time to increase profit margins. So while we see as a side effect of capitalism the diversification of literary translations we can acquire as teachers, scholars, and general readers, there is at the same time a careful control and manipulation of desires and markets in the production of such translations. That is to say, for every Arundhati Roy novel that is translated into twenty-seven languages and that secures profit margins, dozens of other South Asian novels don't even make a blip on the radar. Finally, that translations are tied to a profit-driven marketplace also affects their quality. With the conglomeration of publishing houses, profit becomes more interesting than quality, and so the "foreign literature" category suffers. As Rabassa remarks in an interview with Bondo Wyszpolski, "It is sad, but the business seems largely in the hands of the philistines right now, and there is little we can do to right it" (31).

This acknowledged, the following questions continue to nag: Is translation everywhere—in bodies that move across national boundaries, the way gender, race, ethnicity are performed and so on? Can the act of translation really deform the nation? Can the translator reproduce and/or critically dismantle patriarchal, capitalist, imperialist, colonialist hegemonies? Can a less "refined and sensitive cultural/linguistic translation" and/or a less aware act of translating otherness make our global world "less hospitable"—even cause it to "founder," as Sandra Bermann seems to suggest ("Introduction" 7). Can "a focus on translationality" "urge rethinking of globalization itself in more carefully defined, more humanistic terms" (Bermann 7)?

Indeed, to posit that literature (hybrid, monolingual, or otherwise) is a cultural artifact that forms the identity of a nation is a contradiction in terms. History and culture specific to a given author or a given nation can inflect a literary work, but they do not delimit and determine its shape. Likewise, identifying literary discourse as a shaper of culture doesn't a nation make. As iterated emphatically in chapter 4, the nation is not an imagined community.[10] Neither is the nation a signifying system or a linguistic construct. In the absence of nation as a political framework in which wage workers can struggle to obtain and to protect their basic rights, exploitation and oppression would be complete. So, whether formulated as "double-writing," "third-spaces of hybrid resistance," and/or a vehicle of patriarchal, colonialist/imperialist ideology, these theories seem to get us no closer to understanding the process of translating, say, an English novel into Spanish; nor get us any closer to understanding what we might gain and/or lose when reading a translation; nor shed light generally on the function of a translated work in the shaping of world literature.

Translation is in the air we, as scholars of literature, breath. Since the invention of the printing press and the concomitant opening up of cultural markets worldwide, novelists, chroniclers, poets, and dramatists have increasingly encountered translated works and/or seen their works translated. I think readily of some of the authors I read in English as a teenager: Dante, Voltaire, Stendhal, Dostoyevsky, García Márquez, and so on. During this period I also began to read what others had to say about reading in translation. I was especially drawn to the various meditations of polylingual authors such as Vladimir Nabokov and his idea that to translate is to reproduce with absolute exactitude the original; Milan Kundera and his choice to translate his work himself because translation is "everything"; Borges's idea of translation as a rewriting of the original; Octavio Paz's notion of translation as a "glossary" that guides the reading of the original.

More recently, I've been thinking about the issue of translation when conceptualizing and teaching comparative literature courses in an English department. In a course on the metafictional "Anti-Novel," for example, I was careful about which books I chose based on the available English translations. Authors like Aristeo Brito, Elena Garro, and Julio Cortázar, to name a few, made the cut, but many others didn't simply because their books didn't read well in their translation. Here, I asked as well, what would a first encounter of Garro be like in translation?

At some point in our reading lives, we're going to encounter the pleasures of a novel written in a language that is not our own; we know from reading meditations by and biographies of even the most polylingual of authors that translations have been read. To read should be to read widely, and therefore to read authors who fall outside our proximate language zones. This doesn't mean we need to stop asking questions when reading translations. For example, when I pick up and read Joaquim María Machado de Assis's *Dom Casmurro,* I wonder if I'm missing something by not reading it in its original Brazilian Portuguese. This sense of the translation being a deficient double haunts such a reading experience. It is why even established literary translators like Rabassa, whose work has been praised by the authors he's translated, such as García Márquez (who considered the translation of *Cien Años* an improvement on the original), considers his translations somehow deficient. (See Wyszpolski's interview with Rabassa.)

As I've already begun to suggest (and will continue to discuss later), the translation should be considered differently from the original: it should be treated as an original that is *guided* by another's work.[11] In this case, when we teach translations in monolingual classroom settings, we guide an analysis of the text that is as attentive to nuance of language and detail as we would if dealing with the original. As Rainer Grutman notes, translations "are rarely meant to be read side by side with the original texts (except, perhaps, in a classroom setting)" ("Multilingualism and Translation" 157).

The literary translator translates ideas, notions—feelings—but as constrained by both the source text and the host language.[12] However, this constraint is merely a frame within which a constrained innovation *must* take place if the redressing process is to occur. On a very basic level, the translated text has to sound right in its new language, and yet it must also deploy certain narrative and rhetorical strategies to engage and/or disengage its readers in a fashion similar to that of the source text. In this sense, the translator is an innovator. So while the translation stands on its own proudly displaying its new garb, it does so in relation to an original. That is, the translator is more innovator than originator. As Jeffrey M. Green states, "Translators begin with someone else's finished product. They don't have to create something that never existed before, and their area of creativity is relatively restricted. In fact, if translators are too creative, people will no longer acknowledge their work as translation" (23). Hence, Green likens the translator to the master craftsman who requires "skill, knowledge, judgment, aesthetic and emotional sensitivity, and one that can be brought to a very high level—like pottery, silversmithing, or cabinetmaking" (26).

Perhaps, however, the literary translator is more like the tailor: redesigning an already made dress for another occasion. Or we might consider the translator an editor given great revision power—not only to sharpen the prose, but to do what it takes to convey the feeling and intent of the original. Yet, if we consider the translator to be an editor, we must also see him or her as both constrained and free to recreate. For example, when reading *Cien Años de Soledad* in Spanish with the idea of translating, one makes a version of the whole novel in one's own words, and this version thus follows rules of syntax not exactly laid out by García Márquez when he wrote the novel. In so doing, the translator becomes more of a paraphraser who decides when to preserve and when to recreate in order to convey what Green identifies as an "honest equivalent" (20) of the experience of reading the original. In this constrained divergence, so to speak, one must both be master craftsman and bring a sense of humility in the submission to the original's feeling and worldview. The task is difficult and "unselfish" (23) and requires the "deepest kind of reading" (25), as García Márquez remarks of his experience in translating Giacomo Leopardi's *Canti* ("The Desire to Translate").

Of course, the work of translating varies according to the requirements of the original: for nonliterary translations, in which the writing is fairly uniform and questions of point of view and style are not significant, the undressing and redressing are much more straightforward; for the literary translation, the process can be much more complex. In the latter, much of the work is intuitive, requiring not only a knowledge of the material, but a certain degree of empathetic connection. It also requires a certain amount of self-knowledge. Indeed, those few translators who can afford the luxury of choice often comment on how they choose literature that they're naturally inclined toward both in form (aesthetic, structure, and style) and content. For example, Borges's interest in translating William Faulkner came out of a deep connection with his themes (devastation and defeat in the Deep South) as well as an attraction to his mastery of style. (For more on this, see Ilan Stavans's essay "Beyond Translation: Borges and Faulkner".)

Let me clarify further how form and content work in the translation process by looking at how language and thought work as *separable* entities.

In the case of language, just as English has its own system of sounds (phonetics) and its own syntax, so too does Spanish. When I translate from English into Spanish, I'm not translating the English phonological form—its "envelope," so to speak. The envelope changes, but the content remains the same. This is what makes a difference between an accurate and an inaccurate translation: the content of the text in English remains the same content that has passed into the Spanish; what has changed is the form, or the envelope that now contains this content. If we can place content A contained in vessel A into content B contained in vessel B in the translation process, this means that the form can be separated from the content. If this were not the case, then the translation process would be like an act of magic, a transmutation.[13]

The operation of translation, then, doesn't consist in transporting the content from vessel A (English) into the envelope of vessel B (Spanish). It is not the transportation of the vessel A (transporting the English grammar, vocabulary, and syntax) that would be deposited into envelope B (Spanish) and then making the necessary grammatical rearrangements. The latter is what machine translation does, recognizing words and then strings of words as if content and form are inseparable; machines make such bad translations because they're programed on the basis of this premise of the inseparability of form and content. That is to say, when translating, one is transporting neither a grammar nor a content that is separable from its grammar.

This leads to the question of thought. When I read something in English, I have an expression and that expression triggers a thought: what I have in my brain now is a thought. I have therefore in my mind not a linguistic structure nor a grammar and an accompanying meaning, but rather a thought along with the will to express this thought in Spanish. This is also why when I think I'm interpreting from English into Spanish I suddenly realize that I'm paraphrasing the same words in English that I'm not actually translating. This shows two things: First, that I have a thought in language A (English), but I haven't adjusted the direction of my will to express this thought in language B (Spanish). For example, I have the thought in my mind, "I want to go out for a walk," but haven't adjusted my will toward the linguistic expression in B and not A. If I don't translate, it's not because I can't translate, it's because the mechanism hasn't been readjusted toward the language B (Spanish). This directing of the will takes practice and conscious effort if one is to be perfectly bilingual. That is, one needs to be able to recognize English as an object that's different from Spanish, and for perfect bilinguals this requires a tremendous exertion to separate and put a distance between English and Spanish. This is why under stressful conditions the bilingual speaker might think he or she is translating when he/she is simply paraphrasing in the host language.

The operation of translation consists exactly in this. You have a thought and you have the will to express that thought, except that the thought you have you want to express in another language. There is no translation from language to language; what you have is a thought that's going to use one language or another language or another.[14] Thus in the phenomenon of translation we need to keep in mind always that thought as an entity has both form and content. For example, the form of the mathematician's thought differs from the form of a musician's thought or a painter's thought; and the types of thoughts they have are different. So what we see happening in translation is that the thought is itself *of* form and content, and for multilinguals this thought can find an expression in different languages. Finally, then, we must keep in mind that thoughts do not come to the world dressed up in language. Thoughts come to the world dressed up in their own form and possess their own content.

Let me now turn to other translating matters: its role in the shaping of world literature. Authors generally are readers of literary translations from all over the world. For example, translations into Spanish of American and European literature have influenced Latin American writers just as English translations of Latin American literature have influenced American and European writers. We see this especially in the case of writers of the 1960s Latin American Boom period, as in the blisteringly rapid translation of *One Hundred Years of Solitude* that influenced many a writer, including the writings of the Argentinean Cortázar while he was living in self-imposed exile in Paris. This period of massive circulation of Latin American literature in translation made available to authors worldwide a wealth of literary forms and approaches to storytelling.

When authors (as readers) and readers read translations, they do so within larger world literary networks. The translation opens doors and allows for increased dialogues, interweavings, and innovative shapings to take place. For the everyday reader this means more possible worlds will be available to experience vicariously other ways of sensing different historically and geographically formed spaces. So, while there's certainly a material interest behind the abundance of English-authored books translated into other languages as opposed to, say, translations of Urdu-authored novels that puts certain restrictions on what might be caught up and used in this ever-changing expansive domain of world literature, ultimately translations (English or otherwise) do offer readers and writers (as readers) a greater range of possible imaginative engagements with the world.

Literary translation—along with its distribution and circulation—is integral to the past and present sculptings of world literature. Translations of certain texts inflected with a strong sense of history and culture also give readers in different countries a sense of the specific sociohistorical and cultural contours of a given original: for example, Mexico in Fuentes's *Christopher Unborn* and Colombia in García Márquez's *Death of a Patriarch*. However, the literary translation is not just about conveying the uniqueness of a given culture. Just as the author is not the "sole property of an individual culture" (639) as Stavans declares, neither is the translated fictional work only a key to the original author's culture. Such a view only encourages us to see novels and the human imagination, Stavans continues, "as a series of loosely interrelated ghettos, each controlled by its own self-righteous inhabitants" (639).

Translations and their host fictions do grow from within specific cultures and histories, but they ultimately exist in a no-man's-land unmoored from nationalist-identified cultures. In *What Is World Literature?*, David Damrosch identifies such a movement of translated texts beyond their national confines as the move into the "sphere of world literature" (6). Here, Damrosch informs that we might do well to read such literary translations with what he calls a "*like-but-unlike*" (12) perspective—a reading practice that shuns the ethnocentric and/or exoticist approach by both acknowledging the specifics of the text and also its differences.[15] Kwame Anthony Appiah identifies a similar approach when discussing the "thick and situated" (428) translations of African proverbs; it is an approach to such translations with the understanding that a translation "meets the need to challenge ourselves and our students to go further, to undertake the harder project of a genuinely informed respect for others" (427). And Stathis Gourgouris likewise proposes that we attend both to the specific historical and social details of the literary translation's production as well as to how the original's "genetic code" (18) transcend's locality and allows for the original to enter into the world-literary marketplace without being reduced to its idiomatic translation.

To use the common parlance of today's theory, literary translation is local and global. That is, authors located in a specific social and historical moment create innovative fictional works in their encounter and dialogue with other world literary texts (translated or otherwise). For example, Arundhati Roy's *The God of Small Things* was written in English but takes place mostly in Kerala, India; it also alludes directly to Faulkner and García Márquez in form. The novel has been translated into twenty-nine languages; it, too, has become taken up into the vast sphere of world literature; it is a sure bet that an author from some part of the world will be touched by this novel in translation and will henceforth use it as a springboard to create something new.

The massive production and flow of literary translations we're seeing today is a kind of Miracle-Gro that seems to be accelerating at a rapid pace the inherent tendency of literature to become world literature. Even before the conquest of the New World, the development of the printing press, and full-blown capitalism in the nineteenth century, this has always been its fate. Of course, increased industrialization has over time increased the flow of literature, but literature has always been a product of communication between author and those outside. Homer must have heard somewhere stories told in whatever form before he began to tell them himself; and this we can hypothesize as a process all the way back to the Upper Paleolithic, when *Homo sapiens sapiens* first began to tell and retell stories, all the while making the familiar unfamiliar and new. All authors of all times write and rewrite stories both as a talking to and a talking back to translated or original works. A Spanish-speaking author can refashion the tragic story of Leo Tolstoy's Anna Karenina if he or she should so please because of having access to the Spanish translation. So, from the very first moment we told stories as Upper Paleolithic *Homo sapiens sapiens* to today, the internal motor of literature has been propelling it to become a planetary phenomenon—and translation has been a decisive factor contributing to this planetary outreach.

Translation is shaped by language and thus governed also by the central tendency of language: to communicate with that beyond itself. As literature is one product of language, so too, then, is the translation of a literary text an act of communicating beyond itself.

Perhaps even more fundamentally, translation is language that communicates meaning. We know from post-Saussurean advances in linguistic research that language does mean; language is not, as I've discussed earlier in this book, indeterminable, an infinite semiosis, an endless play of signs leading nowhere.[16] To briefly reiterate, if there were slippage between signifier and signified we would write and speak nonsense. While it is true that we might not find words exactly to express a particular intent or meaning, it is not true that the sign and referent are arbitrarily related. Nor for that matter does it mean that vagueness and ambiguity do not happen in language—but this is not news. By 1914 Bertrand Russell had written an article titled "Vagueness" that analyzed this problem and recognized the central importance of vagueness in the communication process. Others have continued to study this topic at length, including Dan Sperber in his book *Relevance: Communication and Cognition,* and John Searle, identifying vagueness as a prerequisite for everyday acts of communication. In short, if our everyday language functioned according to a semantics of logic formulated by Rudolf Carnap (and others) that implied a one-to-one correspondence with reality or a one-to-one correspondence to all that is implied by the sentence, then we would not be able to communicate. Vagueness—all the meaning that surrounds the utterance—is necessary for us to create shortcuts that allow for communication to take place.[17]

However, this is not the way in which vagueness in language has been picked up and used by those like Derrida; as already discussed at length, his misuse of Saussure to identify the indefinite deference of meaning would mean the words he writes or those I write now could not be understood by you, the reader.

Where does this leave us, then, when thinking of translations? The translator Emma Wagner sums this up best when she states that it isn't "particularly helpful for theorists to tell us that translation is impossible or that perfect equivalence is unattainable. Let alone that words are meaningless and there is nothing objectively there" (25). For Wagner, when translating a text there is always something "objectively there" (the overall intention of the author, for example), and it is the job of the translator, she continues, "to decide which it is, dig it out and put it into a usable and approximately equivalent form" (25). Perhaps Wagner says it best when she playfully remarks, "I hope that when Madame Derrida sends her husband to the supermarket with a shopping list marked with the words *fillets de sole, beurre, farine* and he comes back with some paper clips and a packet of Gauloises, she hits him over the head with the frying pan" (25).

For theories of translation to make sense, they must acknowledge that language is made up of a finite set of rules and words and that the specific combination of rules with specific usage of words produces a linguistic expression of humans' language faculty.

This brings me to Chomsky's parametric theory of universal grammar. English, French, Spanish, Urdu, Hindu, Senegalese, and so on are specific manifestations (or elements) of a more general set: the universal grammar. One of Chomsky's students, Mark C. Baker, clarifies:

> Words are *not* all there is to language; there is also grammar, the principles for combining words into sentences. One might think that if words are arbitrary and fluid in their meanings, larger constructions built out of them would be even more arbitrary and fluid because the indeterminacies of meaning would compound and magnify each other. Yet the opposite is true. Sentence structures are more rigidly

and universally specified than word meanings are, as determined by the basic recipe for language together with its atomic variations, the parameters. Thus, whereas the lexicons of different languages vary widely, their grammars do not. (204–205)

Baker identifies here the basic understanding of language based on the parametric theory—at the level of syntax as universal grammar and also at the level of syntax of individual speakers' actual use—to identify the relation between universal grammar and particular languages (specific lexicons) that communicates ideas within like-languaged communities. Here, Baker also points to how different lexical ingredients of one system will manifest as, say, Urdu, and that this also involves the process of combining certain elements—all while the universal grammar holds all languages together.

Common knowledge tells us that there is no language that cannot be translated into any other language. Keeping the universal grammar in mind, however, we see how translation works as a lexical system cross-culturally; how literary translation works within the verbal system of world literature. As *Homo sapiens sapiens,* then, we share cross-culturally a universal capacity for grammar, and this is expressed in various lexical systems we call English, Spanish, Urdu, French, and so on. In other words, we're biologically hardwired as a species with the capacity to process and convey linguistic contents manifested in, say, Spanish (or any other language) and thus, even if sound patterns differ from one language to another, because of this universal grammar we likewise have the universal capacity to convey the linguistic contents embodied in what we call Spanish, by means of another language like Senegalese. This is what we call translation.

Contrary, then, to Derridean-based notions of indeterminacy (or even the social-psychological linguistics formulated by Sapir/Whorf and seen in today's social constructionism), we know from Chomsky's parametric theory as well as the commonplace experiences of translators like Wagner (among many others) that when one translates one doesn't translate words and one doesn't translate rules. The French word *bois* refers to "wood" and "forest/woods," but in French there is also the word *forêt*. In Spanish the word *madera* is used for "wood," and there is only one word to describe woods/forest: *bosque*. For Eskimos there are thirty different words for snow, whereas in Spanish there is only one, *nieve*. Namely, when one translates, one is not translating words because vocabularies are different. While there is sometimes an overlap, Spanish and

English have fundamentally a different vocabulary. You see this if you open any dictionary. This also goes for rules, or what we call grammar. English grammar differs from French which differs from Senegalese and so on. When translating, one isn't translating rules: the rule concerning the use of adjectives in English will be not be used when writing in Spanish because in many cases it will be of no use: in Spanish the rule might transform an adjective into an adverb, verb, or noun. It thus follows that the translator of literature is faced with the task of also capturing the play of one language's verbal puns in a language that has a different set of correspondences between sound and meaning.

Literary translation shares with language another of our higher-minded capacities: it is a product of mental activity—a mental phenomenon—and thus participates in our universal capacity as *Homo sapiens sapiens* to change something whole into a fragment, then to rebuild such a fragment in a different way. I think here specifically of the mental activity of reconstructing literary texts from fragments (as with archival work), but also more basically of our everyday acts of paraphrasing and summarizing; such activities involve fragmenting parts from wholes as well as rebuilding from fragments new wholes in our minds.

This mental activity—our capacity to imagine "holographically"—takes place when we translate texts. The role of the translator is to break down the original text into summarizable components, then rebuild these fragments into a new complete, whole text. Here, the translator uses the holographic capacity of the mind, where the fragment allows one to see the whole contained in the fragment. This holographic capacity is what allows Borges to translate Melville's *Bartleby the Scrivener*: the original story is absorbed, paraphrased conceptually, then translated into Spanish without the original's baroque style. Borges's *Bartleby, el escribiente* (1984) is lacking in ornate vocabulary that would indicate its precariousness. Yet Borges's *Bartleby, el escribiente* is absolutely faithful in terms of content. He's turned Melville into a Borgesian text. That is, if the book didn't have the signature "Melville," the implied author that comes to mind when reading most certainly would not be Melville, but Borges. Borges's ego is such that he will not only reproduce the text through the translation, but will furnish an entirely new implied author: himself. As if the story—the way to tell it—belonged to Borges and not Melville. Now, another translator might choose to stay closer to the impression one receives when reading the book and in constructing an image of the implied author. Here, one might try to reproduce the novel's content and form with a stronger image of the implied author kept in mind. Often, too, we see how some translators (I think here of Edith Grossman and Rabassa) can serve as a kind of *redactor*, or editor, of the original in the act of reading, absorbing, and even sometimes improving on the original.

This translation process also requires maintaining a certain distance from the text. Even if they could, polylingual authors more often than not do not translate their own works. Here, the polylingual author translating his or her own work knows firsthand his or her intentions and thus doesn't have the requisite distance from the original to enact a holographic process that would keep in balance the shaping of a new text with gestures toward the original. Usually what happens is the author takes such liberties in the paraphrasing and reimagining process that the text that is produced is nothing like the original. The distance to the original that an outsider has makes the process of creating a text anew without completely rewriting the original much easier.[18]

The holographic process helps explain why literary translations can reproduce the feel of the original and to varying degrees give a sense of its newbornness. It also points us to yet another of our universal capacities: the different degrees of our making present the original text that we reshape in our retelling. Indeed, innovation in the verbal art of storytelling operates in similar ways: absorbing the original, paraphrasing it in one's mind, then innovatively retelling and inventing a story anew.[19] Given our cognitive and emotive hardwiring, it's not surprising that extensive research on story prototypes cross-culturally shows that we basically practice such innovative moves on only a handful of paradigm stories: the epic, the story of suffering, and that of romance. (For more on these paradigm stories, see Patrick Colm Hogan's *The Mind and Its Stories*.)

This also leads us to clarify again the difference between translated text and reality—mind and what is not mind—often confused in the theories of translation discussed at the beginning of this chapter. A study of literary translation—language—involves the articulation of the conception of what reality is. By consensus (not definition) reality is everything that is out there plus the mind, so the study of the mind implies that you have a position or point of view or at least an opinion about what the relation is between mind and what is not the mind. For example, translation is not and cannot be the translation of rules or words (or lexical items). As already discussed, translation is the undressing, fragmenting, and paraphrasing of thoughts and the subsequent redressing into a whole of those thoughts in a different way and by different means. This implies that thoughts can exist without being embodied in sounds, words, language. Thoughts and language are separate entities: this is itself an ontology.

So, while translation takes place in language, it doesn't necessarily follow that the translated text is equal to the material (social, historical, biological) facts of our ontological makeup. We know from advances in cognitive science and Chomskyan linguistics that as a species we are not constituted in and through language. Contrary to the social constructionist and relativist paradigm, what we speak and/or write doesn't necessarily affect what thoughts we can have. If it were true that all knowledge originates in experience and that our apprehension of all reality is filtered through language (an experientially constructivist model of reality), then the words spoken and/or written in a given language would affect the thought one intended to express. Again, common sense tells us otherwise. If the language we speak determines what thought or intentions we have, then translation would never be possible.

If we don't think in language alone, then we have to reassess certain declarations of what translation can do. Undeniably, language—and thus translation—is a basic and necessary part of everyday culture the world over. However, while it is our nature as evolved organisms to spin out culture, this act does not serve the same shaping function of the world as, say, physical labor and/or the organization of social movements. Of course, the translation of language is an act of communication that can share knowledge, help organize people, and ultimately act as a tool of the organized masses to communicate demands and so on. Acts of translation can have consequences on your everyday life. One might translate for a non-English-speaking parent at the Immigration and Naturalization Service office, which can lead to certain material gains like citizenship. One might translate Marx's manifesto, which can provide the critical tools for understanding the economy under capitalism and the basis for solidarity and collective action on the part of the people. One might translate a novel and make available an author's work (its aesthetics, themes, rhetorical devices) for other authors (as readers) and readers worldwide. This doesn't serve the same function as Marx's manifesto, but it can potentially open more readers' eyes to other ways of seeing and experiencing the world that might or might not lead to the critical repudiation of racism, heterosexism, and so on.

CONCLUDING REMARKS

The act of translation: One reads an English text (literary or otherwise) from sentence to sentence (fragment to fragment) with its own set of grammar and words that are tied to concepts (content), then one undresses (disembodies) the words and rules coming from English so that the concepts (content) appear naked and pure, then one redresses these concepts (content) in the new clothes (the grammar and words) of, for example, Spanish. This undressing, then dressing up anew is a skill; it is also what makes the difference between a bad translator who translates word for word and who tries to force the clothes of English (grammar, syntax, and words) into the wardrobe where only Spanish clothes hang. This results in a sartorial misfitting: a messy sounding and plodding "Spanish" translation. The translator has allowed the rules and denotative word definitions of English to contaminate those of the Spanish. It's a fact that one can't translate rules of Spanish because they belong to the Spanish language, just as words belong to Spanish language. That is, Spanish grammar is the recipe that provides the translator with ingredients to follow, and if you change the ingredients you can change the product.[20]

The style of translation shapes the image readers form of the implied author of the original. I think here of reading in English, then in French, translation Kawabata's *Beauty and Sadness* (originally written in Japanese), where the former translation's swift, precise, and agile style gave one impression and the heavy, slow-paced French translation an entirely different picture of the implied author. This can have material consequences. The style of the translation—if too heavy and awkward, for example—can determine the fate of the original within the world literary marketplace: whether it will be reprinted, circulated widely, and thus whether it will influence other world literary authors. The translations of Rabindranath Tagore into Spanish circulating today make him sound like a poet who uses inflated, gaseous lines; he comes off more as a third-rate mystic than the brilliant poet that he is. This has contributed to his work's lack of influence in shaping Latin American letters. So, while the style of a literary translation and our forming of an image of the implied author of the original are crucial in determining the fate of the original, they can also alter the material reality of the author.

Of course, this isn't the only reason some novels are translated and published worldwide and others not. To repeat, translations are part of a profit-driven publishing marketplace, so it's more likely that dollar-backed formulaic novels like those of Danielle Steel, Sidney Sheldon, and Jackie Collins will appear in translation in Mexico than a Tagore.[21] Here, however, we must not take the misstep of identifying such imbalances in the literary translation market with patriarchal, colonial, and/or imperial violence against other peoples nor as the power to construct patriarchal, heterosexist, racist national identities. Here, we would blur the line between actual violence in the real world and cultural phenomena such as translation which are based on an entirely different set of functions and registers. In a sober response to Venuti's rather speculative formulations on the role of translation, Jeffrey Green reminds us, "Violence is physical. Violence kills, maims, and traumatizes. Violence is used to oppress and terrorize people, to rob them, to drive them from their homes, to exterminate them" (85).

The exploration of literary translation—its process and function—sheds light on the inherent worldliness of literature. It also sheds light on the difference between how we are constituted as thinking and imagining subjects independent of language and also how language has become necessary for our survival. It also speaks candidly to how world literary translations are not acts of imperialist domination, but ways for authors and readers to communicate with one another as more imaginary worlds are made accessible. In a country like India where a panoply of languages are spoken, English translations of novels written in Hindu, Urdu, and so on have allowed schools and colleges to widen, as Sujit Mukherjee writes, "our horizons by giving us access to ways of living and dying, thinking and judging, feeling and doing, that are not familiar, hence limiting" (21). Moreover, speaking from the perspective of teaching in India, Mukherjee remarks, "Since we can and do take Russian or French, East European or Latin American literature in our stride while reading it in translation, why should we stumble over Oriya or Gujarati, Panjabi or Malayalam, Asamiya or Kannada literature in English translation?" (21).

As scholars, teachers, readers, and authors, we would do well to heed Mukherjee's advice: to treat literature—translated or otherwise—as governed by language and thus inherently about communication between peoples. That is, while translation requires great skill in the undressing and redressing process, there is no great mystery behind literary translation. It simply adds new dimensions to our experiences and also allows for other possible means for the pleasure of communicating, sharing, and the ultimate delight in the building of knowledge about ourselves, others, and the world.

NINE

CAN MUSIC RESIST?

INTRODUCTION

There's much interest in the cultural study of Other music: from East LA Chicano rap, U.S./Mexico border Norteño-techno, to Turkish-German hip-hop. Such interest can lead to interesting musical encounters that give rise to new rhythmic expressions; it can tell us something, too, of distributional paths governed by global capitalism. However, just like the dominant trend in approaches to the study of the self, society, language, translation, and cultural phenomena thus far discussed, so here too we see an enduring presence of a philosophical idealism. Whether identified as an alternative literacy program, as a politics of resistance to global capitalism, or as a site of identity negotiation, such studies detract from the actual building of a knowledge of such musical expressive forms.[1]

In this chapter, I will explore what works and what doesn't work in the analysis of Latino-borderland identified music. I ask how much can a *frontera* (borderland)-identified musicscape—and music generally for that matter—actually function as a textual expression of resistant hybrid identities and experience, as some claim? How much can it actually function as an intervention into the political sphere? How can music act either as a symbolic and/or real resistant site to dominant capitalist/ colonialist hegemonies? Can a so-called borderland music really exist outside a popular music economy driven by dollar profiteers? Is music really a text that can act as a motor of social and political transformation? Finally, what might be the value of studying and teaching students Latino borderland music? I hereby anchor my chapter in a discussion of the Tijuana-based Nortec Collective's music.

First, what is Nortec? It's a complex musical form that draws from and recombines many genres with its own sound patterns and conventions.

The drum-'n'-bass lines and cut-'n'-mix synth dips/arcs and pulsations characteristic of techno fill out and dominate the tambora, tuba, and accordion riffs characteristic of northern Mexican and Tejano *conjunto*.[2] Hence, the "-tec" suffix in "Nortec," which situates its soundscape firmly within the genre of techno. As we know from the techno critics Simon Reynolds and Roy Shuker, this is a soundscape developed in the contact zone between European New Wave synth beats and Detroit funk rhythms in the early- to mid-1980s. Shuker sums up nicely:

> Techno emerged as a musical style and meta-genre in the 1980s, partly associated with new, computer-generated, sound/composition technologies available to musicians. Techno is often conflated with house and ambient music, or used contiguously with the whole corpus of contemporary dance music. Techno became closely associated with a particular social setting, being the stable music at large-scale parties, or 'raves'. Along with the use of the drug ecstasy, these generated considerable controversy (and moral panic) in the early to mid-1990s in the UK and internationally. (153)

Techno was a genre produced by young, middle-class African Americans living in the white suburbs of Detroit in the early 1980s. One generation away from the factory line yet living in the white suburbs, many young African American proto-techno wizards combined the mechanical and repetitive/industrial synth sound of Germany's pop group Kraftwerk with the funk of George Clinton and Parliament. For example, Derrick May used the mass-marketed Roland TB 303 Bassline—originally sold as a bass-line synthesizer to partner with the Roland 606 drum machine for rock guitarists in 1983—to strip down Parliament's funk sound and recombine with a severe pounding rhythm that he spread across an expansive landscape of instrumental techno sounds. In this spirit, May produced the club hit "Strings of Life," which put this new sound on the map and allowed him, as he contends, "to tap into history in a way we could never do before, and that gives us the opportunity to create our own perspective of what we've been brought up with all our lives" (cited in Timothy Taylor 41).

One of the Nortec Collective DJs, Pepe Mogt, also began his early synth play after using high-frequency radio to tune into Kraftwerk, New Order, and Depeche Mode, who were being transmitted on the airwaves across the border in San Diego. This was important to Mogt's cultivation of a musical sensibility, as most of the music he would hear in Tijuana was of the *conjunto* and *norteño* variety. Somewhat similar to May's story, in 1986 Mogt managed to get his hands on a Yamaha Portasound and began to recombine Eurodisco with break beat patterns and synth sounds. Unlike May, Mogt's sounds would take over a decade before becoming visible in wider circuits of production and consumption. May went on to develop a sophisticated synthesized soundspace in which the Euro-pop beats of Giorgio Moroder cut 'n' mixed into Motown favorites like Donna Summer's "Love to Love You Baby," repeating rhythmic patterns that allowed listeners to dance to identifiable sound patterns. He introduced listeners to a lyricless, rearchitectured soundscape where synthetic and processed sounds talked to each other and had the power to stimulate listeners into trancelike movement.

Without a middle-class youth (Latino, African American, or Anglo) with disposable income to purchase who had access to new sampling and synthesizer machines, the tec in Nortec would not have been possible. As computer chips developed, so too did the sophistication of samplers and digitizing recorders. The combination of sampled and created sounds became infinite, as production moved away from traditional instruments to I/O binary converters. So where May's Roland TB 303 and Mogt's Portasound served as "quote" machines, by the late 1980s and early 1990s new technologies allowed a proliferating number of DJs in Detroit, Chicago, and New York to warp and wrap sounds into sophisticated sequences on a massive scale. The end result: deep house and Italo house, jungle, drum'n'bass, trance, trip-hop, acid, garage, techno-rave, the sped-up hip-hop identified as breakbeat, tribal, and the Chicago-based, palsied techno known as minimal jack.

Nortec certainly has a story to tell. As the sound splintered, so too did its audience. By the early 1990s, techno and its subgenres were no longer identified solely as African American. Panoptic surveillance systems identified that DJ-ed techno musicscapes such as Chicago's acid house scene and New York's Garage scene (mostly as brown/black and/or gay inhabited) were sites of "perversion" and contraband drug exchange and use. This drove the scene underground and across the Atlantic. As ebbs and flows of different surveillance systems enacted to control like populations of clubgoers across the Atlantic in metropolitan centers like London, the techno-scape continued its migration to places like Ibiza, Manchester, and Bristol.[3] Today, after many transmutations and transmigrations, the soundscape has found a place back along the Mexican/U.S. border.

If techno is the site of surveillance of outlawed bodies, then one might theorize a musicscape like Nortec—in its reconstitution of transracial, diasporic cultural forms—as a site of symbolic resistance within ideological structures that delimit and segregate sexual (gay/lesbian and straight) and racial (black/brown and white) communities. And certainly, in clubs where Nortec thumps, there can be seen a confluence of dancing bodies. A globally formed musicscape like Nortec arguably appropriates then recombines capitalist-generated technologies to create a space for differently desiring and racialized bodies to crisscross on the dance floor. In this spirit, Celeste Fraser Delgado and José Esteban Muñoz identify pan-Latino syncretic music and dance (salsa and the Brazilian fight-dance, *capoeira*) as forms of resistance. Such syncretic New World musicscapes and dances are identified as sites of resistance to yesteryear's hegemony (the conquest and colonization of the Americas) and to today's exploitive transnational capitalism. For example, they write,

> The intricate gesticulations of New World dance form inscribe and are inscribed by three broad historical movements: (1) the reorganization of the world produced by conquest, colonization, and the institution of slavery; (2) the consolidation of capitalism and the building of nations characteristic of modernity; and (3) the transnationalization of global culture effected by the incessant flow of capital characteristic of postmodernity. These broad movements are not discrete stages nor do they form any kind of direct linear progression from one moment to the next. Rather, we take the polyrhythm as a metonym for history that allows for an understanding of the simultaneous sounding of incommensurate historiographies. (13)

Read accordingly, Nortec's techno and *conjunto* hybrid musicscape would function as a counterhegemonic site of "polyrhythmic" resistance and as trace memory of a past marked by conquest and colonialism.

Can this *frontera* musicscape be a form of political resistance? Nortec is a soundscape that the media—and the Nortec Collective itself—have identified as expressive of a hybrid, borderland identity.[4] However, can one identify this as a musical aesthetic that expresses a new hybrid identity or a site of capitalist/colonialist resistance? Or is it simply a specific patterning of noise to make sounds that move bodies? When a Nortec track pulsates, clubgoers' (real) bodies respond, but is this a way to resist those generationally, racially, and sexually controlled *frontera* zones? Or is this simply one example of many soundscapes that lead to a kinesthetic response? If the musical sounds are patterned and combined with the listener in mind, the soundscape will create, as Richard Middleton argues, a "gestural center" that taps into specific neural networks that trigger kinetic reflexes ("Popular Music Analysis and Musicology" 109).

Such a musicscape with its controlled pitch-contours and harmonic rhythms can also have the power to tap into the brain's neural network, inducing different mental states and emotions. Of course, people do not exist in a vacuum. So while certain combinations of sound might trigger a kinetic response, the shape of this response looks different from community to community. Cognitive responses to music are hardwired in their raw form; the way the body looks as it responds to the music is as learned as the phatic, or gestural, in everyday speech-acts and determined by locally acquired conventions.[5] Hence, it is possible to read body reflexes to music as formed within and manipulated by a dominant capitalist ideology: where each sound and its concomitant gesture are part of the hegemonic discourse that controls subjects by asserting just how bodies move and are seen; where each sound controls just how the subject exists within socially, sexually, and racially inscribed hierarchies of difference. So that, according to a racialized, primitive (body) versus civilized (mind) hierarchy, brown/black bodies would "naturally" have rhythm and the white bodies would "naturally" not have rhythm. Thus it should come as no surprise that dance becomes theorized by the likes of Jane C. Desmond as "a discourse of the body [that is] especially vulnerable to interpretations in terms of essentialized identities associated with biological difference. These identities include race and gender and the sexualized associations attached to bodies marked in those terms, as well as national or ethnic identities when these are associated with racial notions, as they so often are" ("Issues in Dance and Cultural Studies" 43).[6]

To analyze the body's rhythmic response to patterned sounds, then, is to formulate what Desmond calls a "kinesthetic semiotics" where, for example, subaltern subjects express a "bodily bilingualism" in opposition to otherwise segregated social/sexual/racial spaces ("Issues in Dance and Cultural Studies" 33). However, for those cultural studies critics who choose to theorize a subaltern kinesthetic semiotic, they must read dance as more than a body's physiological response to sounds. It requires that a body's response to music be read as a countercultural expression that articulates a counter consciousness and history. It is to make visible and articulate what Fraser Delgado and Esteban Muñoz identify as a "politics in motion" ("Rebellions of Everynight Life" 9, 23). Accordingly, then, music and dance are theorized as Other histories that speak to a disenfranchised community's violent subjugation and oppression from "the conquest of the continent to California's passage of the racist Proposition 187" ("Rebellions of Everynight Life" 9).

In sum, theorizing dance and music for these scholars is one way to understand better how marginalized cultures and peoples become the invisible Other within dominant fantasies (white, heterosexual, male) of nationalism. It requires such critics to speak of "imagined communities" whereby texts—from narrative fictions and political treatise to musicscapes—have the power to create nation. As such, music/dance can also be *read* as a text invested with an ontological weight similar to that of reality. Hence, the theory of a "politics in motion" (23) that reads the kinesthetic semiotics of the Other as an act of the subaltern subject's resistance and intervention within a racist and heterosexist nation-state.

If the nation-state apparatus wields power discursively and dance/music is a text-act invested with the same weight as, say, a political treaty or a mass movement social protest or revolutionary force, then it too can radically alter the reality out there. This line of thought also follows the model discussed in chapter 2 that theorizes power as discursively constructed and that is everywhere—and thus nowhere. Accordingly, music does not, Josh Kun writes, "respect places precisely because it is capable of inhabiting a particular place while at the same time moving across several places—arriving while leaving" ("Against Easy Listening: Audiotopic Readings and Transnational Soundings" 288). Namely, if music can inhabit the same nonposition as power, then it can also have the power to deconstruct and shatter such a power structure. Dance/music produced by those inhabiting ontological margins thus has the discursive power to intervene into what is posited as a discursively constructed and imagined nation-state. Hence Kun can conclude,

> Music creates spaces where cultures can be both contested and consolidated, both sounded and silenced. Moving through space, music performs a double act of delinquency that unsettles both the geopolitical boundaries of the modern nation-state and the disciplinary boundaries that govern the study of music in the academy. (288)

For Kun, *frontera* musicscapes such as The Brat and Los Cruzados, Los Illegals, and Kid Frost all have the power to "unsettle" geopolitically inscribed nation-state boundaries.

According to this line of theorizing, Nortec would also function as a rhythmic cartography symbolic of a hybrid, borderland community with the power to unsettle nation-state boundaries. Nortec would also be an example of a *transfrontera* resistant text-act with an identifiable semiotic that critiques dominant capitalist/neocolonialist systems that systematically exploit and deny basic human rights to subaltern border crossers. Nortec as "politics in motion" or as a subalternized "rhythmic cartography" would have the power to transform the everyday life of the *indocumentado/a* throughout the Southwest.[7] It would express a kinesthetic semiotics of the Other with the same ontological value as the "real" struggles by (im)migrant subjects daily. It would resist and unsettle sexist, racist, and classist master narratives. It would be a text-act that leads to a revolutionary politics.

To clear some muddied waters, let me begin by asking, What does language do that bodies don't? At the most basic level, there is a fundamental difference between a body moving to music and that of bodies en masse fighting for political reform. The former is a reflex that can be crafted and recrafted to perform within different sonically sculptured scenes; the latter functions as a phatic, bodily extension to emphasize political demands for radical reform. To put it simply, a body's kinesthetic response to music that can be shaped into dance is not equivalent to language (sign and phatic gesture) that is necessary not just for the survival of the human race, but for the communication needed to build solidarity between proletariat groups worldwide for revolution to take place.

So while the impulse might be to read dancing bodies as counterhegemonic rhythmic cartographies that resist dominant paradigms and articulate a subaltern history, culture, and consciousness, music and/or the body's movement in response to music quite simply does not have the same ontological equivalence as language.

This is not to say that a rhythmic cartography such as Nortec does not cross borders. As the brief discussion of techno above points out, Nortec participates in a rich history of techno's diasporic movements and hybridizing of musical genres. However, this connection to hybridizing at the level of music culture and genre is not to be confused with acts of linguistic communication—whether counterhegemonic or not. Musical rhythms and body movements might jell together and form communities, such as Latinos with salsa or meringue, Tijuanenses and Nortec, thrash metal and white suburban male teenagers, or ska and British underclassers. However, such dance/music cartographies are not text-acts equivalent to the linguistic structures that inform language. They could never be, then, considered the same as the language required for communication in order to build coalition and incite revolution. Nortec, or any dance/music rhythmic cartography, cannot do what is required of hundreds of thousands of people gathered together on the streets to overturn the formation of nation-states by bourgeois elites with its drawing of boundaries, establishment of institutions, and laws (judicial and legislative branches) and government (executive branch) to enforce the material reality of the existence of these borders that delimit the territory within which the ruling class can rule.

So what are we to make of scholars who conflate language and dance/music compositions?[8] What are we to make of the formulation of music/dance as a counterhegemonic discourse where power is no longer locatable in bourgeois institutional centers used to command, to dominate, to oppress and to exploit in the hands of one social class and its institutions (the State)? Where the text is the world and therefore dance/music is a text invested with the weight of the power that exists in the real of reality.

The tendency of such scholars is to posit these musicscapes as referential, and therefore as potential sites of ontological transformation. Such scholars can theorize music as having a magical power to reterritorialize the restrictive capitalist nation-state because they identify it as a discursively referential construct. However, if the nation-state is neither a textual construct nor an imagined community, but rather the very real drawing up of boundaries, establishment of institutions and laws by a bourgeoisie to enforce the very real and violent oppression of the working class, then we must reassess such declarations. We must reassess the reading given subaltern-identified "rhythmic cartography" or "audiotopia" as referential acts equivalent to speech-acts or text-acts invested with the equivalent power to destabilize a real global capitalism.[9]

This confusion of a cultural form with ontological fact embraces the type of relativism and constructivism that I stand against at the very outset of this book. Such criticism muddles musical aesthetics and dance compositions with ontological fact that does little to build an understanding of music and its function. As Keith Negus aptly reminds, "Music cannot simply *reflect* an individual's personality or life, a nation, a city or 'the age we live in'. That word, reflection, is one that slips very easily into both academic discourse and everyday conversations about popular music. But no music can be a mirror and capture events or activities in its melodies, rhythms and voices. The world, a society, an individual life, or even a particular incident, is far too complex for any cultural product

(book, film, or song) to be able to capture and spontaneously 'reflect'"
(*Popular Music in Theory* 4).

So, what can a musicscape like Nortec actually do in the world? Certainly, Nortec is a soundscape that draws from many different genres and therefore many different musical aesthetic histories, including Mexican *conjunto* and *norteño*, which speaks to a history of hybridizing German polka sounds with *bajo sexto* rhythms and African American and Anglo Detroit/Chicago/New York and London/Manchester rave beats.[10] As such it is caught up in world diasporas often dictated by sociopolitical (less) and economic (more) forces. It is a musical aesthetic that is tied into a government and media rhetoric that applaud NAFTA. For example, the Mexican government sponsored a five-day conference titled "Nortec 2000" to celebrate Nortec as a reflection of a post-NAFTA harmoniously hybrid border reality. It was identified in a special issue of *Time* titled "Amexica" as representing a blended expression of the new Mexican/American cultural and racial identity.

Whether identified as *Amexican* or as reflective of new U.S./Mexico diplomatic and trade relations, this does not mean that Nortec is reflective of a real *Amexican* subject who has, say, real citizenry in both the U.S. and Mexico; nor does it mean that it is a cultural form that will somehow allow for truly equal economic and political relations between a dominating capitalist power such as the United States and its struggling sibling Mexico. Nortec's crossing genres does not mean either that it is reflective of a site of diasporic collectivities that resist dominant capitalist paradigms.

Nortec—like all music of its kind—is simply a popular cultural form. That politicians or journalists deem it something more than a popular commodity mediated by patterns of economic and social organization is pure fantasy—a fantasy with exploitive economic motivations in mind, of course. Its hybridizing of genres should be read as nothing more than the Nortec Collective doing what musicians do all the time: introduce, recombine, and create new variations out of a finite set of rhythms and beats for appeal and for consumption. So when one of its DJs, Bostich, cuts 'n mixes in Tijuana street sounds (car horns and the trombones/trumpets heard on Revolución Avenue), its new *formas sonoras* are not an expression of a resistant street poetic, but a way to make the old sound patterns such as techno and *norteño/conjunto* more interesting. The *New York Times* reporter Frances Anderton is right to celebrate Nortec for revitalizing the techno genre, which had "degenerated into monotony or esoteric meandering," concluding that it is "saturated with a sense of discovery" (3). The music industry encourages this type of "hybridizing" heard in Nortec because the tendency of music is to be monotonous; consumers are always looking for something new.[11] So, while today Nortec might be all the rage, tomorrow it will be something else.

Moreover, such repatterning and hybridizing of sounds take place with instruments produced through capitalist technologies. Electronic samplers, software, sync instruments, for example, are among the more or less recent instruments created to invent new sounds with a view to enliven dying musicscapes, and these are heard by young ravegoers wearing the latest in hip sartorial garb and often under the influence of synthetic drugs and/or alcohol. In other words, even at its most basic level, there is nothing radically transformative about Nortec. Like other music generally, Nortec is not a site of transgressive *Amexican*-ness nor is it an example of a "politics in motion" that can magically reterritorialize hegemonic nation-state spaces and/or resist capitalist/colonialist hegemonies.

Nortec's creation, composition, and modes of distribution (www.millrecords.com) and consumption place it squarely within a capitalist-governed popular culture. Nortec uses sophisticated, expensive technology to fill dance club spaces; its music is distributed widely via record stores and the Internet (one can sample, then buy and download Nortec Collective albums via a Paypal system on the Internet); it has been sampled in television commercials selling forty-five-thousand-dollar Volvos and featured in popular indie hit films such as *Y Tu Mamá También* and in the U.S. box-office hit *Traffic*. Nortec is far from "resistant." The DJs who make up the Nortec Collective such as Bostich, named after a German electrical appliance, is similarly telling. Other names such as Plankton Man and Hyperboreal are in the capitalist lingua franca, English, as well as the title, "Tijuana Sessions Vol. 1." Like all music, this album functions within a capitalist system governed by production/consumption models to ensure profits.

Even when the music is in its most, say, audiotopic expressive form, when clubgoers are high on Ecstasy and lose themselves in a sea of trance-beats and seemingly reach a collective sense of higher being, it is still caught up in exploitive systems of profiteering: it's tied into a huge global drug trade in which capitalist CFOs and Mafia drug lords work together to ensure massive revenue.[12]

Put simply, Nortec is music and therefore part of a huge money-making music industry dominated by U.S. state capitalists that manipulate and artificially create (the media being one of its main appendages) audiences and target markets within the logic of capitalism: to maximize profits. Nortec is a part of the global network of leisure and entertainment corporations and media conglomerates such as RCA, EMI, Sony, Warner, and BMG that exploit working-class populations worldwide. There is nothing transgressive or romantic about it—or about any musicscape generally. (When one listens to a Talvin Singh and his techno banghra beat, one must remember that its "hybrid" soundscapes might have very well been produced in places like Sri Lanka or along the U.S./Mexican border, where labor is cheap and bodies easily exploitable.) Even if one were to posit that such a musicscape simply uses the mechanism of capitalism to distribute a resistant text—investing the music and its listeners with a resistant capacity—such reader/listener-response theory simply does not measure up to the awesome power of centralized media institutions such as BMG, which spend millions of dollars creating musicscapes (from promotion and marketing to production and distribution) that undeniably manipulate consumers. In 2000, as Roy Shuker comments, "the Recording Industry Association of America observed that, as the world's universal form of communication, music touches every person of the globe to the tune of $40 billion annually, and the US recording industry accounts for one-third of that world market" (27).

Many theories of popular music reflect a fundamental tension between the creativity of the artists and music as an aesthetic and the potential for resistance and its place within capitalist consumption/production/distribution. However, Nortec's appropriation and recycling of sounds in no way makes for a localized, resistant symbolic space. You could be in Tijuana, Frankfurt, London, or at a rave in Ibiza, and the music and scene would be the same massive act of conspicuous consumption. The more music is considered an industry, the more it can be seen as a world business dominated by a handful of record companies. There is no place within this hugely manipulated arena for the production of alternative cultural politics in which individuals can reinterpret and then construct oppositional and/or disruptive sites of meaning.

In identifying an audiotopia or a "politics in motion," one unwittingly reproduces a reading of music like Nortec as an authentic site of the exotic and resistant. Such a celebration and show of anthropological interest in the exotic—Nortec's resistant syncretism—is dangerous when such critics use it to discuss politics of resistance in music/culture under capitalism, precisely because it can romanticize very real problems that people on the border face daily; it can deflect attention from exploitive legislative policies (NAFTA, for example) to musicscapes such as Nortec and ultimately lead to inaction. In *Critique of Exotica,* John Hutnyk says, "A pro-hybridity stance does not seem to me to offer any guarantees of a revolutionary project, since the place for articulation of hybridity is also a space which already seems all too easily articulated with the market. Hybridity and difference sell; the market remains intact" (36). Finally, then, more than setting out to critique romantic idealizations of the Latino/a musicscapes as subalternized epistemologies that disrupt capitalist hegemonies, I ask, So what if Nortec uses technology? So what if its soundscape appeared in a television commercial to sell high-priced, slick Volvos? After all, we are only talking about noise harnessed and patterned into soundscapes that elicit certain neural, somatic, and emotional responses.[13]

No matter how obvious the power of capitalism is in its production, distribution, and consumption of musicscapes, the idealist theories of music as resistance are alive and kicking—and not just in academia.

The musicians themselves participate in such rhetoric, claiming, for example, in the sleeve of their CD, that the Collective is not just about music, but about building of borderland communities replete with graphic artists, architects, fashion designers, remixers, producers, listeners, and clubgoers. As the self-techno-titled Bostich tells *Village Voice* reporter Enrique Lavin, "Nortec is not a genre but a way of life" (vol. 46, no. 15, April 17, 2001: 71). One of the non-DJ members of the Collective, the architect Raul Cardenas Osuna, even has promised to design what he calls "the Vertex project"—a spaceship-shaped art gallery that would span the U.S./Mexican border and feature multimedia art—which will destabilize the boundaries between the two national cultures.

Of course, the Nortec Collective want to participate in utopian fantasy. This has a material consequence on their lives. The more people buy into this lifestyle, the more money they make and the more their lives—and only their lives—change. For example, after the dance club success of the track "Polaris," Mogt quit his twelve-hour shift at the local *maquiladora* as a chemical engineer mapping formulas for face creams. So, rather than really altering the oppressive reality for the millions of poor and starving people trying to survive along the two-hundred-mile-long border, the Nortec Collective subculture simply make clear the potential of any media form: that a lifestyle, or subculture if you will, can be formed around a particular musical aesthetic but that this always serves an economic end. Such a lifestyle will, at best, form a subculture produced and contained within dominant capitalist economic practices. Such a lifestyle will never have the power in the real world to resist and/ or revolutionize restrictive colonialist/capitalist-produced social spaces.[14] As much as a Nortec Collective performance (the Collective often tour independently) might stimulate a high kinetic response from hundreds of clubgoers, when the performance ends, the bodies cease stylizing and unifying and return to a real-world *hors* soundspace; along the border this would be the reality of the *maquiladoras/narcotraficantes* and extreme poverty.

Even if one were to posit this as a subculture made up of disenfranchised youth, like all subcultures it reflects a lifestyle, not a site of political collectivity and agency that might have the power to alter social realities. Namely, as much as Birmingham School cultural studies critics romanticized youth subculture formed around music as an expression of a self-determined agency and resistance to an officially sanctioned mainstream culture—I think here of Dick Hebdige's *Subculture: The Meaning of Style* (1979), in which he identifies a subversive punk and ska youth subculture by deciphering its participants' appropriation and recycling of sartorial fashions, body postures, argot speech systems, and hair style—music and its ancillary lifestyles are only ever about the escape into and utter consumption of capitalist mass culture.

This does not mean that Nortec's reliance on technologies of capitalism is less resistant than other music subculture forms. This would assume that other music scenes and subcultures are more authentic ways of producing agency and the real transgression of social and racial hegemonic structures. For example, Paul Gilroy falls into this trap, celebrating certain musicscapes as expressions of a resistant, de-essentializing black Atlantic diasporic culture—reggae, r 'n' b, rap, among others—and denigrating others, such as techno, as musicscapes that have lost their "ethical flavour" and that are therefore void of any sociopolitical interventionist possibility. For Gilroy, techno is simply another example of a hollowed out capitalist world in which stimulation and spectacle predominate. ("Analogues of Mourning, Mourning the Analog" 262). Of course, Gilroy not only continues to participate in an authentic/inauthentic paradigm, but also wrongfully invests musicscapes with the power to be inside or outside capitalist production and consumption.

Musicians and producers of music want to sell their music; they want people to listen to their music. Talvin Singh samples bhangra beats in his Indian brand of techno/trance just as much as Chuck D raps a "fight the power" lyric to identify a black mood. Both dress up their own cultures to sell CDs. That's why all popular soundscapes—rap, r 'n' b, soul, trance/techno, rock, and so on—employ "hooks" in their songs/tracks to imprint through repetition (beat/lyric/rhythm) in the listener's mind for commercial purposes. Theories of the authentic fail to see music as fundamentally an object that circulates in and through circuits of consumption and pleasure.

Let me distinguish further the difference between cultural phenomena like Nortec, language, and acts of political intervention. Nortec—and music generally—is a part of culture. Why, then, can it not be theorized as an oppositional site of resistance to a dominant culture? To answer this, one must first ask, What is culture? Is it the meaning generated in and around certain objects—art, music, food, fashion, language, literacy education, for example—that allow people to collectively determine group identity and collectively define group experience? In *Keywords*, Williams describes culture as "a particular *way of life*" (12), whereby "music, literature, painting and sculpture, theatre and film" (90) reflect "a general process of intellectual, spiritual and aesthetic development . . . applied and effectively transferred to the works and practices which represent and sustain it" (90–91). Williams captures in his definition several aspects of culture but does not cast his net wide enough.[15] According to this restricted definition, culture is the means through which groups of people infuse meaning into their everyday social existence—and this is especially so for people who are increasingly alienated within a global capitalist governed world. In such a world, Nortec stripped down is essentially a musicscape that becomes a part of the U.S/Mexico cultural landscape simply by providing an object for people to gravitate around and interact with in the production, distribution, and social consumption of its soundscapes. In this case, then, Nortec and *all* cultural artifacts exist as products of capitalism and consumption. And, while Nortec is hybrid, to identify it as representative of a subculture is to confuse the historical fact that all modern culture is a product of cross-cultural encounters; it is to ignore the basic fact of human history that culture is the result of hybrid cross-pollinations—music being only a small by-product of this process.

Music is a part of our culture and as such is a way to make meaning out of reality, but not to the same degree of sophistication and metarepresentation as language. Yet, for those cultural studies critics who consider music an interventionist force, music functions the same as language in the altering of reality. Thus, music is formulated as a speech-act with the power either to resist and/or uncritically reproduce dominant capitalist hegemonic structures. In this spirit, Middleton theorizes music as carrying the same linguistic properties—what he identities as a "generative-transformational grammar"—as language. This allows Middleton to ask, for example, "What exactly is this text? Where is it located? What kind of things does it do?" (*Reading Pop* 2). After proposing that "both language and music originate in broader processes of semiosis" (11) and that both are semiotic constructs that evolved through "never-ending, historically contingent" intertextual exchanges, he says they both operate "between utterances, texts, styles, genres, and social groups" (13). For Middleton, then, if musicscapes are the same as linguistic systems and reflect social groups, then any music that crosses genres is not only, as he writes, "multiply voiced" (13), but can be likened to the destabilizing of otherwise segregated social groups (racial, sexual, gender identified). A further instance of this way of thinking is Philip Tagg, who reads sounds in music as signifiers and signifieds to establish a formal relationship between humanly organized nonverbal sound structures and listeners; further, he identifies a reader-response-like method of analyzing how different groups decode the communicated messages, or what he calls a "museme"—a minimal unit of expression that covers over ideologically and manipulates its listeners ("Analyzing Popular Music: Theory, Method, Practice" 94). Also, in his essay "Reflection of a Disappointed Popular Music Scholar," Lawrence Grossberg theorizes music as a Foucaultian "discursive apparatus" that can critically engage with, as he writes, "the apparatuses of power that mobilize different practices and effects to organize the spaces of human life and the possibilities of alliances" (27); music as text—and by extension the world as text—then allows Grossberg to posit it as a way to engage with today's "new and urgent political struggles" (30). In their confusion of music with text (spinning out Derrida's and Foucault's textual-idealist view of culture and reality), Tagg, Middleton, and others can then proceed to locate a politics of resistance—an intervention into discursively constructed ideologies—in music or anything.

Such scholars assume much when they theorize music-as-text. Namely, they take off from Derrida's distortion of Saussure's linguistic definition of the sign. To reiterate a point I made earlier in the book, Saussure's characterization of the sign showed that it is a construct of two *inseparable* phenomena: the "signifier" (or acoustic image or pho-neme), which identifies those sounds that are different to the sounds recognized as noise within language, and the "signified" (or the "mental image"), which identifies how the speaker of a language categorizes an aspect of reality in the particular way of that language. Here Saussure clarifies also his idea of the "arbitrariness" of the sign, remarking that it is not as indeterminate and the choice entirely of the speaker, for the speaker does not "have the power to change a sign in any way once it has been established in the linguistic community" (68). He continues, "The arbitrary nature of the sign explains in turn why the social fact alone can create a linguistic system. The community is necessary if values that owe their existence solely to usage and general acceptance are to be set up; by himself, the individual is incapable of fixing a single value" (69). The meaning of a given word is not arbitrary, but rather defined within a system of terms; for if there is not system, there is no communication. Meaning in language is thus a complex operation of a sign as an insepa-rable signifier/signified unit used in a specific community of language participants. Linguistic sounds (phonemes) are recognized as belonging to either language A, B, or C (German, Spanish, English) by speakers of such languages. Those sounds (Saussure's signifiers) are a physical phe-nomenon (vibrations of waves in air) that produces an "acoustic image" in the mind of the hearer and, I remind, are inseparable from notions formed in the mind of such a hearer at the moment he/she transforms sounds (vibrations, etc.) into concept (Saussure's signified). This sign is unity of signifier and signified—physical and mental phenomena—these two elements are as inseparable as the two sides of a sheet of paper. You might be able to tear the paper apart, but you cannot eliminate the fact that it has a front and a back. To speak of a signifier as separate from a signified is thus, strictly speaking, nonsense.

When scholars theorize music-as-text by way of a Derridean *différance*, they misread Saussure's theory of the sign as the inseparable "acoustic" image with its concept, confusing the signified with the referent, or the "out there." As I discussed in chapters 2 and 3, such a muddling of Sau-ssure's formulation allows cultural studies critics to wrongfully theorize music as textual construct and to read music as text-act that *performs* between the lines of capitalist and/or colonial language paradigms.

From every point of view, whether social, psychological, anthropo-logical, linguistic, or ontological, music and literature are two entirely different entities. Where literature's raw material is a complex language system, music's prime matter is noise submitted to certain patterns of regularity and differentiation. So, to conflate music and literature and therefore language is not only a category mistake, but also a utopic, unrealizable aspiration.

What is the value of analyzing Nortec or any musical form, then? If music is not to be read as a text-as-world discursive act with the power to alter and/or reflect reality, then what is its function? Why "read" music? We analyze music not because we are deluded into thinking it holds the promise to revolutionize the world, but because of an interest in understanding the neural/emotive response mechanisms to sounds and a concern for the development of a vocabulary (genres, rhythmic structures, macro and micro tonal patterns, and so on) for appreciating music consciously. As Christopher New clarifies,

> Musical notation has no other function than to represent sounds, or qualities of and relations between sounds, whereas the written sentences of literature that require to be read or spoken aloud (and, of course written sentences in general) standardly have the additional quality of being meaningful—a quality they possess whether they are read in silence or aloud. The reading of a musical score is in this sense a merely auditory affair—we either imagine the sounds represented in it, or directly produce them—while the reading of a literary or an other written work is not. Music . . . does not have a semantic dimension in the way that literature does. (7–8)

So, although we might employ linguistic metaphors for "reading" music, these are useful analogues and not to be confused with the actual grammars and syntax that govern language. Thus when one describes music one can use literary metaphors—identifying, for example, how an Alanis Morissette lyric is hymnlike or how Nirvana employs the ballad. And one can talk about a poem being musical and discuss the musical rhythms in poetry. However, this is always figurative and never literal.

Meaning in music relies on recognizing and/or physiologically responding to patterns of repetition and difference as shaped by sonic themes and clusters. This meaning exists at the somatic and emotive level. (Without the recognition of difference, music's finite sound patterns would pass unnoticed and therefore would be unable to move its listener.) When we hear a musical sound, a Nortec beat, say, these are a series of vibrations that pass through the air and hit the ear, which then triggers a neural response. Sound meaning, then, is a completely physical phenomenon, not a sign in the Sausurrean sense with signifier and signified. The musical sound is devoid of meaning.

The Nortec DJ—or any musician for that matter—creates shapes and forms with sounds; his raw materials are sounds either as noise or as recognizable music that vibrate through the air and trigger a physiological response. The only difference between the use of noise and music is the value we attribute to the different sounds: whether the accident of noise or the deliberate sound of music. So a musician or DJ can create patterns of repetition and difference by alternating the musicscape identity by putting notes together in certain ways. These same notes can *sound* differently when other notes are introduced and new clustered patterns mixed.

Music is not a language and therefore cannot communicate or transmit meaning. However, it is not meaningless. There's certainly something to the fact that we've been making and listening to some form of music for the past one hundred thousand years or more. It's near-ubiquitous presence in all aspects of our daily activities tells us something of its importance today: in the gym it's used to increase physical stamina and on other occasions to alter one's mood. The neurobiological research shows that music's vast array of sound patterns, loudness, pitch, contour, tempo, timbre, and rhythms engage nearly all of our brain's neural subsystems. Indeed, as Daniel J. Levitin argues in *This is Your Brain on Music,* there's a deep adaptive dimension to music: "Knowing whether something is generating noise or moving toward us or away from us, even when we can't see it (because it is dark, our eyes aren't attending to it, or we're asleep) has a great survival value" (42). We see this adapative faculty in our ability to discriminate timbre when, for instance, the voice of a loved one is heard over a crowd of hundreds of different voices. It is why cross-culturally there's a hardwired response to sharp, shrill, loud sounds (alert) and to longer, quieter sounds (calm). This is why across cultures people undergo a similar experience when they hear music: when sound enters the eardrum, it is segregated by pitch, timbre, contour, and rhythm.

There is no, say, music module in the brain. The processing (composition, making, listening) of music takes place over many regions of the brain. In the making of and in listening to music like Nortec, we experience both lower-order (amygdala) and higher-order cognitive neural activation: memory (hippocampus), motor cortex, timing circuits (cerebellum), sensory cortex, and planning regions, for instance. We all know that the random playing of a tune on the radio can create direct neural paths to a memory of a time and place. When we distinguish notes and identify rhythms and melodies, we use the same part of the brain as when we parcel auditory sounds into phonemes to make meaning of language; the same part of the brain fires (Broca's and Wernicke's areas) when we hear lyrics in music and when we hear a shift in cadence during conversation. While ultimately the processing of sound splits for music and language, it makes sense, evolutionarily speaking, that they would share at least some of the same neural circuits; we see this in children, who as they mature begin to carve out distinctive neural pathways and neuronal clusters in increasingly specialized processing of music and language activities. This is why adults who suffer brain damage to the left hemisphere, where speech processing is primarily localized, do not necessarily lose their musical ability.

We know that while there might be shared neuronal regions of activation, music and language are not ultimately processed the same way. What the above brief discussion should emphasize, however, is that a musical form like Nortec matters, just not in the same way that language matters. It matters as a subject of study because it can help us understand better how genres form and reform in different times and places. It matters more deeply because, as the evolutionary biologists suggest, music most likely paved the way for our ancestors to be able to process what eventually manifests itself in the very complex cognitive and motor reflex mechanism involved in oral communication. (We also used mime to communicate, which also requires motor skills; but it is through much more symbolically complex oral communication that we became able to more completely break the shackles of an existence imprisoned by the present, recalling a past, and imagining a future collectively.) Further, music matters when talking of language. As mentioned, it's the variation of rhythm and timbre that can make a difference in hearing sarcasm or not in a conversation; its direct link to our memory faculty is why authors might choose to tell their tale in rhythmic manner. As Levitin sums up, "As a tool for activation of specific thoughts, music is not as good as language. As a tool for arousing feelings and emotions, music is better than language" (261).

CONCLUDING REMARKS

Lavin celebrates Nortec as a musicscape that radically revises the tourist's preconception of Tijuana, celebrating its "cuts and pastes" of an environment filled with, he writes, "*la migra,* prostitutes, the assembly-line tech industry, FBI 'Wanted' posters of the Arellano brothers drug bosses" (April 11–17, 2001).

It is this kind of idealism that pervades the study of a musical form like Nortec. Perhaps, however, it is time to pause and reflect on what's being said about Nortec and music generally. In this case, theorists of music might be mindful of the distinction between music, language, and material reality. Often the counterhegemonic methodologies theorized by cultural studies scholars of Latino music and music generally differ from the methods used to accomplish social change in reality. Certainly, a shared history of colonialism and capital globalization increasingly equates experiences of marginal groups in Los Angeles to those of marginal groups in the San Ysidro/Tijuana borderland. We need to be mindful of the difference between theories of "audiotopias" and *transfrontera* "rhythmic cartographies" that celebrate hybridity and borderless worlds, and the often less emancipatory reality of working a three-dollar-a-day shift at one of the *maquiladoras* that line the U.S./Mexico border. This said, we need to be mindful in our scholarship and in our teaching of the differences that really make a difference when studying why music matters and how music works.

TEN

THE "CULTURAL STUDIES TURN" IN BROWN STUDIES

INTRODUCTION

"My political work takes place when I teach my students how to be critical of racist stereotypes in film; it takes place when I affirm positive representations in our culture," a graduate student declared during a seminar. I had pushed the students a little, asking where we might find proof that scholarly "cultural work" had led to political change. I had asked the question because in one way or another, having an all-out faith in representations, students would make mind-blowingly smart and sophisticated rhetorical moves to argue either the text's assertion of a transformative politics of resistance or its normalizing of hierarchies of racial, sexual, and other differences. I wanted them to think through their approach and conclusions—just as I aim to do here by exploring recent turns to cultural studies in contemporary Chicano/a and Latino/a cultural studies. In this chapter, I will focus on several representative works to discuss and disentangle the cultural studies turn that has taken place in today's Chicano/a and Latino/a studies: Monica Brown's *Gang Nation: Delinquent Citizens in Puerto Rican, Chicano, and Chicana Narratives,* Curtis Marez's *Drug Wars: The Political Economy of Narcotics,* Michelle Habell-Pallán's *Loca Motion: The Travels of Chicana and Latina Popular Culture,* and the various essays collected in Michelle Habell-Pallán's and Mary Romero's edited anthology, *Latino/a Popular Culture.*

Brown analyzes gang literature; Marez studies drug war iconography in literature, film, and music; Habell-Pallán focuses on various types of performance art; and the essayists included in *Latino/a Popular Culture* examine a wide range of other cultural phenomena. Yet these scholars apply similar methods to "read" cultural iconography and aesthetic acts as textual sites of Chicano/Latino political (symbolic and real) resistance and intervention into dominant, patriarchal (white and brown), capitalist/neocolonialist "norms."

Gang Nation explores the many texts by and about Chicano and Latino gangs to excavate sites of political and social acts of resistance. Brown analyzes authors such as Edwin Torres and Piri Thomas (Puerto Rican) as well as Xyta Maya Murray and Mona Ruiz (Chicana), theorizing this array of gang autobiography, narrative fiction, and drama as making "real" and human those subjects otherwise one-dimensionalized and marginalized within a racist United States. Gangster textualities do more than send a shiver down one's spine. They shake up those power structures, she argues, "that have been held in place by the mechanisms of a monolithic 'national culture' invested in maintaining the status quo" (xxvii). *Drug Wars* analyzes a number of texts, from Leslie Marmon Silko's *Almanac of the Dead* to popular *narcocorridos* and Robert Rodriguez's *El Mariachi,* to show how both drug wars and cross-border drug traffic justify and extend the nation-state's oppressive juridical and militaristic powers within and outside the United States and also a "resistance to capital and the state" (x). Of the latter, Marez declares, "Whether in the form of crime, violent rebellion, labor radicalism, or oppositional cultural production, marginalized groups have directly and indirectly opposed the expansion of state and capitalist power that drug traffic supports" (x). *Loca Motion* excavates a Chicano-Latino cultural politics of resistance in the performance art (and poetry) of Luis Alfaro, Marga Gomez, and Marisela Nortes, as well as Chicana feminist punk and the revisionary rock 'n' roll of El Vez. And, finally, *Latino/a Popular Culture* runs the gamut of cultural analysis: from Puerto Rican Barbie's *jíbara* roots (hair and land) to *fútbol* as televisual means of community building; from punk *rock en español* and Guillermo Gómez-Peña's border-crossing performances that hijack high-tech media venues to circulate revolutionary slogans, to English-language Latino rap riffs of resistance. All popular culture by and/or about Latinos is up for grabs here, reflecting how "cultural and political debates, conflicts, and social expression of identity, gender, sexuality, community, and nation are staged and performed" (6).

I will begin by exploring here how the cultural studies turn has shaped Brown's *Gang Nation*. Having taught literature by and about Chicano and Latino gangs, Brown found students and herself asking, Why the attraction to stories so violent and bleak? What value, if any, could such texts have? To find answers, Brown immersed herself in a formal study of the many different genres—drama, novel, short story, and autobiography—that work as vehicles for conveying the many different modes of being and concomitant range of feeling and experience that inform Chicano and Puerto Rican identity at the extreme margins of society. Rather than narratives that lead to stultifying dead ends, Brown discovers within these texts a kinesis of consciousness that halts cycles of violence and has the potential to begin anew the much-needed process of societal healing.

This wide range of gang narratives—spanning over thirty years and extending from coast to coast (New York, Los Angeles), and including national identifications (American, Puerto Rican, and Mexican) and gender divides—depict a number of critical and uncritical engagements with the dominant and oppressive political, judicial, economic, and social institutions that make up the United States. These texts make apparent, she writes, "the links between youth violence and systemic, historically based racism, structural inequities, colonialism, entrenched poverty, failing educational and health care systems, a debilitated infrastructure, as well as the seeming lack of hope and the existential despair that accompany these material conditions" (xiv). Some authors more than others, according to Brown, present gang life as a counterhegemonic site of resistance to such a nation-state. Some more than others attempt to revise, according to Brown, common misperceptions of urban brown youth as being a dangerous, ever-threatening presence that exists within nation-state boundaries and that has the power to invade and destroy the everyday sanctimoniousness coveted by the coalescing Anglo masses. More broadly, these texts reverse the gaze and site of power from that traditionally invested in the Anglo citizen-subject to that of the traditionally coded "delinquent" or "perverse" ethnic-object specimen.

We know from such sociological studies as Arturo Hernandez's *Peace in the Streets* and James Diego Vigil's *Barrio Gangs* and *A Rainbow of Gangs* that gangs form mostly within the poorest of poor urban communities. This can be traced back to the mid-nineteenth century when poor Irish and Italian immigrants formed gangs in East Coast urban centers. Of course, with class intersecting at the site of racialized bodies, there's the mushrooming of Chicano, Salvadoran, Vietnamese, and African American gangs in *barrios* scattered all over Los Angeles, for instance. For young men of color struggling to survive in urbanscapes that offer very few jobs and extremely low wages, severely underfunded school systems, substandard and scarce medical care facilities, overzealous and often racist crime fighters, and shattered family life, the appeal of joining gangs is obvious. They offer youngsters protection on the street (of course, from the gang itself as well as from neighboring rival gangs) and, as some argue, alternative forms of familial affiliation and belonging. Ex-gang member and writer Luis Rodríguez reflects in *Always Running* that it was the violence "permeating every aspect of his being—his home life and his life on the street" (Brown 66)—that led him to embrace gang life for protection and a sense of belonging. In Miguel Durán's fictionalized autobiography *Don't Spit on My Corner*, the reader follows the life of Little Mike, who, born without the silver key that guarantees access to the kind of education and employment that usually lead to middle-class opportunities, turns to gangs—or, as Brown writes, to other "locations for community identification and empowerment" (xxv).

Of course, as Brown rightly points out, gang affiliation is both empowering and hugely destructive. While it might provide an ad hoc family structure, its very function is exploitive and violent. Not only do gangs expose, as Brown point out, the "oppressive facets of dominant culture's construction of nation and an American 'national symbolic'" (xvii), but they participate directly within a violently destructive, oppressive, and exploitive capitalist system. The more a gang succeeds at controlling the ebbs and flows of parcels of capital—through drug peddling, money laundering, and organized prostitution, for example—the more it offers an attractive form of "making it" to those otherwise locked out of a "legitimate" surplus-value extortion system.

In a vicious and almost always unbreakable circle, the more one is involved in gang life and organized crime, the less likely one is to have access to education and to employment in legal activities. Gangs promise the good life, but, as the many narratives that Brown analyses demonstrate, they usually lead their members to incarceration and often tragic death. Edwin Torres's novel *Carlito's Way* is a case in point. Torres tells the story of a second-generation Puerto Rican, Carlito, who turns to gangs not for a sense of belonging, but as a means to acquire money and power. Here, the racially and socially marginalized Carlito is not concerned with, as Brown writes, the "uplifting of his people or other ghetto youth but rather financial gain at any cost" (27). Carlito is murdered by the Italian Mafia and, Brown concludes, "Carlito is a 'victim' of the system who chooses to mimic dominant social systems and is unrepentant and undeterred in his quest for the American 'goodies' denied him as a child" (35). Whether Puerto Rican Carlito or Italian gangbanger, there is nothing romantic about this power-by-any-means modus operandi made possible through bloodshed and vicious exploitation.

Torres's novel is unremittingly bleak. Piri Thomas's autobiography *Down These Mean Streets,* on the other hand, unfolds a redemption narrative. As the story develops, Thomas critiques not only a life of crime that ends up closing down his options in life as he does time in high-security Sing Sing, but also, as Brown contends, critiques the "existing social structures and institutional limitations present in El Barrio" (35). Thomas takes to the streets to get away from the deep hurt he feels at home. As the one with the darkest skin in the family (the mother calls him *negrito),* the father's internalized racism expresses itself through his fists, with which he beats Thomas. Unlike Torres's Carlito, Thomas's journey is not so much about the acquisition of power as about an exploration of identity: he endeavors to figure out where he fits. Because of what Brown identifies as a "politics of skin color" (13), he is not allowed to identify culturally as Hispanic—even though he's Puerto Rican at home and within society at large—because of his African features, and he is not allowed to be African American because he's culturally Hispanic. Being caught in between and fitting nowhere leads him to the street and eventually to a life of crime and ensuing incarceration. However, this isn't the end of the road for Thomas. In jail, he gains the tool that will help him achieve "legitimate" success. He becomes literate and self-empowered. He acquires ability to write *Down These Mean Streets,* invigoratingly written in a rhythmical, street-slang hybrid Spanish and English. Having managed to leave the streets and find salvation, he thus not only finds his sense of place in what Brown calls the "there-but-hereness" (4) within a racist family and society, but also provides a living testament to future generations of outcasts.

In a dramatic turn away from male-authored narratives, Brown analyzes Xyta Maya Murray's novel *Locas* and Monica Ruiz's memoir *Two Badges* to explore how gender and race inform gang life. While a Durán or a Rodríguez might articulate the complex and often contradictory impulses that inform a brown masculinity within a racist society, they do so while caricaturing women. For Brown, most Chicano- or Latino-authored gang narratives represent women either as hypersexualized whores or passive virgins. They one-dimensionalize and therefore effectively erase the presence of women. In her analysis of *Locas* and *Two Badges,* Brown seeks instead to make visible the complexity of Chicana gang life to critique the "rubric of nationalistic discourse set up in many male gang narratives" (82) that reproduce mainstream representations of Chicanas as dangerous bodies. Taking her lead from Rosa Linda Fregoso's formulation of the empowered *pachuca*—a figure that defies the virgin/whore/malinche paradigm that permeates heterosexist Chicano culture—Brown reads Murray's character Lucía, for example, as a figure of Chicana resistance and an agent of oppositional politics. Lucía embraces gang life as "a substitution for all that the national symbolic promises for majority members" (84–85) and becomes empowered as the leader who uses "the rhetoric of community and civic pride" to control her territory.

For Brown, Chicano/a and Latino/a gangs and lifestyles as represented in these narratives are alternative responses to nationalist discursive and judicial acts that criminalize and deny full citizen rights to brown, urban subjects. These texts also represent how codes of loyalty and honor and territorial pride are similar, according to Brown, to the way nationalist rhetoric informs the American nation-state. According to Brown, these gang narratives that gravitate toward subjects who are denied rights of citizenship imagine alternative communities and alternative forms of engaging with the nation-state. More than just making visible the violent effects of a dominating nationalist identity that criminalizes and makes Other the urban brown subject, these narratives represent how "organized resistance, through the recognition of a shared social, historical, and geographic reality" (xxvii) can form into sites of "counter-nation" resistance and political intervention.

Surveillance, countersurveillance, representation, and counterrepresentation all operate in Curtis Marez's *Drug Wars* to redraw the history of drug trafficking and drug wars: from its early importations and prohibitions that helped fuel the building of the British empire (opium) to its function in today's U.S. imperialism in Latin America (coca) and the increased surveillance of minorities in the United States in the "production of criminality" (258). Rather than approach the topic from a strictly political or economic point of view, Marez seeks to uncover a contradictory function in the cultural imaginary of the nation; more specifically in the tension as "subaltern and elites struggle over media representation" (31). For example, he identifies the "automatic-weapon aesthetic" in *El Mariachi* as a symbolic counter to "both dominant media and military conventions" (17). Seeing *El Mariachi* as an "insurgent" (17) film made outside of Hollywood, he considers the director Robert Rodriguez a "media guerrilla [who] condenses multiple, divergent histories of subaltern rebellion against state power that centrally involve participant observation by media makers" (17).

In the battle over cultural production, the drug war film acts as a form that both constructs an oppressive nation-state (*Scarface*) and/or that can also destabilize it (*El Mariachi*). And texts like Silko's *Almanac* and soundscapes like *narcocorridos* "cut alternative channels of media production" and provide resistant "visual and aural technologies by immigrants" (36). So while the mainstream media have used the drug war to criminalize and suppress "domestic dissent" (249), if we turn to Silko's *Almanac,* as Marez does, we will see the real workings of power: that the U.S. war on drugs is aimed not at ending the drug traffic, but at "annex[ing] it to state power" (249) and funding "rightwing military proxies such as the contras" (249) to insure the capitalist, imperialist expansion in Latin America, the Middle East, Southeast Asia, and beyond.

In *Loca Motion* Michelle Habell-Pallán explores the work of performance artists like Marga Gomez and Luis Alfaro as well as the performed poetry of Marisela Norte, the feminist Chicana punk rock sounds of The Bags and The Brat, among others. All such artists reside in the cultural margins, but discover means of intervening in the dominant modes of representation (film, television, print) to represent themselves in "their own terms" (6). They variously invent subaltern hybrid identified cultural forms that, as Habell-Pallán writes, provide "alternative circuits and media" (5); their countercultural strategies, including irony, humor, and bilingual wordplay, are "subversive" and provide hope for an "America that has yet to live up to its democratic possibility" (6). In Marisela Norte's performance piece about nieces and lascivious uncles, Habell-Pallán considers the feminist theme of survival and Norte's "postpunk femme fatale look" as "edgy enough to front an East Los Angeles punk band" (45) and that resists both Chicano macho nationalism and mainstream representations of the Chicana as exotic. And she considers the Chicano rock 'n' roll performance artist El Vez as "double-edged": he transforms "the dominant culture's imposition of social codes that attempt to define 'Mexican immigrant' or 'Mexican American' identity and place in society" (189); he also unfixes an otherwise essentialized gendered and sexualized Chicana/Chicano identity. Ultimately, El Vez "suggests that breaking with Chicano nationalism does not signify a break with Chicano politics" (189). And the bicultural Cuban/Puerto Rican lesbian performance artist Marga Gomez embodies a critical *mestizaje,* and her performances not only offer sites of healing but also, in her use of "bittersweet humor," require "a new type of literacy, a critical reading practice that frames and interprets power dynamics from the perspective of those excluded from mainstream society" (115). The so-called

DIY (Do It Yourself) Chicana punk subculture embodied in Jim Mendiola's protagonist Molly in his film *Pretty Vacant* as well as the localized Chicana punk vocals of Alice Bags and Teresa Covarrubias express, according to Habell-Pallán, a "private rage about restrictions placed on and the violence done to their own bodies and to their mothers' bodies" (156). This punk sensibility gives voice to a working-class Chicana experience whereby women like Covarrubias can "reimagine the world she lives in [and] where she could see herself as an empowered subject" (156). Habell-Pallán concludes of Luis Alfaro's exaggerated gestures and expressions in his solo performance pieces ("Pico-Union") that they are critically resistant as acts of validation of his gay Chicano identity. Alfaro's nationally performed solo pieces clear a space "for coalition building [to] challenge . . . racism, misogyny, and homophobia" (91). Finally, for Habell-Pallán, the analysis of Chicano/Latino artists' strategies of resistance—humor, irony, punk aesthetics, exaggerated gesture, for example—allows for both a critique of "cultural representations and expectations" (41) and the opportunity for us "to re-imagine status quo power relations within and beyond national borders" (206).

The essays in Michelle Habell-Pallán's and Mary Romero's *Latino/a Popular Culture* explore a wide variety of Latino/a cultural phenomena that make up a so-called "transnational imaginary" (7). These function as "counter-sites" that can help—or hinder—the struggle for social transformation within otherwise restrictive paradigms of nation. The hip swirls and pop rhythms that Ricky Martin performed at George W. Bush's presidential inauguration are not just a show of Republican support: they betray a nation-state's history of "imperialism, racism, class domination, patriarchy, and heterosexism" [2]. The essays have in common an understanding that popular culture is more than an object to be consumed to make everyday life more pleasant. Rather, because cultural phenomena inform our everyday lives, and subjects are constructed through everyday engagement with discourse, then by critically dealing with Latino/a pop culture we can, as Habell-Pallán and Romero propose, "publicly imagine new ways of constructing racial, ethnic, gendered, and economic identities" (7).

The introduction of Puerto Rican Barbie to Puerto Rico in 1997 is a terrain that Frances Negrón-Muntaner tills to critically deal with larger neocolonial and imperialist discourses that inform Puerto Rican nationalism. In her essay "Barbie's Hair: Selling Out Puerto Rican Identity in the Global Market" Negrón-Muntaner details at length how the production and consumption of Puerto Rican Barbie, with its peasant characteristics and Euro-Spanish features, concerns a postnationalist Puerto Rico that has ceased defying American cultural imperialism and is earmarked for a conservative administrative and business class elite characterized by its persistent nostalgia for plantation life. Negrón-Muntaner sums up, "The doll was a triumph for Island elites: corporate America gave them what reality denies them—a purely plastic Puerto Rican identity—and they enjoyed it without financial or political responsibility" (55). However, the doll was critically received by mainland and island Boricua nationalists who considered it something like, as Negrón-Muntaner identifies, a "Trojan horse of identity destruction" (39). That Puerto Rican Barbie's hair was straight—and not curled to identify the *jíbara's* Afro-Hispanic roots—was also a source of conflict and anxiety between the elites and the Boricua nationalists. The straightening of Barbie's hair worked, according to Negrón-Muntaner, "to manage anxieties about the transculturation of future Puerto Rican generations" (45–46) as well as naturalize a colonialist ideology internalized by Puerto Rican elites that continues to uphold a *pureza de sangre* Euro-Spanish identity politics: the lighter the skin and more European-featured the person, the more civilized they will be. Puerto Rican Barbie, Negrón-Muntaner concludes, "is the consummate nationalist elite product bred by the contradictions of the commonwealth: a modern packaging (plastic) of a premodern essence (rural Puerto Rico), for postmodern nationalists (colonial survivors)" (47).

Just as a careful consideration of Barbie can reveal conflictive narratives of nation, so too does the cultural phenomenon of music present a complex web of discourses that inform Latino/a identity and experience. In "Encrucijadas: Rubén Blades at the Transnational Crossroads," Ana Patricia Rodríguez seeks to reveal how the music and lyrics in Rubén Blades's albums "*La Rosa de los Vientos*" (1996) and "*Tiempos*" (1999) act to build a transnational imaginary and enact a process of historical revisionism and neocolonial resistance. For example, she reads the Panamanian-born, Nuyorican-identified Blades's concert to commemorate the country's newly acquired control of the Panama Canal (December 1999) as "the (re)construction of national, regional, and transnational Central American identities and cultures" (85). More specifically, Rodríguez reads Blades's lyrics in the song "Mar del Sur" as his articulation of a violent colonial past: the colonization that ensued after Vasco Núñez de Balboa sighted the Pacific Ocean off the coast of Panama in 1513 and led to centuries of oppression that climaxed in the American invasion of Panama. Not only does Blades's song offer an alternative historical narrative of colonialism and neocolonialism in Central America, but, she continues, it also "becomes a discursive site for enacting transnational linkages between Central Americans (in the South) and Central American Latinos (in the North)" (97).

With similar transnational zeal, Raquel Rivera's analysis of Puerto Rican hip-hop seeks to expand what it means to be Nuyorican by studying English-lyric rap that shuns a *latinidad* identity politics and that is largely neglected by the Latino media for not using Spanish. Just as Rivera and Rodríguez analyze the lyrics as countersites of resistance, so too does Josh Kun read the music videos produced by the punk/thrash rock band Tijuana No! Here, Kun explores how the band uses technology and capitalist modes of production—they were signed by BMG International and run their videos on MTV—to disseminate an antiimperialist, revolutionary (pro-Zapatista) message. In so doing, Tijuana No! "urge us to develop a new grammar of globalization that disarticulates dominant ideology from technical systems of material production, one that properly accounts for the way musicians and video makers are manipulating mass media against their will as modes of emergent citizenship and tools for social change, while denouncing and dismantling the prescribed models of citizenship and the structures of racism, imperialism, and colonialism that these tools are packaged in" ("The Sun Never Sets on MTV" 103).

Brown's *Gang Nation,* Marez's *Drug Wars,* Habell-Pallán's *Loca Motion,* and the essays collected in *Latino/a Popular Culture* certainly open new paths and broaden the critical purview of Chicano and Latino studies. And they obliquely pose interesting questions: Who is given power to represent? What voices are allowed to speak? What types of images and music are allowed to circulate? What effect do such stereotypes of Chicanos and Latinos have on the population at large? How do novelists, musicians, poets, playwrights, performance artists, and filmmakers complicate such representations?

Clearly, the focuses of the books differ, but the method of approach is similar: all sort of narratives (novel, autobiography, or dramatic play) or cultural phenomena (film, music, or football, etc.) can be decoded as texts that either engage critically or participate uncritically in hegemonic discourses of capitalism, neocolonialism, imperialism, nationalism. The cosmopolitan *jíbara* Barbie, complete with low-cut peasant dress can be decoded as "eager to do the work of the nation, and willing to serve as a (non)maternal reproductive machine" (53) for today's *criollo* administrative and business elite. For another essayist, Alberto Sandoval-Sánchez, such decoding uncovers Paul Simon's dramatic staging of *The Capeman*, as a "new politics of diversity, difference, and multiculturalism" ("Paul Simon's *The Capeman*" 158) covers over the unequal and unidirectional flow of capital and culture: the Haves like Paul Simon continue to possess the economic means to appropriate and profit from the Have-nots. Such decodings allow Juan Velasco, for instance, to assert that Guillermo Gómez-Peña's border-crossing performance art carries "forward not only the importance of decentering privileged Eurocentric assumptions about nation and identity, but also the need to initiate the conditions for a critical form of Latina-o performativity that alternates between sincerity and subversion, irony and compliance" ("Performing Multiple Identities" 217). It allows Ana Patricia Rodríguez to decode Blades's lyrics as a "discursive field . . . that is bound to a whole system of historically produced economic, political, and social relations and conditions of living that may be shared by Latin American and Latino subjects across the spaces they occupy" (97). And it means that Christopher A. Shinn can decode *fútbol* as a "deep and abiding transnational connection with Latin America and symbolizes the cultural figure for Latinos, forging new gendered, pan-ethnic, and corporate structures that seek to create and capitalize on an emerging sense of homeland in the United States" ("Fútbol Nation" 241). Finally, it allows Monica Brown in *Gang Nation* to make visible an entire corpus of Chicano/a and Puerto Rican gang narratives that, she writes, "complicate instead of solidify the notion of criminality" (159). Such textual decodings allow her to sidetrack attention from these narratives' aesthetic elements and functions and to see them fundamentally as representations of counternations with the power "to intervene in the exploitative cycle of the demonizing and dehumanizing of minority youth in popular culture" (162). Such scholars not only share a similar understanding of narrative and culture as decodable essentially as political texts, but also settle on similar conclusions: that Chicano and Latino narratives and cultural artifacts are little more than political texts that have, as Habell-Pallán and Romero write, the potential to help "us imagine and construct what [the world] could be in the future" (7) and act as sites of "intervention, critique, and pleasure" (16).

For all the aforementioned scholars to assert that certain cultural artifacts and narratives have the power to effect real social change in the world out there, they must conflate fiction, entertainment, and other cultural phenomena with the political and social action of the laboring population as well as the juridical texts and other institutionalized guarantees (freedoms of speech, organization, and collective bargaining, for instance) obtained by means of the class struggle; they thus must infuse narratives and mass entertainment with the same ontological weight and transforming power as the acts of thousands and sometimes even millions of people mobilized to effect real political and social changes in the world out there.

Herein lies the problem. The study of cultural phenomena began largely in Great Britain under the impulse of Raymond Williams and E. P. Thompson. In their studies of working-class youth populations and the analysis of, for example, the mugging phenomenon, they identified sites of subcultural resistance to the dominant adult- and bourgeois-operated mainstream society. Of course, to search for a political potential of resistance and revolution in subcultural groups, as any perfunctory check of the enormous amount of evidence available readily shows, there is absolutely no indication to suggest that a subculture has the power to alter social reality in a revolutionary fashion. In fact, the opposite has been usually true. For all its radical posturing and anarchic fanfare, youth subcultures have never broken with a capitalist outlook and have been readily turned into massive consumers of goods and services produced within the confines of the capitalist mode of production—music, clothes, Italian Lambrettas, hair products, and so on.

Though the study of culture is by its very nature an ever-expanding and ill-defined activity devoid of clear methodological contours—culture, after all, appears to be ubiquitous, and its study is based on a vast range of very different and conflicting approaches—the field became even more vague and ethereal when British cultural studies (especially the social studies of Williams et al. that came to be associated with the Birmingham Center for Contemporary Cultural Studies) shook hands with French poststructuralism in the late 1960s and early 1970s and made the trans-Atlantic crossing to the United States. (See Todd Gitlin's "The Anti-Political Populism of Cultural Studies.") James W. Carey identifies this as a "fateful detour" (17) that shuns not only fieldwork (such as interviews and the collection of empirical data) but also all attempts at formulating scientifically based hypotheses, favoring instead an unlimited proliferation of opinions, beliefs, impressions, judgments, and personal convictions parading as theories.

Poststructuralist cultural studies dropped heavy anchor in the United

States at the time when the Reagan administration was in full stride attacking workers across the nation, undermining civil rights, busting up unions and strikes, privatizing health care systems, making extensive budgetary cuts in education and welfare, developing at a gigantic pace the most parasitic and speculative trends of financial capital on Wall Street. With little hope of a real and effective political resistance, it's not entirely surprising that the academic left gravitated more and more toward a vast array of mythical—even mystically self-proclaimed—theories of rebellion and toward one guise or another of the political populism shaped in and by cultural studies.

Once nested in literary departments in the United States, cultural studies practitioners held staunchly that both the subject and the world were constructed through discourse and that power was everywhere. The study of literature became mostly an act of decoding sign systems in political and social terms, just as social and cultural phenomena were now seen as texts in need of this same treatment. It then became good enough simply to theorize about culture without any empirical or scientific constraints. Thus, for instance, if the world is a discursive construction and something like the nation is an ideological master narrative, it suffices simply to decode these phenomena as constructs and to declare that such and such aspect or element of culture (or that such and such subcultural occurrence) acts as an accomplice or as an agency of resistance to oppressive social and political discursive forces. Some cultural phenomena were willy-nilly identified as discursive appendages that enforced hegemonic master narratives to control the subject, and others were identified as discursive interventions that could reshape dominant master narratives and therefore reshape reality. As Carey summarizes,

> The emergence of the text further reduced the entire domain of culture to ideology and all social relations into surrogates for power, a vicious self-fulfilling prophecy. The complex culture of a people and an adequate understanding of its formation were exhausted by grasping one limited part of its formulation. Moreover, by discovering ideology in the texts of popular culture, by searching for it in the enacted ideas of the popular practice of everyday life—shopping, commodities, music, television and leisure—political culture was reduced to the most managed and instrumental parts of life and the common-sense understandings of politics were completely evacuated. (17–18)

The upshot: As the text-as-reality was born and the ubiquitous genealogies of power became an intellectual fashion, not only were the search for verifiable facts and the application of ethnographic methods lost but so too any attempt at studying sociocultural phenomena and politics in ways that could be verified and/or empirically refuted.

Today, the idea that the text is world/world is text and that the subject is discursive construct permeates nearly all aspects of cultural studies and literary criticism in the United States. This allows the nation-state to be identified as a discursive construct (an imagined community) built of contradiction, which can be transformed through counter discourses that have been variously called resistant performativity, counternation, alternative citizenship, symbolic reterritorializing, discursive political praxis, mimicry, radical hybridity, politics of a savagism, and localized epistemologies. Now, if the nation-state is an imagined community in which power is not concentrated anywhere but is found everywhere and in which the division of labor and the existence of social classes are of no practical importance and are never even acknowledged, then it is good enough to posit a radical hybridity or a "racialization and sexualization and genderization" (see Caren Kaplan et al.), and so on, to radically reform reality. Decoding a film, music, drama, and other cultural phenomena from a social, gendered, and racial point of view—as seen in Habell-Pallán's and Romero's collection—is to be considered in itself an act of political change and social transformation. Thus Kun can read the sounds emanating loudly from the tracks of the band Tijuana No! as anti-imperialist and as a tribute to the Ejército Zapatista de Liberación Nacional (EZLN) and therefore as an act of resistance and radical social transformation. He can decode the supplemental rock video and the "make-believe murder" of California's governor Pete Wilson as an act of symbolic "retribution for political injustice" and a social critique of "legislatively sanctioned nativism and xenophobia" (106). Kun's radical politics by other (critical cultural) means also hails from the idea that hegemonic culture—those master, discursive narratives that define and inform subjectivity—can be harnessed and deflected by the use of alternative (resistant) discourses (cultural and literary).

Brown's formulation of gangs as counternations that destabilize nation-state power structures also resonates with the formulation proposed in the 1960s by an early cultural studies practitioner, Herbert Marcuse, and his locating of a revolutionary force in the lumpenproletariat. In *One-Dimensional Man: Studies in the Ideology of Advanced Industrial Society* (1964), Marcuse asserts that capitalist society has reached a stage where it has managed to overcome its class contradictions (class struggle has been replaced by a universal consensus in favor of capitalist's values and ideologies). Within such a society, there is no place for working-class resistance en masse or for individual struggle. All objects and subjects have adopted the "commodity form" (57) that liquefies the difference between the social and the cultural, the political and the economic. Such a society, Marcuse writes, becomes an "omnipresent system which swallows up or repulses all alternatives" (xvi) and is characterized by "democratic unfreedom" (1).

For Marcuse, in this new system the working classes "no longer appear to be the agent of historical transformation" (xii–xiii) because, as he later explains, they are a "prop of the established way of life" whose "ascent would only prolong this way in a different setting" (252). So, Marcuse locates the place for resistant and revolutionary possibility within a "new Subject" (252), untouched by capitalist hegemony, that belongs to, he writes, that "substratum of the outcasts and outsiders, the exploited and persecuted of other races and other colors, the unemployed and the unemployable" (256). This description largely corresponds to what Marxist literature has termed the lumpenproletariat—that most violent and openly criminal part of society. And Marcuse invests the people forming this "substratum" with the power to effect massive social change. He invests the lumpenproletariat with this power because their lives represent, according to Marcuse, "the most immediate and the most real need for ending intolerable conditions and institutions" (256). Thus, he concludes, "their opposition is revolutionary even if their consciousness is not. Their opposition hits the system from without and is therefore not deflected by the system; it is an elementary force which violates the rules of the game and, in doing so, reveals it as a rigged game" (257).

Marez's resistant *narcocorridos* and Brown's gang nation resonate loudly here with Marcuse's positing of a revolutionary lumpenproletariat. For example, Brown asserts that gangs provide "an alternative citizenship in a counternation, one that fulfills fundamental needs not accorded by the state, one that provides a sense of economic security (most often through delinquent behavior), one that establishes its own moral and juridical authority with a history tied to territory, and one that provides a sense of communal identity, belonging" (xxiii). Gangs, somewhat like Marcuse's lumpenproletariat, offer alternative networks of "meaningful solidarity, nationalistic, territorially based families" (158) that can destabilize a racially exclusionary nation-state identity.

Marez's and Brown's formulations do not take into account what history and present reality show in a clear and unequivocal way, namely, that the lumpenproletariat is and has always been an ally and even an instrument of the ruling classes in their struggle against the working classes. For the lumpenproletariat, all laws applying in society at large are obstacles that should be destroyed by any means. From the point of view of the interests of the lumpenproletariat, there should be no rules and no legislation of any sort meant to protect anyone, least of all the working classes. In every country, the lumpenproletariat replaces in more or less large segments of society the rule of law by the rule of brute force and unabated violence, oppression, and exploitation. History shows that no gang, no organized group of the lumpenproletariat has been "turned" to progressive politics and coalition building. Indeed, as an ex-gang member (who wishes to remain anonymous) told me in a conversation, the very idea of politicizing gangs is a dangerously naive, wishful, and utopian dream: "If you're lucky, you can get out and turn to a life of community activism, but if you're in a gang and you show any sign of political activism, you're as good as dead." Those who have tried to "turn" East L. A. gangs in the past have systematically met with a bullet with Mexican Mafia written all over it. Nor is the gang a place for transnational coalition building. Members of a Chicano gang have no problem taking out members, for instance, of a Salvadoran gang. Gangbangers will kill, maim, or betray anybody to protect turf and control prostitution, extortion, and all other money-making forms of oppression and exploitation, in particular the ebb and flow of drug production and consumption; drugs are the most visible bridge between the so-called underworld and the "legitimate" world of capitalism, and they play an essential role in the functioning and perhaps even survival of capitalist society today. To repeat, the gang is anything but a show of transnational solidarity.

Brown's phrase "gang nation," then, is an oxymoron. The gang is the quintessence of that very part of society that most needs to destroy all laws and regulations—and therefore to destroy the legal framework that constitutes a nation. The gang is not a nation—nor can it ever be. As Diego Vigil writes in his ethnography of gang life, *A Rainbow of Gangs,* "We are not two nations, we are one; we are not two separate societies, an inner city and everything outside it" (168). Not only is Vigil insistent on the distinction between nation and gang society, but he has no romantic illusions about the gang as a potential resistant force. For Vigil, it is not about how the gangs can radically reform the nation, but about how we must radically change the society that breeds these most violent and destructive organizations. As Vigil writes, gangs are the result of "economic insecurity and lack of opportunity, fragmented institutions of social control, poverty" (7). And, with current high school drop-out rates for Latinos at 30 percent (compared with 7.7 percent for Anglos and 12.6 percent for African Americans) (cited in Vigil, 163–164), it is more likely they will end up in jail than go to college. Vigil correctly perceives that "to eliminate this marginalization process and the resultant street socialization would require massive changes in our way of life at the macrostructural level" (15). It's to a great extent all about economics. As Vigil writes, "A natural outcome of a free-market economic system based on competition, such as ours and those that are spreading widely into other areas of the world, is economic inequality—winners and losers. The greater the economic gap between winners and losers, the more structurally embedded the marginalization of large segments of the population becomes, usually along racial and cultural lines" (166).

Whether in Marcuse, Brown, Marez, Habell-Pallán, or others mentioned above, the notion of a counternation, whether formed by the lumpenproletariat or otherwise, circulates without any sense of practical consequence. Brown's misstep begins when she identifies how those excluded from "dominant nationalism" (125) and the "shared national symbolic" "highlight the crisis of national identity" (125). It continues when she misrepresents the nation itself. If, as she would have it, a nation is an imagined community or a master narrative that manipulates its subjects, it could not be the real and very compulsory framework where the struggle between classes takes place and where the laboring population has conquered all those basic rights that prevent the ruling class from exerting total arbitrariness and complete exploitation. And the same goes for Marez when he locates in "drug-war music and film" (9) representations that critically revise and reinterpret the drug war as part of our imagined nation. This same slip happens when Marez locates resistance to exploitation and oppression in novels like *Almanac of the Dead* and films such as *El Mariachi*, which "provide competing representations of state power, transnational capitalism, the mass of the world's poor, and the role of the mass media itself in the war on drugs" (9). Thus *narcocorridos* like those of Chalino Sánchez are analyzed as promoting "subaltern agency" (22) in rural villages in northern Mexico and in the Southwest and Los Angeles and come to represent "fantasies of a world turned upside down in which poor black and Mexican characters become rich and powerful social actors who battle with and often triumph over the police and other representatives of state power" (23).

Implicit in Brown's and Marez's proposals is actually the destruction of all protection for the vast majority of the population, formed by workers and their families. In a foreword to Doug Stokes's *America's Other War* Noam Chomsky links drug war profiteering to the massive increase in the suppression of working-class movements in Latin America and also the Middle East. In 2002, 184 trade unionists were assassinated in Colombia, "85 percent of the total worldwide in 2002" (viii); and in 2003, he states, "the worldwide total of murdered union leaders . . . was reported to be 123, three quarters of them in Columbia" (viii). And Stokes mentions that in 1985, the year the United Confederation of Workers was formed, "230 members [were] murdered in its first year alone" (77). As far as the available statistics show, it is the narco-bourgeoisie that benefits and the rural "subaltern," the peasant and the labor organizer, who suffers in the drug war.

The gang as counternation or the drug deal as "insurgent" act (9) would actually mean a world controlled by the lumpenproletariat and the total slavery of the people—an outcome we have seen happening to a large extent in the former Yugoslavia, in the rule of warlordism in Afghanistan, and in the near destruction of many African countries, like Uganda or Somalia today. Any underworld operation is concerned only with destroying the independence of labor organizations and the civil rights of the people.

Brown, Marez, Habell-Pallán, and the other scholars mentioned are not alone in theorizing a counternation that resists the nation. Fredric Jameson makes a similar claim of Third World discursivities that "necessarily project a political dimension in the form of national allegory" (65). Indeed, for Jameson, Third World texts are allegories of "the embattled situation of the counter-nation" (65). In like spirit, Homi Bhabha theorizes colonialism and nation building as textual constructs that can be resisted by discourses uttered from the racial and social margins and "between the lines" and thus "against the rules and within them" (*Location of Culture* 89). The postcolonial text, then, has the power to disrupt, according to Bhabha, "cultural, racial and historical differences that menace the narcissistic demand of colonial authority" (88). For Jameson and Bhabha, too, narration is invested with an ontological power identical to the one possessed by the real, materially existing nation; this allows both authors to theorize the deconstruction of the colonial and national by reformulating the real capitalist and colonialist systems of exploitation and oppression as cultural phenomena.

When Latino cultural studies scholars like Brown, Marez, Habell-Pallán, and Romero theorize a gang and/or cultural phenomenon as "counter-nation," "counter-site," and so on, they perform, wittingly or not, a poststructuralist acrobatic trick. They establish an equation between cultural phenomena taking place within a given nation and the nation itself. In other words, they mistake the part for the whole. Another trick is to equate cultural phenomena with Saussure's notion of sign and/or J. L. Austin's conception of performative words or sentences. Thus, Ana Patricia Rodríguez decodes Blades's lyrics as performing the role of "enunciating transnational subject [that challenges] the injurious, degrading language that has been used to produce *tropicalized* images of Central America" (95).

According to Saussure's theory of the sign, formulated nearly a century ago, it is a conceptual entity formed by two *inseparable* mental units: the "signifier" or "acoustic image" (the latter called "phonemes") by which the listener/speaker identifies certain sounds as belonging to his/her language and therefore recognizes them as not being simply noise, and the "signified" or "mental image" or "idea" that is formed in the mind of the speaker/listener of such and such a language when he or she hears sounds identified as belonging to his or her language and by means of which he or she categorizes such and such an aspect of reality or the world out there. A third element, not belonging to the sign as an inseparable mental unit, is the referent, that to which the sign refers or makes reference to. So the poststructuralist use of the Saussurean concept of sign is, strictly speaking, nonsensical. It is totally absurd to assert, as poststructuralists do, that a sign can be manipulated at the point of slippage between signifier and signified. There is no such "point of slippage" possible in Saussure's theory of sign, since for that to be possible would necessarily imply that signifier and signified could be separated and still constitute a sign. In fact, what is central to the existence of human language is the human capacity for language, so that each language is the particular manifestation of a set of rules and sounds of what contemporary linguistics identifies as a universal grammar with which all members of the human species are genetically endowed. In Saussurean terminology, the unbreakable unit of signifier and signified is linked by rules to a referent in ways that are particular to each language, and it is this complex psychological mechanism that allows the sign to communicate meaning between members of a group who speak the same language. Alluding to Jacques Derrida's conception of language, Mark C.

Baker writes that "great metaphoric significance [is attached to] this arbitrariness and conventionality at the roots of language" (204). However, if this were the case—that meaning in language is arbitrary—then how would communication be possible? We would simply speak and write nonsense. So while the words that express a meaning within a given language might vary widely from one language to another, as Baker rightly points out, "their grammars do not" (204). Now, as Baker rightly concludes, this has led to "the bewildering and ever-shifting post-modernist view of the world, in which nothing has a lasting or general meaning" (204).

Certainly, much of our identity as individuals is shaped through culture; much of what we know and do is expressed to and by us in the language of our community. However, language is not tied to culture in any sort of one-to-one relationship. As Mark C. Baker explains, "The grammar of a group's language does not seem to be correlated with other identifiable features of their culture. As we look at how the different language types are distributed around the world, there is no hint of a significant interaction between language type and cultural type" (201).

After demonstrating that there is no causal relationship between one group's grammatical system (Japanese and Mongolians as "head-final" ruled languages, for example) and its culture and worldview and another group's language system (Chinese and Arabic as "head-initial" ruled languages, for instance) and its corresponding culture and worldview, Baker concludes, "Is there any causal relationship between how they order their words and how they experience life? So far as anyone knows, the answer is no" (201). In fact, research proves that a culture of a group is more likely to be similar to that of its neighboring group than to those who share a language system. Baker gives the example of the diverse groups of American Indians in California that shared similar cultural values and worldviews despite their huge linguistic diversity. So, to sum up, there is no cause-and-effect relationship between language and culture or, restated in the language of poststructuralism, between discourse and reality, between gang, *narcocorrido,* and nation.

Today's Chicano/a and Latino/a cultural studies practitioners are fundamentally interested in decoding texts—cultural or literary—as sites of possible resistance to discursively constructed hegemonies. They often, as we have seen, locate such textual sites for scholarly excavation within subcultural groups—gangs, Latino performance artists and musicians, films, and so on—that are assumed to stand outside a nation-state hegemony. Subcultural groups and subcultural artifacts are invested with the power to resist and even transform dominant social organization paradigms. Gitlin has summed up this feature of the cultural studies project generally in the following way: "It is charged with surveying the culture, assessing the hegemonic import of cultural practice and pinpointing their potentials for 'resistance.' Is this musical style or that literary form 'feminist' or 'authentically Latino'? The model tends to be two-toned. The field of possibilities is frequently—usually, I would estimate—reduced to two: for or against the hegemonic" (32–33). And, of course, academics often romanticize those at the margins as the "true" voice of nation. Witness the Birmingham Center scholars' (Williams, Hebdige, Hull, Gilroy, for example) mysticizing of working class and racially disenfranchised groups, and long before that the early nineteenth-century Brothers Grimm's romanticizing of the *volk,* the late nineteenth-century Nicolai Gogol's and Ivan Turgenev's mysticizing of the Russian peasant, and the early twentieth-century Federico García Lorca's sentimentalizing of Spanish gypsies, to name a few. Of course, Ana Patricia Rodríguez's celebration of Blades's lyrics as a sort of *vox populi* with the power to reclaim an otherwise U.S. imperialist-controlled Panama belongs to this same mystifying and mythifying tradition, just as Brown's gang nation does. As Marjorie Ferguson and Peter Golding comment, "In retreat from the crudities of economic reductionism and the base-superstructure model, cultural studies' construction of culture has become entirely detached from economics, and largely from politics too" (xxv).

So no matter how down and out, unemployed, exploited, and drugged-up people are—and the numbers increase daily—according to pop cultural theories, these same people go not only undefeated, but are the true source of resistance to the system that generates unemployment, poverty, exploitation, and massive use of drugs. As Gitlin angrily exclaims, "However unfavorable the balance of political forces, people succeed in living lives of vigorous resistance! Are communities of African Americans or Afro-Caribbeans suffering? Well, they have rap!" (33). Cultural studies speculation, then, diverts scholars' highly specialized skills and capacities from true research and true theory formulation, based on facts that might bring true understanding and therefore really help people in their struggles to transform our socially unjust and exploitive world. Thus, instead of speculating about the social-transforming power of Blades's lyrics, Rodríguez might have asked, with respect to Blades's campaign to become president of Panama (only briefly mentioned): What was this musician's and performer/actor's political agenda, and how did he propose to apply it, taking into account that he has never had any links with the organized labor movement, has never been an activist, and has had no experience as a trade unionist or as a member of a political party? Where did he intend to obtain political support, within the laboring population, the middle classes, the landowners, the American ruling class, or the Panamanian ruling elite? How, in short, did he intend to enact real economic and social reform?

If we look at some examples of recent history, we can see that not only scholars but also the mass media have given cultural phenomena the power to radically alter reality. For instance, in the late 1960s the media and liberal cognoscenti considered the Woodstock music festival a watershed moment, for this gigantic gathering of young people had had the effect of spreading the gospel of peace and love worldwide and would therefore change deeply and permanently the behavior of, first, the young, and then their elders, quite soon too. Woodstock, in so many words, was to enact a massive social paradigm shift that would make for a better life across the globe. The reality, of course, is that no music festival to date—and no youth subculture for that matter—has even made a dent in the adverse living conditions of the laboring population in any country. The fact is, as just discussed in chapter 9, musicians and producers of music are very much caught up in a system that makes mandatory a massive consumption of tapes, CDs, DVDs, and videotapes to survive in a highly unstable, ever-changing market. A music festival—whether in the name of African American emancipation, like the Blackstock that took place outside of Washington, D.C., in 2002, or for the benefit of starving children in such and such a country—is simply another cog in the capitalist machine. In an article entitled "Music can Rock, just not the World," I conclude, "If American imperialism learned something from the Sixties, it is that all youth festivals, and in particular gigantic MusicFests, are great vehicles for the spreading of drugs and cynicism among the disenfranchised, to turn them away from real politics and any real attempt to organize in the hundreds of thousands and to fight for certain basic democratic rights such as equal access to education and the right to representation for all" (www.Bad Subjects.org).

Of course, it is not just the cognoscenti who invest popular phenomena with revolutionary potential. Many individuals who move into the limelight of popular culture—musicians, actors, directors, and so on—have taken up the cause. At the height of his fame, Bob Dylan proclaimed in his songs that the young would revolutionize society. Of course, not only did he not effect political and economic change in his day, but it was this same Bob Dylan who performed in front of thousands of young Catholics in celebration of the pope—the head of one of the oldest, most obscurantist and conservative institutions in the world, the Catholic Church. And in the early 1970s, when the Beatles had reached the pinnacle of fame and glory, George Harrison claimed that society was going to be revolutionized by the new forms of internationalist solidarity he was launching with the concert he masterminded for the benefit of the poorest people on earth, the people of Bangladesh. That concert included the most famous American and British pop artists and was a big economic success. So much so that it deepened the trend already begun by Woodstock: to promote concerts in the name of social protest and/or solidarity to generate huge profits (cutting of records, music conglomerates' signing of bands, high-priced admission tickets, peddling of drugs and all kinds of commodities at the concert site, and so on). Again, not only are these concerts meant to bring in big dollar profits, but very often the performers themselves are blatantly reactionary. U2's Bono, who continues to figure prominently in many solidarity concerts, is a case in point. He toured Africa with the ex-CEO of Alcoa and former U.S. Treasury Secretary Paul O'Neill. Together they had been encouraging a series of African countries to continue paying their debt to the International Monetary Fund, even though those countries have reimbursed that debt not only once, but many times over by paying the exorbitant rates of interest imposed on them; in addition, they were obligated not only to reimburse the IMF in increasingly expensive dollars bought with their ever-more-devalued currencies, but also to adopt drastic budgetary cuts and stringent "adjustment" conditions that have ravaged the economies of Africa and turned the whole area into what economists have called "a lost continent." (For more on Bono and his goodwill trip to Africa, see Ted C. Fishman's essay, "Making a Killing: The Myth of Capital's Good Intentions.") There was also the Live 8 concert, which also made a big to-do about Africa while making its musicians, producers, and corporate sponsors even wealthier. Show business is always *business* in the strict sense of the word.

Cultural studies (Chicano/a, Latino/a, or otherwise), as practiced in the ways I have analyzed here, is not conducive to arriving at a deeper understanding of human behavior and experience. Rather, it diverts from scholarly research and many intellectual resources that could be invested more beneficially in empirical studies leading to verifiable or falsifiable conclusions and therefore giving us a deeper understanding of the cultural products of humanity in all their complexity and variety. Of course, there is value in many remarks and points of view expressed in the studies I have been commenting on here. But it is just not true that it is possible to build some form of shared and solid knowledge using only opinions as raw material. The endless production of opinions does not constitute science. It just leads to an endless fragmentation of approaches in the tackling of cultural phenomena, with no progress whatsoever in the building of knowledge. The affiliation of these approaches with academia confers an aura of seriousness to this endless fragmentation of scholarly work never leading to any theory in the strict sense of the term. Thus, in the name of a left-leaning worldview, cultural studies actually replicates and reinforces a trait developed within capitalist society: the tendency to fragment and divide more and more the social objects of study, to a degree that they become blurred and even irrelevant. The result, ultimately, is that no real knowledge can emerge and no real understanding can guide the efforts of the working populations seeking to improve their lives.

CONCLUDING REMARKS

We live in a world where violence, crime, war, massive unemployment, and extreme poverty are becoming the rule, not the exception. And there is hardly a glimmer of hope that this might change in the foreseeable future. Even mainstream films in which the imagination is allowed to run free are mostly bleak; those set in the future, like *Impostor, The Island, Code 46, Children of Men, 28 Days,* to name a few, often fill up their plots and detail their settings in ways that expand on what is a dismal reality for people today: famine, mass unemployment, generalized violence, and the increasing presence of a two-tier social system. From this point of view, it's understandable that many scholars, including Brown, Marez, Habell-Pallán, Romero, and the others discussed, turn to theories seeking to show how cultural phenomena and literary texts might offer ways to overcome and transform such a hateful reality. While this is a comprehensible impulse, it is, of course, naively utopian.

It is also, in many ways, irresponsible. As I have already discussed at length in discussions of real gangs, they are far from interested in making our world a better place to live. Only the wide availability of decently paid jobs, education, medical services, day care centers, dense networks of public transportation, and well-equipped parks and recreation centers will keep kids from joining gangs in the first place. For this to happen, we need the functioning of a nation-state that ensures the total freedom of members of the working population to build their own independent political parties and trade unions and to freely associate in the struggle to improve their living conditions as well as those of their families and fellow workers. This is not going to happen as a result of the activities of gangs, or as an effect of reading gang literature, or as a consequence of analyzing cultural phenomena.

So what would a workable method of cultural analysis be if not that presented in *Gang Nation, Drug Wars, Loca Motion,* and *Latino/a Popular Culture?* It would have to be less wishful and more realistic. It would have to stop pretending that a small cadre of academics decoding cultural phenomena have the power to change the world in the same way, or in substitution of, as the working population can when it organizes itself independently and moves toward the achievement of its self-designed goals. If the aim is to do politics, then "let us organize groups, coalitions, demonstrations, lobbies, whatever; let us do politics. Let us not think that our academic work is already that" (37), as Gitlin succinctly remarks.

Finally, if the field of cultural studies is to have any value today, we will need to turn to rationalist and empirical methods of gathering and analyzing data and formulating hypotheses that might help us better understand the reality we live in as well as the actions that really transform it.

PULLING UP STAKES IN LATIN/O AMERICAN THEORETICAL CLAIMS

INTRODUCTION

Often the students in my courses on postcolonial (Latin American and otherwise) literature and film, one way or another, begin to question whether or not a given fictional narrative can open eyes to injustices in the world or act as anticolonial manual, especially when the characters they encounter are ethically twisted and contradictory. In some form or other, they ask how the study of a postcolonial phenomenon like Latin American literature can make visible past and present conditions of exploitation and oppression. They delve into questions of genre and style: Is realism or magicorealism more politically resistant or conformist to the status quo? They ask if there shouldn't be some type of accountability on the part of the authors and their characters as well as in their own work as scholars of the postcolonial. Such interrogations usually grow out of a heavy dose of Latin American postcolonial theory read over the course of the term.

In this chapter I explore how the various permutations of the textualist-based ethical turn in Latin American postcolonial studies scholarship and the theories they spawn might (or might not) lead us to a deeper understanding of how such cultural phenomena as literature shape attitudes and behaviors that are politically resistant (or not) within oppressive nation-states and global capitalism generally.

Let me begin with an overview of the postcolonial Latin American theoretical terrain. Dorris Sommer's *Proceed with Caution* explores a variety of writers over a long stretch of time: from Walt Whitman to Julio Cortázar, from El Inca Garcilaso de la Vega in the sixteenth century to Mario Vargas Llosa in the twentieth, from Rigoberta Menchú to Toni Morrison. Here she carves out a transnational frame for approaching the literature of the Americas while simultaneously paying attention to a given text's specific location within history and the social polity. In this fashion, her ultimate goal is to formulate a theoretical approach that contributes, in her words, "toward a rhetoric of particularism" (x). To this end, then, Sommer's analytic frame sets out to situate the social and historical locus of enunciation of "minor texts" to show how such texts incorporate rhetorical structures that prevent their mastery by outsiders. She identifies the intended readers of these texts not as "co-conspirators or allies in a shared culture" (9), but as Western outsiders who seek to turn the "minority" subjects into the fetishized object of a conquering gaze. Thus with respect to Menchú's *testimonio,* Sommer says she is "being coy on the witness stand, exercising control over apparently irrelevant information, perhaps to produce her own strategic version of truth" (115). In this case, as in others, such as Morrison's *Beloved* and the verse of Whitman, to name a few, the non-Guatemalan, Western outsider is the target of that figure traditionally identified as the silent, Third World Other. Sommer demonstrates how Menchú skillfully provides information and then elides with strategically placed silences. She engages the reader "without surrendering herself" (4). Menchú fends off the totalizing impulse of the ethnographic Western reader, who would otherwise mistake the individual—Rigoberta Menchú—as a voice that speaks to the truths of her people and Latin America generally.

Sommer similarly uncovers the particular rhetorical strategy Vargas Llosa used in *The Storyteller/El Hablador* to reveal how the author "stages" the movement in and out of the "slippery space" of language and identity to destabilize the meeting of *mestizo* and Jewish bodies and texts in Latin America (269). She also finds Whitman's *Leaves of Grass* to be more than a text that has become part of the aesthetic patrimony of Latin America (via its multiple translations, notably one by Jorge Luis Borges). It is an example of the creation by a poet of an "aesthetics of liberal democracy" (39). *Leaves of Grass* provided an antidote to divisive particularities and inequalities not with words but within the "gaps that Whitman left between the fragments" (39). Sommer's reading of the more contemporary Robert Young's film adaptation *The Ballad of Gregorio Cortez* exemplifies how a text can perform a "pattern of refusals" inscribed in a racist, Tejano justice system (97). Editing techniques of fragmentation and elision set the "trap for its Anglo viewers and eludes their efforts to grasp its meaning until the end" (98).

For Sommer, how these texts perform their narrative—controlling the ebb and flow of information through narrative fragmentation, use of parodic narrative technique, and blurring of the border between genres—becomes the degree to which they fend off and/or "sting" a reader's desire to master the Third World subject as Other (8). For example, the violent movement back and forth of forced "forgetfulness" in Morrison's *Beloved* becomes an act of staging the "confrontation of *intimacy versus information*" (161) as well as drawing attention to her uneasy juxtaposition of the "chronicle, personal confessions, slave narratives" (161). Morrison's text, then, not only prevents the reader from achieving complete textual mastery, but performs a history of forced silence on African Americans. Sommer's readings aim to highlight how Menchú, Morrison, Whitman, Vargas Llosa, and Young—to name a few of her "resistant authors"—deliberately disrupt the outsiders' desire to conquer and master meaning. Sommer's minority texts, then, formally empower those kept at the textual, social, and political margins.

In *Local Histories/Global Designs: Coloniality, Subaltern Knowledges, and Border Thinking* Walter Mignolo similarly seeks to trace the particulars of localized knowledge and enunciating text acts. Mignolo interviews a wide range of people in Latin America, from taxi drivers to writers and politicians, for example, to show that transitional alliances and connections can be built to transcend the shortcomings of nationalist rhetoric, all while being located in the local and specific interests of the people: the Zapatistas being a case in point. Mignolo reads across a variety of disciplines—history, culture, and politics—as they crisscross at different moments in time and geographic space (pre- and postcolonial as well as modern and postmodern) and crystallize into what he identifies as the "subalternization of knowledge." Subalternization of knowledge is the system of understanding self and world as conceived from a resistant place. In other words, while the West imposed on the native of the Americas a knowledge system that worked in favor of colonialism and, later, imperialism, these imposed ways of being and self-reflecting were not digested and internalized *sans résistance*. Contact "from the exterior borders of the modern/colonial world system" led to a transcultural, subalternized knowledge system articulated from within those spaces traditionally marginalized and identified as Other. Key to this formulation is the idea, not unlike Sommer's, of the double-voiced articulation. In Latin America, Mignolo remarks, "every act of saying is at the same time a 'saying against' and a 'saying for'" (25). Subalternization of knowledge results from contact and transculturation of nativist and Western systems. Identifying a text's double-voiced articulation allows one to locate in the specific text-act how subalternization of knowledge exists at the "intersection of local histories and global designs, and at the intersection of hegemonic and subaltern grounds and undergrounds" (25).

Like Sommer, Mignolo sets up his project against poststructuralist theory. Both see the poststructuralist theorists as using the Third World subject and text as static objects that articulate a theoretical difference at a distant remove from the local social, political, and cultural discourses that shape individual Latin American bodies and texts. Mignolo seeks to infuse the local back into the global by formulating a theory of Latin Americanism that arises from outside the "borders of the system" (Mignolo 315). Subalternization of knowledge (identified as the "colonial epistemic difference") spins out of the local and, as Mignolo amplifies, "emerges in the *exteriority* of the modern/colonial world" (315). Indeed, new ways of localized enunciating and thinking could be obtained only through a localized reading of the responses—"the *colonial epistemic difference*"—to historical, political, and social circumstances that mark the Latino/a and Chicano/a body.

Globalization is a contemporary incarnation of colonialism. Just as history has proved that the West turned to the Americas for raw materials and labor exploitation, globalization—in the form not only of capital but also of poststructural theory in the academy—seeks to suck the life out of "*local* histories" (ix). Seen from this angle, such a poststructural theory is clearly obsolete. Mignolo addresses the characterization of the West-as-center and the Third-World-as-periphery, emphasizing the point that in today's world, where the peripheries are now in the centers (Third World subjects inhabit First World centers), the local space is not to be found only across bodies of water. The erstwhile Western centers are filled with bodies and texts traditionally identified as inhabiting the geopolitical margins. Subalternization of knowledge is the process of adapting, rejecting, integrating, and confronting "two kinds of local histories displayed in different spaces and times across the planet" to produce what he calls the "coloniality of power" (ix).

In his formulation of the local/global subalternization of knowledge, Mignolo turns to the example of language. He celebrates the multiply voiced linguistic act—Caribbean creole and Chicano/a *caló*, for example—which are examples of a localized celebration of the impure (tainted English, French, or Spanish) perspective that speaks to a subalternized epistemology. The three languages (English, Spanish, Nahuatl) the Chicana writer Gloria Anzaldúa uses in her book *Borderlands/La Frontera: The New Mestiza* are an example of what Mignolo identifies as a "new way of languaging" (228) that celebrate worldviews suppressed by monolingual ideologies. Nahuatl takes center stage and is no longer a displaced language; similarly, Spanish is no longer "displaced by the increasing hegemony of the colonial languages of the modern period (English, German, and French)" (237). The Jamaican writer Michelle Cliff further exemplifies how such "polylanguaging" threatens to disrupt essential cultural codes of national identity based on artificially imposed narratives of pure (French) language. Cliff's creole comes out of the knowledge system that deliberately anchored language and identity to territory but as attuned to a localized history and culture that result from contact. In this way, then, the act of speaking creole is linked to Créolité—that knowledge system defined "by a mode of being rather than by a way of looking" (242). Thinking and writing in a subaltern language like creole is an expression of being and not a theoretical construct. Polylanguaging is an act of mapping, producing, and distributing a local, subaltern knowledge system. Cliff's creole and Anzaldúa's polylanguaging, then, are acts of "changing linguistic cartographies [and] implies a reordering of epistemology" (247). Thus, by speaking in multiple registers Cliff and Anzaldúa denaturalize the tie "between language and territories" (229) that traditionally oppresses the subaltern subject. Moreover, their celebration of the linguistic fractures become texts with the power to transform everyday political and social practices as margins reform centers of empire. Mignolo contends, finally, that "the idea of national languaging and, indirectly, of national literacies and literatures in Europe as well as in the United States" (236) is being challenged by today's migratory movements toward those areas. This leads to a new way of thinking about how "linguistic maps, literary geographies, and cultural landscapes are being repainted" (236).

In a like spirit of textual analysis, in *The Other Side of the Popular*, Gareth Williams reads a number of texts—from gangbanger testimonio to Mario Vargas Llosa's *La utopía arcaica,* from the journalistic essay and photographs of an insane asylum to Manlio Argueta's novel *One Day of Life*—to uncover "languages, worlding, narratives, and relations that point us toward those realms of experience, knowledge, and commonalty that promise meanings other than those that are immediately handed over to the history and reproduction of instrumental reason's relation to cultural and social hegemonies" (*The Other Side of the Popular* 276). Ricardo Piglia's novel *La ciudad ausente* is a text that speaks to the "limits of the nation and of national cultural history" (14) and that ultimately acts as the "tenuous affirmation of the remaining distant sound-senses that resonate as echoes, as discontinuous alterities, and as

haunting singularities from within the remains of interruption's enactment" (170). And the "part-*testimonio*" of the Salvadoran/South Central
LA gangbanger Mirna Solórzano is a "linguistic transmission of cognitive trembling," an "active self-insertion into [the] language of postnational belonging," and a text that reveals "both the ground of popular
incorporation and the desires of disciplined institutional reflection"
(213). For Williams, it is such "subalternist thought" that allows us to
"reflect on, [and affirm] the nomadic savagery of subaltern instructional
commonality" (213). In an analysis of Diamela Elitit and Paz Errázuriz's
photographs of the inhabitants of an insane asylum outside of Santiago
de Chile, Williams reveals not only a "negative community" that refuses
mastery, but a "mad love" that radically deconstructs "reason's constituted histories, genealogies, institutional paradigms, and epistemological
configurations" (303). It is the "mad love" of the insane that offers a localized "radical constructivity" (303) that can "keep thought open to the
potentially constitutive force of finitude; open, that is, to finitude's endless repertoire of possibilities and alternative imaginations that we have
been able to claim as our philosophical and political inheritances" (303).
Thus our social and political conditions of existence lie in the hands of
this "scattered and potentially multitudinous site of loving promise, at
which institutional/administrative configurations (asylums, universities) cease to reproduce their mastery" (303).

In *Latin Americanism* Román De la Campa expresses similar interest in identifying the local articulations of Latin American knowledge
and its power to transform the cultural, social, economic, and political
reality. De la Campa is critical of poststructuralism as an approach to
a Latin American epistemology. To this end, De la Campa explores not
only Borges, but other Latin American "native" figures such as Sandino,
Cortázar, Che Guevara, and others whose texts are "unprotected by literary and political canons" and allow him to develop an analytic frame
for a wide-ranging and, in his words, "hopefully freer, sense of textual
historicity" (ix). Each of these author's "unprotected" texts highlights the
"production and articulation of Latin America as a constellation of discursive constructs" (viii). Like the texts authored by the figures he references in his work (Spivak, Benítez-Rojo, Bhabha, and Judith Butler to
name a few), language (its figures of speech, construction, mode, etc.)
ultimately translates into how one relates to the world and how the world
is related to one. But if reality is a text, then, as De la Campa proposes,
language can also be considered a "rhetorical praxis and agency" (vii).
From this standpoint, for De la Campa, Borges's uniqueness as a writer

"is his Latin American provenance, a historical sense of political and intellectual liminality not devoid of a sense of epistemic violence that is now observed on a global scale" (34). Moreover, Borges's revolutionizing of "cerebral essays and detective narratives riddled with epistemological twists filled with their own sense of violence" ultimately speaks not to his uniqueness as an individual, but to his experience of the deeper contradictions that inform a Latin American culture "so laden with ludic uncertainty" (35).

De la Campa investigates Latin American writers and theorists (including the Caribbeanists Edouard Glissant and Antoñio Benítez-Rojo) alike whose text-acts reach beyond their formal boundaries to transform their everyday reality. On one occasion, he celebrates the Latin American critic Angel Rama's posthumously published *The Lettered City* as a text that addresses "a broad spectrum of cultural and social articulations" (121). Rama turns to themes and techniques seen in *modernista* poetry and later in more contemporaneous novels that rupture master narratives—constituting epistemic breaks—and destabilize one's understanding of structures that naturalize hierarchies of difference in colonial relations. With a similar energy, he turns to an analysis of how the Sandinista revolution was the result of reading Rubén Darío not as an apolitical aesthete but as a political icon (40). Also, examining Julio Cortázar's fragmented, episodic factual/fictional "Apocalypse at Solentiname," he concludes that this is an "experiment to bring revolution to the world of art" (46). Cortázar's text epitomizes the Latin American resistant text through its "self-reflexive fusion of technological novelty, Sandinista spiritualism, and his own memory of politically motivated violence in Latin American liberation movements" (50). On another occasion, De la Campa identifies Che Guevara's body as a text that literally acquired political meaning that led to revolutionary transformation as it was moved from Bolivia to Cuba (36). In so doing, De la Campa locates the text within the interplay of political and economic intersections that, he writes, "deconstruction generally dissolves or invalidates" (40). Thus for De la Campa, textual production and the subsequent transformation of reality don't have to take the form only of writing and reading: the dissemination of resistant knowledge can take many forms. Finally, De la Campa uses these as examples of texts in which the "uncertain interplay" (vii) between aesthetics and epistemology (what he calls "episthetics") intersects in Latin America to inform and incite everyday revolution and transformation.

Just as De la Campa keeps poststructuralism at arm's length, in the collection of essays edited by Mark Thurner and Andrés Guerrero, *After Spanish Rule: Postcolonial Predicaments of the Americas,* we see the questioning of the utility of a postcolonialist method and approach in Latin American studies (especially history). Understanding that theories of the postcolonial were based largely on claims made concerning the Middle East and India, they question whether or not the postcolonial can provide an adequate paradigm for understanding Latin America's history, society, and culture with its own set of terms generated out of its own historical, political, and social experience. For Thurner and Guerrero, colonialism and "its after" happen in different historical moments and in different ways in different geographical spaces; indeed, for Thurner colonialism has never ceased in the Americas. So a postcolonial theory devised in relation to other times and spaces (the colonization of India and Egypt, say) would have at best a tenuous relationship to Latin America. Nonetheless, Thurner and Guerrero consider an abstract theory of coloniality and postcoloniality to be useful in understanding the formation of the *subalterno.* For Guerrero specifically, a Latin American postcolonial theory must be attuned to how its histories are "embedded in local processes" (7); for Thurner specifically, it is to keep in mind that a plurality of colonial and postcolonial histories are always operating within a global capitalism where the development of one part affects the development of the whole system; keeping an eye on how the part (local) affects the whole (global) will allow for the development of just such a plurality of postcolonial scholarly approaches.[1]

In this same collection, Mauricio Tenorio Trillo also questions current postcolonial approaches to Latin American studies—but from the point of view of nationalism. He seeks to identify the construction of a true Mexico that is "indigenous, egalitarian, and tolerant" from the time of the Mexican Revolution of 1910 through the present and that in one way or another romanticizes the *indio* ("Essaying the History of National Images" 68). Modern nations are "imagined communities" for Trillo and thus, he writes, "the people who did not participate in the imagining may not necessarily possess the real image of the nation. The 'falseness' of nationalism rests not in some or other form of 'imagined community,' but in the very attempt to come out with such a thing as a national image. . . . Ironically enough, national imaginaries have become more real than ever, but they are not more or less genuine than they have ever been" (61–62). In the face of this reality, the dominant nationalist ideology has been the ideology of *mestizaje*. For Trillo this ideology has reemerged of late in the academy with its new forms of "primitivism and liberalism" (69). To this formulation he adds another important observation: along with this neoprimitivism is the erasure of the working people and real politics. He writes, "In essence national images, nationalisms, and identities are no longer mere historiographical or ethnographical issues, but important ethical challenges. That is why academic literature on nationalism is full of (implicit or explicit) quasi-moral categories (e.g., good, authentic, real, fake hegemonic, counterhegemonic, popular, liberating, dominant, empowering, agency, resistance)" (76). So, Trillo suggests that we launch "another historiographical experiment—a rethinking of national images, nationalisms, and identities in a disenchanted, nonnationalist, pragmatic, and yet wishful fashion" (76).

In many ways, without stating it as such, Trillo is responding to another theoretical thread in Latin American postcolonial scholarship: one that considers the nation to be not only narration, but also, in its establishing of an "American Hemispheric" studies, the recovery of lost texts that disrupt erstwhile traditional literary canons.[2] Several such scholars, including Sybelle Fischer and Rodrigo Lazo, turn to the archives to recover newspaper articles, stories, essays, articles, and poems, usually from the nineteenth century, to reshape North and South American literary canons and to push Europe (Spain) from center stage as a shaper of history. For example, in *Writing to Cuba* Lazo recovers dozens of texts written around the 1850s by Cuban exiles living in the United States. Because these exiled writers express, as Lazo writes, "the nation as a desired ideal and a territorial reality, both present and absent from their immediate context" they support the notion of the nation as a "textual production" (13) and imaginary community; so even though these narratives ("transnational writing") of nation failed to generate support in the United States and Cuba for revolution, the fact that they cross "languages, national borders, and sociocultural contexts" (15) expands the notion of nation beyond Cuba's borders. Thus for Lazo, they remap the "contours of literary history" (20) as well as expand the "nation-state's limits without negating the historical importance of the nation" (20). In *Modernity Disavowed: Haiti and the Cultures of Slavery in the Age of Revolution* Fischer recovers nineteenth-century documents from the Caribbean (mostly Haiti) to make visible another history of revolution: that the Haitian uprisings of Toussaint Louverture and his comrades led to several subtextual revolutionary ripples all along the Caribbean and into the United States.

While she has not produced an archival recovery as such, Josefina Saldaña-Portillo likewise seeks to crisscross the U.S./Mexico border in her analysis of texts by Gloria Anzaldúa, Rigoberta Menchú, Che Guevara, Subcomandante Marcos, and Malcolm X, among others. In this hemispheric bridging Saldaña-Portillo considers it necessary to analyze "literary production" alongside "public economic policy" because in "any revolutionary movement, these are the two areas dedicated to that task of transforming subjectivity and consciousness" (*The Revolutionary Imagination* 13). She ultimately identifies an alternative revolutionary imagination for the Americas (in Menchú and Subcomandante Marcos, not Malcolm X and Che Guevara) that defies a developmentalist logic (Walt Whitman Rostow) because it is anchored in a sense of social class and "ethnic particularity" (260); a revolutionary imagination that clears a space for the formation of the "radically other: as coterminously national citizen and Indian" (287).

It is a recurrently observed phenomenon that, when society is confronted with deep, rapid transformations, there is a widespread replacement of reason and science with irrational thought. Mysticism and esoteric belief systems are packaged as methods for people to master reality. Today, Latin American postcolonial theory—and postcolonial theory generally—seem to have taken up this role. To reiterate a point I make throughout this book, theory becomes a substitute for actual political activism and is packaged as empowerment to the public. Such and such a public is expected to use such and such theory (one among the many constantly cranked out by academia) as a means to break out of the prison house of language, surmount the master narratives, and revolutionize all spheres of life under capitalism that restrict being in the world. Mignolo, Sommer, De la Campa, Williams, and others seek empowerment in a radically changing reality.

Martín Hopenhayn's *No Apocalypse, No Integration: Modernism and Postmodernism in Latin America* offers a tongue-in-cheek critique of such approaches that, in the wake of the failed master narratives of anticolonial Marxism, a capitalist developmentalism, for example, turn to the prioritizing of individualism; that is, approaches that turn away from a sense of making society a better place piece by piece and instead embrace an "ad hoc" way of being, a giving up of our autonomy with respect to dominant ideas and material conditions in which we live and an acceptance of the inevitable and "inexorable" fact of social fragmentation in the world out there (3–5). Finally, to rediscover life's joy we must learn to occupy "the interstitial areas, the areas in-between" (10) and to take "pleasure in forms" (10) whereby "the skin becomes a second form of consciousness" (11). One way or another, the responses that Hopenhayn critically parodies ignore the reality of a violent world where employment, safety, and social mobility can no longer be taken for granted. He asks pointedly,

> Do these motives of joy—seduction by vertigo, the lightness of ties, the interstitial adventure, the adventure of in-between places, the bet on individual passion, the exaltation of forms, and the consequent loss of substantiality—favor social, national, Latin American integration? Is integration conceivable from vertigo, lightness, the in-between, passion, the aesthetic? Or, on the contrary, is there no more solid directionality, no firmer connection required? (11)

We can see such a utopian thread in Latin American postcolonial scholars. With Saldaña-Portillo it is locating a revolutionary *conciencia* in Menchú, who performs neither at the margins nor centers of hegemony, but vacillates between the two; she performs an "authorial, autobiographical, revolutionary 'I' [and] repeatedly insists on performing the position of authentic indigenous Other for the Western readerly subject" (171). The Zapatistas "occupy both the particularity of Indian identity and the universality of abstract citizenship [and thus] challenge the developmentalist paradigms of the Mexican Revolution embodied in the contradiction between ethnic and economic identities" (224); they also "present us with an alternative modernity [eschewing] the antimodernist position of nativist movements because their particular indigenous forms of democratic representation were produced by modernity and modernization" (256).[3] And while Fischer does do a certain amount of archival work, because ultimately there is no record of evidence of the Haitian revolution's influence on the rest of the Caribbean and beyond—hence her "modernity disavowed"—she must turn to the speculative theories of Freud, Lacan, and Žižek in her formulation of her speculative hypothesis based on highly speculative evidence. So, while she acknowledges that a large part of her work is speculative, she doesn't clearly trace the boundaries between, say, acceptable and nonacceptable speculation; ultimately, in her turn to Freud, Lacan, and Žižek, she pulls the ripcord on that text-as-everything parachute to attempt a safe landing.

I think here also of an earlier period in Latin American history: that of *los modernistas*. These writers and thinkers also mistrusted grand narratives and understood reality as a series of intersecting correspondences between discourses that worked to maintain the status quo; they also sought in their writings to destabilize the text in order to empower the people and alter reality. *Los modernistas* fragmented poetic form to shock and revolutionize social hierarchy, yet many served as ambassadors in European capitals, set their sights on intellectual life in such urban imperialist centers, and were attuned to the latest in the European dandy look (Rubén Darío had a particularly strong penchant for Parisian sartorial wear). They did all this while using medieval beliefs such as occultism to fend off change and thus actually dancing to the tune of ideological conservatism.

Postcolonial Latin American studies share the same contradictory bind: their authors promote theories aimed at radically altering a capitalist reality, yet they materially rely on a huge industry based materially and ideologically in that reality to promote their theory.

Theory has appeared in many guises since the ebb of structuralism, changing with every whimsical whirl of intellectual fashion. But, generally speaking, for theory to appear as having the power to alter social conditions, the world must be a text and the text the world. For Mignolo, De la Campa, Sommer, Williams, Fischer, Lazo, and others mentioned above, the text-act in the form of literature is a living social text akin to a political and historical document. Their theory aims, inter alia, to show how literary and other texts advance or hinder a critique of racial, gendered, sexual power relations. For Sommer, it is her identification of "minor" texts and their detainment of the reader "at the boundary between contact and conquest" (ix) that becomes an act of political mobilization. Here, for instance, Whitman's fragmented poetics promises to deliver "America, citizen by (free) citizen, like an infinite machine of (equal) interchangeable parts" (60). Whitman's *Leaves of Grass* is invested with the powers of a political machine, a political party rallying millions of people in the cause of equality and democracy. When De la Campa writes, the "articulation of Latin America as a constellation of discursive constructs" (viii), the world is a text, and textual analysis is political praxis. Theorists agree that deconstructive theory erases the local textual designs and subalternized knowledges present in Latin America.[4] Therefore, they have sought to carve paths that acknowledge, as De la Campa writes, the "local in the global; the here, the there, and the in-between loci of enunciation" (ix). However, ultimately they believe that the text is a "rhetorical praxis" that can transform reality (vii). Hence, it comes as no surprise that De la Campa identifies the Sandinista revolutionary spirit as spinning from the moment when the Sandinistas and the Nicaraguan people in general reread Rubén Darío not as an apolitical aesthete but as a political icon, and he concludes that their "form of cultural revolution" was the Sandinistas' "love for poetry" (40). Although postcolonial theorists might claim to distance their theories from poststructuralism, they must ultimately follow closely its central tenet: the political sphere and the space of cultural production not only overlap and are in fact indistinguishable, but they are also part of an imagined community in which a rhetorical praxis originating in postcolonial theory may convince the powerless that they can become empowered if they destabilize the master narratives that control the imagined community.

It is an inescapable fact that the academy—including postcolonial Latin America—exists within a capitalist marketplace. No matter how hard theorists announce their distancing and withdrawal from this economic frame, they must ply their trade to exist within a society in which the academy, publishing houses, and all their sources of income are governed by the market economy characteristic of capitalism. In his foreword to *After Spanish Rule,* Shahid Amin is quite clear about this. The publication of certain types of books that will be recognized when it comes time to grant tenure, the building of star departments mustering prestige to increase fund-raising capabilities, and the reproduction of theoretical legacies by making disciples out of graduate students are some of the main means open to secure one's position in an increasingly precarious economy. One must work within the machine to stay alive, and this within the conditions of the economy that are rapidly deteriorating everywhere, including the United States and Europe. (Recall *los modernistas,* who secured their incomes as journalists, civil servants, ambassadors, or lower-rank diplomats all while using esoteric beliefs as a critique and counterknowledge system to imperialist materialism and technology.) De la Campa and Amin in particular (but not exclusively) reflect on the Latin American scholar who is forced to use English instead of Spanish if he is to be marketable. For example, De la Campa writes, "Their academic future demands it" (15–16). Under the impact of increasing pauperization and unemployment and underemployment in Latin America, these theorists have moved to the United States, where, in cities like Los Angeles and New York, they now outnumber the total number in Latin America. This leads De la Campa to declare, "More than a field of studies, or the literary articulation of a hybrid culture, Latin American literature and criticism are perhaps best understood as a transnational discursive community with a significant market for research and sales in the industrial capitals of the world" (1).

It would seem, then, that postcolonial Latin American scholars today, one way or another, are compelled to work within a declining market economy that governs the academy and society as a whole. They must formulate theories that, in today's academic marketplace, must yield to a social/political reading of textual production that claims for itself the capacity to replace real political action by its textual ersatz. Thus, to produce a marketable commodity, theory must lay claim to a power to transform reality through the textual/theoretical and to empower people.

The contradiction presents itself again. For all of these theorists' talk of empowerment within globalization, their work cannot help mirroring the financial speculation taking place in today's gangrenous economic system. Like today's declining capitalism, which both creates a society of spectacle and uses speculation in a massively increasing way to prevent the fragile spectacle from crashing back to reality, Latin American and multicultural theorists must pump more and more theory to hold up both their positions in academia and the sand castle theoretical frames they have built to obtain such positions.

Several of these scholars' theories of a Latin American knowledge seek to reveal how the local structures make particular texts—the imagined community—unique. Sommer identifies a "rhetoric of particularism" (x) that contours the local to counter the outsider's desire to master and universalize nativist (or "minor," as she calls them) text-acts of the Americas. In her opinion, this has the pragmatic effect of promoting a liberal education wherein readers become "sensitive to textual markers of the political differences that keep democracy interesting and honest" (4). Certainly, García Márquez's skies that snow angels or blossoming flowers should not be the only stand-in for artistic, exoticized expression of an entire continent. And just as assuredly, charting the local can open readers' and students' eyes to a Latin America that is complexly layered and not simply a sign that refers to so-called Third Worldness. However, for Sommer and others, magical realism merely stands for a simplified sign of a text that critiques and/or buys into neocolonial discourse. Its own complex expressive modes are lost, and complexity is given over to reductive declarations; the world is the text—again.

For these theorists, identifying patterns and structures would be equivalent to believing in a reality that is objectively out there. Thus for them structural analysis is anathema. Yet, the contradictory bind surfaces again. Sommer, Mignolo, De la Campa, Fischer, Lazo, Williams, Thurner, Guerrero, and the others discussed are obliged to recognize patterns and structures even when they posit a subalternized, localized text-act that, they assure, can resist and transform master narratives. When Sommer sets up an analytic method to articulate a rhetorical specificity that identifies the intentional silences in her so-called minor texts, she references the paragon of structuralism, the French narratologist Gérard Genette. Thus, to argue for the power of the literary text to disallow interpretation, she is forced to identify a recognizable and shared rhetorical system: "The challenge for readers of 'minority' literature is to develop that system to include tropes of multicultural communication that block sharing" (24). Yet, the poststructuralists' world-is-text theory equates text-act with social/political-act: to write/read the revolutionary text is tantamount to doing the revolution. But when Sommer informs her readers that Rigoberta Menchú strategically denies full mastery of her text/life and identifies this as a form of "respectful, nontotalizing, politics" (137), she is compelled to identify essential rhetorical structures that make up the testimonial act. So, for the local to be articulated, Sommer and other theorists must fall back on that very procedure they claim to have banished: structural analysis, which allows one to identify, compare, and contrast independent features and even realize a transnational, universal-gesturing analysis.

As I have mentioned, these Latin American theorists rely on a conception of language and the world that reads all texts—social, political, literary, even the body—as effective and effectual acts. When Mignolo discusses the U.S. territorial expansion into Mexico's northern territories in 1848, then into the Caribbean between 1898 and 1959, he identifies the link between "territorial configurations" and "imperial languages and linguistic (colonial and national) maps" (249). The equation reality is text has been present in one guise or another in the different versions of poststructuralist theory. As Steve Woolgar has put it, poststructuralism "is consistent with the position of the idealist wing of ethnomethodology that there is no reality independent of the words (texts, signs, documents, and so on) used to apprehend it. In other words, reality is constituted in and through discourse" (312).

Now, of course, the denial of an extratextual reality is not only counterintuitive (nobody in everyday life confuses words with their referents, nobody believes that the word *salt* will make his meat taste better), but oxymoronic (literally, pointedly foolish). If the world is a text, all but a few sciences would be superfluous: grammar or linguistics would suffice for us to know or to investigate how all matter—from atoms and subatomic particles to human brains and societies—functions. Yet postmodern and postcolonial theorists need to posit this assumption as an uncontested and incontestable postulate in order to be able to claim that the "revolutionizing" of a text is identical to the "revolutionizing" of minds and society. Hence, a postmodernist or a postcolonialist critic is, by definition, a revolutionary. Thus for Mignolo, speaking in polylingual "other tongues" is an act of articulating an "other thinking" that has as a matter of consequence the power to reclaim the colonized territories. Cherríe Moraga's bilingual writing in *The Last Generation* is another case in point. Mignolo writes, "Bi-languaging is no longer idiomatic (Spanish, English) but is also ethnic, sexual, and gendered. Spanish and English 'recede' as national languages, as the language of a nation called 'Queer Aztlán' arises" (269). But when Mignolo identifies a poetics of Queer Aztlán and remarks that it is irrelevant that both English and Spanish are "hegemonic languages of the empire and the nation" and that their use is "unavoidable due to globalization and the consolidation of hegemonic languages" (269), he must base such considerations on the identification of essential linguistic structures. According to Mignolo, "linguistic maps are attached not only to literary geographies but also to the production and distribution of knowledge, changing linguistic cartographies implies a reordering of epistemology" (247). In other words, Mignolo and the other scholars discussed here must both acknowledge structures and at the same time deny them.

And we see in Sybelle Fischer's *Modernity Disavowed* self-acknowledged speculative assertions. Now, speculation is not a sin. And given the dearth of documentation available that might allow one to *avow* that historical moment when Haitian revolts rippled across the Caribbean and the Atlantic to Europe, this is somewhat allowable. But these speculations are themselves built on the highly speculative theories of Lacan, Žižek, and Freud. So what we see in Fischer (and also Lazo) is a poststructuralist maneuver of textualizing all cultural phenomena. It's the same kind of maneuver we see in Williams when he turns to García Canclini, Derrida, Nietzsche, Deleuze, Hardt and Negri, and Baudrillard, to name a few, to identify his posthegemonic-subaltern resistance in the *testimonio* of a Salvadoran gangbanger, Mirna Solórzano, living in South Central LA and/or the insane asylum in Santiago, Chile. In such culture-as-politics approaches, claims of nation, revolution, political reform, the struggles that guarantee the rights of the exploited and oppressed are seen in culturalist terms: if you disseminate an antiknowledge, anti-representation, antiontology, and so on within mass culture you will effect social and political change.

Unfortunately, when Hopenhayn dismisses the fantasies of a Latin American poststructuralism—our occupying of "the interstitial areas" (10) taking "pleasure in forms" (10) as resistance—he promotes in its place a developmentalism styled in the manner of that of the Economic Commission for Latin America and the Caribbean (CEPAL): the promotion of a mixed economy in which the state would have direct control over certain industries. He proposes the establishment of a new utopia characterized by being of this world: it would be both a product of the imagination and at the same time it would not have that totalization (totalitarianism) that traditionally typifies the erstwhile utopia. To obtain this, we need a utopia that supports and brings together, he writes, "autonomy and communitarian participation, local nativism development and/or the ties of solidarity within spaces on the micro-scale" (128). So while he dismisses the poststructuralist approach, his alternative is just as problematic. He's offering what the antiglobalist movement folks (like the Association pour la Taxation des Transactions pour l'Aide aux Citoyens [ATTAC] and NGOs generally) call a "participatory democracy" and "participatory budgeting." That is, just as ATTAC and all those who attended the antiglobalist meetings in Porto Alegre (attended also by high-level government dignitaries and billionaire speculators like George Soros and Bill Gates), Hopenhayn sidesteps the issue of social class, its organization, conflicts, and struggles. It is this participatory democracy that has worked toward the destruction of the independent worker's movement and of the principle of accountability inscribed in the principle of democratic representation. In participatory democracy nobody is accountable; there is absolutely nobody to whom you can address your demands. In a so-called participatory democracy one addresses oneself to civil society—and not a political party, class organization—and thus one is addressing oneself to individuals as a concerned member of the community and thus not accountable to anyone or anything. Finally, Hopenhayn seeks to make a space in Latin America for an "intercultural utopia" that combines an "ideal of participatory democracy" and "a utopia of communication that provides widespread access to symbolic interchange by way of the culture industry" (150–151). If this model were actually applied you would have the total atomization of the people.

This is poststructuralism in another guise; that the present organization of society (capitalism) will never change and is eternal. We have no further history, as it has ended precisely with today's capitalist society. The only alternative: to invent utopia. Hopenhayn thus concludes,

> An open utopia requires a change of rationality, and its efficiency for promoting it is what makes a political practice out of utopic speculation. The utopic construct should rescue as means and ends attributes such as solidarity and participation, social identity and freedom, belonging and work, communication and affection, collective creativity and cultural diversity: these possess value in themselves and radiate effects which are desirable beyond themselves. The continual realization of necessities and the progressive actualization of potentialities is, simultaneously, a road and a utopia. (152)

In so many words, Hopenhayn is really telling us to leave the nation-state with its machinations of power and coercion alone. Rather, the solution, according to Hopenhayn, is to inject a dose of utopian imagination into society to create what he calls a "democratic coalition" (153). So, while Hopenhayn critiques (almost satirizes) postcolonial Latin American scholarship that spiritualizes reality, his solution—to establish a participatory democracy in Latin America—does the same.

Given that Hopenhayn is a researcher for CEPAL, this shouldn't be too surprising. Funded by the UN, CEPAL can't be separated from other imperialist entities like the 1960s Alliance for Progress and Peace Corps; and today's avatars like ATTAC. We see this clearly when Hopenhayn theorizes a need to push for "autonomy and communitarian participation, local nativism development and/or the ties of solidarity within spaces on the micro-scale" (128). This is the same position of the alter-globalists (ATTAC) in their push for a "participatory democracy" and "participatory budgeting"—positions that the president of the World Bank and billionaires like Gates and Soros, no less, applaud—that suppresses any talk of social classes and their organizing. Under the guise of "fighting against globalization," then, Hopenhayn simply falls back into this complacent space that absents class warfare. Hopenhayn writes, "Maybe this contamination will sharpen the spirit of the social scientist and allow for a rediscovery of new incipient tendencies in which there are new rationalities and utopias in the process of gestation" (139). In spite of his incisive critique of poststructuralist Latin American theory, he finally accepts the whole conception of reality as stated and proscribed by postmodern theory: the disappearance of class struggle and therefore of the whole horizon of radical transformation of society by the destruction of capitalism and the establishment of society on a completely different economic basis. He thus concludes, "Utopia that would not necessarily be universal, rational, western. But neither would it be reduced to a bucolic purism that in a short period of time would reflect the heterogeneity of our continent. Utopia that reduces, that mixes, that hybridizes, that combines and recombines anew the scarcity of the present in order to suggest the plenitude of the future. Utopia that is both a factual impossibility and a cultural necessity, a political challenge and a threat, dreams to trick both integration and the apocalypse. (153)

Let me reflect a moment also on Mauricio Tenorio Trillo's declaration of the need to rethink "national images, nationalisms, and identities in a disenchanted, nonnationalist, pragmatic, and yet wishful fashion" (76). While critical of those scholars who conceive of the nation as fixed in the imagination of a people, his so-called "nonnationalist, pragmatic" approach (that nationalism does not depend on geography, on a fixed image, on any kind of regime, or on a fixed ideological characterization) erases the class struggle from politics. That is, he doesn't consider how working-class struggles created a network of public services (social security, postal services, roads, communication systems) for all the people inhabiting the territory we call Mexico. So, here we see what happens when politics no longer has as its subject matter an analysis of the class struggle: it turns into ethics. One no longer sees the social world formed historically in the antagonistic interests of the two classes, but rather as a social world formed by good people (authentic) and bad people (nonauthentic). Hence, we continue to see politics transformed into a politics of image, locality, identity, and where everything turns into ethical divisions of good and bad and/or into quasi-moral categories like agency and hegemony. Yet, we know from history that the domain of the political is always the domain of the state. It relates to the state because the political is the domain of the antagonism between the social classes—and this has been true ever since the development of society. That is, in the move from a hunter/gatherer society to larger groups whereby historically a minority dominated a majority (the exploitation of others' labor through slavery), specializing in trades and other activities (soldiering and so on) allowed for the division of labor. With this process was born the state: the sum total of institutions used by the ruling class to maintain their status as ruling class. The state is thus a product of this deep division of labor in society and it is the emergence of social classes within this society.

From its origins, Marxism has been committed to fostering the radical (as opposed to partial) transformation of society in each country and throughout the world by means of the self-liberating action of the working class organized with its own totally independent organizations (both trade unions and political parties nationally and worldwide). This program has been distorted or, more accurately, turned into its opposite in the myriad guises of reformist and counterrevolutionary policies adopted in the labor movement in Latin America and elsewhere during the twentieth century. Most likely as a result of this failure, it has become fashionable for Latin American scholars to regard the classroom, the textbook, the essay, and the treatise as ersatz means of empowerment and liberation of certain members of society in lieu of the actual mobilization of an autonomously organized youth and labor force.

CONCLUDING REMARKS

A focus on how literature, photographs, film, and, indeed, all material culture function to sway readers and provide anticolonial and/or ethical guidelines to fashion a better future reality becomes simply what the theorist persuades his readers it is, and not what it actually is. So from the point of view of a theory of knowledge, such Latin American theorists claim that nobody can know what reality really is: reality and truth (its correlative) are entirely reliant on a Nietzschean perspectivism. Much like the Neoplatonic conception of the poet, the theorist is now a visionary; the theorist's truth, a visionary truth—and anything that challenges this is swept aside. This has material consequences, of course. If you go against the theorist's truth and instead seek to understand the actual functioning of texts as texts, as well as their modes of production and their modes of reception, you risk being locked out.

I emphasize to my students that to acknowledge structure is not to sell out. I tell them that in the field of postcolonial Latin American literary analysis, hypothesizing, then testing, to see how various storytelling structures work (point of view, narrative voice, theme, characterization, for example) to convey meaning and engage readers can provide a model that others in the field can build on. I remind them that this, of course, does not mean that objective analysis is foolproof, only that there are certain basic patterns we can identify as structures and on the basis of which we can build, accumulate, replace, and/or modify hypotheses with a view to interpreting texts via a more solid understanding of them. We can determine, for instance, how García Márquez, Cortázar, and Borges utilize and modify genres and storytelling techniques used by others in the Western literary canon as well as how they alter structures to work against existing canons. For example, reading García Márquez's *One Hundred Years of Solitude* only locally would yield an interpretation that saw it simply as an allegory of imperialism and foreign hegemony that takes Macondo into Latin American modernity, which is tantamount to reducing the complex layers present in its pages. Forcing the literary text to correspond to an a priori agenda makes readers reduce the text to a singular message instead of open the door to engaging its rich complexity. Close readings of texts and identification of their essential structures or basic patterns can offer new ways of asking large questions concerning those texts, their authors, and their readers. I remind my students that we are all accountable for what we do and say. Therefore, we need to develop theories and analyses that others may verify or refute in order to build productively the field of Latin American postcolonial studies.

TWELVE

FUGITIVE THOUGHTS ON
JUSTICE AND HAPPINESS

INTRODUCTION

In a recent undergraduate course I taught on postcolonial literature I assigned my students J. M. Coetzee's *Disgrace*. I chose the book not only for its masterful use of a third-person present tense voice, but because it offers a filtered look at postapartheid South Africa through the eyes of a middle-aged, white South African, David Lurie. At this stage in the course, this type of narrative presented a radical shift from the South Asian, Caribbean, and Maori voices we had encountered. *Disgrace* put the students on a terrain where their sense of justice and injustice, freedom and confinement was turned upside down and inside out. Lurie is fired for having sexual relations with a student (who is "Colored") and moves from the city to his lesbian daughter Lucy's house in the country. During a burglary, she's raped by a gang of Coloreds, becomes pregnant, and chooses to keep the child; in exchange for protection, she agrees to a form of concubinage with the Colored character, Petrus—a figure formerly exploited as a laborer by Lucy. The students unanimously enjoyed the novel, I suspect because its prose hurls the reader down its roads at a breathtaking pace. But when it came to talking about the issues of right and wrong presented in the work, they didn't know where to stand. They were tempted to dislike the novel because of Lurie's sangfroid and belligerent sexism, but they sympathized with his anger at his daughter's passivity; they were drawn to Lucy yet were openly spiteful of her "white liberal" acceptance of her rape; they hated that she acted out of a sense of white guilt, repenting for the long history of white supremacy in South Africa. And they felt frustrated because at the novel's close they still didn't feel they'd been given a moral compass.[1]

One of the students in this postcolonial literature class recommended I watch John Boorman's film *In My Country*—an adaptation of the

Afrikaner author Antjie Krog's *Country of My Skull*. I did so. The film, like the novel, textures the mid-1990s postapartheid period stretched at the seams with social and political struggles and contradictions. Unlike the novel, the film focuses directly on the Truth and Reconciliation Commission's (TRC) hearing of testimonies of both the victims and perpetrators of apartheid. It's told largely from the point of view of an Afrikaner journalist, Anna Malan (Juliet Binoche), who becomes aware of (to a degree) her silent complicity with those who committed heinous crimes and who contributed massively to the genocide of black South Africans. The film has little to redeem its Hollywoodish romantic depiction of the TRC; however, it does ask us to be wary of the role of the Catholic Church in the TRC and the dangers of embracing a multiculturalism—the call for an *ubuntu* justice whereby the victim/assailant's testimony leads to reconciliation and forgiveness.[2]

Of course, novels and films are not responsible for *doing* the right thing; nor should we hold them accountable for providing or not providing political, moral, and ethical compasses. I mention *Disgrace* and *Country of My Skull* not so much because I want to explore these texts any further, but simply as an entry into this chapter, which will focus on issues such as the function of justice and law within and between nations and within a capitalist economic world system. I hereby map, then remap, contemporary theoretical inclinations in the field of literary legal studies and more generally scholarship that deals with issues of law and justice as they rub up against race and nation.

In certain branches of literary studies, there's been a turn to law.[3] For example, in her introduction to the coedited collection *Un-Disciplining Literature* Linda Myrsiades considers this turn a vital—even "restless" (9)—response to erstwhile disciplinary boundaries that are "showing signs of age" (9). In her conception, the turn to law will make for "demilitarized zones and border traffic" that will not only allow us to "fish in each other's waters" (9), but will open up literary scholarship to new adventures along a "frontier territory between disciplinary lands" (9).[4] In their edited volume *In the Grip of the Law: Prisons and the Space Between,* Monika Fludernik and Greta Olson bring together essays that explore how literature and film reflect criminalization processes in society and/or their affiliative "parameters of resistance." The literary text points the reader toward the "injustices, imbalance, and slantedness of the legal-penal system" (xviii). For the editors of a special issue of *MELUS* (2003), Gaurav Desai, Felipe Smith, and Supriya Nair, the analysis of literature also offers a site of social critique as well as acts of resistance specifically on the part of those most targeted by injustice in the United States: the racialized ethnic-object specimen. For these scholars, an analysis of multiethnic literature that shows how literary and legal canons have created hierarchies of difference can open, they write, "a space for the resolution of social inequities, not by virtue of a fantasy projection into an unproblematic future, but by a determined impulse to set the record straight about the lived experiences of ethnic Americans" (7).

Much of this turn to law flows in one way or another out of the earlier work of Stanley Fish and others, like Richard Posner, who, respectively, made the turn from literature to legal and the turn from legal to literature. We see, for example, in the seminal work by Fish, *Doing What Comes Naturally* (1989) and in his essay "The Law Wishes to Have a Formal Existence" (1991) the establishing of a theoretical framework that allows for literature and law to be considered as equals. In both works, Fish considers that meaning in language is conveyed not by its constituent parts (its syntax, grammar, semantic functions) but by context—and thus, as I'll show, by its rhetorical effect. That is, whether we're discussing legal or literary texts (sentences) for Fish there is no direct, clear ("literal") meaning because each sentence's/utterance's meaning is dependent on context; and yet is not completely limitless. That is, Fish positions himself somewhere in between what is known as legal positivism and legal naturalism. I'll return to the specifics of these approaches shortly.[5]

For now simply keep in mind that Fish's theory of how language communicates meaning puts the emphasis on rhetoric, allowing one to analyze law in the same way one might a novel. Meaning resides, according to Fish, in the "marks or sounds produced by an intentional being, a being situated in some enterprise in relation to which he has a purpose or a point of view" (99). It is this intentionality that constrains the reader's interests when interpreting the meaning of a given utterance. In "The Law Wishes to Have a Formal Existence" Fish gives the example of a parole evidence rule that invites interpretation of otherwise "unambiguous contracts" in the admission of parole evidence:

> In the first its presence on the "interpretative scene" works to constrain the path interpreters must take on their way to telling a persuasive story (an account of all the "relevant" circumstances); then, once the story has been persuasively told, the rule is invoked to protect the meanings that flow from that story. The phrase that remains to be filled in is *persuasive story*. (178)

How is this achieved? For Fish, "the persuasiveness of a story is not the product merely of the arguments it explicitly presents, but of the relationship between those arguments, and other, more tacit, arguments—tantamount to already-in-place beliefs—that are not so much being urged as they are being traded on" (178). For Fish, then, the listener/reader (in this case, those in court) chooses the most plausible narrative—that which not only corresponds to something verifiable outside the statement, but is also the most persuasive. So while the meaning of the sentence (literary or legal) is arbitrary, it is constrained by the context (the author's intention) and in this way law and literature, according to Fish, continually create and recreate themselves as "spectacle" in a world "without foundational essences" (203). Ultimately, then, the legal or literary utterance means something not just because of the author's intention, but because of its power to emotively move and cognitively direct its audience in specific ways.

The turn to law in literary studies has broadened to include all variety of U.S. ethnic cultural phenomena.[6] In *Fugitive Thought,* Michael Hames-Garcia considers writings by so-called "prison intellectuals" like Malcolm X, Angela Davis, Miguel Piñero, Pancho Aguila, and Oscar "Zeta" Acosta not so much to provide a "history of legal thought, prison movements, or leftist activism in the late twentieth century," but rather to present more generally the "resistant practices of the oppressed" (xvii). And, while he will use the "tools of literary analysis to examine writings by legal theorists and prison intellectuals" (xvii), he does not aim to provide a literary study, but rather "to reinvigorate political discussions on the left that have reached an impasse due to a suspicion of key moral terms like justice, solidarity, and freedom in a postmodern, post-Civil Rights era" (xvi). His is a study that seeks to critically engage the laws in the United States that contain and control racialized, sexualized, and gendered bodies.[7] In his analysis of testimonies, autobiographies, poetry, and legal writings as "resistant practices" (xvii) Hames-Garcia ambitiously aims to contribute to the field of critical legal studies, but as well as to "intellectual debates about social transformation and moral theory" (xvi). In this regard he seeks to realize and make actual (in the Aristotelian sense) the vision of justice and freedom that Martin Luther King Jr. could only "gesture toward" (37).[8]

As I mentioned, *Fugitive Thought* is not to be considered a literary study, or a history of racialized law in the United States, or a discussion of the U.S. legal system (with its tripartite separation of powers).[9] Rather, it is to be seen as the theorizing of a *"postpositivist* and *antifoundation-alist"* (xxiv) epistemology and ontology,[10] what he also calls a "critical moral realism," that radically surpasses existing positivist and naturalist theories of law.[11] His path, as he asserts, is neither

> an absolutist project that demands unquestionable foundations or to-tal certainty, nor a relativist one that gives up on the importance of "reality" in conditioning our experience and knowledge of the world. Instead, it contends that accounts of causal features of the social world can yield accurate, reliable, and *revisable* understandings of reality. (xxv)

Thus, it is to be read as an epistemology and ontology that radically sur-passes existing positivist and naturalist theories of law. This move be-yond naturalist and positivist law comes into play when, for example, he analyzes Assata Shakur and Angela Davis, who faced directly the "injus-tices of positive law" (xliii).[12]

To assert his critical moral realist method and approach, Hames-Garcia in one way or another does away with a whole series of phi-losophers and social thinkers, including Aristotle, Epicurus, Spinoza, Hobbes, Mill, Sartre, de Beauvoir, Merleau-Ponty; some, like Hannah Arendt,[13] are taken up more than dismissed. And because Left-identified critical legal theory—and Marxism generally—has reached a dead end, according to Hames-Garcia, we thus dismiss Marx completely.[14]

What exactly are these two positions Hames-Garcia supposedly leaves in the dust? And can one really move beyond a legal positivism and legal naturalism when, as I'll show, they are two sides of the same coin? Let me explain. Legal positivism, strictly speaking, is embodied in the work of Thomas Hobbes. In *Leviathan* he formulates a position vis-à-vis hu-man nature that runs counter to what he considers a philosophical Ideal-ism in Aristotle and Plato: as it exists in various social and political sys-tems in Europe and in a Rousseauean "state of nature" outside of Europe. Hobbes drew several conclusions. First, that it is not in man's nature to exude Christian charity, good will, and so on. Second, that it is man's nature to be bad, predatory, like a wolf. Third, moments of relative social equilibrium are short and in no way defined by either man or society.[15] If man's nature is bad, then to restrain this badness you have to create laws and then give authority to decide matters concerning both the creation of laws and the application of laws. According to this theory, this would then lead to the creation of a nation-state with its borders and punitive machinery; and to maintain its sense of identity as a nation-state, there would always need to be an enemy; one must always be in a state of war.[16] Finally, the positivist approach doesn't see law and its modification as divinely ordained, but rather the result of sheer raw human nature; human nature dictates everything. This is why many legal positivists speak of laws as having only laws as their foundation.[17]

Legal naturalism (as found in Plato, Aristotle, and Aquinas, for example), on the other hand, is law that is external to man and whose existence is justified not by the norms and customs of man, but by something greater; its origin lies within a transcendental morality, ethics, or reason (as seen in the eighteenth-century *philosophes*). It is Kant's categorical imperative: "Thou shall not kill." It is God, humanity, or any other higher order entity. It is the effect of a cause that is external to the law.

Naturalist law and positive law are one and the same. What causes God to will (to cause) natural laws? If that origin of law is reason, then the *what* is reasonable. If reason is the external cause of natural law, then what is the cause of reason? If we say that law is justified by reason, then we can ask, what justifies reason as being the source of law and as making life and society better? That is, we ask, what is the cause of origin of the cause in an infinite regress? We see the same thing in the positivist approach where laws beget laws that beget laws ad infinitum.

So, even if legal theorists agreed, say, that God or reason or ethics is the foundation, we still would have to establish how the universal principle is connected to contingent laws established in time and place. We would have to ask, how is this law connected to any universal principle? In the case of the antisodomy laws that exist in several states today in the United States, one could say that it goes against the will of God: sodomy doesn't reproduce and the Bible wants us to reproduce, as decreed by God. Others might justify the law by saying that sodomy should be condemned because it's *contra natura*. According to natural law it is assumed that all lawmakers (Congress/courthouse) will stop and think, we need a law and this law should be done according to principles laid out by God, and thus my laws should be formulated in a way that will not contradict the universal, natural order established by God, ethics, and/or whatever foundation you find for laws. According to the legal positivists, this law needs no justification outside of law. So even though positivism indicates that there is nothing external and naturalism does, both end up positing an external source. In the case of legal naturalists, the source is God; in the case of legal positivists, it's our inherent badness. In both cases, we are still talking about universal, abstract categories. In both cases, therefore, we are still talking about foundational categories.

If positivism and naturalism are one and the same, then where does this lead us with Hames-Garcia's assertion of a new moral critical realism? Nowhere. Not because the division of positivist from naturalist law is false, but because of his abstraction of reality, and because he sees his third way as an end in and of itself.

To further clarify, let me turn to the four main categories of legal thought in the United States, as formulated by Guido Calabresi. These render obsolete any further deliberation by Hames-Garcia regarding positivist and naturalist law. I summarize his four main categories as follows:

- "Doctrinalism, or Autonomism" approach: characterized by the view that "law is autonomous and distinct from other fields of learning" (2115). Such an approach would thus analyze "the rules of laws consistent and coherent with each other, so that like cases are treated alike" (2115). It attempts "to rationalize and render coherent the rules that derive from the great Codes of Law" (2115). Legal positivism falls under this approach. We see this embodied in the German positivist Hans Gelfin's *Formal Theory of Law,* which attempts to build in a very abstract way a perfectly legal theory of law in terms of formal logic: all elements within the theory were to be consistent and coherent with all the other elements so there would be no contradiction. As a "doctrinalist," the reactionary member of today's U.S. Supreme Court, Justice Antonin Scalia, would fall under this category.
- "Law And" approach: characterized by its view of law as "functionalist" (2119); its aim is to break out of the self-contained system of legal values seen in "Doctrinalism, or Autonomism." This category includes law and literature, law and psychology, law and cognitive science, and so on, ad infinitum. To avoid the "tyrannies of mystical conservatism, of revolutionary ardor, and of simplistic majoritarianism" this set of legal scholars does not feel bound by the "self-imposed limits of the underlying disciplines [but rather] follow the insights of these disciplines beyond the points where the economist, sociologist, etc., would go, meld them with those of other disciplines, and come up with highly imperfect—but perhaps the best available—guidelines for reforming (or confirming) the legal system in its attempt to serve the current needs of the people. (2120)

- "Legal Process School" approach: characterized by the comparative examination of courts, legislatures, administrative agencies, executives, juries, and so on, in order to shed light on the "particular attributes of each of these that would make a given institution especially suited to decide some issues rather than others" (2123). This is an approach or school that focuses on finding out how the law is established and by which institution. These theorists are more interested in the process of law making and thus in the analysis of the institutional analysis of law making.
- "Law and Status" approach: examines how "laws and the legal system affect specific categories of people. It asks that all law be questioned and criticized on the basis of its treatment of certain preselected groups. While in theory this could be done with respect to any category, e.g., the elite or the nobility, in practice, in America in this century, the focus has been on groups that have been viewed as exploited, disadvantaged, or otherwise dominated" (2127). This approach focuses on how laws affect the common man and woman and how they came to be. It is an eclectic approach that focuses on the status of people that pulls from the other big categories and has played a central role in U.S. legal scholarship that gravitates around identity politics. This is Hames-Garcia's approach.

Certainly there are overlaps and crosscurrents among the four categories; Calabresi likens them to a kind of musical chair game in terms of which one is or is not in fashion. But this isn't why I summarize each category at length. The typology is important because it allows us to put some order to what could otherwise be an endless discussion of an endless number of approaches concerning law. It's a typology generated by a scholar who seeks to understand things as they are in reality; as they exist. That is, it is useful because it's a means that allows us to make order out of our reality.

What does this tell us about Hames-Garcia's approach? It tells us little more than that it fits into the "law and status" category; it tells us that essentially whether we choose a doctrinalist approach, like that of, say, Justice Scalia, or a law and status approach like Hames-Garcia's they are all equally valid. Why? Because, as Calabresi makes clear, they are useful for whatever purpose you consider them to be useful: to advance a career, to put into law a reactionary conservatism, or whatever. Now—and this is the main point here—if they are all equally valid and useful depending on the value one attributes to any of the four approaches listed above, then they are also just as automatically not useful as an approach. That is, neither theory contains criteria for any kind of rational critique or study.

Where does this leave us, then? To begin to answer, let me provide a rather crude example. Suppose a field is observed by a geologist, a cognitive psychologist, and a lawyer. Each will use his or her own instruments, methods, and approach to study the field; the geologist might excavate to observe and classify the rock formations; the cognitive psychologist might measure those perceptual processes and mechanisms of memory involved in perceiving the field; the lawyer might consider boundaries and property laws. While the study of the field changes depending on the method and approach of each specialization and each person's interest and ability, the field remains the same. Moreover, the three specialists can discuss their data and conclusions among themselves. There are questions, methods, instruments that distinguish one approach from the other, yet each can potentially contribute to the other to add to our knowledge of the field.

This brings me back to my point about law and justice. If in the assertion of a critical moral realism the distinctions made between positivism and naturalism don't ultimately make a difference (in method and approach as they depend completely on subjective purposes and personal abilities), then it will never make the difference that *makes* a difference.

A quick glance again at how positive and natural law have been used historically reveals approaches that in one way or another can be seen as having value (good) and not having value (bad). Let's take the naturalist approach: its foundation of law based on universal principles of good, fairness, and/or reason was used to justify the establishing of the inferiority of some and the superiority of others. Yet, the positivist approach, whereby laws are founded on laws of man, also led to the passing of laws adopted, for example, by the Reichstag and by Philippe Pétain's parliament, which forced all people of Jewish origin to wear a yellow star on their clothes. From the positivist point of view, this law is fine because it was the democratically elected German and French parliaments that instituted these laws, and thus they represented the French and German people who adopted this law; according to this positivist approach, it doesn't matter if you agree or disagree with such laws because they are established by legal institutions vested with authority to create laws. Finally, we see both approaches in action when Adolf Hitler was legally and legitimately given the equivalent power of prime minister by the president and the majority of representatives of parliament; this transmission of power happened under the legal Constitution of the Weimar—a constitution built on the basis of law. That is to say, the positivist (the writing of the Weimar Constitution) approach gave him the authority to turn to a naturalist approach once he gained power legally in 1933.

In Hames-Garcia (and in a whole host of others not mentioned) we see a similar abstraction of law and reality that ultimately gives us nothing of any scientific or practical value.[18] Whether doctrinalist or law and status or any of the other approaches, if one abstracts law from time (history) and space (concrete situations) and if one doesn't make distinctions between one approach and another that make a difference, then one will never add to the knowledge of the field of law.[19] Law is always concrete; it always refers to concrete situations: to a moment in time and a place in space. Thus it is only an approach to law that takes into account concrete situations in time and place that will further our understanding of our reality governed by law—and the reality of law.

Let's revisit the field in concrete terms. Law appears only in societies; we know that society developed historically in the development of the dominant and subordinate social classes. We know also that in classless societies there are norms of behavior, good manners, ethics, and so on, and not laws. Within society, laws require a coercive apparatus. I can impose certain rules of behaving in my house, but to enforce these rules I don't need a tribunal, a court, a judge, or a sheriff, a police officer, a prison, a warden, and guards. I don't need a state apparatus to forcibly make people in my house obey this norm. That is, norms belong strictly to the private sphere and laws to the public sphere. This doesn't mean that the private and public aren't connected. The moment the state establishes a law that prohibits, say, what happens in the privacy of your bedroom, then what happens in your bedroom is no longer part of the private sphere, but now part of the public sphere.

An approach to law must take into account that it exists within the public sphere and within a society that is necessarily split in two: the ruling class, which stops having direct physical involvement in the production and reproduction of goods for the continuation or maintenance of the reproduction of humans and that devotes itself entirely to overseeing and paying a coercive body (soldiers, police, and so on) to ensure that the much larger group work to guarantee the surplus required to pay the soldiers, police, and so on to defend the society (and to bring war and enslavement to other groups).

Society is composed of the ruling class and the rest of society. In society you have the state apparatus and thus laws; and as far as we know (nobody's proven otherwise), historically the state, no matter how complex, represents in all cases the social and economic interests of the ruling class from which it emanates. In the United States most of the laws are produced by Congress (the meeting of the Senate and the House of Representatives together); the president of the United States has the authority to produce laws that emanate from the executive power. In defense of the Bill of Rights, the Constitution, and democracy, we have rules that have become laws that allow the U.S. government to occupy Iraq and kill its people, for example. And within the state apparatus there are rules and regulations produced within the bureaucracy: departments of health, education, and so on, that create regulations that are as binding in intent and fact as any law. There are hundreds, probably thousands, of sources for the making of rules that are applied publicly and that we are unaware of. Indeed, any rule or regulation coming from any state organ has the potential to become a law. History also shows us that within this ruler-ruled structure every time the working class has made gains in preserving and improving its existence as a working class, it has happened as a result of force applied in one way or another to the law-generating organs of the state (ruling class) to make the laws.[20]

If in today's capitalist system it is always the institutions of the ruling class that determine laws—and of course these can be influenced by pressures exerted by the subordinate class—would the implementing of laws that insure justice and equality also guarantee the subordinate group's freedom—and more generally, their happiness? Should we look to the writing of "prison intellectuals" and their "intimate involvement with" the "injustices of positive law" (xliii) and their "participation in struggles for freedom" as "theorists of the material nature and possibilities for expanded notions of freedom" (xliii), as Hames-Garcia would have us do? Should we look to King as the figure who "transcends liberal conceptions of law and justice and gestures toward an acknowledgment of unrealized possibilities for human existence and social organization" (37)? Should we conceive of freedom as an incomplete state of becoming that ceases once the struggle for justice is won, as Hames-Garcia also posits?

While it's true that freedom was a central concern of writers and thinkers of the Enlightenment (a period Hames-Garcia and others have written off as a repository of social and political wrongdoing), as a concept it was already circulating widely among thinkers, writers, artists, and intellectuals in the Renaissance. It's certainly true that during this period, when such thinkers were concerned with freedom, the conquest of the Americas occurred, bringing destruction and genocide; this was certainly the beginning of what would become an even more widespread and brutal imperialist expansion under capitalism. But Europe during the Renaissance was itself deeply contradictory and plagued with tensions over an increasing divide that was forming between a bourgeoisie and a laboring class. In spite of this, within Europe we also see a moment of massive creativity. This was a watershed in terms of writers and thinkers conceiving of the actualization of their potential. It was also for the first time a period when people began to see that diseases, poverty, famine, droughts, and war were not the result of God's will or the will of God's vicar, the pope, but of human action and decision. Moreover, the discussions between figures like Giordano Bruno and Giovanni Pico della Mirandola show an understanding of the social relations (man's role as producer) as the determining force not only in social existence, but also society in its potential capacities. For these figures this was articulated in the exertion and development of social and individual potentialities as fully as possible. This goal went by the name of Happiness.[21]

Happiness was conceived of neither as something to possess nor as an emotion (pleasure or joy, say) that expresses a subjective state of mind delimited by time, but rather the realization of a state of affairs; it's the passage from potentiality to actuality, and this on both the social and individual levels. The conditions for this passage from potentiality to actuality in the individual are subordinate in the historical, social, and economic sense to the realization of potentiality to actuality at the social level. Leonardo da Vinci's helicopter or submarine were conceived of as potentially present but not yet realizable because of the lack of technology; following Newton's scientific explanation of what gravity is, da Vinci saw very clearly that these things could be realized, could be created and produced; at the same time he was extremely aware of the fact that as a subject situated in a specific time and place, he couldn't make actual a helicopter or submarine; the materials, the knowledge, and the technology present in his society were insufficiently developed for the actualizing of an object that could defy gravity.

Society had not yet furnished the means for all people to have enough to eat and enough for all to have a minimum of clothes to keep them warm, and already in the Renaissance an abundance of writers were inventing utopian society; the impulse to write utopias as a genre barely existed before the Renaissance. In other words, already in the Renaissance there were people fully aware that a society of happy individuals is very important and worth attaining; at the same time they were aware of the fact that their present society could not provide the means for this potentiality to become an actuality. In Darrin McMahon's careful tracing of an intellectual history of happiness, he discusses at length the shift from an earlier conceptual linking of happiness and luck or fate—a Judeo-Christian promise of a "perpetual felicity to come" (138)—to a more terrestrial-bound concept in the Renaissance; here the concept of happiness is caught up both in a Judeo-Christian web of faith (be good on earth and eternal happiness awaits) as well as in a state attained through reasoned acts in the here and now. It was a period in which Renaissance humanists defended the pursuit of happiness more broadly outside the sanctions of the church. (For more details of this era's crisscrossed tapestry of Christian theological and humanist conceptions of happiness, see, in McMahon's *Happiness,* the chapter titled "From Heaven to Earth.")

By the time of the Enlightenment, McMahon demonstrates, happiness was presented "as something to which all human beings could aspire *in this life*" (13). This conception of happiness as a stable, long-lasting state of existence whereby one could realize both individual and social potentialities fueled the French Revolution, for example, and the abolition of slavery—to abolish forms of society whereby the authority of the few delimited the realizing of a state of happiness of the many. It is the declaration that "all men are created equal" and that we have the "inalienable rights" to "life, liberty and the pursuit of happiness" that became the mantra of the building of a United States of America.[22]

I mention this because if we are to achieve happiness, then we must be able to shape a society that allows as much as possible for all its members to actualize potentialities; to act with the knowledge of one's possibilities and limitations and what these possibilities are within the society we live in. You can't observe the dictum "Know thyself" if you see yourself only through the lens of the self and not through the lens of what you actually are: the social self as constituted through the lens of the society in which you live and that you can potentially become in the surmounting of obstacles. To emphasize yet again: whether formulated in a postpositivist realist epistemology or otherwise, to separate the individual from the social is nonsense.

There is, of course, not just a social, but also a biological component to happiness. Cross-cultural psychobiological research shows that most of us have a fairly steady level of happiness in our lives. Indeed, to prove the point made above, the research shows that it is when individuals experience prolonged periods of not being able to actualize potentialities—extended periods of unemployment or employment under exploitive conditions—that one sees the development of a less than adequate everyday emotive coping mechanism and sometimes a radical reorganizing of neural-network activity that leads to permanent depression. Many of us know this first- or secondhand; my father's emotive system, for instance, can no longer hold at a critical distance the horrific events conveyed through the newspaper media. When he hears of hundreds dying in Iraq or in Africa, his emotions peak in intensity the same way they would if here were directly experiencing such deaths. This, of course, only deepens further his unhappiness, resulting in increased isolation from the social. Just as he lacks the capacity to rationalize, or find meaning in, negative experiences, in his isolation he increasingly eliminates the possibility of surprise—something our brains need to boost levels of joy.

Being able to experience positive emotions is essential to a healthy life, but the more we make such experiences predictable, the less joy we derive. The healthy individual keeps emotion and reason in fine balance. In "Making Sense of Emotion" Arne Öhman identifies a human adapative strategy that favors the evolution of an emotion system that has assisted the evolution of our capacity to reason.[23] We continue to get the big cognitive and emotive payoff when we engage in basic survival activities like eating, having sex (orgasm), vanquishing rivals, collecting resources, and so on. From the perspective of our evolution, as Öhman continues, "an important priority for any culture is to domesticate emotions that are likely to generate conflicts and threaten group cohesion. An essential component of socialization, therefore, is to acquire the ability to regulate emotion. As a result, the successfully socialized individual has a cultural self with goals that may differ from (but are likely to be less evocative than) the goals of the evolutionary agenda" (38–39). The research thus far shows that there is both a reflexive-emotion system (nonconscious and subcortical direct activation of the amygdala by emotional stimuli) and a reflective-emotion system that involves what has been identified as an appraisal process. This second-order emotive appraisal processing involves a series of evaluative mechanisms. I quote Öhman's overview of appraisal process theory:

> The most basic evaluation is relevance. "Relevant" in this context typically refers to whether the stimulus has any consequences for one's current goal scenario. If it has no goal relevance, there is no emotion. But if the stimulus has the potential to enhance or impede one's prospects of reaching a valued goal, it will evoke positive or negative emotions, respectively. Goal-congruent stimuli basically induce hap-

piness: if one can attribute the enhanced goal prospects to one's own effort the likely emotion is pride; if they are attributable to another person the likely emotion is mutual affection or gratitude. (42)

At the National Institute of Neurological Disorders and Stroke in Bethesda, Maryland, a research team that includes Jorge Moll and others is at work on identifying the neural substrates to moral cognition; their neural mappings show that motivated moral behavior is linked to moral emotion (those that are linked to the welfare of others) as well as our social knowledge (Theory of Mind ability, for instance) of the world. They present neurobiological evidence that our moral emotions, moral values, and moral cognition have neurological correlates in the brain that are responsive to "context-dependent knowledge," "semantic social knowledge," and "motivational states." (See, for instance, Moll et al., "The Neural Basis of Human Moral Cognition.")

In the psychobiological work of Marc D. Hauser there is a radical break from the blank-slate concept of morality. Building on extensive research on children, Hauser determines that children show a perceptual and action competence far beyond the limits of their exposure to an impoverished environment. After several detailed analyses of various research results, Hauser discusses how we necessarily must be endowed as a species with a moral faculty that enables us to "unconsciously and automatically evaluate a limitless variety of actions in terms of principles that dictate what is permissible, obligatory, or forbidden" (36). This isn't to say that the social doesn't count. Hauser contends that, like language, "the specifically expressed and culturally variable moral systems are learned in the sense that the detailed contents of particular social norms are acquired by exposure to the local culture; the abstract principles and parameters are innate. The role of experience is to instruct the innate system, pruning the range of possible moral systems down to one distinctive moral signature" (422). For Hauser, it is this "universal moral grammar" that ultimately provides us with "a sense of comfort" and a shared understanding of each other (426).

Hauser's work is interesting and at same time not so interesting. His grounding of action, perception, and causality as hardwired components of our moral grammar, however, easily spills over into a *faith in:* that our moral grammar is always acting for the better good of the species. I think, of course, of the way capitalism has been destroying the environment as it makes all of human life depend on massive consumption of oil and gas.

While I hold more to the work of Moll et al. and less to a faith-based utopianism like that of Hauser, the point is that in the various materialist, ontologically grounded perspectives we learn that morals don't come out of the blue; they are part of human behavior that is social behavior materialized and embedded in individuals and thus in our biological makeup. Although still in its infancy, this research reminds us that there is a biological and a social component to understanding ethics, justice, values, morality, happiness, and freedom.

Put simply, the research reminds us that we are biologically constituted and share universal faculties as a species (the capacity for language and morality, for instance), but that we don't exist in a vacuum or as isolated, atomic entities.[24] We are social beings, and thus whatever we do, think, and feel is done, thought, and felt within a social context and according to behaviors that are socially accepted or condemned. We therefore also interpret and understand other people's behavior within the social (context and semantic social knowledge). Thus we can see how the realizing of a basic emotional state such as happiness must take into account both unconscious, reflexive actions (in the Pavlovian sense) toward moral issues: that microsecond impulse to help a person in distress or that immediate feeling of disgust when seeing an Iraqi civilian torn apart by a bomb.

The point is that there can be a materialist ontological and realist epistemological understanding of emotion, cognition, and motivation. Moreover, while the "contextual cues that link moral emotions to social norms are variable and shaped by culture" (Moll et al. 806), such moral emotions evolved from universal prototype emotions that we all share as a species; at base, we are all equally biologically endowed. Iraqis, South Africans—all people—experience the same kind of reactions to death, pain, grief, that we do in the United States.

There is a reality (social and biological) out there that we can know more and more in ways that will allow us to make ethical judgments that are justifiable and that are selectable. The more scientific knowledge we have about how we are built and how we are able to act according to how we are built, the more difficult it will be for politicians to uphold so-called moral or ethical statements that go against the scientific knowledge we have about ourselves.

Such research gives us a materialist basis for understanding how the self as a biological and social self experiences stimuli as well as how such stimuli are processed: how we shape our world in ways that impede or enhance the ability for all to actualize potentials.

When talking of being able to shape a world in which we can all fully actualize our goals—make real our dreams and create from our imagination—we are always talking simultaneously about the biological and social. Indeed, this sense of freedom for all is enveloped within this sense of happiness. Just as happiness is not a *thing* but rather a social relationship, so too is freedom. To use an oft-misquoted phrase first voiced by Hegel, then Marx: "Freedom is a consciousness of necessity." If you want to be free, you have to be aware of the rules or laws governing nature and the rules governing the human being and society. I can spend all my life yearning to be free of the laws of gravity, but unless I extend as deeply as possible my knowledge of gravity—and thus of reality—I will never be free of it.

Freedom, therefore, is both a goal and a means: it is necessary for the actualization of one's potential and it feels good to be free. It is only living as equals that we can exercise our rights, be fully responsible for our actions, and feel valued. It is through our collective actions in the preserving and gaining of rights that we can create a society that will foster this possibility of living as equals.

Indeed, the struggle to make such a society where we all have the right to actualize potentialities will not happen in a scholarly play of ideas or in a literary analysis of law or in the application of legal theory to literature. It will not happen either if we continue to approach law from any of those above-mentioned categories identified by Calabresi. Rather, to break from a society like that of the United States today, which incarcerates one person out of every one hundred and forty and whose executive power makes rules into laws that lead to the disappearance of people without a right of defense or representation, we need most urgently to see clearly how laws work, how they gain authority, how they can be used and overturned. More than scholarly play, living in today's world, where the working people's struggle has been greatly weakened, we need more urgently then ever to know how ethics, justice, action, happiness, and freedom spring from our social and biological self.

CONCLUDING REMARKS

It should be clear by now that a turn to law to understand literature or to literature to understand law is not the direction that will lead us either to understand *Disgrace* (or *In My Country*) better or how this fiction might shed light on law. This isn't to say that we should be ignorant of laws that allowed for apartheid and to the establishing of so-called tribunals like the TRC. However, to look to literature (or film) for answers to questions of justice and freedom in the realm of law is not the way to proceed. As Patrick Colm Hogan summarizes of the literature-as-law (and law-as-literature) approach: "These problems suggest that the narrative analogy most often adds little to our understanding of law *per se,* and in many cases even impedes that understanding" ("Fictive Tales, Real Lives" 271). While such interdisciplinary work might stimulate the imagination, its value as "a research program" (273) is questionable. Moreover, unless the approach—whether critical moral realist or functionalist—makes a distinction that makes a difference and that is grounded in reality, then it will only lead us away from areas of research that might potentially yield much fruit.

Laws are the legal tissue that envelope all aspects of life in society. There are thousands of laws that we aren't even aware of: those between countries, those that govern the movement in international waters, to name only two, each carrying big binders of rules and regulations concerning a vast amount of activities from fishing to sanitary health conditions to gambling, and so on. One of the characteristics of this tissue that envelops all social relations in every country and worldwide is that it is constantly changing and evolving through additions and subtractions. So while laws and regulations are a constant out there, this tissue is always changing; and their application, interpretation, and enforcement are also always changing.

This doesn't mean that we can't understand this tissue of law. It is as much a reality and a part of our real world as the cars we drive, the buses we take, the food we eat. Thus, we should be able to determine a set of criteria as well as an approach and method that will allow us to study this phenomenon as part of our measurable, objective reality. For example, we know that a legal system is not eternal—that it has a history—so we might begin by asking how this legal tissue is formed historically. In Europe, for example, we know it developed from feudalism; that it became dominant as a legal system with the radical triumph of capitalism. We know that laws are modified, so we would also have to study the circumstances in which laws within the general legal system have been modified. This is to assert once again that one can choose any number of approaches—positivist, naturalist, and/or "critical moral realist," for example—but if this approach doesn't give us a scientific explanation of what is out there, such as how laws have changed and what the historical and social factors involved in the change are, then they will always lead to dead ends.

It's not only a matter of interpreting the world, it is a matter of changing it, as Marx would say. Yet, we know that laws do not change favorably for the people who are going to bear the burden if there is no social movement to support the change. Those who are to bear the burden are those who should have exclusive right to make the law. In the case of abortion, say, it should be women who vote to decide this right. Soldiers in the army (mostly working class) are the ones that will be maimed and killed, so they should be the ones and the only ones allowed to vote on whether to invade Iraq or not. Likewise, since the consequences of decisions taken during war are matters that concern them in the same way, then the rank-and-file soldiers should also be the only ones electing their officers. In strictly democratic terms, since they are the ones concerned then they are the only ones who should take the decision by voting. And this applies to all people. If workers consider that all workers should have access to medical care and social security in general, then this is something that concerns the workers directly (male, female, active, retired), and so in the decision-making process the decision makers should be exclusively the workers. Namely, the study of law, law making, and the institutions connected to juridical process as a whole should show us the way to extend democracy, extend the rights of people, and eliminate (as much as possible under capitalism) the distortions caused by the fact that the power of decision is not restricted to the people that will carry the burden of the decisions taken.[25]

There is something particular about law in general. On the one hand it's an objective mechanism, something out there that we can study as such. But precisely because it's a net covering the whole of society, it is something that can and does change by society itself, by social means. To assure that the changes are made to benefit those who are most concerned by the change is to make sure that those who carry the burden of this change will be the ones solely allowed to vote on this change. What's more unjust than having old men in offices decide to invade Iraq when they themselves will never be in the war?

It will not be Martin Luther King Jr., Desmond Tutu, Nelson Mandela, or human rights groups like the Center for Legal and Social Studies or Mothers of the Plaza de Mayo in Argentina, who will bring justice; it will not be Hames-Garcia's "critical moral realism" that will free the real political prisoner, Mumia Abu-Jamal, in the United States. It will not be my teaching of law in a postcolonial literature course or the teaching of a morally complex novel like *Disgrace* that will transform conditions of apartheid, which continue to exist today; nor will Africa's children be saved by a Live 8 music concert that simply "mourned a corpse while forgetting to denounce the murderer," as Jean-Claude Shanda Tonme writes (A21). Overturning injustices will not happen in the hands of one or two or three people. It will only happen in organizing marches, boycotts, strikes; and we know this from the Montgomery bus boycott and the protests over the wrongful conviction of the Scottsboro Boys, as well as with the civil rights gains generally. We know this from those anti-Vietnam War marches that brought whole cities like San Francisco and New York to a stop. Freeing the political prisoner Mumia will not happen in a cry for a freedom to come. It will only happen if we mobilize to ensure that he receives a fair trial.

Stanley Fish's op-ed piece "Intentional Neglect" (July 19, 2005) discusses, in light of the nomination and election of a new Supreme Court justice, the interpretation of the Constitution or other juridical texts as not infinitely decipherable, but rather constrained by the intentionality of the author. And, for Fish, it is this intentionality that keeps us engaged; when we discover that the word "help" on a rock formation (his example) was not etched by man but rather was the erosive work of wind and rain, we lose interest. What Fish doesn't mention is that this activity is not language or text dependent. It is part of our universal interpretive faculty. Just as my dog, Mei-Mei Bruno, can't help but sniff out his world, we can't help but fill in the blanks and ascribe meaning to those things that catch our eye, tongue, ear, nose, and skin.

This leads me to another point—suggested but not developed by Fish. Whether we're interpreting an object or a piece of language in the Constitution, in one way or another the relationship between the interpretation and the reality is determined by some correspondence to the verifiable (otherwise known as the "correspondence theory of proof"). That is, we can determine the intentions of the author in a careful examination of the text along with what the author meant, as Fish points out. However, I would add that such an examination must include a careful look at the context and circumstance in which the text was written. To better determine the intentionality of the author and the text, you have to know the "state of affairs" in which the author was reacting. This leads to another point: the decisive differences between laws that pertain to, say, physics and those that concern, say, the minimum wage in the United States. That is, the former differs decisively from the latter in intention: the understanding of the law of gravity might help you understand better why you might fall from the tree in your backyard, but it doesn't presuppose an institutional punitive mechanism; that is, you might break an arm because you forgot how gravity works, but you won't end up in jail for breaking the law. When the Supreme Court voted in favor of a woman's right to choose to have an abortion in 1973, they interpreted a piece of the Constitution that guarantees the right to privacy and in so doing decided that the punitive capacity of the state (with some exclusions) could not be directed against women who had abortions. Moreover, the Supreme Court did so within a particular historical context: civil rights struggles and anti-Vietnam War marches. Thus when talking about intentionality, historical context matters. And when it concerns our study of law, and in the United States the Constitution (the heart that beats at the center of our juridical system) we especially need to keep in mind the three-part relationship between interpretation, intentionality, and reality. Not so much to determine whether or not we're comfortable with a given nominee's style, as Fish suggests, but rather, to know that we have the strength and material force (as did our foremothers) to exert the kind of pressure necessary to ensure that the Constitution serves, protects, and advances the civil rights of the working people of America— and the world.

THIRTEEN

WHY LITERATURE MATTERS

INTRODUCTION

This chapter is inspired by that moment (usually midway through a semester of teaching an upper-division literature course filled with mostly smart and curious English majors) when brows furrow quizzically and that mental ticker-tape starts clicking: Why are we reading and analyzing books when no one I know even reads? Why not get up to speed with the times and analyze something more relevant, like film? What value does this all have in the bigger scheme of things anyway? I usually take pause from the work at hand and throw the question back out to the students. They come up with a variety of answers: Literature helps us think better! It sharpens our critical vision of the world! It makes us more well rounded! It's fun! I take up such questions and responses in this chapter in a first step toward identifying the pieces to the complex puzzle: What is literature and why does it matter?

I'm in the profession of teaching and studying literature. This means devoting hours and hours everyday to the reading and teaching of novels, short stories, poetry, plays, and the like. It means having committed hundreds of hours to reading and analyzing literature as an undergraduate and graduate student with the aim of becoming a professional scholar and teacher of literature. Yet, when I look at the National Education Association report or the Census Bureau report[1] and see the steady decline in U.S. readers of literature, I ask myself: Why would anyone want to devote so much time to this? Why do a certain number of my students want to follow this path? Certainly, there are fewer people who are reading. However, as far as I can tell, students still want to study English in college, and some even want to become professors—and not just because we supposedly have long summer holidays. And I still see people riding the train to work in places like Mexico City, London, and San Francisco and soaking up a few pages of a novel.

Literature clearly continues to matter. And it matters differently for different scholars and their different definitions and inclinations. There are those who approach the subject from a genealogical perspective, seeking to find answers in tracing the debates and theories back to Plato and Aristotle. I think readily of a book I've used often to teach under-graduates, Richard Harland's *Theory from Plato to Barthes: An Introductory History* as well as Jean-Marie Schaeffer *Pour quoi la fiction?* Others look at formal features like syntax, rhythm, and other structures to iden-tify literature's uniqueness and its special role. I think readily of Gérard Genette, James Phelan, Robert Alter, Seymour Chatman, Marie-Laure Ryan, to name a few such scholars. And there are those like Thomas Pavel who consider it important because its fictional worlds provide "alterna-tive sets of situations, thereby putting the actual world into perspective, challenging its supremacy" ("Fiction and Imitation" 529). For yet others, it matters because it can open eyes to social injustices as well as help us, as John Horton writes, "to see the value in commitments and ways of life which from our own moral perspective may seem empty and worth-less" ("Life, Literature and Ethical Theory," 94). For others, like Frank B. Farrell, it matters because it allows us "to form a more complicated selfhood" (152–153). For still others, like Brett Bourbon, it matters onto-logically: fiction is a "quotational form" (13) that comes into existence as literature only as a result of the reader's "ontological commitment" (13) to it as literature; it matters for Bourbon because we make it matter in our attitude toward its sentences and textures; it matters because of our on-tological commitment. For the scholar Denise Gigante it matters because of its unique expression and cultivation of taste: taste as in aesthetics and canon formation and taste as in what happens within the storyworlds. Thus by attending to taste we can see how "aesthetic judgment" is formed and also how this speaks to a given author's "sense of self" (2). For Sianne Ngai literature matters because it can express "ugly feelings" like envy, anxiety, paranoia, irritation, or what she calls "stuplimity" (3).

Other scholars declare it is important because it sheds light on such topics as evolutionary biology, cognitive science, cognitive linguistics, and cybernetics, to name a few.[2] Katherine Hayles, for example, consid-ers literature the place where we can understand how metaphor oper-ates (as per Lakoff, Turner, et al.), not only as the guide to our everyday thoughts and actions, but as the bridge between our interior thought and what we perceive exterior to ourselves. For Hayles, literature is a particular expression of metaphors that organize the mind/brain according to both objective and subjective (embedded in body and language) constraints. Literature is simply a unique expression of this "constrained constructivism" (145) that informs our everyday activities and existence. We see this also in Sämi Ludwig's *Pragmatist Realism* and the identification of a "cybernetic, cognitive-constructivist" (5) analytical frame to study nineteenth-century American realism. For others who have made this linguistic cognitive turn, literature can point us to a deeper understanding of metaphor as that roadmap of our conceptual domains that are enabled by cognitive structures. The more we know about how the mind/brain works, the more we can understand how literature works—and vice versa.

In the turn to evolutionary biology, literature matters because it is tied to ancient survival strategies that coevolved with our mind/brain as we moved from a hunter/gatherer system to agriculture to a more permanent settlement society. As a by-product of the mind/brain and also something that has in turn shaped the mind/brain, it matters because it is intimately interconnected with, as Michelle Sugiyama writes, our "long history of evolution by natural selection" (233). Likewise, in *Madame Bovary's Ovaries* David P. Barash and Nanelle R. Barash consider that its connection to our biology is the key to understanding "literature and, in the process, ourselves" (9). As we are more alike than different as a species, we can understand why "Othello's jealousy, Huck's rebelliousness, and Emma's urges" (2) have captured readers' attention for so long: "It is the breath and beat of living organisms embodied in an organic world of sex, blood, food, fear, anger, love, hopes, trees, animals, air, water, sky, rocks, and dirt" (251). Literary Darwinists like the Barashes consider that literature matters because it reflects universals such as mate choice, kinship relations, social hierarchies, to name a few. Thus, literature matters for such scholars because it reflects and "artfully" reframes and defies biological behaviors and truths. (For an overview of this approach to literature, see John Whitfield's "Textual Selection: Can Reading the Classics through Charles Darwin's Spectacles Reawaken Literary Study?")

While such scholarly approaches certainly provide interesting insights, I ask, do any get us closer to understanding why literature matters? Some say yes, and some say no. For example, those who "dissolve the aesthetic into cognitive clarity . . . may miss the mark" (216), according to Hans Adler and Sabine Gross. Adler and Gross consider that such turns, at least to cognitive science, flatten the "aesthetic-affective potential of literature" and don't account for "the range of readings we are capable of" (216). We might ask as well if this doesn't simply try to harden a social constructivist approach to literature-as-text—Hayles's theorizing of a "constrained constructivism" and "posthuman consciousness," for example—that idealizes the real cognitive functioning of the mind/brain? Here we might do well to ask, is language inseparable from thought, as Hayles and others posit when ascribing to the "embodied" mind/brain position? It is true that knowledge is made possible partially because we are built biologically (bipedal, a certain average height, and so on) and cognitively in specific ways determined by our species; and, we transmit knowledge in writing and through oral communication and this has allowed for the cultural phenomenon language to exist and evolve. However, can we claim that these elements play the same important role in a theory of literature, language, and narrative?

What I consider to be the drawback for those who look to study literature as an expression of an embodied knowledge is that it is used ultimately to negate that there can be any knowledge, any truth about literature or any other matters concerning our existence and experience in the world. If our mind/brain is not equipped to get at the essence of things like the essence of literature and is only equipped to know the appearance because our perception of reality is always embodied (linguistically), then why study literature?

This leads to a related point. When turning to other fields like cognitive linguistics, evolutionary biology, ethics, and so on in our study of literature, do we enlarge too much our domain of inquiry? Maybe we should begin by asking not what literature is (expression of embodied knowledge, biological truths, and so on), but rather what its most salient feature is.

Literature's most salient feature is that it is fictional. Fiction *is* the defining, indispensable component of literature. If it's not fiction, then it's not literature. On a very basic and general level, fiction is formed by a collection of fictional "tokens" that form systems. These fictional systems solidify into what we typically call genres. Whatever the differences between one work of literature and another—between one tradition in one country and another—there are at least three big divisions: (1) short stories and novels; (2) drama (theater); and (3) poetry. Within each of these three broad genres there are subdivisions. For example, there's the genre novels (or long short stories) like the romance or murder/mystery; in theater there's tragedy and comedy and a whole number of subcategories, like the comedy of errors, and so on; in poetry there's the epic, lyric, and a hybrid narrative form of both, as seen in Browning's "The Ring" or Byron's "Don Juan." Finally, within these three large divisions you have tragedy and comedy, and within these two bookends many combinations and permutations.

I'm most interested in the novel, so I'll focus on this fictional genre. The novel is capable of mixing all the other genres; it metabolizes all these genres but does so while maintaining its identity as a novel. Whether it cuts and pastes historical nonfiction, uses the language of philosophy, medicine, quantum physics, or Marx, it can be about any aspect of reality—as long as it maintains its fictional quality as a novel. By this I don't mean some formal limitation like length—it can be long or short; nor do I mean that it must carry a certain content; as mentioned, it can be about any aspect of reality, psychology, physics, history, and so on. Rather, I mean that it maintains its identity as a novel—as fiction—in the way that it points to the real world. For example, Amitav Ghosh's *The Glass Palace* relates a real historical period of time in the history of the former Burma; it refers to real characters, events, dates, and times. Ultimately, however, its making real of events and characters is in accordance with the terms of the fictional narration and not the conventions of the work of history; that is, it's "will to style" asks the reader to do something other than go to the archives to check its accuracy.

But fiction as a category is still rather fuzzy. Do we thus turn to its unique use of linguistic, rhetorical, and stylistic elements in the identification of what some scholars have called the "literariness" of literature? Not exactly. The formalist approach to a definition of fictionality separated fiction from nonfiction on the basis of just such a study of its literariness. That is, an exhaustive list of formal (syntactical, lexical, rhetorical, thematic, and so on) features that pointed to a given fiction's fictionality. As every feature declared to be unique to fiction had dozens of examples to disprove this assertion, we then moved onto a fictional worlds approach; this used the logic of "possible worlds"—that something is true not only with respect to the world as it is, but also with respect to all "possible worlds" (all white is white, not only with respect to what we can observe now, but also in all possible worlds)—to assert that what defines or characterizes fiction is that fiction is always tautological because it is necessarily true or false only within the diegetical worlds: To find out if its statement is true or false we need only look within the fiction.

Both the formalist and fictional worlds approach are ultimately limited because they don't explain why both the author and the reader can follow a story and understand it (imagine its setting, context, character, and so on) by constant reference to the actual, real world. That is, the problem of what distinguishes fiction from nonfiction can't be solved only by an immanent, logical, or formal linguistic approach. This is why we must also develop a method that includes the contextual, or worldly, aspects of the fiction: the author's will to style that directs the reader's framing or intentionality vis-à-vis the text.

This leads me to the matter of aesthetics. How the reframing of an object (real subjects and real experiences that make up everyday reality) can be engaging, produce pleasure (and pain), and even redirect our perspective on that object—and therefore on reality.[3] I think here of an interview with the Afro-Caribbean émigré author Caryl Phillips and his response when asked if in the writing of novels that juxtaposed the slave trade with the Jewish Holocaust he aestheticized suffering. He remarked,

> As far as I'm concerned, a novel concerns a group of people about whom one attempts to give voice to their experiences, and sometimes their experiences are unpleasant, difficult and painful, even tragic. One wants to render these experiences as synthetically as one can, and obviously part of that is to use language, is to use form, is to use structure with as much finesse and as much elegance as possible— that's the only type of aesthetics I am interested in, it's the form, formal aesthetics. (36)

He then distinguishes between the aesthetics of his novels and the suffering in the actual lives of the people, declaring that "people who suffer suffer" (36).

To talk about a literary aesthetic, then, is simply to distinguish between the mimetic drive of narrative fiction and the real facts that make up our reality. Indeed, as Winfried Fluck writes in "Aesthetic Experience and the Image," the aesthetic "denotes a distinct mode of communication and experience without which we could have no object in literary [studies] and no good reason for the existence of a separate field of study" (11). The distinct reframing of an object carries with it an experiential dimension. Fluck defines this experience as twofold:

> (1) An aesthetic object is created by taking a certain attitude toward the object in which its non-identity is foregrounded; (2) This non-identity, in turn, creates the necessity of a transformation that becomes the basis for articulating otherwise inexpressible dimensions of

the self and permits us to stage ourselves as somebody else, so that we can be ourselves and another person at the same time. (21)

This, of course, also raises the question of how the structures and narrative techniques used in literary aesthetic engage authors (as readers) and readers generally.

Just as painting, say, has a finite number of techniques (based on a finite number of colors we recognize in the light spectrum and range of perspective our vision affords, for example) so, too, does literature have a finite number of structures and techniques that authors can use to transform the use function of real experiences, people, and objects into an aesthetic function—but all keeping in mind that such and such a reframing will necessarily engage its readers. Narrative devices such as point of view, play with time, characterization, mise-en-scène, and so on are verifiable and finite and also do certain things to cue and trigger certain emotive and cognitive responses. I think of Umberto Eco's notion of the "limited semiosis" of the "open work" as posited in his *The Open Work* (1989).[4] As he discusses, even a seemingly impenetrable novel like James Joyce's *Finnegans Wake* works according to a number of finite structures. Eco's notion of literature ultimately posits it as both finite and infinite in its production and in the reader's engagement. Now, this doesn't mean that readers will necessarily react to the same book in the same way; indeed, the finite number of techniques available to authors (working at the level of language, story, and discourse) can solicit an infinite number of responses; this is largely due to the fact that while an author might use certain techniques to cue and trigger specific emotions, because we don't all share the same memories, different parts of the text—even different words and images—might resonate with us in different ways. This is to say, the fictional work is finite in its openness.

Such memories are as infinite as the readers'/writers' experiences that have created the memories. Again, the mind and brain have verifiable cognitive processes, but also an infinite amount of space for personal memory to put a spin on how we map universal prototype, schema, and Theory of Mind (ToM). Readers and authors (humans generally) have experiences. Such experiences leave two types of trace markers in the mind: one representational and one emotive. At any given moment, one might be more active than another. That is, we might be more conscious of one experience than another; we're not continually in a state of constant sensitivity to all trace markers and all their memories. We can see how this might help us understand that an author's specific use of words and phrases not only forms images, themes, and events in narrative as a whole, but do so by activating (to varying degrees) memory traces that trigger certain emotions or ideas—and this can be felt directly and/or understood clearly or more fuzzily. The author employs certain narrative techniques to prime those traces that can trigger our long-term memory: sometimes we are more cognizant of why we feel/perceive the way we do and at other times, it's much more fuzzy (those thoughts we have before we've managed to put them into language).

The mind's process of identifying those cues in a text that render meaning are also context dependent. In *The Mind and Its Stories* Patrick Colm Hogan writes, "When we read or hear the syllable 'mon' at the beginning of a word, we begin searching the lexicon for a 'fit.' When the topic is Wall Street, we will reach 'money' first; when the topic is animals related to apes, we will reach 'monkey' first" (56). And such lexical networks, if not triggered regularly, will, Hogan continues, "drop quickly out of the buffer if they are not repeatedly primed" (57). Hogan further identifies three types of substructure within a lexical item: schema (hierarchy of definitiveness: conception of human as organic), prototype (concretization of schema, concept of men, say, those more different to women, sadness as sadder than average), and exemplum (specific instances of a category, say, man). We employ all three in cognition, not only in responding and interpreting the world and people in terms of abstract schemas, but also by reference to prototypes and/or salient exempla.

This helps us clarify several points regarding the reading and writing of fiction. First, an author works within a finite range of cognitive processes; this allows an author to use a finite range of techniques (lexical units) that will make "maximally relevant" (63) the narrative as literature as well as prime his/her reader for both a finite and infinite range of experiences. Narrative techniques (style, phrasings, characterizations, point of view, etc.) work both at the level of idea (representation) and emotion as they prime a given reader's memories.

This is not to propose an intentionalist mode of interpreting literature. The author does this wittingly or not. When an author reads his or her work out loud, he or she is not only hearing how it reads—as Gustave Flaubert would do in his special spot at the end of his garden to fine-tune his style—but also to feel his/her phrasing. The revision process includes this sense of fine-tuning how an author wants to *move* the reader. As Hogan remarks, "Being a person like his/her readers, the author will experience some comparable priming of memories, and so on, whether he/she knows it or not" (63). In the phrasing of words and the inventing of ideas, characters, events, and plots, then, the author undergoes his/her own cognitive and emotive priming of memory. This process happens by accretion and in a loop feedback system. Just as memories help guide the author's choice of details (phrasing, conditions, character, etc.) to further enhance the holographic effect of the narrative, so to do such memories guide the author-as-reader into such an invented world.[5]

Indeed, we can identify (and revise and discover anew) the techniques authors use to engage readers precisely because we share like-cognitive architectures as readers and authors and also cross-culturally. Thus our engagement (either as reader or author) follows a set number of cross-cultural rules (prototypes, schema, and exemplum). It is infinite in the sense that a given set of rules, say, those that govern narrative prototype, can be re-formed by the author and/or reader and because it is ultimately a massively plastic container: literature talks about everything. Namely, an author like Amitav Ghosh is free to choose a finite number of prototypical genres—romance, heroic, and suffering (see Hogan), for example—but once the rules are acknowledged, he can re-form the rule of the genre infinitely (provided, of course, he guides the reader in this reformation). And, of course, a novelist can fill a prototypical form with characters that evince an infinite number of behavioral schemas. Philip Roth fills his novels with characters that are at once abhorrent and fascinatingly attractive; Dostoyevsky can tell the story of a murderer in such a way that the reader feels deeply empathetic. And an author can use the rules of storytelling—third, first, or even second person point of view that will achieve this or that effect—but the author also has at his or her disposal an infinite range of other storytelling tools. In Laurence Sterne's *Tristram Shandy,* we turn a page and the narrative literalizes the character's view of night sky: black fills up the page. This is also why studies that try to determine what is specifically "literary" about literary language only end up putting a straightjacket on literature.

So, when trying to understand better how literature works and why it matters we must attend to both how a fictional work like, say, *Finnegans Wake* stretches into the infinity in its abundance of possibilities and openness (our concerns and experiences are limitless) as well as the finite and verifiable number of tools (and we have yet to discover them all) that work to prime, cue, and trigger not just a cognitive engagement (clearly more likely with *Finnegans Wake*) but also an emotive engagement.

We can inhabit worlds filled with events, spaces, people, things; we can imagine in the present such holographic worlds of time past and future.

To do so we believe, empathize, and have a temporal sense of self: what I might be in the future. In terms of literature, when we read and/or write we reconstruct story (plot/event) as the discourse unfolds (point of view, temporality, genre, mood, and so on). Authors, as I mentioned, play with this double chronology: play with how the story-time (plot, event, description, etc.) might slow down/speed up, fall out of sequence, etc., according to how the author chooses to order/organize the information (flashback, etc.). Narrative technique cues, primes, triggers the cognitive process necessary to figure the puzzle out—to make meaning. When we read/write, procedural schemas are set into play that allow us to distinguish between the discourse (how it is told) and the story (what the story is about). As we read/write, we puzzle out the story from the discourse. Such a construction involves, as Hogan clarifies, "the application of a vast wealth of information—prominently including an array of representational schemas—from our experience in the real world" (*Cognitive Science* 117). That is, we store in our memory schemas from our real-world experience (as well as representational schemas gathered from reading/listening/watching narratives) that allow us to fill in the blanks while reading—most of the time, unless a narrative cues us to do otherwise, in a rather automatic way.[6] Because the mind works procedurally (mnemonic structures), we can understand why in poetry, for example, we find prototypical line lengths and rhythmical structures. So while there is a seemingly infinite capacity for expressing just about anything in literature, because we have specific cognitive architecture and procedure, a writer's techniques for expressing this are not infinite.

This isn't to say that we process schemas in the same way in all historical times. For example, the scholar Reuven Tsur demonstrates how our brain's process versification structures can be influenced/shaped through repeated social transmission (monemes); here the mind and the social are not binary oppositions, but mutually reciprocating, and an understanding of this can help us see how cultural phenomena reflect the "complex relations between the mind, the world that at once determines it and is determined by it, and the cultural forms that spring from this interaction" (85). This can allow us to understand better, for example, how our continual production of cultural objects instigates new ways of thinking that, in our collective engagement, require the shaping of prototypical procedures. Namely, evolution has provided us with certain cognitive capacities to process phenomena out there, but because changes in our social/cultural environment occur so fast, adapting to such changes requires both the biological ability to evolve and also the ability (identified with short-term memory) to process and adapt swiftly to new stimuli. For Tsur, this allows us to understand how short-term memory and gestalt rules of perception—"the conditions that maximize our tendency to perceive a stimulus pattern as an integrated whole" (Tsur 73)—determine why we have breaks (caesuras) in syllabic and in syllabo-tonic metric verse patterns.

All of this leads us to yet another piece of the puzzle: How do we feel emotionally moved by, say, a character we know to be fictional? Not only in the sense that the author might play with temporality or the editing of a story for readers to experience, say, a rush and thrill when certain events unfold, but also how the story activates memories.

We know from cognitive research that emotional experiences we've had are linked to our collective memory deposit; often, the emotional experience is the path that leads us to specific memories in the present. As Hogan clarifies, "When we feel fear, anger, sorrow, or joy as we felt it in the memory, not (necessarily) as it is relevant to the current situation" (*Cognitive Science* 156). And, in everyday life, the priming of memory can be swiftly supplanted by the priming of another memory. In contrast, when we read a novel we reexperience the emotion of certain memories, and these the novel can sustain for long stretches of time. So, while memories might trigger emotions in our everyday life, they shift rapidly and thus are unpredictable, varying in type and degree. When we read a fictional work, our memories can remain primed for longer stretches of time and thus create a more coherent and sustained emotion. As Hogan simply states, "A love story will continually prime memories of romance" (158). This also helps us understand better why we respond differently to different texts: our memories determine this and also change over time; we might not like reading *Ulysses* in high school but like reading it in college, depending on how our new experiences have created memories and therefore how these new emotions are triggered by a narrative that connects with these new memories.

There are other techniques that authors can use to trigger our everyday cognitive and emotive faculties. The way an author chooses to detail, say, a lamp can give a setting the feel of the nineteenth century, for example. Moreover, the way an author uses different details of character primes and activates another of our everyday functions: our ability to read others' actions and infer emotion—or, that universal "mind-reading" ability more technically known as ToM. Just as we can infer from someone's movement and gesture (for example, we can infer from gestures whether someone running fast toward us is going to attack us or is simply eager to see us), when reading a fictional work and registering a character's gestures, we also infer from minimal detail his or her behavior and internal emotional state.

Literature works because it is good at tricking the mind, and part of this process spins out of ToM capability: we read characters as we would people. It has been conclusively shown that autistic children neither show an interest in stories nor have this capacity of inference and empathy; they can't infer from details of gesture, behavioral schema, and so on, the internal state of others, and this lack is directly linked to their disinterest in story. This is to suggest that ToM (and its affiliative cognitive and emotive functions, such as inference and empathy) is a central element in why we engage with literature, why we can derive so much pleasure from reading a story by an author that plays with behavioral schemas and to varying degrees challenges us to infer interior emotional states. I think here of Virginia Woolf—an author who invents a narrator who makes only sparse evaluative comments about the characters, and thus the reader must look to the smallest of gestures to learn anything about a character. As Lisa Zunshine says of Peter Walsh's trembling hand in *Mrs. Dalloway,* "Rather than provide details of character through an over description ('he trembled with desire for Clarissa, but was too shy a man to . . .', for example), Woolf simply provides a flash of a detail of his 'trembling' hand; here context and our ToM faculty work to fill in—and pleasurably—the blanks about his character and ultimately we come to see a rich array of intentional stances" (273). Our ability to empathize, or "read minds," sheds light on how a reader can infer from a "trembling" Peter Walsh that he trembles with love—and not from, say, delirium tremens. From such a small detail, Woolf cues us to fill in much detail about his character, his relationship to the other characters, his actions, and so on. Woolf can do this because she can assume that certain details will direct a given reader to map the behavior of a given character's emotional state. So, while Woolf's narrator challenges us to infer from minimal gestural cues (we map this across our stored behavior schema, which is informed by our everyday encounters with people), this also happens with authors who challenge less by giving us more direct information about the character's interior state; I think here of a Mary Higgins Clark novel that offers us more information but still ultimately relies on our ability to map behavioral schema and the like in order to engage with the characters portrayed. That is to say, Woolf (or any writer) is also a reader and is also a human being with the faculty of being able to empathize and experience ToM. Such a capacity allows one to rehearse in one's mind any possible scenario in life without direct consequence. And so it's not surprising that we see it so significantly employed in the creating of fictional works.

When we read literature we refer to specific schemas and prototypes not only to infer from a person's behavior and internal state, but also to help us fill in large holes in the information provided. In literature, this is the mind creating constantly wholes from fragments.[7] This happens from a young age and helps explain why children the world over gravitate to picture books that are nonphotographic based. Paintings generally work to engage audiences more than photographs because they don't provide all the details. (This is also why we often feel disappointed in a film when, after seeing it, we read the novel on which it is based.) The artists who draw the illustrations of such books are careful to paint the general features of people, actions, and scenery so that children can experience the pleasure of filling in the blanks. We see this tendency at work in comic books also. From panel to panel, the action is represented in a static, two-dimensional drawing, so any character's movement must be imagined by the child based on the few elements provided by the picture.

This process of moving from fragment to fragment and the making of imaginative wholes—what we might call the gestalt effect of narrative fiction—allows us to powerfully relate and imagine ourselves in the shoes of the characters. This is especially the case with teenagers when they speak of liking the novel because they identify with the character. ("I can feel that character's pain," "I can relate to that character because I've felt that way before," and so on.) Here, the author has created a fictional work with a certain amount of detail that engages the reader's emotions. If the depiction of character and place is too precise, the reader might not have the opportunity to experience the pleasure of relating to the character and experiencing this gestalt effect. This also leads to adolescent readers becoming interested in the author biographically as well as in other books the author has written. Adolescent readers tend to immerse themselves in fictional works, in which they discover an enormous number of possibilities—worlds, emotions—and that helps them understand that world because it helps them understand *their* own real world.

This leads to an engagement with the fictional work on yet another level: that of not only identifying with characters, but needing to create a fuller picture of the author. That is, the gestalt effect extends beyond the pages of the given fiction and into the pleasure we derive in our reconstruction of the author. Even if the author has been dead for centuries, if the narrative involves one—that is, if his or her will to style engages and gives pleasure—then one seeks out not only extratextual details (biography and so on), but also other books written by the same author—that projected image of the author (implied) whom we've formed an image of while reading and delighting in their work. So although Dostoyevsky wrote the novel *The Adolescent* when he was turning fifty years old, a teenager might feel he wrote it for adolescents, potentially leading them to read it. So, the author becomes an extension of his writing. In a way, the author becomes yet another part for whole in the pleasure of experiencing the gestalt effect.

Understanding how an author intensifies the reader's experience of the gestalt effect (both at the textual and implied/imagined authorial level) can help us understand better why we spend so much time reading works of fiction. It also complicates and ultimately dismisses as specious highbrow as opposed to lowbrow arguments regarding the value of literature. Whether a child "reading" a picture book, an adolescent reading young adult fiction, or an adult reading *Ulysses,* readers' cognitive processes work in similar ways: to transform fragments into wholes.

To summarize thus far. One reads a comic book the same way one reads Proust, as both fictions engage and involve the imagination in similar ways: the former in the imagining of oneself in the shoes of the comic book hero, and the other in the double imagining of oneself in the shoes of the character and in the imagining of the author as the pieces of the narrative fit together.

When reading we engage everyday cognitive processes—power of empathy, our mind-reading capacity, the selecting, storing, and accessing of memories and emotions, and so on—that can powerfully create a "holographic effect": the virtual simulation of feeling, seeing, tasting, smelling invented worlds as if they were real. However, while fictional works trigger this holographic effect we have always in the back of our mind (and at the tips of our fingers as they touch and turn a novel's pages) the sense that this is simulated. Even if we empathize deeply with a given character about to be attacked by a lion, our legs might twitch but our mind doesn't fully switch into a flight-fright escape mode. We don't start running. (The same thing happens when we see a film—and this arguably even more powerfully as its visuals tend to generate an even stronger holographic effect.)

Even though we have this stereoscopic capacity—real and unreal—the leg still twitches and we're still moved. How can something we know to be fictional affect us in the same way that a real everyday event might affect us? Why do tears of sorrow or joy well up in our eyes at the movies or while reading a novel even though we're fully cognizant of the works' fictionality? Why are we moved when we engage with situations that have nothing to do with our lives directly? Evolutionary biologists contend that it is part of our adaptive machinery: to engage with a virtual experience (as, say, homo erectus with mime) as a way to put into play our survival mode. The story of an attacking mammoth told in mime (or a modern-day mugging depicted in film) increases one's heart beat and adrenaline flow in much the same way as a real situation of fear and threat. Indeed, an author employs certain techniques to dupe the mind so as not to keep audiences at arm's length emotionally; there must be sufficient detail of character and scene, for example, as well as a certain play with the temporal flow of events to trigger such emotive responses in the reader. This, many argue, plays right into off-line adaptive strategies: the brain's ability to both dupe the rest of our system into thinking the virtual is real and at the same time it's ability to remind us that it is play.[8]

Fictional mimesis as off-line play is only part of the picture. The other part involves going more deeply into how our mind works when we feel emotions (the key ones being sorrow, anger, fear, joy). We know from research on the brain and the processing and releasing of emotions that they remain latent as long as certain memories remain latent. However, as soon as a certain memory is activated, so too are its associative feelings. Hogan suggests that the way literature communicates emotion is similar. We feel sorrow and anger when, say, Madame Bovary ingests arsenic to commit suicide because the passage has triggered those trace memories (nodes of neural activation) that allow us, Hogan writes, "to reexperience the emotion of that memory" (*Cognitive Science* 156). Of course, this doesn't mean that we have had to experience suicide directly to feel this; our brain can store such trace memories from virtual, or holographic, experiences (the reading of other novels, viewing of films, listening to stories, and so on). That is, an author will use particular phrasings and images to affect his/her reader because this author has also had experiences of feeling fear, anger, sorrow, or joy as associated with stored experiences (virtual or direct). Furthermore, the use of certain techniques and language can guide us toward feeling such emotions as fear, sadness, disgust, temptation, etc., but as empathetic (at a virtual remove) and not as directly experienced. When we experience the sorrow of Anna Karenina throwing herself in front of the train, we don't directly experience that fear and sadness, but rather experience what Hogan calls, "empathetic fear" (81). Moreover, although everyday experiences produce the same emotions (sorrow, fear, anger, happiness, disgust) as those elicited by virtual experience, how they are activated differs. Hogan suggests that the way literature triggers memory and thus its associative emotion is "fairly consistent and continuous for particular primed items" (158). As Hogan further clarifies,

> A love story will continually prime memories of romance. This is important because priming effects decay rapidly. In daily life (e.g., in ordinary conversation), a memory will be primed once, but then it will fade, replaced by other primed memories in rapid succession. When this occurs, the primed memories are likely to have led to limited emotional consequences. In contrast, the suggestions of literary works keep the emotion-laden memories primed for long stretches of time. Thus their cumulative effect may be very strong. (158)

In other words, unlike the randomness and varied experiences that fill our daily life, literature is absolutely organized by an author who invents certain types of characters who have a specific range of experiences. That is, while we might, when reading, experience emotions similar to those we feel in our everyday life, how we experience them differs: literature is much more consistent and controlled than that of our everyday random and chaotic life.

As already suggested, whether we like T. S. Eliot's "The Waste Land" or not largely depends on our emotional engagement with it. If emotion is linked to memory, then this also helps explain why we might change our minds about liking or disliking "The Waste Land." As one grows older and accumulates more memories (either through virtual or direct means), one's relationship to a given text might change. New experiences create new memories, which create new emotions that might be triggered in new ways by Eliot's phrasings, for example. And, conversely, as we know also from research, formulaic writing or filmmaking weakens audience response; that is, writers and directors need to vary their techniques for engrossing us because our minds become desensitized by repetition.

Emotions also govern how genres have been evaluated and organized historically. Hogan suggests,

> At the lowest level, we find melodramas and works of propaganda that pass the expressive threshold for dysphoric emotions, sorrow, and

anger. The middle level is occupied by comedies, especially romantic comedies, that surpass the expressive threshold for euphoric emotions, such as mirth. Perhaps, slightly above these, we find works of euphoric emotion (e.g., more serious romances, such as those of Jane Austen) that pass the orientation threshold, but not the expressive threshold. At the very top, we find tragedies that pass the orientation threshold for dysphoric emotions, but not the expressive threshold. (*Cognitive Science* 172–173)

Generally speaking, the shaping of genre is governed by how a given narrative triggers emotions that are tied to the realization of and/or lack of realization of the goal of happiness (autonomy and in-group security). In *The Mind and Its Stories,* Hogan further surmises that "most if not all societies appear to establish romantic union as a—indeed, *the* prototype eliciting condition for happiness. This is no doubt partially based on a biological given, the sex drive. But it is also the result of human society. After all, cross-culturally, romantic union is far more than sexuality. It is a matter of living together, of sharing intimacy and affection, and of having children. It is, in other words, a very complex aspiration, and one that arises socially, even though it arises universally" (244). So, whether biologically innate or socially constructed or both, what's important to realize is that the realization of happiness is how we plan, plot, and organize our lives. We shape our everyday life with a larger plot of happiness in mind, and this, not surprisingly, is a powerful determinant of prototype genres: romantic tragicomedy, heroic tragicomedy, and sacrificial tragicomedy.

Hogan suggests that genres are consistent in goals and development of narrative events that prime a reader's memories to "produce a coherent emotive effect" (65). Hence, the three prototypical genres Hogan identifies are defined by the characters' ability (or inability in the case of tragedy) to court, overcome obstacles, and realize a romantic union and/or political/social power. While happiness and sorrow, for example, can dominate a narrative (those enduring emotions Hogan calls "outcome emotions"), Hogan is careful to explain that a given narrative might have several interacting and working emotive prototypes (anger, happiness, sorrow) triggered simultaneously and in conflict. This is when the reader takes pause (what Hogan identifies as "junctural emotions") and (wittingly or not) begins to assess the character's position in an "imagined trajectory of actions and events as they seem likely to play out relative to some goal" (91). This is also where ethical evaluation enters the picture and can become central to our response to a given narrative. Hence, in

the heroic tragicomedy (a more common genre cross-culturally) the exiled hero overcomes obstacles and returns home to win back political
power; in the romantic tragicomedy, the separated lovers are reunited.
Happiness prevails, but only after readers have experienced sorrow (exile
and imprisonment, for instance). That is, prototypical genres constrain
and pattern how authors invent possible worlds and how readers engage
such worlds.[9]

An essential ingredient in understanding why literature matters is the
author's innovation. This involves exploring the author's will to style
and also how the author's creative reshaping of cognitive prototypes and
schema engages the reader anew.

How do readers learn anew to engage with the slight spins an author
might put on a prototypical genre? And we've seen, deliberations on authorial muse, a Harold Bloomian anxiety of influence, Lacanian chasing
of infinitely unreachable signifier, and so on, have not led to interesting
results. As authors and readers share the same cognitive architecture,
perhaps a look at how cognitive structures and processes work can help
us clarify how they play out in literary innovation.

Just as our cognitive and emotive architecture leads to the manifestation of prototypical genres (Hogan's romantic tragicomedy, heroic tragicomedy, and sacrificial tragicomedy), so, too, does the use of such genres
guide our cognitive processes and emotions. It's a circular, loop-back
system where a given emotion prototype governs what types of stories
are tellable and determines what is interesting to the reader/author as
well as works as a guide to what is ultimately, as Hogan states, "effective and engaging" (*Mind and Its Stories* 88). As I mentioned, while we
all have prototype emotions and a hardwired cognitive architecture (the
brain's thought, language, memory modules), this doesn't mean that
there isn't room for creative play. An author might employ a prototypical genre (that spins out of prototype emotion and cognition) and yet
innovate within this genre. He or she can engage with conventions of
genre only to re-form the conventions. In *One Hundred Years of Solitude*,
García Márquez can variously use the prototypical genres of the romantic, heroic, and sacrificial, but use them to re-form the conventions of
the picaresque storytelling mode. He adds the element of self-reflexivity
(parody) to slowly readjust the reader's expectation of and emotional engagement with the prototype genres.

Although much mystical fanfare might surround those considered to
be a genius because of their masterpieces, artistic innovation stands on

much sturdier ground. As already discussed, we all share the universal capacity to imagine other worlds (exist temporally in a past and a future as constructed by an other) as well as to propose and share hypothetical situations with others, and so on. That is, *Homo sapiens sapiens* has the capacity to imagine. So how does the act of innovation enter into imaginative representation (literature, film, music, art, and so on)? To rethink and give new shape to prototypical genres—to think outside the box, as they say—is not the exclusive right of those considered geniuses. To varying degrees, all ordinary people exercise this capacity in their everyday problem-solving activities. So, is it that those who spend their lives becoming experts in mathematics, painting, or the writing of novels understand prototypes and schema better than those who don't and therefore are more likely to innovate? As Hogan succinctly states, "To write poetry successfully, I need to have enough familiarity with various aspects of poetic form, the historical resonance of different terms, the ways in which images interact with themes, and so on. Otherwise, I will not be able to orient my poems to a readership. I cannot have these crucial sorts of familiarity unless I know a good deal about poetry" (*Cognitive Science* 69).

Certainly, knowing one's field is necessary for innovation, but not everyone who becomes a specialist in, say, physics wins a Nobel Prize. It would seem that those who specialize without looking outside their field make few radical breakthroughs. This is where research in cognitive science provides some clarification and insight. While we all imagine during our everyday cognitive processes and while those who work at writing novels, say, engage with respective prototype and schema sets, it is the individual who reaches beyond his or her respective set of prototype and schema that is most successful at innovation. Again, this might be as simple as someone who knows well—has a greater degree of aptness for—which streets to take in order to get to work and then reaches beyond this given set to come up with a radically new approach and route; or it could be as complex as García Márquez's aptness for writing and his knowledge of world literature that leads to a more freely associative approach to his own writing of novels. Or, in the case of Jeanette Winterson's novel *Gut Symmetries,* innovation occurs when she reaches far into another schema/prototype set all together: that of biology and chemistry. In both cases, we see how an author reaches beyond his/her conventions to other schema/prototype sets that innovate their literary forms (host domain): García Márquez's reach takes him beyond the more proximate conventions of realism to create magicorealism; Winterson moves her novel beyond the conventions of nineteenth-century realism to create a fresh and exciting antirealist (self-reflexive collage/pastiche) narrative.

Innovation is a cognitive process—and not one of divine and/or muse inspiration. It entails not only an artist knowing well the prototypes/schemas that inform the conventions of his or her artistic domain (poetry, narrative fiction, sculpture, music), but also the borrowing across "non-identical" (*Cognitive Science* 69) domains; hence, in fiction we might find poetry or iconographic scrawls. Finally, innovation entails a sense on the part of the author/performer/teller of how his/her audience/reader/listener carries certain domain-specific baggage that will need to be reshaped. That is, if an author/artist reaches too far from the given prototype/schema set in their innovation they risk losing their audience. And here it is usually the author/director's built-in sense of what "feels right" that helps govern how far he or she can innovate, how far he or she can push the reader to re-form given prototypes and schemas.

Clearly, when we read and/or create works of fiction much happens, including an intensification of the real world in its reframing of our perspective. This experience—which moves us back and forth between the aesthetic reframing and the reference to reality (which, while distinct, do coexist)—leads to a further question: To what degree can reading works of fiction affect us in a lasting way? As noted, authors can use certain techniques to generate deep empathetic ties with characters that can cause us to react in different ways. I think of my uncontrolled outbursts of laughter while reading Zadie Smith's *White Teeth* in a cafe. But these reactions are usually short-lived. What happens once I've turned the last page of *White Teeth*—a book that not only draws one inside its story, but complicates how issues of race, class, and gender inflect and transform notions of what it means to be living in late-1980s London? The same could be asked of how the injustices of slavery represented in Toni Morrison's *Beloved* affect me and other readers? Or how the rape of a white woman by black South Africans in J. M. Coetzee's *Disgrace* does or does not intensify our sense of the value of human life? What happens to our sense of right and wrong after we've finished reading such books and entered the real world once again? Do we now see the world differently and a have different sense of right and wrong? Does this lead to some sort of action?

John Horton and Andrea T. Baumeister write that works of fiction "best represent the complexities of political experience and the open-texture and necessarily incomplete character of real political arguments"

(13). They consider the lifelike representations in works of fiction as powerful shapers of the readers' ethics and ideals. Such a turn becomes especially forceful in postcolonial approaches to literary analysis. Ramu Nagappan declares in *Suffering and South Asian Narratives,* for example, "We must not be so squeamish as to ignore the ethical underpinnings of our work" (4). Thus in Nagappan's analysis of Amitav Ghosh, Rohinton Mistry, and Salman Rushdie, showing how they "bring their audiences face to face with their own responsibility for social good" (5), we must do more then "gesture toward" (21) other disciplines if we are to foster an "important dialogue about injustice and cultural loss" (21). Finally, as Daniel Schwartz sums up, we must be attuned to the fact that "texts demand ethical responses from their readers in part because *saying* always has an ethical dimension *and* because *we* are our values, and we never take a moral holiday from our values" ("A Humanistic Ethics of Reading" 5). The basis of ethical criticism for Schwartz is this sense of a "strong connection between art and life" (5) along with his belief that when we enter other worlds and lives beyond our own, we gain a heightened understanding of the world.[10]

The work of Martha Nussbaum is another case in point. In Nussbaum we see a placing of value in literature not only in its nuanced, complex rendering of life, but also in that we spend so much time deliberating and debating the role of literature. Ethical and moral deliberations as to literature's role in the world themselves become grounds for its importance—especially vis-à-vis our everyday civic practices. In *Poetic Justice,* for example, Nussbaum traces the long history of literary debate and inquiry back to classical Greece to demonstrate how fictional works have served as the unifying center for community: the sound board for individuals to question norms of conformity, resistance, and the ethical conceptualization of society. More specifically, fictional works echo and shape the sense of ourselves as "judicious spectators" formed by our ability to enter into and vicariously experience the imagined lives of others—"the concrete ways in which people different from oneself grapple with disadvantage"(30)—and thus have the potential to shape our ethical attitudes toward human life.[11] And this forming of ethical thought Nussbaum reserves for literature because of its plasticity of form, which provides a richer understanding of life and its complexities.

Perhaps, however, the picture is a little more complicated. First, Nussbaum's idea of literature doesn't fully acknowledge how authors often employ a variety of techniques whereby the story and its characters conflict with the narrator's worldview, say, and thus that present readers with a reality that is not so clearly ethically directed. Second, fictional works lay out readerly contracts that, if we agree and sign and then enter its worlds, don't guarantee that we will encounter an ethical and/or moral didacticism.[12] This does not mean, of course, that we cannot learn from reading fictional works, only that these are not the sole examples of fiction's "truths" and that therefore it doesn't provide some privileged access to values based on consensus and customs (evaluative ethics) and/or ideologies (Judeo-Christian moralism that divinely ordains right from wrong). Third, reading a novel like *White Teeth* doesn't necessarily mean that one will change and/or give up one's identity. Fourth, not all good readers necessarily make for good judges or lawyers—or even political leaders. As Horton perceptively declares, "One can be a highly discriminating reader of such texts while being morally shallow and corrupt. . . . one can be a person of considerable moral sensitivity and depth without having the literary skills to fully comprehend the refined and elaborate prose of Proust or late James" (89). So it would seem upon second glance that perhaps there is no clear-cut link between one's literariness and being, say, a good person.[13]

While we can't point to specific links between novels read and ethics formed, we do know instinctively that literature can and does engage our ethical evaluative practices. Indeed, Hogan takes a step back to assess the function of our everyday ethical evaluations and how a sense of "ethical excellence" functions as a "sort of norm against which we evaluate our goals and actions that lead to the achievement of those goals" (*Mind and Its Stories* 132). Identifying our ambition as a way to achieve happiness (social fulfillment), we learn that the very genres an author employs as containers of their stories (heroic, romantic, tragic, for example) are linked to this cross-culturally shared ethical evaluative process.[14] Following the principle of ethical evaluation and its hierarchy (happiness at the top), this also determines how we relate—or not—to characters: our sympathy can either gravitate toward the hero, the victim, or even the villain.

It makes a certain amount of sense that literature matters not so much in how it shapes our ethical principles and/or moral concerns directly, but in how an author plays with prototypes and schemas of behavior— for example, bravery and defiance in protecting one's group, compassion, even "the sustaining emotion of love" (136)—that work to enhance or to diminish the pull toward the attainment of happiness and social and individual freedom. But content is only one of many ingredients in literature that matter; if it were the only one, then there would be no difference between entering the ethically tortured and upside-down world of *Crime and Punishment*—Raskolnikov murders a neighboring pawnbroker, is troubled psychologically by his action, and falls in love with a prostitute—and a *soap opera* melodrama. That is, in the quest to understand why literature matters, one must include an exploration of content and form as well as of the text's pragmatic effect; of both its rhetorical formal features as well as its contextual features that include the reader's and author's cognitive and emotive engagement in the consuming and creating of the fiction. So here we have to go beyond that which fills up content.

To clarify, let me use the example of the painter; like the author, who employs sentences, tenses, points of view, the painter follows a syntax and grammar to combine colors and to create textures, dimensions, and so on as governed by the medium; this with a will to style aimed to engage its audience in specific ways. Along with this syntax and semantics of the painting there's a pragmatic dimension: this huge sphere of emotions, reflections, thoughts (cognitive and emotive mechanisms) set in motion by the painting, and these are "willed" in the sense that the artist knows he or she wants certain reactions and engagements. Of course, not all such reactions happen as the artist intends. When the Impressionists first showed their work, the art world turned up its nose with indignation; when Picasso made his move into cubism, many said that their child could draw better. Most artists know this, but instead of caving in to what the viewers are already accustomed to seeing, what they do is persist and educate the sight faculties of the viewers to make them *see* the paintings properly. We see the same will in literature. And in fact, it is the degree of the presence of this will to style that, in my opinion, makes the difference between a Barbara Cartland novel and *Crime and Punishment*—the latter teaches the reader how to read it, and the former simply tells a story. So, the question of why literature matters must include this important contextual dimension of how the degree of the presence of the will to style of an author carves out and fashions material to guide the reader's cognitive and emotional reactions and engagements—and obtain along with this (and to varying degrees) a lasting *permanence* in the reader's memory.

Before concluding this chapter, I'd like to return to a more abstract and general concept: our cross-cultural "fiction-making" ability that spins out of a more basic and primal "world-making" capacity. Let me distinguish the two. Our survival as a species does not rely on our fiction-making capacity and its expression in verbal and visual art generally. If all our made cultural objects—literature, buildings, art, music, and the like—were destroyed tomorrow—provided our species wasn't entirely wiped out—we would still survive as a species. However, our survival does rely fundamentally on our universal capacity for "worldmaking"—a term coined in the 1950s by the American logical positivist philosopher Nelson Goodman and adopted by scholars like Paul Hernadi. World-making is not to be associated at all with social constructionism, but rather, as Hernadi writes, with "literature's evolutionary reasons for being [that] presupposes that the social, the natural, and the personal are intertwined dimensions of being human" (23). Much like Karl Marx's conception of working society as being simultaneously natural, social, and personal, our world-making capacity points to how we evolved through work: that man is an animal and a part of nature, but through work has transformed all of nature. Hence, Hernadi's worldmaking is neither ahistorical nor a total abstraction of what is fundamental to human beings: where we came from, the process of production within and transformation of nature and thus the transformation of the individual and humankind. This said, while we are "higher-minded" organisms constituted biologically by the total working of our cognitive and affective processes—the neuronal, synaptic, and biochemical activities that allow for the selection, storing, and retrieval of memory and emotion—we are also capable of reflecting on all aspects of nature as well as of modifying all of nature that surround us. That is to say, we evolve through processes of self-generation—one part of our nature—that produce what we call society and culture. So, just as the spider is inseparable from its web (the mode of existence that allows it to reproduce and eat and continue living) so, too, do we have to spin out culture and society to live: literature is one such by-product.

Our world-making capacity, which is expressed in our ability to inhabit holographically a past and a future in the present through mime, pictograph, and story, has had a positive influence in the evolution of protohuman and *Homo sapiens sapiens*. On the other hand, our fiction-making capacity is a coevolutionary function[15] that assumes many different forms: from painting to mime to novels. It has evolved over time into a hardwired part of our cognitive architecture and perceptual equipment; there are cognitive and emotive processes involved in fiction making: imaging and relaying to others in the present a past and future world. I don't mean to propose that we follow Gilles Fauconnier's model of the mind as literary mind (also seen later in Mark Turner's work) or

Lakoff's and Jackson's notion of embodied metaphors (the dominant shaper of the way we live)—all of which ultimately subordinate the study of literature to speculations about the mind.[16] Rather, I propose that we need to understand how fictional works are products of our fiction-making capacity that require a more basic world-making capacity and thus the full functioning of the mind's cognitive and empathetic processes.

This leads to issues of temporality. Works of fiction involve readers and authors in time: the present tense of the reading (and of the author's writing) that takes us back into a past and also proximate future (both as a reader's experience and also as the author's imagining of a future readership). Of course, to be able to enter into time-past and time-future in the present (not just of reading, but of listening or watching, as in the case of mime), we must have the cognitive capacity to do so; and, likewise an author/teller/performer must also know what to use to cue, prime, and trigger cognitive and emotive responses in the audience. Just as an author/teller/performer might rehearse his or her lines/phrasings to experience how they *feel*—how they cue, prime, and trigger memories and their associative emotions—so too do they play with time (in the more sophisticated use of flashforwards and flashbacks, for example) to engage audiences.

Porter Abbott insightfully draws from hypotheses made concerning man and language in the Upper Paleolithic era. In "The Evolutionary Origins of the Storied Mind" he proposes that the presence of mime is evidence that there was narrative before language. This leads to several important insights. If "story" is defined as a succession of events involving existents (as per the classical definition), then mime is an example of narrative prelanguage; it requires neither language nor a narrator (discourse). This also sheds light on the thought/language problem. It is true that even if one did not have thought as a phenomenon organized in language—if language did not exist, yet thought did—one would still use a means of communication—mime—to ensure one's survival. Our prelanguage ancestors (*Homo erectus*) could mime that an animal was about to attack, and so they had an evolutionary edge over other species. And this miming could be an enactment: not the telling of what was happening in the present, but of a past and/or a future possible occurrence of an animal attack. That is, the mime is a narrative with a succession of events involving existents, but *sans* language.

Our ability to inhabit in the present a past and a future allowed for the evolution of a new temporal and spatial mode of meta-awareness.

With storytelling—mime or otherwise—we begin to see the development of a distinction between tenses: past (what saw), present (what enacting), and future (the miming of an imminent predator attack).[17] This "living within time" (250) marks the evolutionary moment when we became aware through storytelling of our reality in ways that distinguished us from (as far as we know today) other animals. Abbott proposes that "narrative time is constructed time according to creatural priorities" (250). His hypothesis gets us closer to understanding how tense is central to narrative. The telling of a story in the present that recalls the past (as being in the present moment of telling) that imagines a future that does not exist. In this present moment of telling—or miming—communication creates community as both teller/performer and listener/audience inhabit a present that involves an imagined past and future.

Although we can't locate exactly when language first appeared, we do know that language allowed for the infinite multiplication of expressions of narrative enactment. Language is especially suited to this, as it is an extremely flexible form of communication. Chomsky shows that a finite set of elements can give rise to an infinite number of combinations. Moreover, as Abbott advances in his hypothesis, language and narrative opened up the possibility for us to organize time according to our own free will and not according to dictates of nature (the inhabiting of only a present tense) and that eventually our evolution of more sophisticated forms of storytelling (verbal and visual) allowed for the splitting of narrative into a double chronology: story and discourse. Written storytelling allowed for new markers to appear that allowed audiences and readers to inhabit multiply-layered temporalities as the story unfolds. This, of course, helps us understand better why an author or director can manipulate narrative point of view, lighting, diegetic sound, and so on not only to tell a story, but to engage audiences and readers on a number of different levels.

Our "living within time" radically altered our relationship to the world: not only as a way for us to communicate experiences, but as a means for us and others to inhabit different temporal spaces simultaneously. Our species was no longer caught in an eternal present: this, of course, opened the door for us to evolve cognitive capacities for speculating a future. Our species' specific capacity to situate ourselves in time and to communicate through story (visual and/or verbal) and therefore connect to the world in chronological terms implies necessarily also the added enormous advantage of being able to operate in the world according to the "fictional mode" and the "scientific mode." Moreover, our faculty to imagine objects in time and spaces not of our direct experience in the present is the basis of our ability to imagine—and share with others—scientific hypotheses: imagine cause and effect before actually doing the experiment. Just as time opens the possibility of fiction—increasingly complicated as we move from mime to oral to written storytelling modes—so too does this reflect a like faculty at work when we explore through scientific means our reality by imagining all sorts of possibilities in reality.

CONCLUDING REMARKS

In closing, let me return briefly to Farrell's *Why Does Literature Matter?*, which identifies literature's raison d'etre as essentially to provide readers with a means and a forum for reflecting more wisely and more fully on the self and on the world we happen to inhabit. Thus, according to Farrell, authors like Virginia Woolf and James Joyce, Dante and Shakespeare, Marcel Proust and Samuel Beckett, to name a few in what would necessarily be a very long list, come to be singled out because their writings successfully and artfully portray those "subtle and hard-to-grasp patterns that make human relationships what they are" (12). Their works have become an essential part of a durable world canon because, as Farrell states, like all "exceptional works of literature," they "require us to form a more complicated selfhood" (152). Resisting the "postmodern thinning out of the social world" (152–153), Farrell considers that, by delving deeply into the "self-formation" of characters or by engaging with the depths of their "rituals of self-undermining" (240), the reader reaches a perspective (the "stance" designed by the author) that will allow him or her to move self-reflexively inward as well as outward, each time seeing himself or herself and the world in new, richer ways. When this happens, literature has accomplished its proper task.

Now, the nature of the enterprise Farrell pursues in this quest relies on a definition of literature generally characterized as (1) a body of writing in any language of the world that has been given a metered or an unmetered form (verse or prose or a mixture of both); (2) arranged in so-called genres and subgenres or in any of their various combinations (fiction, drama, and poetry; novel, long story, short story, tragedy, comedy, tragicomedy, and melodrama; essay, biography, and autobiography, to mention the most common classifications); and (3) preserved, valued, and deemed worthy of study. These three factors, together or in isolation,

are at the source of the many complex kinds of expectations and gratifi-
cations experienced by the reader.

I imagine everyone would agree that reading literature matters above
all because it is fun, that is, because it engages the imagination and sets
off many sorts of emotional and cognitive reactions that are lively and
pleasurable, at the same time that it does not demand any specific action
or impose any kind of more or less forced behavior. This said, one may
ascribe importance to literature on many grounds. Farrell, for example,
underlines those features of literature that may heighten our perceptions,
our experience, and our knowledge of the world and other humans,
through formal and thematic means that make reading and rereading
a uniquely gratifying and enlightening activity. (This is a position that
I myself propose in my earlier book, *Postethnic Narrative Criticism.*) He
also insists on the relevance of literature as an imaginative exploration of
worldviews, circumstances, and psychological characters. And he never
loses sight of the aesthetic devices (what I have been calling the will to
style) that are brought into play each time in a unique way in order to
create a significant and lasting work.

On the other hand, many people consider that literature matters because it "reflects" an epoch or a people or a certain way of perceiving the
world in a particular circumstance. Others restrict this assumed mirroring effect of literature to certain demographic groups considered politically or socially significant within a population. The notions of Orientalism, postcolonialism, nation building through literature, ethnic identity
and gender as literary constructs as well as many others still circulating
in academia are based on this idea that literature somehow not only represents (and distorts) reality but creates it. Literature in this case is given
the tremendous power once assigned to social classes and to the state
and its institutions. It becomes the Gnostic Demiurge, the creator and
controller of the material world. It is turned also into the only remaining instrument of critique, at least in the minds of those who hold such
notions.

First, as discussed above, I do consider one fiction to be better than
another because it has a greater power to transform us. Some authors
more than others use the fictional ingredients in their will to style to
leave lasting memories in our minds. Second, as I discussed earlier, the
most salient feature of literature is that it is fictional. As fiction, it implies a certain contract with the reader and implies therefore a certain
attitude on the part of both author and reader and thus a specific intentionality: you are to read it as fiction, not as nonfiction. This leads us

to the point made about authors. Authors are flesh-and-blood readers, so in writing stories they have in mind not the idiosyncrasies of every individual reader, but a sense of how their finite number of techniques (characterization, mise-en-scène, style, mood, temporality, point of view, for example) will trigger specific responses in themselves as readers and thus in readers generally. It is this contextual or worldly dimension that directs us to those insights made in other fields of inquiry, like cognitive science.

Indeed, this can prove a powerful tool in our exploration of why literature matters. As Hogan says, cognitive science is itself a research program, one that "has connections with virtually every discipline in the modern university" (*Cognitive Science* 29). Knowledge of our universal capacity for memory (working memory and deep memory) and its attendant emotions is central to understanding how we read fiction. Reading fiction, for instance, involves "an incorporation of primed memories," and these memories "are the source of the reader's emotive reaction to the work" (*Cognitive Science* 160). Hogan reconstructs "the basic algorithmic sequence" of this complex phenomenon in the following way. Just as we don't really remember the past but rather "reconstruct it—often in a way that reflects our present concerns as much as our past experience" (*Cognitive Science* 161)—so, too, our working memory synthesizes from "fragmentary observations" (162) a coherent sense of scenes, characters, and events. Of course, this also means that a given author can reorganize time (and space) in ways that engage our minds in interesting and challenging new ways. For example, when we encounter a murder mystery "much of our cognitive effort is a matter of placing events in their proper order"; conversely, when we encounter the typical Hollywood film the "story is presented in its actual temporal sequence" (123). This also means that an author or director can use certain details (and not others) in a mise-en-scène to describe a particular space around human acts (live, walk, swim, fly, sleep). Because we share a universal capacity to imagine other times and spaces not present in the here and now, authors and filmmakers can resequence time and warp spaces both to stimulate our imaginations and to transform generic preconceptions. Our engagement with verbal and visual art is not just a matter of puzzling out and imagining spatial and temporal spaces; it is also a matter of how a given film or fictional narrative triggers our capacity to empathize. As Hogan discusses, our ability to feel happiness, anger, disgust, fear, and sadness (directly and vicariously) is so powerful that such emotions can override reasoning. For instance, if we are about to be attacked, we don't contemplate running, we simply run, and we experience this same process when watching a film or reading a novel.

Of course, because our minds are organized hierarchically, while we respond to the moods and/or actions of others (simulated or not), we share the universal capacity to *know* that we are reacting in such and such a way. We can become absolutely invested in a story because we feel (sometimes conflicting emotions) for a character and at the same time think beyond the character's direct experiences; we can simultaneously feel sad and angry as well as formulate positive outcomes for the character. Our capacity for emotion is a key ingredient in both our engagement and creation of verbal, aural, and visual art.

We have to keep in mind, however, that like any of the turns (ethnic, ethical, biological, aesthetic, interdisciplinary, and so on), turning to cognitive science in the study of literature will only get us closer to understanding why literature matters if it is considered as one tool of many that we may or may not use depending on what a given narrative asks of us. It is one tool among many that can help further our knowledge of why fiction making (chirographic, gestural, and/or oral) matters cross-culturally to engage audiences (readers, listeners, and viewers). To know well all the taxonomic compartments of this toolbox (biological, cognitive, linguistic, narratological, and so on) can help us better understand that the many elements that make up literature depend on and can potentially modify other elements. This can further our knowledge of how literature works and why it matters and also allow us to better understand the way verbal, aural, and visual artists use certain techniques to transform everyday experiences (how we remember, emote, experience, interpret) into memorable aesthetic activities. Since we all share the same mental and cognitive architecture, we can build a shareable knowledge base that will clarify how authors worldwide invent certain characters; how they use certain details to prime and activate memories; how we as readers infer cause and effect from such details; how we respond emotionally to certain narrative techniques; and how we create empathetic bridges with both characters and those who exist outside of the world of fiction.

In the study of fiction, we need to keep in mind always this worldly dimension of fiction: that the reader and author share common faculties (language, memory, emotion, and so on) and that within the domain of fiction it includes potentially all existing and possible worlds. That nothing human is alien to fiction, so both in form and in content fiction can be about everything and anything and can be materialized and/or expressed in the most surprising and unexpected ways. Think of Cortázar's *Cronopios y Famas,* in which he transforms a manual for using a toaster or the act of winding a watch into stories that engage us and leave a permanent trace in our memories; think also of film adaptations of Shakespeare like Gavin Bedford's *Street King,* in which the story of Richard III radically mutates and transforms into Chicano street gangs in East LA. So, an approach to why fiction matters must consider that fictionality in all its forms (film, theater, novel, short story, and so on) will incorporate all the useful elements that we can identify using the tools of narratology (the syntax of point of view, time shifts, mood, and so on); it must also consider, as do those who ascribe to the possible worlds theory, that fiction is always tautological because it is necessarily true or false only within its diegetical worlds; that is, questions of its truth or falsity come from within the fictional world itself.

Finally, to all this we must necessarily add the dimension of the real, historical, biographical author and reader. This means that we consider not only how the will to style creates a gestalt of the "implied author" and "implied reader," but also how flesh-and-blood authors transform the everyday activities and events in the world we inhabit into objects that engage us in new and interesting ways. Moreover, it is to see how authors look beyond the atomized self and reach into a world that we have collectively been radically transforming and that has been, in turn, transforming us.

FOURTEEN

INTERPRETATION, INTERDISCIPLINARITY, AND THE PEOPLE

INTRODUCTION

In response to a conference on the role of theory in society held at the University of Chicago on April 11, 2003, the *New York Times* reporter Emily Eakin concluded, "These are uncertain times for literary scholars. The era of big theory is over. The grand paradigms that swept through humanities departments in the 20th century—psychoanalysis, structuralism, Marxism, deconstruction, post-colonialism—have lost favor or been abandoned. Money is tight. And the leftist politics with which literary theorists have traditionally been associated have taken a beating" (9).[1] In this chapter I look at how several scholars have responded to this general sense of a crisis in theory: what it can and can't do in the world at large. I first reflect on the Modern Language Association's (MLA) 2004 publication of its journal *Profession*—a "report from the field"—call to interdisciplinarity and then consider the work of John McGowan, specifically *Democracy's Children*. I keep centrally in mind the following question: What is the role of teaching, writing, and theorizing in and out of the classroom?

The crisis in the humanities springs not only from a sense that theory has failed to make the world a better place, but also from a material fact: the massive monetary cutbacks seen by literature departments and others in the humanities. As the MLA report from the field in *Profession* (2004) clearly shows, when an increasingly shrinking pie is being divvied up, it's the humanities that gets the crumbs. Hence the sounding of the clarion call to establish an interdisciplinarity in English. In their essay "Engaging in the Humanities" Jonathan Goldberg and Cathy Davidson, both directors of interdisciplinary institutes, see the humanities playing a central role in the university and society that is otherwise ignored by both. The humanities is "broadly and flexibly" defined to include traditional departments, ethnic, gender, and area/global studies as well as all the arts, theoretical social sciences, "policy studies, legal theory, science, technology, and information studies" (43). While the humanities does not produce the discoveries that one finds in the hard sciences, it does produce "insight, analysis, logic, speculation, historical knowledge, linguistic mastery, geographic precision, aesthetic production, and complex religious understanding" (44). For Goldberg and Davidson, that the central role the humanities plays in the university isn't recognized is either because of a lack of self-advertising or because it doesn't produce knowledge in the same quantifiable way as the sciences.

Whatever the reason (and I disagree with the two suggested) the solution lies in a turn to interdisciplinarity. Goldberg and Davidson propose a model of interdisciplinarity that is, they write,

> problem- or issue-based rather than field-specific. It also tends to be less nation- or area-centered than had been traditional in many humanistic fields and more concerned with contact; the flow of ideas; and cultural intersection, which are an intellectual by-product of the globalization that has transformed the humanities in unexpected ways. (45)

Goldberg and Davidson, however, point to a double bind that faces those who make the interdisciplinary turn: almost all hiring in the humanities takes place within discipline-bound departments: English, philosophy, Romance languages, and so on. It is extremely unusual for a university to hire someone across the traditional divisions of the departments. Thus, the turn to interdisciplinarity allows us to address, as Goldberg and Davidson state, "large and complex problems that are not susceptible to analysis (or solution) from a single perspective" (55). The other essays collected in *Profession* (2004) offer several specific models for repackaging our discipline, including collaborative teaching with economists, anthropologists, cognitive scientists, for example, of courses that would encourage the learning of "multiple methodologies" as well as increase the numbers of students (administrations love metrics) taking courses in the humanities (54).

One way or another, the scholars in MLA's *Profession* (2004) consider that those teaching in the humanities should figure out new ways to repackage and sell their disciplines; English professors need to package it as something essential for all professions, trades, and walks of life. The better we package and advertise ourselves, the better chance we have to sell—and thus save—our careers.

In this interdisciplinary repackaging, we see scholars (wittingly or not) like McGowan aiming to show how the teaching and theorizing about literature can make democratic society. In *Democracy's Children: Intellectuals and the Rise of Cultural Politics* McGowan asks, What is the role of intellectual work in and outside the classroom? Can work in the classroom become a model of social democracy? What is the function of literary interpretation? Can it transform minds and therefore direct political action?

To answer these necessary and important questions, McGowan attempts to yoke a humanist belief in universals—to know those facts that make our world unjust and that are necessary for us to fight for true democracy—with a belief that reality is indeterminate and socially constructed. He considers the intellectual a "cultural worker" who has the power to transform the minds of students through literary analysis and, therefore, ultimately to transform the psyche of the body politic. Yet, the cultural worker must also acknowledge history's reminder of a material reality of the "people on the bottom," who know that "they are being screwed" and that "the people on top know they are screwing them" (90). According to McGowan, the cultural worker, then, must realize that, he continues, "resistance to change isn't psychological, a matter of false consciousness or subject formation; it is simply the power of the powerful to maintain arrangements that suit them" (90). It is clear that McGowan believes that to level the socioeconomic playing field by making education and freedom of expression an equal right for all (his primary goals) requires the locating of real sites of power to make visible real targets for social transformation. (At one point even, he is overtly critical of Foucault's anarchistic model of power.) He is weary of poststructuralist theorists who consider the subject and world to be discursive constructs and so claim that decoding texts and symbols will radically alter our world; far from leading to the active shaping of society, McGowan holds, such practice leads to a place of absolute political apathy.

In spite of this skepticism, McGowan believes that if humans work in and through language, then decoding how we work and think within language will lead to new ways of interpreting and understanding the world. It will augment the type of social transformation that takes place by real people. He acknowledges that real people en masse are what bring about social change, mentioning, for example, the civil rights movement.

However, because social injustices continue to exist, McGowan believes that a kind of intellectual cultural work *is* necessary for the realization of "full racial equality and harmony" (24). As such, his criticism of the irrational aspects of poststructuralist theory—the indeterminacy of the sign coupled with a belief in a folkish model of talk therapy—and his grounding of his own political pursuits in the tangible facts that make up reality, slide into a theorizing of social change realized only in the decoding of cultural processes of representation.

In his interdisciplinary turn, he attempts to straddle a constructivist and positivist position, identifying a model of "pragmatic pluralism." Accordingly, as a pragmatic pluralist, what the intellectual/professor does in the classroom has consequences in the world beyond its walls precisely because such classroom discussions articulate, he writes, "concepts, commitments, and visions that legitimate and/or contest the way we live now" (3). Intentionally interdisciplinary and eclectic, his pragmatic pluralism aims to show how "relationships are contingent and hence to be understood as the product of human sense-making" (140) and to understand that all human activities make sense through "performative articulations" (141). To enact this bimodal process is to subvert interpretive paradigms dictated by "elite groups," university officials, and gate-keeping theorists. He thus aims to extend "democratic practices into social sites (the classroom, the workplace) where they are often deemed inappropriate" (6). The classroom becomes a space of "dearticulation" par excellence that enables "negotiations, compromises, arguments, and procedural steps [that will lead to] collective decisions" (267). McGowan's classroom, then, serves as the egalitarian and collective space where "differences and interdependencies" (6) are valued and where the proceedings will help pave the way for the making of a democratic nation-state.

McGowan's interdisciplinary turn ("pragmatic pluralism") is relativism in another guise. Namely, it is another way of stating that what we know of the world and ourselves is contingent on theories that are themselves contingent on other theories. This becomes especially apparent when he identifies "the principle of democratic egalitarianism" (264) as culturally and historically constituted and not a transcendent truth. Here, for example, he states, that a "humanist society can make decisions in the absence of truth" (264). His formulation is tautological. It suggests that we can transform an empirically verifiable reality with tools and information that aren't verifiable and whose meaning is relational and contingent. In *Politics of Interpretation*, Patrick Colm Hogan clarifies, "If I see something as an orange, this has nothing to do with essences, but means only that I construe certain experiences in relation to a schematic hierarchy and in the context of present interests and practices" (61). What Hogan exemplifies is that there is no question of the presence or absence of the orange—in the sense of *essential* presence or absence—but only one of interest, in this case, in that the orange is perceived as a result of verifiable biological and cognitive mechanisms. Our perception of things is, as Hogan clarifies,

> partially accurate and partially inaccurate understandings of the world. They are based upon our previous understandings, including those codified in our linguistic competence, but they are not confined to these. And their accuracy is a matter of the way relevant intentionally discriminated things happen to be, and not the way supposedly essentially discriminated things are (or are necessarily). (61)

Namely, the orange, like all things that make up reality, provides that object that can generate common grounds of interest and information based on empirically verifiable evidence.

To put it more plainly, for McGowan to even be able to state that truth/fact is socially constituted relies on the rules of language that are based on shared understanding of grammar, syntax, and semantics. If there was an absence of truth and empirically verifiable reality, real social change could never happen; it would mean that because I was born in Mexico and raised Chicano my brain works differently from that of Anglos born and raised in the United States and therefore my reason— thought, language, and algorithmic process—operates differently from that of others in the United States. In other words, if we were all social constructs, then no communication could take place between intellectual and worker, and thus no collectivities could be formed for political activism. In such a relationally contingent world, no action would be possible to realize a shared goal of making a truly democratic nation-state. To return to the point made above about the orange. It is good enough that we perceive and verify things and their effects in the world. Claiming that knowledge is relative and that objects and subjects are socially constituted only muddies the water in our attempts to realize the true ideals of democracy.

To summarize thus far. In his version of the interdisciplinary turn, McGowan puts forward arguments that favor the empirical verification of facts—the pragmatic/humanist element—and simultaneously argues that "we should consider the symbolics of power" (98)—the pluralism element.

What can we untangle and salvage from McGowan's formulation? First, as long as we try to hold together contradictory positions (empirical and social constructivist), we will always find ourselves straddling an unbridgeable gap—or moving toward a dead end. Second, it leads us to see if we might be able to answer more satisfyingly questions posed about the role of the teacher-researcher generally.

We know from experience that reading and interpreting literature can open eyes to different ways of existing in the world; we know we can gain something in the process of reading and interpreting a novel—our experience of an Other—even when we are fully aware of its fictionality. However, we must ask, is it really possible for our work as scholars and teachers of literature to influence and single-handedly transform the values and attitudes of the many millions of people required for real social transformation? Can we tell our students that the work done in the classroom in analyzing, say, Ana Castillo's *So Far from God,* is a form of political activism? And can we really liken the place of the classroom to a democratic space where legislation and policy take place?

First, I ask the question, What is our function as teachers of literature? Should we shun a single disciplinary method—one that fears interdisciplinarity—as McGowan suggests in his formulation of a pragmatic pluralism, to enact egalitarian ideals? Does such a single disciplinary method in the classroom lead us, as McGowan suggests, to a state of "rigor mortis" (95)?

Disciplinarity and method are in the air we breathe. Every part of our daily survival as *Homo sapiens sapiens* requires the teaching, learning, and practicing of method within the constraints of disciplines. We go to school where different disciplines determine how we learn to read, write, and use our algorithmic skills. We need to learn rules in and out of the classroom—words in a certain order and hierarchy within this order—to communicate; carpenters learn which tools to use and in what particular order to build houses for shelter; architects and engineers follow methods of designing such structures; pilots learn which instruments to use and in what order to fly us safely through the skies. Even the most randomly conceived of cultural forms requires method. I think of avant-garde art. Here, the artist must choose from a limited number of colors that the eye can perceive (determined by cognitive and biological constraints) and the order in which he or she applies the pigments; in music, there is the order and constraint of time. Our ear and brain can't absorb Haydn's symphony all at once, as in the visual arts, where one can perceive the whole in an instant, and so notes unfold as a sequence within time. And the list could go on ad infinitum.

Creation that involves any kind of conception or innovation thus has to follow a method. If we pause to think about this, we realize that it is precisely in the learning of method, with its respectively defined disciplinary parameters, that we advance our knowledge about the things and activities that fill our world. (To learn to frame a wall does not require the learning of the method for flying an airplane, for example.) Indeed, all the minutiae of our everyday existence entail the teaching, learning, and practicing of disciplinary-specific method.

Even if we were to take McGowan's method-as-mortis model as a critique of scholarly work that fears the interdisciplinary, we run into problems. While I'm all for learning what we can from other disciplines— recent advances in cognitive science, linguistics, and evolutionary biology certainly shed new light on our understanding of how literature works—the knowledge in each discipline is produced precisely through the use of method. Each field of inquiry is productive and even predictive precisely because it limits the number of directions it pursues. For example, the physicist follows a certain method when formulating a hypothesis, knowing that if the hypothesis is to lead to any tangible results, it must have limits. Certainly, these limits are not fixed for all eternity. However, whether in the field of science or in the study of literature, we need to impose limits to *what* we intend to investigate or argue, and we need method to explore this *what*. In literature there is no limit to what can be imagined by a writer, and thus we could discuss and imagine an infinite number of elements that make up fiction. Literature—like all phenomena that make up our culture—is the product of complex human beings and therefore is as limitless as we are. This doesn't mean, however, that when writing, interpreting, and/or teaching literature we should follow no method with no limits. Just as we need to employ method, we also need to reduce the number of elements and questions to formulate a hypothesis that might potentially lead to an explanation of the text at hand. If done well, bounded inquiry based on rational method (what Hogan identifies as an "empirical poetics") can have great predictive power. More precisely, it is the reduction of the number of concepts explored in, say, narratology that can explain an unlimited number of literary phenomena: concept of voice, point of view, etc. Of course, narratology is not the only method, but it does have, as in Gérard Genette's work, great explanatory power.

Of course, we shouldn't impose limits that stifle scholarly and creative exploration. Rather, we impose limits in order to build on and revise what we know of literature—and the world generally. If there is no method and no limit, then anything is permissible, and whatever we say or argue has no particular importance. For example, sociolinguistics (or "pragmatic linguistics") eventually ran into a dead end because, ironically, its field of inquiry had no boundaries. Language is a very complex phenomenon and is immediately associated with millions of human activities and behaviors that are difficult to systematize. Because the terrain was too large, the predictive capacity of sociolinguistics turned out to be worthless. (Chomsky realized that for linguistics to have any predictive power, it must follow the scientific principle of reduction and abstraction. Hence, by reducing the number of linguistic features that appear in all languages, he arrived at his formulation of a "universal grammar.") That is to say, if nothing is ruled out in the large field of culture (everything that is the product of humans' activity), then culture is everything and therefore as a field of study it is nothing. Just as we must have method to survive, we must also set limits to our field of inquiry or else we simply produce *flatus voci.*

As scholars of literature, we can use method to understand better what the critics *make.* What we make are hypotheses based on theories, analysis, and arguments that can be furthered by reaching out to other fields that use the same empirical method to arrive at their own conclusions. As teachers of literature, we need to provide students with the methods they need to sort the seeds from the pulp. Teaching students that eclecticism is better than rigorous method, or that reduction is to destructively essentialize, or that subjects and the world are discursively constructed moves us away from the means by which we can build, verify, refute, and revise our understanding of how literature works.

Method is hardly a path, then, that leads to *rigor mortis.* Indeed, method (with its disciplinary limits and tools to test hypotheses) allows us to formulate within specified boundaries and limits a number of elements that make up a teachable system that can be passed on as a tool for the next generation of scholars to learn, revise, and build upon anew. In the absence of limits to literary exploration, we can conjecture endlessly because all is contingent and arbitrary. As literary scholars, we should be affirming the place of disciplinary method in opening up the possibility for exploratory advancement. Without this sense of disciplinary-bound methods we have a restricting limitlessness.

For McGowan, the classroom should be seen as a democratic space in which interdisciplinary teaching fosters a plurality of voices, tastes, and opinions. The classroom is the last frontier where tolerance for "differences and interdependencies (of various kinds)" (6) can flourish in an otherwise disciplinary-bound university setting. In this schema, to teach without method and to diffuse authority is to further the goals of democracy. The teacher who ascribes to no single disciplinary approach and/or method will awaken "new identities" in the "joining of desire to ideals, of identities with public, cultural form" (72–73).

If authority is everywhere, then it is nowhere. There must be an identifiable center of authority in the classroom that imposes useful limits and rules as required by its respective disciplinary methodological contours in order for students to learn and become independent thinkers. The teacher has trained for a certain amount of time (sometimes years and years) and has acquired a knowledge of things that the students do not have simply because they have not yet devoted as much time and energy to learning as the teacher.

What does this mean? It means that the teacher has a series of tasks and has to be qualified to introduce concepts and categories and tools to deal with the verifiable elements that constitute his or her particular discipline. To suggest that power in the classroom is everywhere follows a belief that power is everywhere. This is necessary, of course, if one believes that we can enact resistance and political intervention through language and cultural phenomena. However, not only does it participate in a formulation of power that dislocates and permanently erases it from real sites—the State apparatus of the real ruling class and the owners of the means of production that assert real power through executive, legislative, and judicial institutions—but it dangerously leads to the type of complacency McGowan himself objects to: academics comfortably situated in their corner of the world destabilizing the symbolic while real oppression and exploitation of real people continue.

An interdisciplinary approach that ultimately provides no method for students to follow will not lead to the clear-sighted thinking necessary to see things as they are outside the classroom, where real political activism takes place.[2] This is why we teach methods and approaches appropriate to the study of literature. We do so to show how, for example, an author like Ana Castillo, John Rechy, or Arturo Islas (some of my favorites) uses specific narrative tools to engage his or her reader's imagination; to enable students to know better how those black marks on the page can create images and sounds in the mind of the reader; to point out how we vicariously feel the pleasure and pain of a character while being simultaneously aware of its ontological status as fiction; to illustrate how the universal human capacity of storytelling might shed light on our capacity to tell the difference between deception and truth, hostility and love, in our everyday social encounters. That is, other disciplines may shed light on our study, but they should always remain ancillary.

I want to return to some issues I raised in the beginning about this interdisciplinarity turn in literary studies. As I mentioned, in one way or another interdisciplinarity is a way to repackage and advertise our goods as useful products. For some this is extremely ambitious—that we can change the face of science or a democracy make; for others this move simply offers a way to change with the times. Interdisciplinary courses and collaborative teaching and research are, as seen in the essays collected in MLA's *Profession* (2004), a way to stay involved in a rapidly changing world.

There are some practical issues to consider here. It is relatively easy for me to decide to coteach a course on Latin American and Chicano/a literature with a professor in the Romance languages department or with a Latin Americanist in history; this doesn't require any additional institutional support. I simply have to organize this interdisciplinary course in a timely manner. This isn't the same thing as building a bridge to, say, the department of cognitive science or linguistics. The more ambitious and complex the interdisciplinarity is, the more it will require institutional support; this also requires that the people you're working with on the project both in your field and the other fields be scholars you can communicate with; and that they be willing to share and explain *their* vocabulary as much as you are willing to reciprocate. If you want to launch a project on the study of metaphor, for example, and you want to include specialists in linguistics, cognitive science, and ethnography, the project becomes more complicated and expensive and involves a lot more red tape. Such a project can be organized, of course, but with great difficulty.

This leads me to another, more serious issue that concerns the institutionalizing of interdisciplinarity in the forms of granting diplomas and how they are valued. First, in capitalist society today—and there's no other one globally—those who attend university and receive a diploma/ degree are being officially recognized as having completed a certain number of years of study in a specified field of knowledge. This diploma then becomes associated in general terms (not mechanically) with a salary. Now, in a capitalist marketplace, the diplomas that sell well—the ones employers are most interested in—are ones that indicate a specialization in one area. If my diploma, rather than saying I can teach English literature, says I know a little bit of history, physics, and French, unless I am in an exceptional situation, I won't get hired. This isn't to say that it's not possible to know well many things; or that it's impossible to have wide knowledge of how things work in many fields. It is to say that in capitalist society the jack-of-all-trades diploma isn't marketable. This is doubly complicated when you think of how one's salary, health insurance, and other conditions under which we are hired are fixed by the way disciplines are institutionalized in academia. No matter what I do within capitalist society, I'll never have the same hiring conditions as a star teacher in law, economics, physical science, and astronomy. Inseparable from the discipline represented by my English Ph.D. are the hiring conditions fixed by the university for this diploma.

That is to say, a diploma is not a social construction that I imagine and that I can change in my imagination; it is from the very beginning something that is attached to material effects and consequences within the academy and in society at large. So, for the interdisciplinary approach to work in reality, one would have to do more than build bridges between departments in a reciprocal way. It would require changing the whole university structure. To do this, we would have to radically transform all of society. More dangerously, if we dissolve the frontiers that separate disciplines, in a capitalist economy we risk participating in the demolishing of departments and thus the loss of jobs for professors and all staff.

CONCLUDING REMARKS

An essay by Robert Scholes in the MLA's 2004 publication of *Profession* identifies the problem in the humanities whereby one's value as a teacher and scholar is tied to one's publication record; with academic presses receiving less and less funding, he foresees a time when there will be so many scholars in search of ever-decreasing numbers of publishers that the whole system will collapse. He suggests we change the criteria used to promote teachers in the humanities, focusing more on research that discovers something. He recounts the "humble work" of bibliographic research and editorial work that is very useful for teachers, writers, and scholars. He considers that scholarship should be considered "in the service of teaching" ("Learning and Teaching" 124), and so we should sometimes ask for assistance from colleagues in other disciplines.

I agree with Scholes. Our time is limited, so if you want to do a good job teaching and writing it's important to go to colleagues and ask about, say, Mexican politics or history and to accept reading recommendations so you don't have to dig through stacks of books to parse good from bad. This kind of interdisciplinarity makes sense: the seeking of guidance from colleagues in other departments.

It is also a practice we can do on our own. The study and teaching of literature have always taken me to other disciplines: cognitive science, linguistics, history, even physics and biology. This is why one day I might be studying some technical articles on the theory of logic or the theory of semantics developed within logic as a discipline; and on another day, I might read Darwin or Marx. This doesn't mean that I'm going to become a logician, biologist, physicist, or philosopher. What it means is that I know literature is the imaginative recreation of the world and that to this extent nothing in the world is foreign to literature; it can deal potentially with any part of the world, with any reality in the world. Thus the study of literature leaves no discipline outside of its scope. At other times my activity will be interdisciplinary in the sense of communicating and working with scholars in other fields. Other disciplines can open new ways of analyzing literature as products of the human mind—that is, products of the human being in all his or her material and historical circumstances: as part of nature (biological) and as a historical being—a being that has made itself and that continues to make itself.

As scholars and teachers of literature, then, our business is the business of literature. This doesn't mean that we should be ignorant of politics. However, our job in the classroom is not that of political activism— building the party and so on—but that of attending to our business as scholars of literature. Neither are we in the business of psychology, sociology, cognitive science, linguistics, and so on. So, while it is important for us to know the research in the field of cognitive psychology or linguistics, it is with the aim of better understanding how literature works. For example, we can posit the not completely unfounded hypothesis that poetry manifested itself before the novel because, as deduced by cognitive research on brain development, rhythm has a mnemonic function. (See Michael R. Trimble's *The Soul in the Brain*.) Such research from psychology labs and neuroscience research gives us useful information in that it allows us, in this case, to better understand our different engagement with prose and poetry. And if we can understand better how language functions by turning to recent research in linguistics—proving that there is no direct link between language and thought—then we can understand how art might stimulate those thought processes that take place prelinguistically. This might lead to a further understanding of how, after reading words on a page we form images in our mind that are nonlinguistic. And recent advances in evolutionary psychology can shed light on whether the concept of the "implied author" is valid or not. If it is valid (empirically verifiable), it will help us understand how it is produced in the mind of reader and the writer. It might also help us understand better how a few descriptive details in a given passage can produce a full holographic effect in my mind; and how the holographic effect is achieved differently in realism and in the fantastic, magical realisms and minimalism.

Perhaps our role is to encourage our students to learn specific methods to understand how literature works and turn to other fields of inquiry, not to become specialists in those fields, but to see how such research might help us better understand how we function as a species universally. It is the recognition of disciplinary differences and boundaries—and not their erasure in the turn to interdisciplinarity—that promises most to shed light on our many activities in the humanities.

NOTES

CHAPTER ONE

1. I'm reminded here of Bishop Berkeley's work in the eighteenth century, in which we see an extreme form of idealism when it comes to understanding the self in the world: the mechanism for perception takes place in the brain, and so what's out there is actually inside the brain. So we live with the false impression that the out there is really out there.

2. Descartes' disciple Spinoza found a much simpler explanation of the self: rather than consider God in the hyphen between mind-body, God simply exists, to different degrees of, say, a Godly concentrated substance, in all things. Accordingly, God exists in a concentrated form in our mind and in a less concentrated form in our body. When we die, God still exists but in a less concentrated form; we have turned into part of the organic matter that makes up the whole universe and thus share this God substance.

3. The twentieth century had the stamp of behaviorism. It was B. F. Skinner's behavioral model that dominated much thinking on the self: the brain as a blank slate that responds to contact with the world through the double mechanism of reward and punishment as well as success and failure; it is through these two basic mechanisms that the child learns everything: to speak, walk, perceive objects in the world, remember things, and have emotions. Here, what is called mind is nothing but traces left on the brain from infancy to adulthood.

4. Unlike yesteryear's neuroscientific research based on the nonliving brain, technologies such as the fMRI (functional magnetic resonance imaging scan) and PET (positron emission scan) have allowed scientists to measure more accurately the biochemical and neuronal processes and their affiliative affective and cognitive operations in living human brains (healthy and impaired).

5. The "principle of identity" (see Leibniz) says that if all properties present in X are also present in Z, then X is identical to Z because you cannot discern a difference between X and Z. Their properties are indistinguishable. Stated otherwise, if all is gray, then there are no colors because all properties of everything overlap with

the property of gray, and therefore gray doesn't exist. (See G. W. Leibniz, *Philosophical Essays*.)

6. Image making and its affiliative goal-driven intentionality are central to the evolution of the human self, as they form the central elements of our universal capacity for "worldmaking"; that is, our ability to inhabit holographically a past and a future in the present. The activation of this universal world-making capacity—much like Chomsky's hypothesis of a universal grammar—requires environmental stimuli to activate genetically hardwired biochemical and neuronal processes that evolve as we grow from infant to adult into an increasingly sophisticated and complex world-making capacity.

7. In the Stone Age, humans lived in more or less small communities that allowed them to transform nature through their work as gatherers and hunters and toolmakers, and by transforming nature (satisfying their needs) they also transformed themselves. As time passed, work became more and more socialized and so involved more and more organization and coordination of increasingly large numbers of people. So, as communities grew, our ancestors had to find new ways of transforming nature: domestication of animals, cultivation of crops, and the invention of more sophisticated tools. (For more on this, see Nicholas Wade's *Before the Dawn: Recovering the Lost History of Our Ancestors*, as well as Merlin Donald's *Origins of the Modern Mind: Three Stages in the Evolution of Culture and Cognition*.) When our ancestors began to organize work on a much larger scale to ensure the survival of increasingly expanding communities, society itself began to transform into one divided by manual and intellectual labor. Hence, the rise of clerical workers, soldiers, priests, architects, musicians, painters, who were sustained by the manual labor of the majority. The increasingly sedentary life of the community led to the private ownership of land by individuals, families, and/or clans. With private property and the tools used to cultivate this private land there appeared two main institutions: the church (any institution that regulates the beliefs of the community) and the state (which has the force to guarantee either the private property or the state property of the land). Indeed, the state in its origin is directly related to power (force) and to property. The self is thus the human mind/body that belongs, along with others, to a territory controlled by a state and a church. At the same time, the self is, from birth till death, an individual.

8. This does not mean an absolute deterministic sense of self. There are many examples of, say, the working class and/or trade leaders defending the interests of the bourgeoisie and those born of the bourgeoisie adopting and fighting for the interest of the working class. And, perhaps less willfully, we see how certain historical moments (the 1929 stock market crash, for example) have given rise to huge shifts in sense of self that result from dramatic changes in the individual's material conditions.

9. The evolution of language and social intelligence has been a central ingredient in this development of a sense of self different from the world; along with this we've evolved the capacity to read intentionality in others; to have a theory of minds. Research led by Giacomo Rizzolatti's team at the University of Parma has isolated what has been identified as a mirror neuron system at the right inferior

frontal cortex. It was discovered that the neurons concentrated here fired up not only when we act with intention—say, picking up a mug of coffee—but also when we watch someone else act—pick up a mug of coffee. Indeed, those with damage to this part of the brain cannot construct an internal model of somebody else's actions to judge whether they are a threat or not. Moreover, this system of neurons differs from others in that they code current actions as well as aspects of logically related future ones, suggesting that they are intimately involved with reading the intentions and behaviors of others as well as predicting it; the mirror neuron system allows us to read interior states of other minds and has in turn led to the increasingly sophisticated development of our social and instrumental skills. In *A Brief Tour of Human Consciousness* V. S. Ramachandran suggests that the evolution of our mirror neurons system took place during our so-called great leap forward (approximately fifty thousand years ago) marked, he writes, by the "explosive evolutionary ability to mime complex actions [which in turn led to the] cultural transmission of information, which is what characterizes us as human" (38). Our imitative and mimetic ability originates at a much deeper level than phenomenal awareness. According to Ramachandran, it is the evolution of this mirror neuron system that "liberated humans from the constraints of a strictly gene-based evolution" (107). (See Maxim I. Samenov and Vittorio Gallese's edited volume of essays *Mirror Neurons and the Evolution of Brain Work;* see also the research of M. Iacoboni, I. Molnar-Szakacs, V. Gallese, G. Buccino, J. C. Mazziotta, et al.)

10. We are fast approaching a stage in our evolution when we might be able to reproduce without these determining biological facts: cloning as asexual reproduction. Even in such cases, however, we are still constrained by the laws of evolution; that genetic variety gives more opportunity for positive adaptive mutation necessary for the survival of the species. Given our biological machinery, if all zygotic reproduction stopped, we would work against evolution and therefore lead our species to an ultimate dead end.

11. I am surprised constantly by a seemingly simplistic notion that it is literature (or any cultural phenomenon) that constitutes the subject. In *How Novels Think: The Limits of British Individualism from 1719–1900*, Nancy Armstrong declares, "The history of the novel and the history of the modern subject are, quite literally, one and the same" (3). For Armstrong, the British novel came into being "as writers sought to formulate a kind of subject that had not yet existed in writing. Once formulated in fiction, however, this subject proved uniquely capable of reproducing itself not only in authors but also in readers, in other novels, and across British culture in law, medicine, moral and political philosophy, biography, history and other forms of writing that took the individual as their most basic unit" (3). Moreover, in its "repeated performances" (142) of the subject, the novel has "wrought significant changes on our culture's standard for gender difference" (142). For Armstrong, fiction "produces identity" and thus "certain narrative strategies" can be "hijacked" and "reworked" in ways that respond to "the needs and desires of the disenfranchised and dependent groups" (142).

12. It's not counterintuitive or surprising to posit that all knowledge is interdisciplinary knowledge and that to understand the world from the point of view of epistemology and fundamental ontology you have to have a systemic view of the world. You have a supersystem—the universe as a whole—formed by as many subsystems as you can identify and many of these subsystems that we identify become disciplines, become objects of research in a particular way (many others don't because they're not considered interesting or considered unmanageable from the point of view of the means of approaching these subsystems).

CHAPTER TWO

1. Ernest Gellner identifies Freud's hydraulic model as a "hydro-hermeneutics," that is, the "driving force behind the agitation of our mind is related to powerful instinctual forces, with a deep physiological basis, and related to the biological needs of survival and procreation" (*The Psychoanalytic Movement* 93). Importantly, Gellner asks whether Freud's "sketchily constructed model of sluices and channels and chambers and locks and water-wheels [is] in any way scientifically serious, as opposed to being mere metaphor" (93).

2. In Freud's words, "We have arrived at our knowledge of this psychical apparatus by studying the individual development of human beings. To the oldest of these psychical provinces or agencies we give the name of *id*. It contains everything that is inherited, that is present at birth, that is laid down in the constitution—above all, therefore, the instincts, which originate from the somatic organization and which find a first psychical expression here [in the id] in forms unknown to us" ("An Outline of Psycho-Analysis" 14).

3. As formulated in *The Ego and the Id,* the ego accomplishes this restraining function by bringing the psychical apparatus into relation with the world, acting as a repressing mechanism and performing its defensive operations in ways that are most often automatic without ceasing to be ruled by what Freud calls the "reality principle." The repressing mechanism rejects from consciousness those ideas and impulses which threaten the stability of the ego in its function of connecting the psychical apparatus with the external world, channeling them towards the id. The connection with the environment involves all conscious and deliberative processes, including an awareness of all sorts of external entities and their characteristics as well as the perception of the subjective qualities of experience (odor, taste, color, and so on) and the recognition of other humans as intentional beings like oneself. Other skills of the ego are the capacity to use and understand human symbolic representations, to establish logical and causal connections, to conceive ideas and communicate them through language and other means, and so on.

4. Freud's ternary model can be summarized as follows: At a certain moment in the life of the child (more or less after the age of five), part of the energy from the id that had been channeled into the ego starts becoming differentiated once again

and, in this process, creates a new agency which will be in charge of forwarding or hindering the pleasure-seeking aim of the id in ways that differs from those used by the ego. The resisting forces of the ego are based on its connection to the external world and its submission to the reality principle, while those of the superego are based on its internalization of parental and (more largely social) ideals and moral values. In the superego one finds a combination, as it were, of the realistic thinking of the ego and the irrationality of the id. Children's dependency is relatively long and teaches them to obey both the reality principle and the precepts, wishes and moral dictates of parents and/or other persons in a position of authority over them in order to secure their approval, avoid pain, and obtain pleasure. After a certain time, the judgmental, censorial, and punitive or rewarding parental action is internalized and becomes the child's own moral code. Thus, the parent's authority, as assimilated by the child, becomes an agency of his or her psychic apparatus. The child's insertion in society follows a similar path, since the prohibitions, demands, precepts, critical judgments, and other practices in the child's environment become part of the larger process of socialization.

5. Karl H. Pribram conjectures that Freud, who lost his place at the University of Vienna to Sigmund Exner, "was thrown back on his clinical practice and had to limit his research to his patients' verbal reports of introspection [because he] had no laboratory" ("A Century of Progress?" 12). See also Freud's "Autobiographical Study," in which he looks back on his career.

6. Whereas Ramón y Cajal won the Nobel Prize in 1906 and Sherrington in 1932, Freud never was awarded the prize. Neither was he rewarded on the basis of his creative ability—an option used by the Nobel committee to honor Bertrand Russell in 1950. For more on the history of the exploration of the brain, see Robert-Benjamin Illing's essay "Humbled by History."

7. Lesley Chamberlain argues that while Freud had scientific ambitions and claimed a scientific status to his work, he was fundamentally an artist. That is, perhaps his considerable achievement should not have been judged as scientific, but rather as a creative expansion of durable myths and an artistic exploration of the imagination.

8. Freud doesn't want to destroy his early work on the hydraulic psychic model of the libido, but rather, as he states in *Civilization and its Discontents*, to bring into "sharper focus a thought arrived at long ago" (75). Given that his work had become such an institution, there were very real material reasons why he wouldn't want to dynamite his earlier speculative work.

9. Freud's attempt to explain the motives and mechanisms for the internalization of social orders resonates with the work of Durkheim and Weber. It is not for nothing that Freud's *Civilization* and the work of Weber and Durkheim are held up by those like Talcott Parsons as pillars of modern social science. As in Freud, so in Durkheim and Weber we see an abstraction of reality. Here I think of Durkheim's concepts of the "social function" and "social fact," which he proposed in *The Rules of Sociological Method*. Accordingly, the study of "social facts" necessitated that one

automatically give up all attempts at theorizing and explaining essential phenomena that are not immediately present to our senses: if what one sees in a factory is the hiring of workers in what appears to be an equitable operation, then one need not research, say, conditions of exploitation or the use value of the commodity; one need not go deeper and ask, say, What is the real nature of this transaction materially and legally? In Durkheim, capitalism is not a social fact and thus has no influence on whatever happens within capitalist society and thus need not be studied. There is a total abstraction of capitalism. Durkheim's theoretical justification for not going beyond the surface of things—thus to not disturb the status quo—masks a form of philosophical idealism; it also promotes a nascent form of a hermeneutical method: the interpretation only of meaning. With Weber's conception of an ideology of Protestantism as the singular force that shapes society, we see yet again a form of philosophical idealism: it is the realm of ideas that shape society, and not the laboring, organized hands of the people. Like Durkheim, Weber doesn't want to rock the boat, and thus he spiritualizes reality as a way to calm and control those who misbehave ("anomie")—the working class. Rather than understand how society really functions, in both we see an abstraction and spiritualizing of reality.

10. According to Saussure, the two components of the sign (the "signifier" and the "signified") are psychological ("mental") entities and are not separable. In other words, contrary to a widely shared misconception, the Saussurean notion of the sign excludes all possibility of a split, a parting, a hiatus, a void, or a slippage between these two components. The sign can exist and function only as a sign, that is, as the most basic unit of linguistic communication, if it remains whole, if it is the undivided mental unity of an acoustic image (what is known as a "phoneme") and a concept (a "meaning"). Many theorists have confused the "signified" (a "concept," a "meaning") with the referent (of necessity, "something" exterior to the sign), thus judging themselves entitled to separate the signifier from the signified, misconceiving the signifier as a word and the signified as a referent, all the while believing that they are following Saussure's theory of sign and language.

11. In chapter 3, I discuss at length Derrida's faith in an ever-arriving "messianicity without messianism." We see a similar formulation of a faith-in in his *Acts of Religion,* in which he writes, "To wait without waiting, awaiting absolute surprise, the unexpected visitor, awaits without a horizon of expectation: this is indeed about the Messiah as *hôte,* about the messianic as hospitality, the messianic that introduces deconstructive disruption or madness in the concept of hospitality, the madness *of* hospitality, even the madness *of the concept of* hospitality" (*Acts of Religion* 362).

12. Notably, a Nietzschean perspectivism had already been articulated by the sixteenth-century Spanish poet Quevedo; he wrote in several lines of a poem that nothing is true, all is a lie, all is true according to the lenses through which it is seen.

13. An important point to ponder here is the following: Foucault's so-called archeological histories that identify the social and political conditions in which, say,

masturbation-as-madness is a reflection of the discursive formation of the subject in a particular moment is not only Western-centric, but limited to France. When he pulls from the archives a book on masturbation and madness written by a doctor in France, does this really say something about the human subject in Mexico, Japan, India, or any other place in the world?

14. In a 1984 interview for *The Advocate* Foucault says that sadomasochism will open the possibility for "an acting out of power structures by a strategic game that is able to give sexual pleasure or bodily pleasure" ("Sex, Power and the Politics of Identity" 27). He adds to this a discussion of how role-play, ritual, and even real physical pain can offer a way to enter and transform the psyche (collective and individual). And in his vision of a future in which "economy of bodies and pleasures" is not subject to the "austere monarchy of sex" (*History of Sexuality* 159), Foucault proposes an aestheticization of self/pleasure that ultimately stands in resistance to external laws. It is only in Foucault's theory centered on the self that the realm of absolutely unregulated pleasure can be conceived and that the positing of resistance to discursive power relations in the "normal" real world can take place. In this theory there is no place for actual collective solidarity, only for self-centered play.

15. Judith Butler's "performative" refers to and builds upon J. L. Austin's identifying an utterance that functions in and of itself as an action rather than as an assertion. First, this notion of the performative appeared in one of Austin's essays that was later edited and published posthumously in *How To Do Things with Words* (1955). Second, Austin himself abandoned his constative/performative hypothesis, noting that language does not work in such a neat, contrasting way and that his formula ultimately failed to account for the contextual factors that determine meaning in everyday speech acts. Hence, he offered a revised hypothesis (the locution/illocutionary binary) to identify those complex aspects of sentences that highlight the thought and/or action expressed. Third, Butler herself has admitted that "performing" gender and sexuality cannot change the system. All it does is give the individual performer of such and such identity the possibility of creative play, as someone would do onstage; when the curtain falls, while the performance might have engaged its audience and even opened the public's eyes to certain social injustices, nothing will have changed in the real world of the real people that suffer daily from those injustices.

16. In contrast to Foucault, we might turn to Hegel, who had conceived of the making of subject always within history. Even though Hegel wasn't capable of going all the way and seeing man as a self-created creature in history (he thought of himself as being at the end of history but in a way completely different from that of Foucault), he couldn't see that his own society was subject to its own deep transformation and still to come a deeper transformation required in the destruction of capitalism. As we see in Homer's *Odyssey*, Hegel's subject is a subject that must overcome obstacles, temptations, and digressive routes. At the end of the quest the subject reaches a stage where it knows what the route has been. We are conscious of our history. That is, man is conscious of how man has built himself/made himself.

CHAPTER THREE

1. In *The Premodern Condition* Bruce Holsinger identifies the "obsession" (4) of French poststructuralists such as Lacan, Derrida, and Bourdieu with the Middle Ages; in their leapfrogging over of an abhorred Enlightenment, "the critical generation" of post–World War II France "turned to the Middle Ages not in a fit of nostalgic retrospection, but in a spirit of both interpretive and ideological resistance to the relentless inevitability of modernity" (5). Holsinger analyzes Lacan's foray into the Middle Ages in his seventh seminar as well as Derrida's apophaticism in *Of Grammatology,* concluding that it might be claimed "as one of the great twentieth-century interrogations of medievalism, the medievalism of Enlightenment rationality and its attendant ideology of periodization, the Enlightenment of Rousseau and his century's attempt to account for the legacy of the Dark Ages to European languages and cultures" (151). And for Holsinger, Augustine's spirit "lives and breaths" in Lyotard's phenomenological critique of Cartesian rationalism (201).

2. See Maimonides' *Guide,* in which he writes, "Upon realizing that there is no means to grasp what can be potentially perceived [of God] but negatively and that a negation cannot teach anything about the truth of the subject, it became transparent to all humans, past and future, that God, blessed be He, cannot be comprehended by any mind, that nobody but He can comprehend He is, that to comprehend Him is the inability to comprehend him fully" (cited in José Faur's *Homo Mysticus* 23).

3. The machines harvest the millions of sleeping humans plugged into the Source to provide the bioelectricity to power the machine city. Neo is identified as the super savior that has the power to reboot the Source program and emancipate humanity from the machines, marauding sentinels, and programs (Mr. Smith) that regulate and surveil the Matrix. There are three distinct worlds in *The Matrix*: the virtual world of the Matrix, the real world, and the Train Station program. Matt Lawrence identifies the Train Station program as the bridge between the machine world and the Matrix and is used to "smuggle programs from the one world into the other" (11). This is the space where the South Asian character, Sati, appears. Interestingly, it is the exotic other, Sati, who also appears at the end of *Revolutions* to create the dawning of a new world. Finally, the characters, including the revolutionary fighters that inhabit the underworld, Zion, simply have faith in Neo—that he is The One. That he will liberate all from the machines. The film's message resonates loud and clear: For revolution to happen, one must have faith.

4. Derrida's nonnaming of such a "messianicity without messianism" can be seen variously in his idiosyncratic use of terms like "trace," "supplement," "hymen," "gram," "incision," "interval" (terms he has used in works since 1967) that variously (un)name a messianicity without messianism.

5. See also Timothy Brennan's essay, "Postcolonial Studies Between European Wars: An Intellectual History," in which he not only identifies (via Derrida) the Heideggerian roots of postcolonial studies, but also (via Foucault) their Nietzschean

foundations. He writes of the latter that this lineage in postcolonial theory "conceals a source-specific elitism and racialist filiation that it wants very much to supersede, and feels utterly uncompelled to explain or distance itself from" (187). He continues to identify Heidegger's sentimental fixation of the peasant, his "mystificatory cult of the soil and of a village craftsman's ideal of counter-technology, all of them joining his orientalist borrowings from Eastern philosophy late in his career" (187).

6. For more on *The Matrix* as political manifesto, see P. Chad Barnet's "Reviving Cyberpunk" and essays by Mercer Schuchardt, Dino Felluga, and James L. Ford in *Taking the Red Pill*.

7. In "Seeing, Believing, Touching, Truth" Carolyn Korsmeyer writes, "An exasperated viewer could conclude that blatant hooey uttered with faux-Zen opacity passes for insight. What could it be but a cheap plot trick to say that if you die in the virtual world of the Matrix you also die in the real. But then I remembered the Hmong and their deadly dreams. Changes in heart rate, breathing, and adrenalized output are among the noticeable physical changes that mental images can bring about. It is a step further for a dream—or a virtual experience—to draw blood, a bridge between what is merely seen and what has a palpable, felt effect—a bridge, that is, between vision and touch" (51). Others have likened Neo's journey out of the Matrix to the prisoner's ascent from the cave in Plato's allegory. Yet others have read the film as a philosophy of mind.

8. Simone Weil spent a year laboring in a factory to experience firsthand the exploitation of workers. In spite of this, she wrote the extremely reactionary and philosophically idealistic *La Pesanteur et la Grace*.

9. On the same page in *Speech and Phenomena* where Derrida characterizes "*différance*" as "neither a *word* nor a *concept*" he also states, "Difference more properly refers to what in classical language would be called the origin or production of differences and the differences between differences, the *play* [*jeu*] of differences. Its locus and operation will therefore be seen wherever speech appeals to difference" (130).

10. In John Caputo's work we see materialize an apophatic Derrida. In *The Prayers and Tears of Jacques Derrida: Religion without Religion* Caputo characterizes how Derrida calls forth a deconstruction "in response to the unrepresentable"—a deconstruction that "is large with expectation, astir with excess, provoked by the promise, impregnated by the impossible, hoping in a certain messianic promise of the impossible" (xix). And, very much in the tradition of negative theology, Caputo remarks generally of Derrida's *Passions* (1993) and *Psyché* (1987) of the sense that there "is no privileged access to a *hyperousios,* beyond the name of God, to some deep truth that arrests the play of traces in the text. There is nothing beneath the surface of the text—*scriptura et traditio*—or the trace that is left in a text that is tormented and disturbed by the desire to efface itself before the wholly other" (34).

11. In *Of Grammatology* Derrida writes, "Thus as it goes without saying, the trace whereof I speak is not more *natural* (it is not the mark, the natural sign, or

the index in the Husserlian sense) than *cultural*, not more physical than psychic, biological than spiritual. It is that starting from which a becoming-unmotivated of the sign, and with it all the ulterior oppositions between *physis* and its other, is possible" (47). He continues, "The trace is in fact the absolute origin of sense in general. Which amounts to saying once again that there is no absolute origin of sense in general. The trace is the difference which opens appearance and signification" (65).

12. Derrida directs his criticism at the humanisms in "current French thought" and that "in a gesture which is sometimes more implicit than systematically articulated, to *amalgamate* Hegel, Husserl and, in a more diffuse and ambiguous manner, Heidegger, with the old humanist metaphysics I purposely use the word 'amalgam,' which joints the alchemic reference, which is primary here, with strategical or tactical reference to the realm of political ideology" (39). The figure that "amalgamates" Hegel, Husserl, and Heidegger is Foucault. Thus Derrida is also leveling a critique at Foucault—the figure in France at the time who was well known for his best-selling *Les Mots et les Choses* and who appeared regularly on television talk shows. Here we see Derrida's demand that his disciples be unconditionally aligned with him. That is, Derrida wanted the whole territory to himself. This is also why, in coded language, he also takes a jab at Roland Barthes; that is, Derrida targets those like Foucault and Barthes who sought to make Sartre look obsolete with their new philosophical tools and perceptions.

13. Right after Sartre's big conference, a disciple of Heidegger's, Beauffret, became the main spokesperson in support of Heidegger in France; in the United States it was Hannah Arendt. Each in his own way looked for ways to diminish his pro-Nazism.

14. See Boris Vian's novel *L'ecume des jours,* which immortalized this lecture.

15. Before the so-called *Kehre* (the turn), Heidegger developed the concept "Dasein" in his *Being and Time* (1927). He makes it clear that he's using Dasein as technical concept that is not reducible, as some translations have suggested, to the concept of a human reality or a human essence. In *Being and Time* Heidegger avoids any kind of explanation that would turn his analysis into a so-called philosophical anthropology, or a philosophical inquiry into man's essence. Rather, he wants to avoid this and any limitation based on an analysis of human beings. His goal is to find out what Being is. Dasein and the analysis of Dasein (or, what is also known as the "existential analytic") is a means and only a means towards the characterization of Being with capital "B." Keep in mind that Heidegger considers that saying something exists is equal to saying that something has existence. The word "is" refers one to a concept of existence, and the concept of "is" is contained within the concept of being. His stated objective is to look into the foundations of metaphysics; to explore and understand the ontology of Being (capital B), beginning with an exploration (vague at best) of "Dasein"—the privileged, circuitous route to the understanding of Being. Accordingly, of all the entities—all the beings out there—the Dasein is the only entity (being) that formulates questions and that is capable of asking the question What is Being? This leads to the question How can a finite being (human

or animal, or a rock, a speck of dust) communicate or enter a relationship with an infinite Being?

Otherwise stated, if man is finite and God is infinite by definition without transforming that which is infinite into finite, how can man relate to God? One is infinite and one is finite, and thus there is no possible way to relate one to the other; no relationship is possible. If he wants to determine that Being is that which *is* common to all beings (entities), then he is saying that Being is a being. Being with a capital "B" cannot be a being, as it would then be an entity. Hence, to maneuver out of this paradox, he makes the detour through Dasein; this, however, ultimately acts as a proxy for another word for human being, and so you end up with the same problem: how do you relate Being to being without turning Being into being.

16. In *Being and Nothingness* Sartre makes a tripartite division: (1) he talks about being-in-itself, a fancy concept for, say, a rock or everything that is not capable of self-consciousness, that is not able to recognize the self as a self; (2) being-for-itself, that is, the being possessing a consciousness (a spirit), the being that has its own foundation; (3) the social reality that he calls "being-for-other." When Derrida makes reference to Sartre's statement, "man is a useless passion" (see Derrida's lengthy footnote 2, page 36), he refers to Sartre's concept of God as that being that is like the being in itself; like rocks or inert matter or animals: they are there. Accordingly, God is there as a being in itself, but at the same time it is a being for itself. It is conscious of itself. It is matter and, at the same time, spirit.

17. *Presence* for Derrida has always carried a great metaphysics. In *Of Grammatology,* he writes that such a weight of presence has meant that all Western philosophy has privileged the spoken word as opposed to the written; the written can be read and reacted to in the future, unlike the present speech-act, which one can interpret immediately and which the speaker can correct immediately; so more truth and more substance lie in the speech-act than in the written word, according to Derrida (and also Heidegger).

18. This might sound rather deep, but in actuality the whole analytic of Dasein in *Being and Time* is a disguised explanation of the Fall of Man. Of course, one can't say this too loudly because it might upset people. But in my opinion, the whole work is a laborious description of man having forgotten God. Man has forgotten Being and, on the other hand, Being has distanced itself from Man because Man has been doing terrible things with science, technology, and war. He has not been "concerned" with Being. So Being has retracted itself from man. So, what he states is that man's concern is with reestablishing proximity with Being and its potential capability to open up toward Being and thus to live in the truth of Being and thus live in truth with God.

19. The distinction between ontic and ontological was made by Heidegger. Ontic is everything or anything that concerns being (lowercase); that is, anything concerning what is also called "entities." And "Ontology" is classically defined as the study of Being (uppercase) and in this sense it is synonymous with Metaphysics or the result of such study.

20. In many vulgarized forms and thanks to Derrida, this has become a sort of cliché used mainly by artists and writers. In several interviews I've conducted with artists and writers they tell me, "I do not paint, painting paints through me"; "I'm not the writer, I'm merely the vessel in which writing takes place." It has become a pseudo-sophisticated way of talking about inspiration. One way or another they follow the Heideggerian formulation: don't force your way toward truth, open yourself to Being, and the truth will happen.

21. In "The Politics of Derridean Deconstruction" Catherine Zuckert argues that Derrida's position is not "conservative" but "anti-revolutionary" (355); that is, his deconstruction of foundational oppositions promises to "generate new systems of meaning" and not "to replace, immediately and completely, one order or system of authority with another" (355). She also identifies in Derrida the absenting of human agency in the shaping of our world. She concludes, "Just as the late Heidegger urged his readers to open themselves to a new 'dispensation of Being' without any assurance that such an event would occur, so Derrida would persuade his readers to rely on the impersonal, unpredictable, although emphatically embodied operation of *différance* without any notion of the outcome. Indeed, Derrida goes even further than Heidegger. According to Heidegger, people living in modern times at least had to make a fateful decision. Derrida suggests we have no more control over our future than we have our past" (355–256).

22. In their introduction to *Early Christian Mystics,* Bernard McGinn and Patricia Ferris discuss how twelfth-century mystics like Bernard of Clairvaux and William of St. Thierry sought to put themselves into a meditative state that would allow them to open to "a direct, immediate, and transformative encounter with the presence of God" (10); for these mystics, the coming of God would never actually feel like a presence "the way a thing is present, because God is literally no-thing" (10). They sum up the mystic's position: "God may become present in a way somehow similar to how two persons are present to each other, especially in the presence of lovers; but God as infinite person so far exceeds the categories and consciousness characteristic of our own finite subjectivity that the divine presence is often realized in forms of absence and negation that mystics have explored with courage, tenacity, and great subtlety. One thing that all mystics insist upon is that when they come to know of God through their yearning for and meeting with the divine presence it is incommunicable, at least insofar as we understand ordinary communication" (10–11). They conclude, "Mysticism is a journey, a path that almost invariably demands long preparation and whose true attainment can be measured only by the effects that mystics have upon others, both their contemporaries and their readers over the centuries. All the mystics took finding deeper contact with God as the central goal of their lives" (12). See also Marion Glascoe's English *Medieval Mystics: Games of Faith* as well as Michael Kessler and Christian Sheppard's edited volume, *Mystics: Presence and Aporia.*

23. Derrida follows Heidegger, not Hegel. That is, he follows *grosso modo* the conception of the self as "thrown/born into world" and thus lacks this crucial di-

mension of how our labor transforms the world in space and time. We simply are worldly beings—beings that exist in the world. In an attempt to add the dimension of time, he adds to this "pro-jection" as a way to insist that the essence of "Dasein" is time; that is, we are temporal beings and as temporal beings, whether we like it or not, we "project" ourselves—and in every instant because the now is the instant that takes place the moment I say "now"; after this instance; accordingly, the future is not present; it is absent, but becomes a presence the moment the "now" is over; the moment the now is over, it is past; thus past now is the non-now and future now is the non-now. Thus it follows that the only reality we have is the "now now"; the instantaneous now. This is the temporal essence of Dasein: the presence and absence, the present past and future. And the "Dasein" can only exist as this "concern" and the care for the future: as a worldly being, you are in the now, but at the same time you wouldn't survive if you didn't care about the future; the only way of living in the future where you can experience a fundamental part of your self that is inexperienceable without your total definitive and absolute absence: that is your death. And one can only experience one's death if you project yourself into the future and thus live the experience of being a finite being. Hence Heidegger's formulation in *Being and Time* that the only authentic existence is the existence concerned with death.

24. In "Ends of Man" Derrida writes, "What is difficult to conceive of today is an end of man which is not organized by a dialectic of truth and of negativity, an end of man which is not a teleology in the first person plural. The *we* which in the *Phenomenology of Mind* joins natural consciousness and philosophical consciousness and assures the proximity to oneself of that fixed and central being for which this circular reappropriation is produced. The *we* is the unity of absolute knowledge and anthropology, of God and man, of onto-theo-teleology and humanism. '*Being*' and language—the group of languages—which it governs or which it opens, such is the name of that which assures this passage by the *we* between metaphysics and humanism" (42).

CHAPTER FOUR

1. For Timothy Brennan, "Cosmo-Theory" not only plays out fantasies of "new world subjects" that can move through the supposedly more permeable borders of the nation in late-globalization, but in such fanciful theorizing of such ease of movement, Cosmo-Theory denies the material reality not only of immigrants who encounter real borders and laws of nation and also denies the very real presence of the nation-state today. For example, he writes, "The trade showdowns that periodically arise between the United States and Japan, the United States and Mexico, or between Venezuela and Brazil [as well as the] national disparities existing in wage levels, ecological legislation, or the rights of judicial redress—disparities that arose historically as a result of the different ethnic compositions of the workforce as well as distinct national-political traditions" ("Cosmo-Theory" 673). Indeed, that

capitalist corporations are at all policed is a result of national governments. Finally, as Brennan soberly makes clear, "nations continue to exist because the major players have a vested interest in their continuing. Working people need nations in order to have someone to complain to; corporations need nations in order to ensure a lack of fair competition and the absence of an equality of law" (673).

CHAPTER FIVE

1. Said's definitions of "Orientalism" are bountiful, slipping back and forth between it as a political program, linguistic construct, textual (literary, ethnographic) representation, and so on. There's no sense of it as an empirically verifiable entity. Perhaps this is why it isn't so readily picked up by scholars of politics, history, and linguistics.

2. The examples of how Said turns to space to spiritualize reality are endless. Latin American scholarly avatars of the Saidean approach are discussed in chapter 11. Saidean inflected publications within the field of what is identified as "hemispheric American studies": Gretchen Murphy's *Hemispheric Imaginings* (2005) and Sara L. Spurgeon's *Exploding the Western* (2005). In the former, the popular novelist Lew Wallace's *The Fair God*, Américo Paredes's *George Washington Gómez*, Lydia Maria Child's *Hobomok,* to name a few, trace "the development of an ideology that impelled and concealed U.S. imperialism inside the imagined confines of the Western Hemisphere and beyond" (26); in the latter, Spurgeon analyzes the novels of Cormac McCarthy, Leslie Marmon Silko, and Ana Castillo to "trace the development of various forms of the frontier myth in the works of three contemporary writers, to offer critical interpretations of its meaning, and to assess its power in shaping the life, thoughts, and politics both of the nation that produced it and the rest of the world that must live with its ubiquitous, colonizing presence" (3). And there are many others, including some in Native studies that I've reviewed for the journal *American Literature*: Arnold Krupat's *Red Matters* (2002), Steven Conn's *History's Shadow* (2004), Martin Padjet's *Indian Country* (2004), and Harry J. Brown's *Injun Joe's Ghost* (2004).

3. In the introduction to *Power, Politics, and Culture* Gauri Viswanathan celebrates Said as a historian of ideas, especially in his redirecting attention in the study of Indian postcolonial history from a "Marxist trajectory that dominated the school of Indian historiography" to its "cultural politics" (xiii); Viswanathan applauds Said for diverting "the scholarly focus from class analysis to a study of the discursive power of colonial texts and their representations" (xiii).

4. Active participants or not in British empire-building conquests, Said proclaims authors like Austen, Dickens, etc., as necessarily implicated; by virtue of their location in the so-called West they are glued to the "rather sordid experience of imperialism" (*The Pen and the Sword* 71). So, to read them responsibly is to "reinsert" them back "in their own history" (71), as with, say, a Jane Austen within a

history of Caribbean colonization; it is also to identify authors like Chinua Achebe who enact a "process of writing back" (71). Responsible reading is thus representation of all texts (representations, myths, voices) to produce a more complete picture of "history" (71).

5. Patrick Colm Hogan, in the introduction to his guest-edited issue of *Journal of Commonwealth and Postcolonial Studies,* considers it important to approach Said in terms of his intellectual and political work to more fully understand the complexity (and contradiction) present in the development of his ideas and goals. Hogan is certainly critical of Said's unwitting poststructuralist bent whereby his claim of discursive power and more than obliquely present sense of indeterminacy means that he cannot point to real reality and truth; he cannot provide a "clear way of differentiating his own assertions from those of the Orientalists he criticizes" (6). Overall, however, Hogan is generous in his critique, declaring them "fallible hypotheses in the course of a research program or set of research programs" (2).

6. As much as Said tries to put thinkers like Foucault and Derrida at arm's length, he is very much a thinker shaped by his time. Finishing his doctorate in 1963 and then working as a professor at Columbia, Said couldn't help but be immersed in that structuralist/poststructuralist stew boiling over in the 1960s and 1970s in the United States. For more, see his 1993 interview with Mark Edmundson, "Wild Orchids and Trotsky."

7. Unlike the Cartesian model, this one does not posit first a mind that imagines (or thinks or doubts about something) or means something and then separately an object that is an image, the meaning, the doubt, whatever psychological function (jealousy, grief, anger, etc.), but rather the mind (consciousness) that constitutes itself at the instant there is this action.

8. George Poulet discusses how a given author's writing is an act of bracketing off reality, and thus he identifies narratives like the novel as the objects that express most directly and purely the author's intentions and perceptions (consciousness). My objection to phenomenology aside, I must say that whenever I've sat down to read Poulet, I feel as if I'm ingesting some strange concoction: an imaginative psychological description of a novel or a poem. There is nothing of epistemological merit here.

9. Language, according to this view, is a massive accumulation of signs where, say, the sign-user simply selects a series of the signs, strings them together, and then sends them out into the world in some kind of mobile container; the container is then received by an addressee, who unpacks from the container the strings of signs with their meaning intact. This focus on rhetorical effect isn't surprising; many manuals of rhetoric discuss some grammar (those rules that need to be learned concerning, say, the correspondence between the plural in nouns and the plural in adjectives), but mostly focus on how, say, figures of speech and word order move audiences.

10. Husserl's conception of language had already been expressed in medieval philosophy. This idea of a container (package, vessel, and so on) packed by the

addresser with certain signs and unpacked by an addressee can be seen in discussions of language as far back as the Middle Ages and especially through the nineteenth century and the beginning of the twentieth. This view, however, doesn't really explain much about how language is acquired by infants and developed by them in conditions where the infant is surrounded by uses of language that are limited and/or grammatically incorrect. It doesn't explain or attempt to explain the universality of the phenomenon of language: why in all human groups there is language. Thus it doesn't make any attempt at explaining Chomsky's universal grammar or our innate capacity for language. It only has something very limited to say about how signs follow a certain order or sequence in what we call "syntactical strings." If there's any discussion that reaches beyond this, it's usually done in a rather elementary way, appearing as some type of primitive theory of mind popular among philosophers and "psychologists" as far back as the sixteenth century. (See Locke's "Associationism," for example.)

11. See also Said's interview with Bruce Robbins in 1998, in which he mentions how in such magazines as *The New Republic* and *Commentary* as well as "in the more outrageous magazines to the right of them" you read "the most horrible things about the natural depravity of the Arab, the crazed ways of Arab culture, the inability of Islam to tell the truth from falsehood" ("American Intellectual and Middle East Politics" 320). To fight racism toward Arabs, one must, for example, take "terrorism" and give it a "historical semantic" dimension, providing alternatives to the notion and locating it in, say, the "violence produced by the politics of identity, of nationalism, of exaggerated patriotism, etc." (paraphrase 332).

12. Paul Bové applauds Said's work as a form of political resistance, writing, for example, how "when the Israelis besiege and shell Beirut, [he] calls for the people to find ways to narrate their experiences, to make the horrible events of their daily lives into experiences by giving them shape as stories that can be shared and remembered, and form a national memory and tradition" (*Edward Said and the Work of the Critic* 3).

13. It seems odd that Said conflates theoretical speculation with political activism, given his clear vision of the need to distinguish between other categories, such as the church from the state, politics from the academy. He states, for example, "I don't think the classroom should become a place to advocate political ideas. I've never taught political ideas in a classroom. I believe that what I'm there to teach is the interpretation and reading of literary texts" (*Pen and Sword* 77–78). And, in an interview with Al Jahdid in 1999 he declares that "the most dangerous and worst scenario for intellectuals is to be involved in both the intellectual and political realms, that is, to combine functions in their political life and political ambitions (seeking positions and offices) and their functions as intellectuals" (*Power, Politics, and Culture* 440). In spite of such assertions, however, he dissolves again and again the role of the scholar and that of the political activist. On yet another occasion he tells Barbara Harlow, "There's only one way to anchor oneself,

and that is by affiliation with a cause, with a political movement" ("The Intellectuals and the War" 366).

14. Said distinguishes his responsible approach to history from that of Foucault, whose theories of power and oppression are not directed to "alleviating human suffering, pain, or betrayed hope" ("Traveling Theory" 216).

15. Said is not the only one. Indeed, as already discussed in earlier chapters, those like Foucault and Derrida, to mention only two, also chose to distance themselves from Marx. As I've already discussed in this book, this posed a huge problem for Derrida and Foucault because the alternative in France was Sartre's Leftist phenomenology; so one way or another and to different degrees they turned to the highly speculative work of Heidegger, Husserl, and Nietzsche.

16. We see Said's turn to a spatial theory in all his work. We see this explicitly when he tells W. J. T. Mitchell that the Palestinian struggle is "all about territory and contested space and dispossession, which means you have to do certain things because you don't have the space or the place. It's hard to regain some substitute or equivalent for space if you don't have it. And the relationship between language and space becomes an issue, above all, the notion of writing and distance, which very much informs my thinking about matters of exile and displacement" ("Panic of the Visual" 44).

17. Said's atomized conception of society and power is identical to Foucault's ontologically atomized conception. As discussed in chapter 2, Foucault's power is everywhere; from lovers to fathers, mothers, sons and daughters, every relationship is a relationship of power. And in this microstructural conception of power, the self is only ever conceived of as atomized: every individual in society exists in a Hobbesean opposition and conflict with one another; we exist in our exertion of power against one another. The theories of Carl Schmitt and the fascist positions of Mussolini, Franco, Hitler, and a host of others also come to mind.

18. As I discuss in chapter 11, the same is true of those scholars in the United States with respect to Latin America; it is very difficult for the so-called Subaltern Group to convince their colleagues in other departments to adopt their approach.

19. There are many smart and learned scholars in the public eye who expose the cracks in the machine of capitalism but who ultimately lead us to a dead end; I think readily of Noam Chomsky, who implicitly offers as a solution to today's exploitation and suffering only a rather reactionary libertarianism. Even when people publish in much more popular venues like the Internet, one runs into the same problem. Those who claim the Internet is a venue for global emancipation are wrong—even if it puts one into contact with thousands more people than a trade union assembly. When one publishes something on the Internet it might reach many readers, but there's no sense of being in direct contact with the audience where you can see people's reactions and move to organize.

20. The personal turns into the political only with a force that moves it out of the personal sphere and into the public sphere whereby it can become a political

weapon with the goal of transforming reality. And this cuts both ways: the modification of reality can be politically progressive (equal rights and protections applying to Israelis and Palestinians as citizens of one nation-state, say) or regressive (today's Israeli/Palestinian fragmentation and destructive debacle, say).

21. It's worth mentioning that since Gramsci's days as a teenager building a worker's party in Italy till the day he was murdered in Mussolini's prison, he was avidly opposed to Stalinist policies (like those that infused the work of Lukács) and always absolutely a Marxist.

22. Just like NGOs that have exerted an enormous pressure to be present and represented in the UN in many agencies like the ILO, they seek the same status as the representatives of governments, of trade unions, and of what they call "civil society"—a term used by those who attend the yearly NGO convocation in Porto Alegre, where they never refer to classes but always to civil society. NGOs are self-conceived as the emanation or outgrowth of civil society, and yet, if you dig a little, you begin to see that most NGOs are financed by the big imperialists of the world.

23. In spite of Said's criticism of Foucault's spatial approach to history, he does the same trick of privileging space over time, geography over history. Said does exactly what he critiques Foucault for doing. Recall Said's essay "Foucault and the Imagination of Power," in which he considers Foucault's early and middle works "deeply compelling" (149) in their theories of "the order, stability, authority, and regulatory power of knowledge" (149). However, while he is drawn to Foucault's "spatial" (149) move toward sites of power that make for a "disciplinary society"— hospitals, prisons, libraries, schools—-he considers him "profoundly pessimistic" and lacking in a real sense of "effective resistance" (151). On the other hand, he is critical of Foucault's pessimism, yet he also considers him correct "in showing how discourse is not only that which translates struggle or systems of domination, but that *for which* struggles are conducted, 'le pouvoir don't on cherche à s'emparer,'" (153). For Said, then, Foucault opens the door to understand "the problematic of the relationship between subjectivity and ideas of justice, for example, or the category of the aesthetic as a negation of power, or of genealogical and critical history as interventionary activities within the network of discourses of knowledge" (155). Recall, too, Said's position in his essay "The Problem of Texuality: Two Exemplary Positions," whereby he identifies Foucault's "*mise en discours*" and Derrida's "*mise en abîme*" as more than "contemplative" activities (673). Indeed, as Said writes, "in our present circumstances criticism is an adversary, or oppositional, activity" (673). Finally, he remarks of his use of both theoretical paradigms "in what is its own best interest since both strike me as indispensable to any cogent critical position" (674).

24. Said not only employs the more idealist and ideological concepts of Gramsci—hegemony, political society, and civil society—but arguably misreads Gramsci's double-valenced, coded prison notes; under surveillance of one form or another and spending much time in prison meant also that Gramsci wrote in code; this has the consequence of leading many academics today to misidentify his writ-

ings, especially categories like "Philosophy of Praxis," a coded name he used to refer to Marxism. So while using Gramsci to situate his work within a Left-identified intellectualism, often he does the opposite. The problem here is that when, for example, Said uses the notion of "civil society" as a Marxist concept, Gramsci in fact meant it to be a code word for fascism, a Mussolinian concept; not that Mussolini invented the term (a term used by Hegel and others all the way back to Francis Bacon). This old notion of "civil society," which actually disappeared from the political vocabulary after Hegel's death, was reborn in the twentieth century and made fashionable by fascist, "Corporativist" ideology (corporativism is another name for fascism mainly in French and Italian).

25. He tells Jennifer Wicke and Michael Sprinker how Marxism as "orthodoxy, an ontology, even an epistemology, strikes me as extraordinarily insufficient. The protestations or the affirmations of belonging to a Marxist tradition seem to me to be interesting only if they are connected to a practice, which in turn is connected to a political movement" (in *Power, Politics, and Culture: Interview with Edward W. Said* 158). This hasn't stopped scholars from identifying Said as somehow Left and/or Marxist; in his essay "Counternarratives, Recoveries, Refusals" Mustapha Marrouchi declares Said's postcolonialism to be a "Fanonist resistance" whereby he exposes "those symptoms of prejudicial thinking—manifest, obsessional motifs, manipulative rhetoric, undocumented blanket assertions, and so forth—which signal the presence of an overriding drive to construct an image of the 'Orient' in line with Western beliefs and policy interests" (212).

26. He writes in *Orientalism*, "I had to focus rigorously upon the British, French and later the American material because it seemed inescapably true not only that Britain and France were the pioneer nations in the Orient and Oriental studies, but that these vanguard positions were held by virtue of the two greatest colonial networks in pre-twentieth-century history" (17). Accordingly, the West (Europe) is only Britain, France, and "American material." I ask, What about countries like Finland, Sweden, Denmark, Germany, and all the Central European countries like Poland, Hungary, Czechoslovakia—not to mention Spain? Spain, after all, is a country that had been occupied by the "Orientals"—the Arabs—for eight centuries or so. Said's focus on space and not history provides his out.

27. In the interview with Anne Beezer and Peter Osborne, Said discusses how he got involved in Amman in 1969 not while living there, but as an expatriate: "I began to write about politics for the first time in my life, to be published in America, and to appear on television" ("Orientalism and After" 209).

28. Although he claimed not to be a member of the Palestinian cabinet, he did work for the PLO, focusing his attentions exclusively on the role of propaganda and public relations.

29. Today, like yesterday, the Palestinians had as a central demand the "Right to Return" to lost lands. This demand implied that Palestinians and Jews would live together in one unique state governed not by theocratic norms and heavily militarized

(like today), but under conditions where Israelis and Palestinians would have the same rights in a secular, democratic state.

30. Said was more than critical of Arafat—he broke completely from him. Here it is important to keep in mind the difference between being critical and breaking from a political party. One can be critical and disagree with, say, the French Communist Party's handling of the recent "riots" in France, but until one breaks with the party, one continues to share in the ideological identity of the organization as a member. It's healthy in political life for disagreement within an organization; everyone has different ideas and all have the right to express their differences, but once decisions or actions are taken, then you go along with the majority; this doesn't mean you give up your ideas or political opinions, it just means that you will continue to support the organization.

31. When Arafat was dying in France, many gathered at his deathbed to hear if he would divulge the locations of accounts he controlled in which he had stashed billions of dollars, money he would dip into to pay soldiers' salaries, build small state infrastructure in the West Bank, and so on.

32. Even a cursory glance at the UN documents from 1948 on reveals that the Palestinians made many declarations of resistance and appealed for peace in the area. Notwithstanding the massive military superiority of the Zionists, armed first by the British, then by the Americans, the Palestinians had always resisted.

33. Of course, I don't possess an encyclopedic knowledge of the history of the Palestinians, but if you simply follow the documents published by the United Nations on the matter of the creation of the state of Israel and how it adopted laws that allowed the Zionist government not only to dispossess the Palestinians of land and houses, but also to create a theocratic state, you will discover the following: citizenship was grounded in the Jewish religion, thus turning those Palestinians who remained into second-class citizens.

34. It had the immediate advantage that this conception of history allows for the identification of power everywhere; thus it turned on the factory conveyer belt of an industry that churned out scholars who examined power relationships in everything that Said examines in particular in *Orientalism* and in all other films, novels, anthropology books, and so on.

35. A different approach to Said can be found in the essays collected and edited by Homi Bhabha and W. J. T. Mitchell, *Edward Said: Continuing the Conversation* (2005). For example, Mitchell calls him a "literary warrior" (4); Bhabha speaks of his "polyphonic voice weaving together his various subjects with a fugal virtuosity" (10); Paul Bové identifies *Humanism and Democratic Criticism* as "a book about the survival of the human species as a form of mind interested in and capable of knowing itself and its works and of desiring freedom and liberty" (37); Aamir R. Mufti rescues Said's "*cultural* emphasis" in understanding imperialism as not "simply an "idealist failure to comprehend the determining impact of material and economic forces" (122).

CHAPTER SIX

1. Some titles and subtitles of these recently filed dissertations in the United States, United Kingdom, Africa, and Sweden include "Modernity and Change in Ethiopia 1941–1991"; "Lesbian Modernity and American Realism"; "Masculinity, Modernity, and the Making of a Jewish National Subject"; "Writing and the Experience of the Body in Modernity"; "Rebirthing Balance between Modernity and the Natural World"; "Biomedicine and Modernity in the Lives of Adults with Cystic Fibrosis"; "Relating to Modernity: A Study of the Authorship of Gertrud Lilja"; and "Figures of Infanticide: Traumatic Modernity and the Inaudible Cry."

2. Modernity as today's academic piñata isn't beaten only by those squarely situated in postcolonial theory. For example, Elizabeth S. Goodstein approaches modernity as a way to understand boredom; modernity and the state of boredom arose simultaneously in Western society. Here, modernity refers to a shift in subjectivity where "nothing means, nothing pleases, nothing matters" (1). Modernity is the "experience without qualities" (1) as one adapts in mind and body to life "in a world where nothing stays put, to an era in which the idea of transcendent meaning seems hopelessly old-fashioned" (1–2). A critical study of the rhetoric of boredom—"a negative configuration of self" (4)—allows for a destabilizing of this "experience of modernity" (6).

3. Modernity is fashionable as a way to describe any period between the seventeenth and early twentieth centuries; some use it to reference the scientific and technical revolutions (telescope/microscope) launched by the new sciences of Galileo and Newton and that corresponds to a period when the bourgeoisie became the main economic force everywhere. Some theorize the end of modernity after World War II, when we moved into a period of postmodernity, an epoch identified by many (Lyotard, Jameson, Hardt/Negri, Baudrillard, et al.) as the epoch of late capitalism, supracapitalism, biopower, or empire and the end of traditional class conflicts and antagonisms.

4. Modernity as a concept allows scholars to expand their spatial (geographic) reach; not only do we see it as the common denominator that allows for scholarships of the Caribbean, Mexico, and the United States in today's "hemispheric studies," but also in English-language studies of Chinese literature. See especially the essays collected in Charles A. Laughlin's edited *Contested Modernities in Chinese Literature* as well as Tani E. Barlow's essay "Eugenic Woman, Semicolonialism, and Colonial Modernity as Problems for Postcolonial Theory" in *Postcolonial Studies and Beyond*.

5. For another use of the postcolonial to identify several modernities (and vice versa), see Vilashini Cooppan's "The Ruins of Empire: the National and Global Politics of America's Return to Rome" in *Postcolonial Studies and Beyond*.

6. In their edited collection *After Spanish Rule*, Mark Thurner and Andrés Guerrero conceive of modernity as developing historically in different moments

and different geographic spaces. For example, sixteenth-century imperial Spain was "postcolonial Spanish America's first 'Europe'" (*After Spanish Rule* 5).

7. We can look to a similar period of dysphoria during the 1930s ideological conflicts of Stalinism, Western liberal capitalism, and fascism (Mussolini, Franco, and Hitler), where there was a tidal shift to the Right among those who supported the Bolshevik Revolution and socialism. See Trotsky's pamphlet *Their Morals and Ours,* at http://www.marxists.org/archive/trotsky/works/1938/1938-mor.htm

8. It's worth noting that C. L. R. James was an active writer, thinker, and activist; during his long sojourn in the United Kingdom he actively participated in the artists' and writers' circles in London and was a Trotskyite active in workers' organizations and groups. Like many others, after World War II James began to feel more and more out of touch with political reality; the revolution had not made the kind of progress imagined, nor had the workers gained power as all on the Left had hoped for. Although he never ceased being political, after World War II James's political analysis lost its sharp focus.

9. At the Bandung Conference in 1956 the heads of the nonaligned states (among them Mumbia, Nehru, the president of Mexico, Adolfo Lopéz Mateos) and intellectuals (Malcolm X and Richard Wright, for example) met to declare their "third path," which would follow neither the way of communism nor that of capitalism but something in between. They declared that the people of these nonaligned states should simply accept their misery and patiently await the arrival of social change; this, of course, was another way of getting the people to submit completely to imperialism.

10. It's not surprising that C. L. R. James had a change of heart when he returned to the *Black Jacobins* in the 1960s. This was supposed to be a time of great anticolonial emancipation and the establishment of worker states and governments in Africa, Asia, the Caribbean, and Latin America; it was marked instead by massive crushing of workers' organizations in these countries. In responding to this reality, the former "utopianism" in James shifted to one of great pessimism; we see this especially in those seven new paragraphs he adds to the 1968 edition.

11. Capitalism is increasingly splitting at the seams with explosive tensions and contradictions. Even several of the U.S. military's top brass and certain members of Congress are today questioning the massive financing of the occupation of Iraq.

12. In "The Living On [sur-vie] of the Postcolonial Nation in Neocolonial Globalization" Pheng Cheah not only divides the world into pieces—the Western versus postcolonial—but goes even further to place the postcolonial (a.k.a Third World) outside a one-world system under capitalism. Cheah variously identifies it as a "prosthesis" and "a specter that haunts global capital" (252). See also Cheah's *Spectral Nationality: Passages of Freedom from Kant to Postcolonial Literatures,* in which he uses a theory of "organismic vitalism" (an indigenous/culturalist-based nationalism) as political/philosophical manifesto of sorts.

13. While many economists considered only economic factors for capitalist growth, Rostow looked to Weber and others to add a psychological and sociological

dimension. We see this mixing of economic analysis and history with sociological and psychological studies in the work of Amartya Sen, who won the Nobel Prize in 1998 because of such cultural and psychological considerations.

14. James Ferguson sums up this New Nations developmentalism as follows: "For those at the bottom of the global hierarchy, the message was clear: wait, have patience, your turn will come" ("Decomposing Modernity: History and Hierarchy after Development" 168).

15. I agree with Aijaz Ahmad's critique, with some reservations; specifically, I'm weary of the implicit use of a factors theory of history and culture in his discussion of uneven production of postcolonial literature. So while he acknowledges the unity "bestowed upon our globe by the irreconcilable struggle between capital and labour," to understand postcolonial literature one must take into account the different factors that leave different traces of influence on the text; the literary scholar has to take into account all the factors to see which one is the most powerful in the determination of the fate of the postcolonial literary text. In chapter 5 we saw this factors theory approach in Said's "Orientalism" (via Foucault via Althusser), whereby single factors—ideas—have the power to change the course of history.

16. History shows us that divisions such as capitalism vs. communism as well as first vs. third worlds are nonsense. Recall that it was in the name of communism that Stalin ordered the Chinese Communist Party to put down their arms to prove their loyalty to the Nationalist Party (NP); naked to the barbarous Nationalist Party, the workers were brutally exterminated by the hundreds of thousands; the leader of the NP, Chiang Kai-shek, even had bodies of certain militants thrown into steam train furnaces.

17. In "Cosmo-Theory," when Timothy Brennan asks, "Were intellectuals not so reluctant to explore their economic roles, they might be championing the efforts—in Southern Mexico, Colombia, Indonesia, Palestine, and elsewhere—of establishing sovereignty—this as opposed to constructing intricate theoretical edifices designed to explode the very ability to imagine it" (686). In resonance with my discussion of Said in chapter 5, I wonder if it isn't precisely this establishing of sovereignty that cut off Palestinians from existing along with Israelis under a "One State, One Law" nation-state that would guarantee them equal rights. In the name of sovereignty, we have seen Native Americans in the United States confined effectively to huge concentration camps. While the nation-state serves the interests of the bourgeoisie, because of its formation within the history of the class struggle, its structures have been used by the working class to gain and preserve civil rights. As discussed in chapter 4, if one takes away the nation (structures of national law) from the Zapatistas, the Palestinians, and the Native Americans, then one only further deepens the reservoirs available for exploitation of peoples.

18. It is true, of course, that tourists feed this huge capitalist plague that damages everything: from the native peoples to the environment. But are those who are forced to work in miserable conditions because they need money to survive really able to resist the tourist gaze? Likewise, when these scholars celebrate the erasure

of the nation-state, we have to look at reality. We've seen in the twentieth century the massive transfers of populations (Israelis, for example) as well as refugees who have been thrown out of cities or areas and who have lived elsewhere because the state structures have exploded and there's total chaos; with this massive creation of refugees, you have the creation of exiles: people who have to leave their country essentially for economic or political reasons. For them it is literally a question of life or death; there are thousands of people in exile because of former military dictatorships in Argentina, Chile, Africa, and the Middle East. And you have those forced into the international sex trade—or slave trade.

CHAPTER SEVEN

1. In her response in *Profession* (2006), entitled "Thinking in Dark Times," and as a self-identified "energetic pessimist" (20), Kristeva claims that we live in a world made up of "prepolitical and transpolitical experiences that render obsolete any appeal for normative conscience or the reason-revelation duo" (17). Moreover, the "opposition reason/faith or norm/liberty is no longer sustainable if the speaking being no longer thinks of himself as dependent on the supratangible world and even less on the tangible world 'with the power to oblige'" (17).

2. As I argue in chapter 9, "Can Music Resist?," many U.S. academics feverishly seized upon French deconstruction and British Cultural Studies during the 1980s, the Reagan era, in which massive cuts were made in humanities programs and the rights of teachers and workers generally to organize unions were undermined.

3. As touched upon in chapter 4, "Imaginary Empires, Real Nations," very often such positions encourage unclear thinking and writing. Recall Spivak's self-serving defense of writing and thinking that don't follow a straight line and also Homi Bhabha's so-called "partial milieu" that resists the "fever of frenetic speeds, appetites for expanding size" that characterizes globalization (*Globalizing Rights* 172). Timothy Brennan, in his essay "Cosmo-Theory," is critical not only of such obscurantist and tautological writing, but also of its formulation of power as a discourse of processes, movements, and unfoldings that identifies intellectuals—and not organized working-class labor movements—as the grand shapers of reality. See also Simon Gikandi's essay "Globalization and the Claims of Postcoloniality" and Laura Chrisman's, *Postcolonial Contraventions: Cultural Readings of Race, Imperialism and Transnationalism.*

4. I recall when a colleague of Homi Bhabha and Henry Louis Gates Jr., a regular contributor to *The New Republic* and *The Atlantic,* was called before the Supreme Court as an "expert witness" (on the basis of his work on the signifying monkey and Ivy League credentials) in the charges filed against the rap group, 2 Live Crew.

5. Carrying the U.S. and British flags at the World Economic Forum in 2004 were such notables as Bill Clinton and British foreign secretary Jack Straw. Here they donned the garb of democracy and humanism worn during the late 1990s

(Straw then as British home secretary and Clinton as U.S. president) that sanctioned the bombing of and trade embargoes imposed on Iraq. Recall, too, Clinton's appearance in 2003 on *Larry King Live,* when he exonerated the Bush administration's manipulation of intelligence and endorsed the war on Iraq.

6. To give a stronger sense of the rhetoric used by "cultural workers," I quote at length here Grant Farred's "Vernacularity": "Vernacularity marks that sociopolitical occasion when the conventional intellectual speaks less as a product of a hegemonic cultural-economic system than as a thinker capable of translating the disenfranchised experience of subjugation as an oppositional, ideologically recognizable, vernacularized discourse. Vernacularity represents the moment of a significant, palimpsestic transformation. Vernacularity signals the discursive turning away from the accepted, dominant intellectual modality and vocabulary and the adoption of a new positioning and idiomatic language. It also signals a turning toward, not in a nostalgic but in a considered and deliberate fashion, and (re)connection to an originary—but not necessary umbilical—community: it marks the initiation of the process when the conventionally trained intellectual is ideologically remade through culture—the culture of the subjugated, diasporic community, those cultural practices that signify an intersection between the dominant and the subjugated, those practices that, while being marked as Other, have transformed both the periphery and the metropolis, that have affected relations between the (erstwhile) colonizer and the colonized, those practices that have reconstituted the diasporized constituencies and the metropolis as a whole" (11–12).

7. In *Democracy Matters,* Cornel West also identifies Christ as a "philosopher of democracy" (214). He sees the Christian movement as privileging visions of justice and compassion and how a "prophetic love of justice unleashes ethical energy and political engagement that explodes all forms of our egocentric predicaments or tribalistic mind-sets. Its telling signs are ethical witness, . . . moral consistency, and political activism—all crucial elements of our democratic armor for the fight against corrupt elite power" (215).

8. In the name of humanitarian relief, such organizations are directly funded by capitalist entities that simply want to obscure the real problems that working peoples face worldwide; their efforts are like the Live 8 performances or U2's Bono traveling with various high-level government officials from the United States and the United Kingdom to Africa, paying lip service to the very organizations that are controlled by capitalist elites.

9. There are scholars like Timothy Brennan, Patrick Colm Hogan, Barbara Foley, and Marcial González, who know the difference between politics and intellectual inquiry; those that uphold values like truth and reason and that understand how the nation-state and power really work. They participate within and extend Bertrand Russell's advocating of the learning of analytical skills, and the use of clear thinking/logical reasoning, which make for a fully participating individual in society and lead to participation on equal terms to achieve common goals which were democratically conceived. (See his *Mortals and Others II: American Essays: 1931–1935.*)

10. We see this played out differently by different nation-state conquests. France, during its colonization of Africa in the nineteenth century, created an institute in Paris dedicated to African studies with the idea of cultivating French, African, and Algerian specialists. This was very systematic and a highly managed operation that sent, for example, Paris-educated Algerian natives to serve as appendages of French capitalists during its invasion of Algeria. We can see this cultivating of mandarins in all the big capitalist countries.

CHAPTER EIGHT

1. It is interesting to note that when Raymond Williams sought to save working-class culture as a focus of study, he identified culture as "a whole way of life" in order to locate resources for resistance in all objects, actions, and feelings (see his *Keywords*). We see this same move in translation studies today as it identifies itself as a "whole way of life" and theorizes that "translated subjects" who code switch have the power to transform the world.

2. While Derrida has written directly on translation or, as he called it on one occasion, "transtextualization," as either a willful collision, "highjacking" and/or cooperation between text, author, and translator, he conceives of language itself as an act of translation (a translation of a translation). Derrida conceives of translation as a series of embedded codes (languages) that come into existence as a result of our search for the right word (that word that is not another word) within language, which is itself a series of languages made up of gaps (*différance*) that describes not what is present in language but what is not present. Translation thus conceived is the backbone of his formulation on language and the *différance* of signification. See his essays "What Is a 'Relevant' Translation?," "Des Tours de Babel," "Living On: Border Lines" as well as his books *L'Ecriture et la différance, Dissemination,* and *The Ear of the Other.*

3. In "The Empire Talks Back" Michael Cronin identifies the role of the language interpreter with that of the Euro-Western ethnographer vis-à-vis the subaltern subject. However, within this imbalance of power, he proposes that if one were to bring a sense of dialogue to the interpretive act, then this would tip the balance and make human (and not objectify) the subaltern subject.

4. Spivak's antifoundationalist rejection of the Enlightenment also proposes that we look to religion as the authentic site of cultural difference. I'm reminded of the discussion in chapters 2 and 3 of Derrida's antifoundationalist foundationalism.

5. Gayatri Spivak puts a pedagogical spin on her theories of the postcolonial as translated body. Accordingly, the postcolonial self (subject and text) translates but doesn't fully deliver a localized epistemology as it circulates within world literary canons. Hence her proposal that when we teach postcolonial literature we teach it as a translated text distorts the cosmopolitan frame of its reception.

6. Many scholars formulate translation as nation; that is, as a discourse that interweaves with other discourses to create the dominant ideology of the nation. In *Translation and Understanding* Sukanta Chaudhuri identifies how European translations of Sanskrit in the nineteenth century used "pseudo-scholarship" with the aim of projecting the "alien cultures" onto the "lower rungs of a hegemony of civilizations determined by the colonial order itself" (19). Others have determined that the tension between original and translation plays itself out in the battles between monolingual and bilingual national identity. (See Dorris Sommer's *Bilingual Games,* in which certain kinds of translation, bilingual code switching, and so on come to identify political acts of resistance to monolingual, bordered nation-states.)

7. Edwin Genztler identifies such a "rough" translation when he discusses how the translator "unmasters" the principles of translation by "'stuttering' through its utilization of material" (253).

8. We see this "third-space" also discussed in Maria Tymoczko's "Post-colonial Writing and Literary Translation." On one occasion, she writes how "the act of writing in English is not 'merely' one of translation of an Indian text into the English language, but a quest for a space which is created by translation and assimilation and hence transforms all three—the Indian text, context and the English language" (42).

9. In her introduction to her edited collection *Nation, Language, and the Ethics of Translation,* Sandra Bermann considers translations, translators, and the work of translation as informing one way or another the construction of nation; and so denaturalizing this imagined nation, decoding the gaps of linguistic slippage, and/or making visible processes of "linguistic oppression" (8) can offer "hope for insight, reciprocity, and therefore creative negotiation, if never perfect resolution, between languages and peoples, between values, enmities and loves" (8). Finally, Bermann invites the readers of her edited volume "to rethink the issues of nation, language, and translation in concrete, linguistically and culturally specific terms. Through such situated readings, a new and surprisingly different understanding of our world, it languages, and the individual cultural and historical perspectives so important to its flourishing begins to unfold" (8).

10. Many attempts at defining a nation have been insufficient because they fail to acknowledge the necessary and sufficient elements that characterize its socio-economic and historical elements. "Nation" is a geographical space inhabited by a population that has a common history, a common language, and a common set of customs or habits (a common culture). Of course, even this definition needs to be further refined as it has many exceptions: in some nations, like Switzerland, for example, the population does not speak one but several languages; in Belgium, people speak two languages. And it would be difficult to say that the United States, with its great cultural diversity, contains one common culture. So, we might further revise this definition: a nation is, on the one hand, a material reality and, on the other, a

psychological affiliation. It is a space inhabited by a people identified by the name given to that geographical space that is limited by borders established and preserved by a state apparatus.

11. Gerald Martin also discusses how translations of book titles, beginnings, and endings can alter the material fate of the original work. He writes, "We know that titles are the first and in some respects most important keys to unlocking a literary work. They are its name and identity but, unlike our own names—at least in this culture—they are also a decisive clue to its meaning" ("Translating García Márquez" 157).

12. Jeffrey M. Green considers the task of translating as "involving a dive through strata of linguistic consciousness" (49). For Green, there exists a "top level of individual words, a lower level of phrases and sentences, and an even lower level of semantic structures beneath any specific language" (49). When moving to the inner core, then, one must know the meaning of individual words, the syntax of the sentence, and a sense of the "way you would write what the text says if you were writing it originally" (50). He concludes, "The deeper you dive into the source language, the more natural the translation will sound, though it might turn out inaccurate" (50).

13. This idea that form and content are separable spills over into concepts of everyday speech-acts: not just when we paraphrase but also when we have to rephrase something because the listener misunderstood the original phrase; what one is doing is transmitting the same content in a different form. Concerning language, then, in any phrase—"I'm going out for a walk"—one can find a referent for "I," "am," "going" and even "out"; even though "out" is an extremely vague word, nobody stops to analyze it or at first sight finds it vague at all: yet it is an extremely general and vague word. The referent is established automatically when you hear it. But there is no referent for "for"; nothing in the world would correspond to the word "for" in this phrase. When I say "I like rice and potatoes" there's nothing in the world that I can point to that is an "and." They are all syntactical operators—words with an indispensable function in English. One can't formulate in an ordinary language an expression without these words. Therefore you can't express, communicate, or transmit thoughts without these words—even though their only function is syntactical (or formal).

So if this is the case, then we have a form and a content that is proper to language and a form and content that belongs to thought. You can formulate phrases that are perfectly understandable and are used in everyday speech that contain sounds with no referential content; their content is only operational or formal. And you have a whole referential vocabulary in language that has its form and its content—its reference to which it points to in terms of content. To bring us back to literature, we see this misunderstanding of the inseparability of form and content also in the New Critics with their "heresy of paraphrase" theory; to show that there is no separate value in the content of the poem and in the form of the poem, they posited the inseparability of form and content. In this diet of form and content, they're saying that the form is the language and the content is the thought; this, of course, denies the fact that thought as, say, an entity has both form and content.

14. We can see the same process working in the example of the paraphrase: a thought expressed in shape "A" (English) that you wish to express in form "B" (the same language as a paraphrase). This happens in the writing of poetry as opposed to prose. I write poetry in English and I want to write a poem in the form of a sonnet; this means that I'm going to exercise my will to express my thought within the language conventions of the sonnet instead of expressing my thought in the conventions of prose.

15. In *World Literature* David Damrosch gives the example of Rigoberta Menchú as a provincial writer who has become subordinate to Western writers and readers and who has become "assimilated to the immediate interests and agendas of those who edit, translate, and interpret them" (25).

16. Indeed, several scholars have variously identified the subaltern (ethnic, postcolonial, hybrid and/or diasporic identified) as particularly able to harness to positive political ends this infinite semiosis. Bilingual speakers experience a "double belonging" for Sommer, and so if one can learn to enjoy the effects of code switching in everyday communication acts then one can potentially "overload" and transform a hegemonic nation-state (*Bilingual Games* 2). Sommer explores this further in *Bilingual Aesthetics: A New Sentimental Education,* in which she argues that the nation-state suppresses resistant code-switching subjects; that if the nation were to recognize itself as a "multilingual nation" it would be much healthier. I see several issues here. First, that Sommer still follows largely an antiquated behaviorist linguistic approach (Bloomfield, Sapir, and Whorf) and not that of current approaches in linguistics that follow Chomsky (this, even though she positions herself within a "post-Chomskyean linguistics"). Second, when one gives the state authority to declare which language or languages should be learned, one divests the people of the authority to decide. It is fine if people want to be bilingual or trilingual in the United States or elsewhere, if this is what they want. Third, Sommer proposes that making a multilingual nation will realize a social utopia. I ask, are the peasants in Oaxaca, Mexico, more exploited and discriminated against because they aren't allowed to be bilingual or multilingual? Is a country like Switzerland less racist because it mandates that all products sold have advertising in three languages? Finally, it is the knowledge of English in the United States (just as it is of Spanish in Mexico or of French in France, for example) that is an essential tool for working peoples to be able to communicate to organize against the repressive mechanisms of state. If, as suggested by Sommer, a "multilingual nation" means a linguistic apartheid (Spanish for Chicanos, Swahili for African Americans, the Uto-Aztecan Comanche for Natives Americans, for example) then what we'll see is a decline toward barbarism.

17. In "Literary Theory and its Discontents" John Searle discusses the necessary function of vagueness in language by using the example of ordering a hamburger. The scenario unfolds as follows. First, he describes precisely what he wants in his hamburger (lettuce, ketchup, etc.). When it arrives, it is encased in a block of

cement. Why? Because he didn't specify that he didn't want it to be contained within a big block of cement. So, he reorders the hamburger, this time specifying that it arrive without a block of cement, yet when it arrives it weighs a ton. There are many examples of such miscommunication in our everyday communication acts. That is, if we had to specify all the details of the hamburger—what it is and what it is not—communication between people would not happen; the infinite number of details needed to identify the hamburger would take a lifetime to communicate. More to the point, we would never fly in a plane knowing that when the pilot receives instructions to land on the runway he might defer meaning for an unlimited time to understand all the layers of meaning and so crash the plane. That is to say, no language would exist without vagueness—it is the element of language that allows us to make shortcuts in our communication acts.

18. There are notable exceptions to this rule. In the preface to *Switching Languages* Steven Kellman writes, "Translingual authors—those who write in more than one language or in a language other than their primary one—are the prodigies of world literature. By expressing themselves in multiple verbal systems, they flaunt their freedom from the constraints of the culture in which they happen to have been born" (ix).

19. Innovation also takes place when an artist reaches beyond his or her own genre's domain. The author of a novel makes old stories innovatively new not only by reaching out to those schemas, exempla, and prototypes that appear in other world literary novels, but also by reaching beyond the novelistic domain and into, say, the domain of visual arts.

20. The translation process works within bounded limits. Jeffrey Green sums this up by likening the translation process to the international currency markets, which, he writes, "set a range within which the value of the local currency can fluctuate freely in relation to international currencies, and when it threatens to slip beyond that range, the central bank steps in. Similarly, the translator is granted a range of freedom with respect to the original text (more in some cultures than in others). If he or she exceeds that range of freedom, the work will no longer be regarded as a translation, but as an adaptation or an aberration" (*Thinking Through Translation* 8–9).

21. Translations of U.S. (and/or British) formulaic authors are sold not only in places like Mexico, but also within European countries. A recent statistic reveals that for every German book translated into English, nine English-language books were translated into German. (See also Josef Joffe's essay "The Perils of Soft Power: Why America's Cultural Influence Makes Enemies, Too".)

CHAPTER NINE

1. Elaine Richardson's *Hiphop Literacies* (2006) captures this idealist impulse well. Richardson aims to "locate rap/Hiphop discourse, particularly, its pop culture

forms, within a trajectory of Black discourses, relating them to the lived experiences of Black people, emanating from their quest for self-realization, their engagement in a discursive dialectic between various vernacular and dominant discourses and semiotic systems" (xvi). For Richardson, it is socially conscious rap/hip-hop that can reveal an alternative social agency struggling "against forces that would annihilate them" (xvi). And, it is worldwide circulation via the Internet, video games, music videos, hip-hop novels, cinema, and the like that has led to, for instance, code switching between German and what the author identifies as AAL, or African American Language. Of a particular video game experience, the author reflects: "I noticed that my voice began to engage the game. I was the one talking more trash than a little bit. In this way the player of the game begins to merge with the game world. My language and knowledge of how to empower myself help me to empower my player-controlled agent/wrestler" (103). Richardson's hope: that her work "will contribute to the growing body of scholarship that encourages educational institutions more fully to incorporate the study of literacy, particularly literacies of popular culture, more broadly into the official curriculum to stem racist social practices in society" (xvii).

2. In the "Unofficial conjunto Primer" Carlos Guerra writes of the birth of *conjunto* in nineteenth-century Mexico "when the *bajo sexto* was added for rhythmic bass-guitar accompaniment. This reed-and-string duet arrangement quickly became popular music form for dances, a basic entertainment form of the lower classes" (5). He describes how "these forms were easily absorbed by the already musically inclined Mexican culture and the process of Mexicanizing them began immediately" (4). The Germans' introduction of the diatonic accordion in Mexico in the last half of the century was embraced by the rural poor, as it could complement the existing harmony of Mexican vocals through its ability to produce both melody and bass parts simultaneously with the push of two adjacent buttons.

3. Importantly, too, the "tec" in Nortec is linked to a variety of associated lifestyles. Techno was first associated with African American suburban kids, then later to a Chicago, New York queer club scene. Specifically, it was techno's offshoot "House" that sampled and revitalized a disco soundscape beaten down by the dominance of a 1980s white, heterosexual-identified rock scene. House became increasingly associated with gay club scenes in the West. The very term "House" was used to describe the techno heard at Chicago's gay nightclub the Warehouse. With police crackdowns, especially at gay nightclubs, techno/house migrated underground and became increasingly associated with a white middle-class, Ecstasy-popping straight rave scene. Hence the claim by the rap artist Chuck D of Public Enemy that techno is "anti-black" and "upwardly mobile" (cited in Reynolds, 24). Today, of course, techno is identified as a border aesthetic. Its diaspora and variously linked lifestyles manifest a series of musico-aesthetic nodes that reflect an evolution of a form with a number of differently contoured consumers attached: African American, queer, white, Latino.

4. In a special edition of *Time* magazine titled "Amexica," Josh Tyrangiel writes of Nortec that it represents a "new frontier" that reflects "contrary realities of a place that's neither First World nor Third World; a culture that is neither Mexican nor American; an economy propelled by the dual engines of drug traffic and high-tech maquiladoras; a large, stable middle class sandwiched between grotesque poverty and excessive narco wealth. The goal, simply, is to transform the strangeness of Tijuana into art" (76).

5. In "Popular Music Analysis and Musicology: Bridging the Gap," Richard Middleton writes that musical gestures are underlaid with "kinetic patterns, cognitive maps, affective movements [that are] probably specific to a culture" (106). He concludes, "People seem to learn to emote, to order experience, even to move their bodies, through locally acquired conventions" (106).

6. There is no such thing as a music that is in any essential way Latino/a or queer: Latino/a and queer are racial and/or sexual categories, and music is a particular way of organizing noises to make soundscapes. Of course, certain sound arrangements and certain styles are associated with and even produced by people described as Latino/a or queer, for example, but this is a social phenomenon, not a musical one. (For more on this important distinction, see Philip Tagg's important article "Open Letter: 'Black Music', 'Afro-American Music' and 'European Music'" in the journal *Popular Music*). While this slips problematically into a racially essentialist rhetoric long denounced by cultural critics such as Paul Gilroy, it is simply wrong to conflate and/or analogize music genres with racial or sexual categories.

7. In *Barrio Rhythms: Mexican American Music in Los Angeles,* Steven Loza discusses Chicano rock/punk groups who hybridize New Wave rhythms with Tex-Mex sounds—Los Cruzados (The Plugz), Felix and the Katz, Odd Squad, The Undertakers, Loli Lux and the Bears, The Brat, and Los Illegals—to "critique society" (111). He concludes of such resistant *frontera* soundspaces: "New wave in the Chicano community of Los Angeles offered musicians and aficionados a vehicle for social statement and at the same time the potential for penetration into a new market" (111).

8. Mainstream music critics also participate in this idealization of music. They not only situate a music by contextualizing and referring to music conventions, but they also influence what is bought and sold; such mainstream critics are cultural gatekeepers who help to cover up a capitalist production/consumption mechanism in their transformation of music-as-object into music falsely invested with epistemological value. As Roy Shuker sums up, "The more crucial intermediaries are those who control airtime (DJs and radio programmers) and access to recording technology and reproduction and marketing facilities (record companies and record producers)" (95). For such critics, the confusion of music as cultural phenomenon with a resistant ontology or epistemology ultimately serves, as Shuker writes, "as a service industry to the record industry, lubricating the desire to acquire both new product and selections from the back catalogue" (98).

9. We can trace this confusion of musicscape with real acts of resistance back to the Birmingham School Cultural Studies critics Stuart Hall, Raymond Williams,

Dick Hebdige, and Ian Chambers. These critics performed ethnographies of youth groups subcultures to identify their appropriation and recycling of mainstream commodities as a form of resistance to a dominant hegemony.

10. Juan Tejada defines polka/conjunto (group or ensemble) as "a specific form of music that combines German, Mexican, Latin American, and U.S. influences. The lead instrument in the traditional four-piece conjunto is the button accordion. The other instruments are the *bajo sexto* (a twelve-string bass-rhythm guitar), bass guitar, and drums. Conjunto music is dance music, and currently its most popular rhythms . . . are the polka and the *cumbia*" ("Introduction" xv). Conjunto's origins go back to the late nineteenth century, when many German immigrants moved into northern Mexico and southern Texas. As a result, salon music (*música de baile*) began to combine and hybridize polkas from Germany and Poland as well as waltzes from Austria with Mexican sounds.

11. House/techno originally was all about using discarded sounds to enliven dead rhythms and beats. As Simon Reynolds writes, techno was created out of "disregarded and degraded pop-culture detritus that the mainstream considered passé, disposable, un-American: the proto-disco of the Salsoul and Philadelphia International labels, English synth-pop, and Moroder's Eurodisco" (24). Like house/techno, all music seeks to make interesting dead and discarded sounds. Tom Waits "invents" sounds out of makeshift "instruments" (cooking pans, for example) and then mixes this music with sounds coming from his barn. His music sells—and well.

12. It was the collaboration between the U.S. government (supported by private corporate interest) and the lumpenproletariat that led to the pushing of heroin (and later cocaine) into brown and black urban neighborhoods as a way to control what was considered to be a growing threat: the rise of brown and black power movements (working-class coalitions) in the late 1960s and early 1970s.

13. One can study music in a number of ways. In the *Harvard Dictionary of Music,* musicology is defined as "the whole body of systematized knowledge about music which results from the application of a scientific method of investigation or research, or of philosophical speculation and rational systematization to the facts, the processes and development of musical art, and the relation of man in general" (cited by Roy Shuker 140). For instance, music literacy is learning how to read noises created purposefully with physical things called instruments that are deliberately built to create sounds. It is learning how to read notes in their combinations and in the patterns and sequences that such notes follow. It is learning how a given musician/composer patterns sequences of identifiable patterns and differences between these patterns. It is also to learn to appreciate the complexity or invention and novelty in the recombination of music patterns. It can also be learning to analyze how music—its melody, rhythm, harmony, lyrics, and performance—affect a listener's emotions and kinesthetic responses.

14. The British promoter Paul Oakenfold (promoter of Run-DMC and Beastie Boys) realized the potential of creating a subcultural scene not in London, but in Ibiza, where Ecstasy was more widely available and the laws less strict. After his

South London club flopped (Funhouse in 1985), he set up shop in Ibiza, renting a villa and flying in DJs from all over the world to create an all-in-one techno subcultural package complete with drugs, lingo, clothing (baggy trousers/ponchos/paisley bandannas), and a behavior. All this was hatched in the summer of 1987. After this success, Oakenfold went on to launch London's Spectrum—a two-thousand capacity gay club (billed as Theater of Madness) that generated huge profits.

15. As I've mentioned earlier in the book, culture is a hugely ambiguous and vague concept. It is used to describe a whole array of everyday practices. It is essentially a term used to oppose the concept of nature: that is cultural, which is not natural (fire in woods caused by lightning vs. fire caused by Neolithic man rubbing wood against stone). This distinction is useful as long as one is aware of its limitations: man is a cultural being who created himself through the transformation of nature, but in transforming nature he transforms himself (the biological being is also simultaneously and inseparably a social being). As discussed at length in chapter 1, in man, nature and culture are inseparable, and the transformation of culture (sedentary lifestyles, for instance) leads to the transformation of nature (road building, house building, etc.), which leads to the transformation of culture (roads allow the passage of cars, etc.), which helps the passage from one type of economic organization—the feudal, for instance—to another—the industrial, capitalist society, and so on and so forth.

CHAPTER ELEVEN

1. In his "Foreword" to *After Spanish Rule* the South Asian historian Shahid Amin expresses a concern over such an abstraction; he's critical of "postcolonial" as a template used to serve all situations, upholding the value of the patient exploration of archives and careful comparative study of the relationship between different documents found in one archive and another.

2. See Anna Brickhouse's *Transamerican Literary Relations and the Nineteenth Century Public Sphere,* Anne Goldman's *Continental Divide,* José Aranda's *When We Arrive,* Kirsten Silva-Gruesz's *Ambassadors of Culture,* Gretchen Murphy's *Hemispheric Imaginings,* Sara L. Spurgeon's *Exploding the Western,* and Carlos Hiraldo's *Segregated Miscegenation: On the Treatment of Racial Hybridity in the U.S. and Latin American Literary Traditions,* to name a few who are shaping American "hemispheric studies."

3. Oddly, Saldaña-Portillo, like many others, reveres Menchú—a darling of the haute bourgeoisie; open a newspaper in Mexico City and you see her photographed as the distinguished guest at all kinds of parties and at the biggest haciendas in Mexico. She's always dressed in haute couture peasant garb. And in Saldaña-Portillo's critique (mostly based in psychoanalytic terms) of Che Guevara and Malcolm X as adherents to a developmentalist economic model, there's no historical, economic, sociological context given to their individual struggles. Hence, Saldaña-Portillo's

critique of Malcolm X as a "leave it to Beaver" type of conservative fails to see how and why the defense of the family—the black working family—as a unity was and still is vitally important. If you don't defend the family unit in the way Malcolm X did, youth fall prey to the world of the lumpenproletariat, becoming what Malcolm had been; moreover, Malcolm X's defense of the family is not, as she can claim in her decontextualized reading, a "romanticized family unit," but a move to protect the working class for the revolution.

4. The storytelling form of magical realism epitomizes this erasing of difference. Postcolonial theorists criticize poststructuralists for identifying magical realism as paradigmatic—what counts as ethnically authentic—of Third World literary production and epistemology. See Spivak's essay "Poststructuralism, Marginality, Postcoloniality, and Value."

CHAPTER TWELVE

1. Other scholars of *Disgrace* and of Coetzee's work generally have often read this novel allegorically as a way to establish a moral compass. Sam Durant sees Coetzee's fiction as a postcolonial response to and reflection of an "oppressive memory of the past in tension with the liberatory promise of the future" (1). That Coetzee leaves his readers without a moral and/or ethical direction in his work is interpreted by Durant as a critical nonaffirmation of identity that opens up the possibility of an Agamben "coming community"—a "co-belonging without any representable condition of belonging" (111). Coetzee textures such a coming community by "indicating what still remains excluded" (111) and whose boundaries "remain perpetually open to the difference of the other, to the possibility of different others and not yet imagined modes of being" (111). For scholars who look specifically at *Disgrace,* it is a picture of a post-Apartheid South Africa where gangster tribalism rules a land filled up with white guilt and the "dregs of the old South Africa" (Kochin 4). For Sue Kossew the novel reflects a "collision between private and public worlds; intellect and body; desire and love; and public disgrace or shame and the idea of individual grace or salvation" (155). Lucy's decision to serve Petrus is interpreted as a compromise and first step in her overcoming a history of racist disgrace that goes beyond guilt and punishment. It is thus, as Kossew writes, a measure of humanity "in a society that has made a spectacle of its inhumanity" (161). Florence Stratton reads Lucy's rape as "embodying the territory or state of South Africa," which continues to be controlled by a larger global patriarchy (98). By drawing a parallel between David Lurie's appearance before the university's disciplinary board for sexual harassment and the Truth and Reconciliation Committee, Stratton is ultimately critical of Coetzee's "assigning sexism a metaphoric status in the narrative" (87). This reveals a lack of real "interest in crimes of patriarchy" (87). For a more general exploration of law and resistance in postcolonial South African literature, see Natasha Distiller's *South Africa, Shakespeare, and Post-Colonial Culture* and also Margaret Urban Walker's

essay "Moral Repair and Its limits" in *The Ethical Turn: A Reader in Ethics, Culture, and Literary Theory.*

2. After spending twenty-seven years in prison, Mandela was released and elected president in May 1994. "The words 'a miracle' were heard on many lips with the realization that this was an unprecedented case of a ruling group relinquishing its monopoly of power without imminent military threat to its continued rule" (xiii), Lyn S. Graybill writes. This was also the time when the government formed the Truth and Reconciliation Commission (TRC). With Archbishop Desmond Tutu as chairman, the TRC professed to follow a precolonial African system of justice: *ubuntu*. This so-called philosophy appears in the final clause of the interim constitution titled "On National Unity and Reconciliation" and reads, "There is a need for understanding but not for revenge, a need for reparation but not for retaliation, a need for *ubuntu* but not for victimization." (The *ubuntu* tradition has since been revealed to be a construct of the writers/thinkers/founders of the African National Congress like Jorgan Ngubane, who later became president of Howard University). As Chief Justice Ismail Mahomed declares in a 1996 speech, the TRC ultimately allows the perpetrators "to become active, full and creative members of the new order, [allowing for a] rapid and enthusiastic transition to the new society at the end of the bridge" (cited in Erik Doxtader's and Charles Villa-Vicencio's *The Provocations of Amnesty* xiv). For Robert I. Rothberg (president of the World Peace Foundation) and Dennis Thompson the TRC remains "the most far-reaching, and the most effective of this genre [and whose] mandate and procedures will become the starting point for all future truth commissions" (*Truth v. Justice: The Morality of Truth Commissions* 19–20). And, for Erik Doxtader and Charles Villa-Vicencio (both affiliated with the Institute for Justice and Reconciliation) the work of the TRC in South Africa forces us to "grapple with the question of whether it is possible to develop and cultivate forms of memory that overcome amnesty's 'forgetting'. We are placed in the uncomfortable position of needing to reconcile the fact that some kinds of forgiveness are a necessary condition of collective life with the belief that there are crimes which defy excuse" (*The Provocations of Amnesty* x). For these scholars, the TRC's "trade-off of truth for amnesty" (x) shed light on the "'motives and perspectives' of those who committed gross violations of human rights during the years of apartheid" (x); for such scholars, this is part of the process of a nation "sharpening its moral conscience" in its transition to "constitutional democracy" (x). Hailed as a new justice system—one of *healing*—it is also seen in developmentalist terms: as a way for South Africa to make the necessary step toward becoming a mature nation-state. Such naive *visions* of the TRC as expressed above hide several important facts. With capitalism and the Catholic Church under threat in South Africa, what better way to obviate that threat than by pairing the church and state as symbols of a new South Africa in the TRC? And, of course, with all the talk of miracles, the fact remains that by April 6, 1999, the TRC had refused amnesty to seventy-nine ANC members and had granted near total amnesty to all those in Frederik de Klerk's apartheid cabinet (http://jurist.law.pitt.edu/world/sacor1.htm).

3. As I discuss elsewhere in this book, English departments are being squeezed financially, and so wittingly or not many scholars of literature are showcasing the importance of literary studies in its usefulness to other disciplines, like law.

4. See, for example, the essay by Richard Clarke Sterne, "The Trial in *A Passage to India*: 'Justice' Under Colonial Conditions," in *Un-Disciplining Literature*. Here, Sterne argues that the legal world of the raj is constructed by the attitudes and perspectives of the characters in the novel.

5. In *Doing What Comes Naturally* Fish summarizes, in so many words, positivism as "a rationality to which beliefs or community practices would be submitted for judgment" (32); and naturalism, in so many words, as "the deconstruction of that rationality [that throws] off those beliefs and practices that now define us" (32). He continues, "When I argue against the first group [positivism], beliefs are forever escaping the constraints that rationality would impose; when I argue against the second group [naturalism], beliefs are themselves constraints that cannot be escaped. Neither stance delivers a finely tuned picture of the operations of belief (or community or practice) because that is not my task, and indeed it is a task which, if taken seriously (as it certainly should be), would prevent me from doing what I have here tried to do. Whether I have done it and whether it is worth doing are questions that are happily not mine either to ask or to answer" (33).

6. The turn to legal critical race theory in Chicano cultural studies can also be seen in Carl Gutiérrez-Jones's, *Critical Race Narratives: A Study of Race, Rhetoric, and Injury*.

7. It's not entirely surprising that in the United States, where 1 out of every 140 adults do some sort of jail time (by 2010, half the population of African American males will be behind bars), our everyday activities one way or another rub against the massive incarceral machine of the nation-state. Literature, film, music, and a whole variety of cultural phenomena reflect this society because it's in the air we breathe.

8. As Hames-Garcia mentions, there are a lot of political prisoners; however, by conflating political with ex-convict and not contextualizing in history and social/material context their political programs, the whole analysis is out of time and out of space.

9. The tripartite separation (executive, juridical, legislative) is supposed to provide those checks and balances that maintain an equilibrium between these fundamental power structures and institutions that make up the state apparatus. However, to keep the equilibrium, there has been historically a need for constant intervention. As one sees today in the discussions about the invasion of Iraq being too costly for American imperialist interests, the state is under constant pressure by the deferring and sometimes opposite interests within the ruling class. That is, within the ruling class there are conflicting points of view concerning the best way to obtain the shared goal: to further the system of oppression and exploitation in the United States and all over the world. Hames-Garcia never mentions the fact that the

state, in whatever form (in the United States it assumes this tripartite form), is the organ that monopolizes power and the means of violence.

10. Several scholars, including Paula Moya, Linda Alcoff, and Michael Hames-Garcia, have made the turn to postpositivist realist theory in their various studies (literary, philosophical, psychoanalytical, and so on) that seek to "reclaim identity" as both real (essential characterizations) and constructed (series of signifiers that assign meaning to bodies). In so many words, the postpositivist realists aim to couple a deconstructionist and an essentialist mode of understanding identity in the Americas (mostly North America) as both unique to localized social, economic, gendered forces and with the possibility of reaching beyond the local. For example, according to the theorists of postpositivist realism, there *can* be an essential, say, woman identity; thus, an individual experiences the world according to her/his perception of herself/himself and his/her interaction with a world where opportunities and resources are distributed according to his/her being identified as a type: black, white, brown, and either woman or man. At the same time, while these scholars believe that identity determines how we experience the world in specific ways (hence their critical stance toward poststructuralist theory that proposes the indeterminacy of identity), they are also careful to declare that they are not empiricists. So while they posit a localized experience of the social, political, and so on, they believe that knowledge of reality is not objective; like the poststructuralists, they believe that all observation and knowledge—and therefore reality—are mediated. Aware of this double bind, they directly acknowledge the possibility of an objective knowledge. However, because they maintain a constructivist stand, ultimately their theory still articulates objective knowledge as framed and determined by language, the individual, and the social. Postpositivist realism, then, isn't so much a new theory of knowledge as it is poststructuralism with a new sartorial cut. See the initial formulation of this theory in Satya Mohanty's "The Epistemic Status of Cultural Identity: On *Beloved* and the Postcolonial Condition." See also Paula Moya's *Learning from Experience* and Moya and Hames-Garcia's edited volume *Reclaiming Identity*. See also Barbara Foley's incisive review of *Reclaiming Identity*.

11. Candidly speaking, *Fugitive Thought* reads a lot like a self-help book; in the selling of a critical moral realism and/or postpositivist realism as an epistemology and ethics, Hames-Garcia makes his reader feel good: you can know prisoners (political and ex-cons alike), feel sorry for them, and not actually have to do anything to change their situation. Its self-declared lack of purpose as an analysis of law or politics or literature leaves it with little else to offer. Since he has nothing to say about political prisoners like Abu-Jamal, he doesn't allow his readers to see their relation to the state (juridical system) and what kind of state is willing to put in prison (even kill) such political prisoners. Rather, the book simply allows the reader to feel good because he or she is told that they're part of a general resistance that *speaks* against power and that doesn't require any real action.

12. My other quibbles with *Fugitive Justice* are as follows: In Hames-Garcia's analysis of the autobiographies/testimonies of so-called "prison intellectuals" like

Angela Davis and Assata Shakur, he mixes apples with oranges. Shakur was a member of the Black Panther Party—a party that had only fleetingly the support of the black working class and that never addressed the concerns of the working-class struggle generally: the need to form an independent party independent from the bourgeoisie. Angela Davis, on the other hand, had been a longtime member of the Communist International Party. And, in the same breath that Marxism is declared dead, Hames-Garcia mentions that Marx had a disdain for the law. For support, he quotes Marx's unfinished, voluminous rough draft "The Gundrisse." If Hames-Garcia had read *volume 1* of *Das Kapital* (the only volume published during Marx's lifetime) he would have seen that Marx devotes whole chapters that show an absolute respect for laws. Finally, Hames-Garcia upholds Martin Luther King Jr as a critical moral realist. First, King was a reverend; that is, he was a man of the church who used the authority of church—that institution that has been used for centuries as an instrument of the ruling class to redirect people's anger and frustrations away from organizing as a material force against the ruling class. (I'm reminded here of Barbara Foley's *Spectres of 1919,* in which she discusses, among others in and around 1919, Alain Locke's *The New Negro* and how the construction of a radical pluralism diffused revolutionary energies as it channeled them into an American exceptionalism.) King was a White House regular who was very much held in the grip of Hoover and Kennedy.

13. Hannah Arendt's work seems to be the flavor of the month in academic scholarship. We see her work providing a main theoretical thrust in much of the Latin American postcolonial scholarship that I discuss elsewhere in this book, informing directly even Dorris Sommer's theories of bilingualism in *Bilingual Aesthetics.* Arendt's work also feeds directly into theories of international relations. In the introduction to *Hannah Arendt and International Relations: Reading Across the Lines,* the editors Anthony F. Lang Jr. and John Williams consider her "ontology of politics" (4) valuable in opening up the field of international relations (traditionally focused on states and institutions) to seeing "individuals as political agents [that are] capable of unpredictable and surprising acts of great political significance" (2). It baffles me that scholars are readily taking up Arendt; in my readings of her work, like *The Origins of Totalitarianism,* I see not only a promotion of an ahistorical and abstract account of fascism that isn't so unlike the totalitarianism of the Soviet Union, Communist China (Nazism and Stalinist Communism are one and the same), but a fear of the people: "the madness of the mob." (Considering that Arendt was Heidegger's student, it's not entirely surprising that she winces at the people.) Moreover, such a general conception of totalitarianism erases not only a long history of working-class struggle and organizing with its foundational logic of universalism, but ultimately upholds a kind of tribalism where the public sphere of politics is eliminated in the promotion of the free functioning of democracy. (This resonates loudly with the work of the reactionary economic theorist Von Hayek among others.)

14. Marx had nothing to say about positive or natural law. Many who haven't read Marx turn him into a kind of Catholic priest, claiming he was a utopian thinker

who considered people to be naturally good. They dismiss their mischaracterized Marx by taking a Hobbesian (man is naturally bad) and a Malthusian economic position.

15. Aquinas conceived of man as created in the image of God, so if man is created in the image of God there would necessarily need to be something in man that is as eternal as God—a soul. Thus, this soul, which constitutes the essential nature of human beings, is also eternal in man. Recall here the debates in tribunals regarding the human status of Native American Indians: did they or did they not have a soul?

16. Giorgio Agamben and Carl Schmitt take their lead from Hobbes. In *Concept of the Political* and *Glossarium* Schmitt formulates a notion of the nation-state's identity as necessarily being at war or in a state of exception. Schmitt considers the function of politics only to direct the "enmity" between the nation and its enemy: "Tell me who your enemy is and I'll tell you who you are" (cited in Mark Lila's *Reckless Minds* 57). As Lila sums up Schmitt's position: "A world without war would be a world without politics; a world without politics would be a world without enmity; and a world without enmity would be a world without human beings" (58). And in *Theory of the Partisan* (1963) Schmitt expresses a certain nostalgia for his theory of human enmity and the state of exception in discussing the end of colonialism, the rise of guerrilla warfare and terrorism. Agamben's state of exception is also a way of conceiving of the nation-state's formation and existence. Agamben discusses how after the king appointed Mussolini the prime minister, the fascist majority in congress gave Mussolini powers that correspond to this state of exception. So Mussolini never had to abolish officially—by decree, law, or any juridical means—the constitution because whatever he decided automatically became law, and thus his decisions simply rendered laws dead or dormant. The same thing happened after Hindenburg offered Hitler the chancellorship. Hitler used his majority in congress to give himself the authority to have the full power of decision. That is, he never got rid of the Weimar constitution, nor did he render preexisting acts and laws obsolete; rather, he simply rendered them dormant one by one. That is, like Bush and others today, Mussolini and Hitler didn't have to modify the whole juridical edifice of the country. Oddly, many scholars today have followed the lead of Schmitt and Agamben; many even on the scholarly Left do so even though Agamben and Schmitt's theories do not take into account the centuries of struggle by working peoples within nations and between nations to ensure that the nation-state serves to protect their interests.

17. George W. Bush used the rhetoric of enmity—"My people are threatened by those that embody pure evil"—to put into place the Patriot Act. We see today how Bush used the executive power to make decisions that automatically became effective as laws: the creating of tribunals that fall into neither civil nor military jurisdictions; hence the unchecked torturing and detention of people at the U.S. prison in Guantánamo Bay. Bush regularly dismisses those who object to such horrendous acts when he declares them unable to see the world as it is. That is to say, in the name

of legal positivism Bush exerts full statal coercive powers against people who are defined vaguely as "enemy combatants" who have a unique legal status as established by the lawmaking machinery of the U.S. government.

18. When studying legal theory and approaches to law in the United States, we need to consider not so much whether or not the Constitution includes natural or positivist law (it includes both), but rather the context in which the law was established. Did the passing of a law fragment and/or destroy trade unions? Did trade unions endorse the law, or did they buckle and accept it? All these questions seek to explore the independence of law in the twentieth century vis-à-vis the working class, either as a whole or in its parts. Regardless of whether one takes either a natural or positive legal theory approach or a combination of both, these questions will remain unanswered.

19. Man is nature, and as nature, at a certain moment in time and space man began transforming nature and in transforming nature started transforming himself, that is, his or her nature. It's one and the same continuous process: man humanizes nature, and nature as an obstacle has to be transcended by human nature, which is in turn creating new natural—and social—circumstances. As articulated in Marx's "Economic and Philosophic Manuscripts of 1844," humans are socialized nature and at the same time they are the agents of the further socialization of nature; nature became social through humans. While Marx didn't quite have the scientific tools to develop this, writing pre-Darwin, through Hegel's work Marx was able to formulate the following principle: "Man is a species being not only in that he practically and theoretically makes his own species among other things his object but also as present and living species he considers himself to be a universal . . . the life of man is physical and man like animal lives by an inorganic nature."

20. In the United States federal laws rule the whole nation, but in addition there are member states of the federal nation with their own lawmaking organs (state legislatures). Like a set of nesting Chinese boxes, the U.S. government, with its bicameral Congress and tripartite institutional organization (legislative, executive, and judicial), represents the biggest box, which contains smaller and smaller boxes that replicate the larger one. There are many other sources of law as well. If you compiled all the laws existing in the United States today, you would fill thousands of pages of texts.

21. In *Happiness: A History* Darrin M. McMahon sums up the intellectual history of happiness as follows: "In truth, the belief that we can make ourselves happy through effort of our own has been a part of the Western tradition since Socrates and the Greeks attempted to wrest eudemonia from the clutches of fortune. Happiness, in their view, was the product of the refined craftsmanship of living—something, at least in part, that we could make on our own. And although the Greeks and their successors restricted this trade—confining the highest human end to life's master artisans, an elite guild of 'workers,' who could build their lives better than the common lot—Christianity and then the Enlightenment destroyed this closed shop, bidding all to work toward their deliverance, and to find deliverance in their work. In

keeping with the greatest good of the greatest number, happiness should be sought in all things, even in sweat of one's brow" (404).

22. In *Happiness* McMahon explains this phrase in Jefferson's writing of the Declaration whereby, as a thinker shaped by the Enlightenment, we see the uncritical folding into one another of the concept of individual interest (private) and the welfare of the people (public) in the pursuit of a greater goal of happiness. There is not the sense that an unbridled pursuit of private pleasures, possessions, and profits doesn't necessarily mean the greater good of the people.

23. Arne Öhman cites Antonio Damasio's research on people who suffer from frontal-lobe lesions: perception, language, attention, and memory function well, but their social decision capacity suffers greatly. That is, they lack a healthy sense of determining or reading shifts in "emotion-related bodily changes" (37) that provide the emotional backdrop for decision-making processes in healthy, functioning people. Those with frontal-lobe lesions, specifically a lesion in the ventromedial prefrontal cortex, as Öhman remarks, "get stuck pondering a multitude of alternatives, eventually making a bad choice" (37).

24. More generally speaking, in *Before the Dawn* Nicholas Wade reminds us that our evolution didn't occur in isolation from our environment. Geographic region and climatic conditions determined adaptive strategies that in turn determined the slight genetic variations in populations (Caucasian, Asian, African, and so on). Today, when determining the use of certain medications, it is important to recognize both a shared biological universality—the "continuing unity of the human family" (194)—as well as these slight genetic differences.

25. I'm careful here when talking about democracy. I see many excellent scholars defend democratic ideals (its series of checks and balances) and actually end up defending the bourgeoisie; this is not because these scholars have reactionary intentions, but rather because they don't see clearly that as a system of checks and balances democracy doesn't exist anywhere today—and this since the late 1960s and beginning of the 1970s. Rather, what we've been seeing is the near absolute giving of power to the executive, which institutes more and more an apartheid division of power.

CHAPTER THIRTEEN

1. Our universal engagement and capacity for story is not to be confused with a sense that all people read literature—novels and so on. Rather, it is to point to how cross-culturally we engage with narratives in one form or another: whether from TV sitcoms, visual or mimed story, to spoken stories. Indeed, in terms of our engagement with written fictional works, there's been a decline in numbers. According to the recent results of a Census Bureau survey of 17,135 people, it was determined that in the United States the number of readers has fallen from 54 percent in 1992 (and 56.9 percent in 1982) to 46.7 percent in 2002. The largest dip in readers was noted

among young adults (18–34). The survey also discovered that men read less than women, that whites read more than African Americans and Hispanics. See Bruce Webster's article in the *New York Times*, "Fewer Noses Stuck in Books In America, Survey Finds."

2. For an interesting discussion of the "linguistic turn" and critical race theories of narrative, see Robert Young's "The Linguistic Turn, Materialism and Race: Toward an Aesthetics of Crisis." For a "turn to a new aesthetics," see Michael Eskin's "Introduction: The Double 'Turn' to Ethics and Literature?" in *Poetics Today* (2004), in which he identifies an "ethics-and-literature" (563) approach that conceives of "art and our engagement with it not in standard aesthetic terms but in what has been called 'poethic' terms" (563). John J. Joughin's and Simon Malpas's edited volume *The New Aestheticism* also makes the aesthetic turn as an approach to reinvigorate and reshape "the direction cultural and literary studies have now taken" (13). In the ethical turn, see the essays collected in Todd F. Davis and Kennedy Womack's edited volume *Mapping the Ethical Turn*. For this ethical turn in autobiography, see Paul John Eakin's *The Ethics of Life Writing*. Here, for example, Eakin identifies Rigoberta Menchú as a life writer who has a responsibility not to "cloud our access to the historical record" (2), to not "violate a literary convention governing nonfiction as a genre" (3), and to not "disobey a moral imperative" (3).

3. This reframing and reorientation of our perspective is best exemplified by Duchamp's "Ready Mades"; nobody thought that a used urinal would be a work of art until Duchamp put a frame around it and displayed it in a museum as a work of art. Here, we see how reframing of an object limits and reorients the way the object is offered as spectacle—as a work of art. When Magritte inscribed, "this is not a pipe" underneath a painting of a pipe, he also directs viewers to bring a new perspective to the object, asking us to engage with it as an aesthetic object. All things can be works of art even if in their original conception they had other functions. The "aesthetic function" is not an inherent quality of a special culturally produced object—as the highbrow vs. lowbrow media and scholarly pundits would have us believe—but rather the reorientation of our perception toward that object.

4. Although in *Does Literature Think?* Stathis Gourgouris doesn't identify his approach as a limited semiosis per se, he does identify the limits of its material production (historical context, linguistic idiom, cultural tradition, and so on) and how the text works as a self-enclosed object with its own "social-imaginary intact" (17) as well as its stimulating of a plurality of responses. In a sense, he follows Eco's line of thinking, proposing both how the text balances between unlimited meaning making and an "intact inner core" (he also calls this a "genetic code" that remains unchanged and that allows us, for example, to translate literature "across languages, historical contexts, and cultural sensibilities" [18]).

5. Lisa Zunshine and Patrick Colm Hogan's discussion of Theory of Mind explores how cognitive science involves the study not only of mind, but also of the relationship between mind and whatever is not mind: the relationship between mind and body, mind and brain, mind and physical reality. From this point of view, a

scientific study of mind involves also an ontology. It entails a conception of what reality is. By consensus (not definition) reality is everything that is out there plus the mind, so the study of the mind implies that you have a position—a point of view and/or an opinion—about the relation between mind and what is not the mind. As discussed in the chapter on translation, we see this at play in translation. Translation is not and cannot be the translation of rules or words (or lexical items); the translation is the transformation—the denuding of thoughts and redressing of those thoughts in different ways and by different means. This implies that thoughts can exist without being embodied in sounds, words, language. Thoughts and language are separate entities: this is itself an ontology.

6. And this is also genre dependent. So while we cross-culturally process schemas, prototypes, and exemplums the same way, each medium (painting, literature, film) employs the techniques relevant (and necessarily so) to its genre. For example, if a film director were not to use the conventions of the "eye-line match," the audience might not understand the relationship between one shot and another.

7. We can speculate, too, that the enjoyment we derive from filling in blanks dates back to our Upper Paleolithic ancestors and their forms of storytelling—miming, painting, and talk-story—where fragments would be made wholly imagined in the minds of a community of viewers and listeners. We can see how such fragmented verbal and visual storytelling survives today in genres like the comic book especially. Comic books work by creating fragments that guide the reader to fill in blanks and experience a gestalt effect.

8. For Paul Hernadi, our ability to both suspend disbelief and distinguish between the real and unreal is an activity we rehearse daily when our brains process, he writes, "certain kinds of stimuli as vehicles of *indirect* communication and *virtual* representation. Such processing seems specifically designed to forestall any immediate impact of a literary experience on nonliterary volition and action" (186). Our mind is wired to be able to switch back and forth between "action bound to the imaginative" (186) and that which is bound to the "perspectival information supplied by grammatical means in communication" (186). He argues, then, that "without mental processing of a specifically literary kind, you would fail to realize that it is neither Shakespeare nor the actor playing Hamlet who refers to himself in the first person whenever Hamlet is represented on the page, stage, or screen as saying "I" (186–187).

9. Specifics of location (geographic and historical) influence the visibility of one genre over another and variously inflect the way prototype genres externalize themselves. An analogy might be Chomsky's formulation of the universal grammar and its externalization in the multiplicity of "I" languages, or ideolects. Patrick Colm Hogan identifies, for example, how "hierarchical, militarized societies in which the poet is patronized by a ruling elite tend to produce a higher percentage of heroic plots. Societies in which narratives are produced for broader, popular consumption particularly emphasize romantic plots. Societies in which famine is a constant threat have a higher percentage of sacrificial plots" (*Mind and Its Stories* 185).

10. In "A Humanistic Ethics of Reading" Daniel Schwartz proposes a distinction between an *"ethics of reading* and an *ethics while reading"* (12): the former "includes who we are and what our biases and interests are" (12); and the latter "that we interpret a given literary work by reading that text from multiple perspectives, acknowledging the differences between authorial and resistant readings, and understanding why and who the original audience might have responded and for what reasons" (12).

11. Even judges and lawyers are not off-limits; Nussbaum proposes that they be required to read novels so as to be made aware of the "good of other people whose lives are distant from our own" (*Poetic Justice* xvi).

12. When people claim that certain fictions are morally wrong, they're confusing how a novel in and of itself functions with those people actually doing immoral acts; the deaths and death threats that resulted from the publication of Salman Rushdie's *Satanic Verses* is often cited as an example. This was also the grounds for censoring Joyce's *Ulysses*: people considered it a book that would incite readers to masturbate, go to brothels, and so on and thus claimed that the novel was immoral in and of itself. As we know, however, literature is constituted by language that even in its most descriptive form is not the same thing as the willful acts of people in the world.

13. In *Sex, Lies and Autobiography* James O'Rourke seeks to complicate the tendency to simplify how literary texts act on people; how the sole function of literature is to derive a general set of ethical principles. He does so by looking at what he calls the "confessional autobiography," which challenges, as he writes, "the narratives that give our lives a sense of ethical coherence" (1); such a novel disrupts the "presumption of a discernible continuity from ethical principle to practice in everyday life" (1–2). A confessional autobiography like *Lolita* acts to "rupture the ethical fabric of everyday life" (2).

14. In *Ethics: The Good and the Right* Mario Bunge puts flesh back on ethics and morality by anchoring it in the biological and social; within the one world we all inhabit and where we share universally biological nutritional needs and require the making of social structures to ensure our well-being: good physical health, psychological contentment, and also the freedom to engage with and actively participate within all of society's resources and activities. See also chapter 12, where I discuss the importance of our constant transforming of our one world so that those societies that are barely able to meet the basic requirement of nutritive survival can have access to all social resources—medicine, education, and transportation, for instance—that allow for the freedom to exercise rights and realize one's ideals and socially responsible goals.

15. Patrick Hogan suggests that fiction making serves as an adaptive function in our survival not only because of its off-line simulation (its "holographic effect"), but because our world is so filled with violence and tragedy that our engagement with art (verbal and visual) is not "wholly lacking in practical value" (*Mind and Its Stories* 263).

16. Mark Turner understands literature as a crucial product of mind, but he places too much emphasis on the bidirectionality of metaphor and the idea of "conceptual blending," leading to vague formulations of how metaphor involves two or more inputs ("*input spaces*") that project some properties of *blended space* and that deflects and refracts the projection in a way that is not direct from source to target. For Turner, this complex blending is not only characteristic of all thought, but *is* all thought. (See Turner's *The Literary Mind*.)

17. Although Abbott hints at this, it is important to add that with mime Upper Paleolithic *Homo erectus* could refer "to time past, present, and time future," as T. S. Eliot would say. However, this necessarily means that one could enact things that never happened. One could mime falsities. Options that refer to future are options that don't exist and therefore are not present and thus nonexistent. By the same token, then, the existence of time (having recourse to tenses) as something organized by a mime or narrator already carries necessarily the possibility of fiction and therefore lies (untruths).

CHAPTER FOURTEEN

1. In *Against the Postcolonial* Richard Serrano remarks more pointedly of such a disconnect in postcolonial theory: where the theoretical claims and the real facts don't measure up. He writes, "There is a curious belief among some postcolonial theorists that close reading (or close misreading) is something of a revolutionary act, giving their work a bizarre messianic tone" (4). And he cautions of such claims that we "should remember that the rise of Postcolonial Studies did not prevent the American invasion of Iraq in 2002" (5). He thus considers the postcolonial project "at worst an immoral and self-promoting enterprise and at best myopic and self-deluding" (6) and instead proposes that we consider that each literary text (he's interested in francophone texts) be studied within the context of its "peculiarities—absurd, contrary, and stubbornly resistant to simple-minded generalization, as every career is—of each writer in his or her specific cultural, geographic, historical, and literary context" (7).

2. If we define the way English is taught in classroom as democratic, as McGowan proposes, we're making nonsense of the very concept. As he correctly observes, the classroom can be a vital place for learning and sharing of ideas. However, democracy remains that which the people wish to turn into law and policy and not that of studying literature in the classroom. Democracy in the strict sense of the term is what is stated in the Declaration of Independence and Bill of Rights: the establishment by the people of the general rules that will apply to all the people. In point of fact, the classroom should not be a democracy. Just as a pilot doesn't submit for a vote to his or her passengers how to land an airplane, neither should the teacher submit to his or her students how and what will be taught. Both spaces are absolutely totalitarian in this sense: neither teacher nor pilot should submit to a vote

any decision he or she makes. Indeed, applying McGowan's so-called democratic approach to teaching—submitting to a vote whether students read the Yellow Pages instead of Julio Cortázar's *Hopscotch,* for example, or to study narratology instead of a book on how to improve your tennis swing—would never lead to our further understanding of how literature works.

WORKS CITED

Abbott, Porter H. "The Evolutionary Origins of the Storied Mind: Modeling the Prehistory of Narrative Consciousness and its Discontents." *Narrative* 8, no. 3 (2000): 247–256.

Adler, Hans, and Sabine Gross. "Adjusting the Frame." *Poetics Today* 23, no. 2 (2002): 195–220.

Ahmad, Aijaz. *In Theory: Literatures, Classes, Nations.* London: Verso, 1992.

Ahmad, Eqbal. "Introduction." *The Pen and the Sword: Conversations with David Baramian/Edward Said.* Monroe: Common Courage Press, 1994.

Alcoff, Linda Martín. "Who's Afraid of Identity Politics?" In *Reclaiming Identity: Realist Theory and the Predicament of Postmodernism,* edited by Paula M. L. Moya and Michael R. Hames-García, 312–344. Berkeley: University of California Press, 2000.

Aldama, Frederick Luis. "Troubled Times: A Conceptual Approach to Understanding Barbarism." www.sulekha.com

———. *Cuba Libre:* Capitalism, Communism, and the Worker." www.Badsubjects .org. Issue 62, 2003.

———. "Music Can Rock, Just Not the World." www.Badsubjects.org. Issue 62, 2003.

———. *Postethnic Narrative Criticism.* Austin: University of Texas Press, 2003.

———. *Brown on Brown: Representations of Gay and Lesbian Chicano/a Literature and Film.* Austin: University of Texas Press, 2005.

Amin, Shahid. "Foreward." In *After Spanish Rule: Postcolonial Predicaments of the Americas,* edited by Mark Thurner and Andrés Guerrero, xi–xv. Durham: Duke University Press, 2003.

Anderton, Frances. "South of the Border or North, Their Futures Are Linked." *New York Times,* March 21, 2002, section F: 3.

Appiah, Kwame Anthony. "Thick Translation." In *The Translation Studies Reader,* edited by Lawrence Venuti, 417–429. New York: Routledge, 2000.

Arendt, Hannah. *The Origins of Totalitarianism.* San Diego: Harcout Brace Jovanovich, 1985.

Armstrong, Nancy. *How Novels Think: The Limits of British Individualism from 1719–1900.* New York: Columbia University Press, 2005.

Austin, J. L. *How To Do Things With Words*. Cambridge: Harvard University Press, 1975.

Baker, Mark C. *The Atoms of Language*. New York: Basic Books, 2001.

Balakrishnan, Gopal, ed. *Debating Empire*. London: Verso, 2003.

Balderston, Daniel, and Marcy Schwartz. "Introduction." In *Voice-Overs: Translation and Latin American Literature,* edited by Daniel Balderston and Marcy Schwartz, 1–14. Albany: State University of New York Press, 2002.

Barash, David P., and Nanelle R. Barash. *Madame Bovary's Ovaries: A Darwinian Look at Literature*. New York: Delacorte Press, 2005.

Barlow, Tani E. "Not Really a Properly Intellectual Response: An Interview with Gayatri Spivak." *positions: east asia cultures critique* 12, no. 1 (2004): 139–163.

———. "Eugenic Woman, Semicolonialism, and Colonial Modernity as Problems for Postcolonial Theory." In *Postcolonial Studies and Beyond,* edited by Ania Loomba, Suvir Kaul, Maffi Bunzl, Antoinette Burton, and Jed Esty, 359–384. Durham: Duke University Press, 2005.

Barnet, P. Chad. "Reviving Cyberpunk: (Re)Constructing the Subject and Mapping Cyberspace in the Wachowski Brothers' Film *The Matrix*." *Extrapolation* 41, no. 4 (2000): 359–374.

Barthes, Roland. "The Death of the Author." In *Image, Music, Text*. Translated by Stephen Heath. New York: Hill and Wang, 1977.

Bassham, Gregory. "The Religion of *The Matrix* and the Problems of Pluralism." In *The Matrix and Philosophy,* 111–125. Chicago: Open Court, 2002.

Bassnett, Susan, and André Lefevere. "Introduction." In *Translation, History and Culture,* edited by Susan Bassnett and André Lefevere, 1–13. London: Pinter, 1990.

Bayoumi, Moustafa, and Andrew Rubin. "Introduction." In *The Edward Said Reader,* edited by Moustafa Bayoumi and Andrew Rubin, xi–xxxiv. New York: Vintage, 2000.

Bellessi, Diana. "Gender and Translation." Transated by Daniel Balderston and Marcy Schwartz. In *Voice-Overs: Translation and Latin American Literature,* edited by Daniel Balderston and Marcy Schwartz, 26–29. Albany: State University of New York Press, 2002.

Berlant, Lauren. *The Anatomy of a National Fantasy: Hawthorne, Utopia, and Everyday Life*. Chicago: University of Chicago Press, 1991.

Bermann, Sandra. "Introduction." In *Nation, Language, and the Ethics of Translation,* edited by Sandra Bermann and Michael Wood, 1–10. Princeton: Princeton University Press, 2005.

Berube, Maurice R. *Beyond Modernism and Postmodernism: Essays on the Politics of Culture*. Westport: Bergin and Garvey, 2002.

Bérubé, Michel. "Public Academy." *New Yorker,* January 15, 1995, 40.

Bhabha, Homi K. "The Third Space." In *Identity, Community, Culture, Difference,* edited by J. Rutherford, 207–221. London: Lawrence and Wishart, 1990.

———. *The Location of Culture*. New York: Routledge, 1994.

———. "On Writing Rights." In *Globalizing Rights: The Oxford Amnesty Lectures 1999,* edited by Matthew J. Gibney, 162–183. Oxford: Oxford University Press, 2003.

Bhabha, Homi K., and W. J. T. Mitchell. *Edward Said: Continuing the Conversation.* Chicago: University of Chicago Press, 2005.

Bilder, Robert M., Christian C. Felder, Neil Lewis, David S. Lester, F. Frank Lefever, eds. *Neuroscience of the Mind on the Centennial of Freud's Project for a Scientific Psychology.* New York: New York Academy of Sciences, 1998.

Billig, Michael. "Lacan's Misuse of Psychology: Evidence, Rhetoric and the Mirror Stage." *Theory, Culture and Society* 23, no. 4 (2006): 1–26.

Boorman, John. *In My Country.* Los Angeles: Columbia Tristar, 2005.

Borges, Jorge Luis. *Bartleby, el escribiente.* Madrid: Ediciones Siruela, D.L., 1984.

Bourbon, Brett. *Finding a Replacement for the Soul: Mind and Meaning in Literature and Philosophy.* Cambridge: Harvard University Press, 2004.

Bové, Paul. "Introduction." In *Edward Said and the Work of the Critic: Speaking Truth to Power,* edited by Paul Bové, 1–8. Durham: Duke University Press, 2000.

Brannigan, Michael. "There Is No Spoon: A Buddhist Mirror." In *The Matrix and Philosophy,* 101–110. Chicago: Open Court, 2002.

Brecher, Bob. "Do Intellectuals Have a Social Public Responsibility?" In *Philosophy and Its Public Role: Essays in Ethics, Politics, Society and Culture,* edited by William Aiken and John Haldane, 25–38. Charlottesville, Va.: Imprint Academic, 2004.

Brennan, Timothy. "Cosmo-Theory." *South Atlantic Quarterly* 100, no. 3 (2001): 659–691.

———. "Postcolonial Studies between European Wars: An Intellectual History." In *Marxism, Modernity, and Postcolonial Studies,* edited by Crystal Bartolovich and Neil Lazarus, 185–203. Cambridge: Cambridge University Press, 2002.

———. "The Empire's New Clothes." *Critical Inquiry* 29, no. 2 (2003): 337–368.

———. "Postcolonial Studies and Globalization Theory." In *The Cambridge Companion to Postcolonial Literary Studies,* edited by Neil Lazarus, 120–138. Cambridge: Cambridge University Press, 2004.

———. *Wars of Position: The Cultural Politics of Left and Right.* New York: Columbia University Press, 2006.

Brown, Monica. *Gang Nation: Delinquent Citizens in Puerto Rican, Chicano, and Chicana Narratives.* Minneapolis: University of Minnesota Press, 2002.

Brown, Nicholas. "Marxism and Postcolonial Studies Now." *symploke* 8, nos. 1–2 (2000): 214–221.

Bunge, Mario. *Ethics: The Good and the Right.* Boston: D. Reidel, 1989.

———. *Emergence and Convergence: Qualitative Novelty and the Unity of Knowledge.* Toronto: University of Toronto Press, 2003.

Butler, Judith. "Values of Difficulty." In *Just Being Difficult? Academic Writing in the Public Arena,* edited by Jonathan Culler and Kevin Lamb, 199–215. Stanford: Stanford University Press, 2003.

Calabresi, Guido. "An Introduction to Legal Thought: Four Approaches to Law and to the Allocation of Body Parts." *Stanford Law Review* 55, no. 6 (2003): 2113–2151.

Carey, James W. "Reflections on the Project of (American) Cultural Studies." In *Cultural Studies in Question*, edited by Marjorie Ferguson and Peter Golding, 1–24. London: Sage Publications, 1998.

Carroll, Joseph. *Literary Darwinism: Evolution, Human Nature, and Literature*. New York: Routledge, 2004.

Caputo, John D. *The Prayers and Tears of Jacques Derrida: Religion without Religion*. Bloomington: Indiana University Press, 1997.

Castro-Gómez, Santiago. "The Social Sciences, Epistemic Violence, and the Problem of the Invention of the Other." *Nepantla, Views from the South* 3, no. 2 (2002): 269–285.

Chamberlain, Leslie. *The Secret Artist: A Close Reading of Sigmund Freud*. New York: Seven Stories Press, 2001.

Chaudhuri, Sukanta. *Translation and Understanding*. New Delhi: Oxford University Press, 1999.

Cheah, Pheng. "Spectral Nationality: The Living On [sur-vie] of the Postcolonial Nation in Neocolonial Globalization." *Boundary* 2 26, no. 3 (1999): 225–252.

———. *Spectral Nationality: Passages of Freedom from Kant to Postcolonial Literatures*. New York: Columbia University Press, 2004.

Chomsky, Noam. *Syntactic Structures*. The Hague: Mouton, 1957.

———. "A Review of B. F. Skinner's Verbal Behavior." *Language* 35, no. 1 (1959): 26–58.

———. *Cartesian Linguistics: A Chapter in the History of Rationalist Thought*. New York: Harper and Row, 1966.

———. *Chomsky on Democracy and Education*. Edited by Carlos Otero. New York: Routledge, 2002.

———. "Foreword." *America's Other War: Terrorizing Colombia*. London: Zed Books, 2005.

Chow, Rey. "The Resistance of Theory; or, The Worth of Agony." In *Just Being Difficult? Academic Writing in the Public Arena*, edited by Jonathan Culler and Kevin Lamb, 95–105. Stanford: Stanford University Press, 2003.

Chrisman, Laura. *Postcolonial Contraventions: Cultural Readings of Race, Imperialism and Transnationalism*. Manchester: Manchester University Press, 2003.

Churchill, Ward. *On the Justice of Roosting Chickens: Reflections on the Consequences of U.S. Imperial Arrogance and Criminality*. Oakland: AK Press, 2003.

Coetzee, J. M. *Disgrace*. New York: Penguin, 2000.

Coopan, Vilashini. "The Ruins of Empire: The National and Global Politics of America's Return to Rome." In *Postcolonial Studies and Beyond*, edited by Ania Loomba, Suvir Kaul, Matti Bunzl, Antoinette Burton, and Jed Esty, 80–100. Durham: Duke University Press, 2005.

Cowell, Alan. "Writers, Spying in the House of Power." *New York Times*, January 29, 2004, section E: 3.

Cozolino, Louis. *The Neuroscience of Human Relationships: Attachment and the Developing Social Brain.* New York: W. W. Norton, 2006.

Crews, Frederick. "Foreword." In *After Poststructuralism: Interdisciplinarity and Literary Theory,* edited by Nancy Easterlin and Barbara Riebling, vii–x. Evanston: Northwestern University Press, 1993.

Cronin, Michael. "The Empire Talks Back: Orality, Heteronomy, and the Cultural Turn in Interpretation Studies." In *Translation as Power,* edited by Edwin Gentzler and Maria Tymoczko, 45–62. Amherst: University of Massachusetts Press, 2002.

Cubit, Sean. "'Maybellene': Meaning and the Listening Subject." *Reading Pop: Approaches to Textual Analysis in Popular Music.* Oxford: Oxford University Press, 2000.

Dagenais, John. "The Postcolonial Laura." *MLQ: Modern Language Quarterly* 65, no. 3 (2004): 365–389.

Damasio, Antonio. *The Feeling of What Happens: Body and Emotion in the Making of Consciousness.* New York: Harcourt, 1999.

Damasio, Antonio, and Hanna Damasio. "Minding the Body." *Daedalus,* Summer 2006: 15–22.

Damrosch, David. *What Is World Literature?* Princeton: Princeton University Press, 2003.

Davies, Todd F., and Kenneth Womack, eds. *The Ethical Turn: A Reader in Ethics, Culture, and Literary Theory.* Charlottesville: University of Virginia Press, 2001.

De la Campa, Román. *Latin Americanism.* Minneapolis: University of Minnesota Press, 1999.

Delgado, Celeste Fraser, and José Esteban Muñoz. "Rebellions of Everynight Life." In *Everynight Life: Culture and Dance in Latin/o America,* edited by Celeste Fraser Delgado and José Esteban Muñoz, 9–32. Durham: Duke University Press, 1997.

Denning, Michael. *Culture in the Age of Three Worlds.* New York: Verso, 2004.

Derrida, Jacques. *Writing and Difference.* Translated by Alan Bass. New York: Routledge, 1978. Originally published as *L'écriture et la différance.* Paris: Seuil, 1967.

———. *Speech and Phenomena, And Other Essays on Husserl's Theory of Signs.* Translated and introduced by David B. Allison. Evanston: Northwestern University Press, 1973; French original published in 1967.

———. "The Ends of Man." *Philosophy and Phenomenological Research* 30, no. 1 (1969): 31–57.

———. *Of Grammatology.* Translated by Gayatri Spivak. Baltimore: Johns Hopkins University Press, 1976.

———. "Freud and the Scene of Writing." In *Writing and Difference.* Translated by Alan Bass, 196–232. New York: Routledge, 1978.

———. "Living On: Border Lines." In *Deconstruction and Criticism,* edited by Geoffrey Hartman, 196–232. New York: Routledge and Kegan Paul, 1979.

———. *Dissemination.* Translated by Barbara Johnson. Chicago: University of Chicago Press, 1981.

————. *Positions.* Translated and annotated by Alan Bass. Chicago: University of Chicago Press, 1981.

————. *The Ear of the Other: Otobiography, Transference, Translation/Texts and Discussions with Jacques Derrida.* Translated by Avital Ronell and Peggy Kamuf. Edited by Christie V. McDonald. New York: Schocken Books, 1985.

————"Des Tours de Babel." In *Difference in Translation,* edited by Joseph F. Graham, 209–248. Ithaca: Cornell University Press, 1985.

————. *The Post Card: From Socrates to Freud and Beyond.* Chicago: University of Chicago Press, 1987.

————. "To Speculate—on Freud." In *The Derrida Reader: Between the Blinds,* edited by Peggy Kamuf, 518–568. New York: Columbia University Press, 1991.

————. *Archive Fever: A Freudian Impression.* Chicago: University of Chicago Press, 1996.

————. "To Do Justice to Freud: The History of Madness in the Age of Psychoanalysis." In *Resistances of Psychoanalysis,* Jacques Derrida. Stanford: Stanford University Press, 1998.

————. "What Is a 'Relevant' Translation?" *Critical Inquiry* 27 (2001): 174–200.

————. *Acts of Religion.* Edited by Gil Anidjar. New York: Routledge, 2002.

————. "For a Justice to Come: An Interview with Jacques Derrida." Lieven De Cauter. April 5, 2004. http:www.indymedia.be/news/2004/04/83123.php

Derrida, Jacques, and Gianni Vattimo, eds. *Religion.* Stanford: Stanford University Press, 1998.

Desai, Gaurav, Felipe Smith, and Supriya Nair, eds. "Introduction: Law, Literature, and Ethnic Subjects." *MELUS* 28, no. 1 (2003): 3–16.

Desmond, Jane C. "Issues in Dance and Cultural Studies." In *Everynight Life: Culture and Dance in Latin/o America,* edited by Celeste Fraser Delgado and José Esteban Muñoz, 33–64. Durham: Duke University Press, 1997.

Distiller, Natasha. *South Africa, Shakespeare, and Post-Colonial Culture.* Lewiston/Queenston/Lampeter: Edwin Mellen Press, 2005.

Dolezel, Lubomîr. "Fictional and Historical Narrative: Meeting the Postmodernist Challenge." *Narratologies: New Perspectives on Narrative Analysis,* edited by David Herman, 247–273. Columbus: Ohio State University Press, 1999.

Donoghue, Frank. *The Last Professors: The Twilight of the Humanities in the Corporate University.* New York: Fordham University Press, 2008.

Dorfman, Ariel. "Resisting Hybridity." In *Voice-Overs: Translation and Latin American Literature,* edited by Daniel Balderston and Marcy Schwartz, 55–57. Albany: State University of New York Press, 2002.

Doxtader, Erik, and Charles Villa-Vicencio, eds. "Introduction: At the End of Amnesty." *The Provocations of Amnesty: Memory, Justice and Immunity.* Institute for Justice and Reconciliation, 2003.

Durkheim, Emile. *The Rules of Sociological Method.* 8th ed. Translated by Sarah A. Solovay and John H. Mueller. Edited by George E. G. Catlin. Chicago: University of Chicago Press, 1938.

Durant, Sam. *Postcolonial Narrative and the Work of Mourning: J. M. Coetzee, Wilson Harris, and Toni Morrison.* Albany: State University of New York Press, 2004.

Eagleton, Terry. *After Theory.* New York: Basic Books, 2003.

———. *Figures of Dissent: Critical Essays on Fish, Spivak, Žižek and Others.* New York: Verso, 2003.

Eakin, Emily. "What Is the Next Big Idea? The Buzz Is Growing." *New York Times,* July 7, 2001, section B7.

———. "The Latest Theory Is That Theory Doesn't Matter." *New York Times,* April 19, 2003, section D: 9.

Eakin, John Paul. "Introduction: Mapping the Ethics of Life Writing." In *The Ethics of Life Writing,* edited by John Paul Eakin, 1–16. Cornell: Cornell University Press, 2004.

Eckstein, Lars. "The Insistence of Voices: An Interview with Caryl Phillips." *Ariel: A Review of International English Literature* 32, no. 2 (2001): 33–43.

Eco, Umberto. "The Poetics of the Open Work." In *The Open Work.* Translated by Anna Cancogni. Cambridge: Harvard University Press, 1989.

Ellis, John M. *Literature Lost: Social Agendas and the Corruption of the Humanities.* New Haven: Yale University Press, 1997.

Eskin, Michael. "Introduction: The Double 'Turn' to Ethics and Literature?" *Poetics Today* 25, no. 4 (2004): 557–572.

Farred, Grant. *What's My Name? Black Vernacular Intellectuals.* Minneapolis: University of Minnesota Press, 2003.

Farrell, Frank B. *Why Does Literature Matter?* Ithaca: Cornell University Press, 2004.

Faur, José. *Homo Mysticus: A Guide to Maimonides's Guide for the Perplexed.* Syracuse: Syracuse University Press, 1999.

Ferguson, James. "Decomposing Modernity: History and Hierarchy after Development." In *Postcolonial Studies and Beyond,* edited by Ania Loomba, Suvir Kaul, Matti Bunzl, Antoinete Burton, and Jed Esty, 166–181. Durham: Duke University Press, 2005.

Ferguson, Marjorie, and Peter Golding. "Cultural Studies and Changing Times: An Introduction." In *Cultural Studies in Question,* edited by Marjorie Ferguson and Peter Golding, xiii–xxvii. London: Sage Publications, 1998.

Ferudi, Frank. *Where Have All the Intellectuals Gone? Confronting 21st Century Philistinism.* London: Continuum, 2004.

Fischer, Sybelle. *Modernity Disavowed: Haiti and the Cultures of Slavery in the Age of Revolution.* Durham: Duke University Press, 2004.

Fish, Stanley. *Doing What Comes Naturally: Change, Rhetoric, and the Practice of Theory in Literary and Legal Studies.* Durham: Duke University Press, 1989.

———. "The Law Wishes to Have a Formal Existence." In *The Stanley Fish Reader,* edited by Aram H. Veeser, 165–206. Oxford: Blackwell, 1999.

———. "Intentional Neglect." *New York Times,* July 19, 2005, A21.

Fishman, Ted C. "Making a Killing: The Myth of Capital's Good Intentions." *Harper's* 305, no. 1827 (2002): 33–41.

Fluck, Winfried. "Aesthetics and Cultural Studies." In *Aesthetics in a Multicultural Age,* edited by Emory Elliott, Louis Freitas Caton, and Jeffrey Rhyne, 79–103. Oxford: Oxford University Press, 2002.

———. "Aesthetic Experience of the Image." In *Iconographies of Power: The Politics and Poetics of Visual Representation,* edited by Ulla Haselstein, Berndt Ostendorf, and Peter Schneck, 11–44. Heidelburg, 2003.

———. "Fiction and Justice." *New Literary History* 34, no. 1 (2003): 19–42.

Fludernik, Monika, and Greta Olson. "Introduction." In *In the Grip of the Law: Trials, Prisons and the Space Between,* xiii–liv. Frankfurt am Main: Peter Lang, 2004.

Foley, Barbara. "Review of *Reclaiming Identity: Realist Theory and the Predicament of Postmodernism.*" In *Cultural Logic: An Electronic Journal of Marxist Theory and Practice* 4, no. 2 (2001). http://eserver.org/clogic/4-2/foley.html

———. *Spectres of 1919: Class and Nation in the Making of the New Negro.* Urbana: University of Illinois Press, 2003.

Fontana, Paul. "Finding God in the Matrix." In *The Matrix and Philosophy,* 159–184. Chicago: Open Court, 2002.

Ford, James L. "Buddhism, Mythology, and *The Matrix.*" In *Taking the Red Pill,* edited by Glenn Yeffeth, 125–144. Dallas: BenBella Books, 2003.

Foucault, Michel. *Folie et déraison: Histoire de la folie à l'âge classique.* Paris: Plon, 1961.

———. "Sex, Power and the Politics of Identity: An Interview." *The Advocate* 400 (1984): 26–30.

———. *The History of Sexuality.* Translated by Robert Hurley. New York: Vintage Books, 1990.

———. "About the Beginning of the Hermeneutics of the Self: Two Lectures at Dartmouth." *Political Theory* 21, no. 2 (1993): 198–227.

———. "My Body, This Paper, This Fire." In *Aesthetics, Method, and Epistemology: Essential Works of Foucault 1954–1984,* volume 2, edited by James D. Faubion, 393–417. New York: New Press, 1998.

———. *History of Madness.* Edited by Jean Khalfa. Translated by Jonathan Murphy and Jean Khalfa. London: Routledge, 2006.

Freud, Sigmund. "Project for a Scientific Psychology." In *The Standard Edition of the Complete Psychological Works of Sigmund Freud,* 1:281–397. London: Hogarth Press and Institute of Psycho-Analysis, 1953–1973.

———. *The Complete Letters of Sigmund Freud to Wilhelm Fliess, 1877-1904.* Cambridge: Belknap Press, 1985.

———. *Beyond the Pleasure Principle.* New York: W. W. Norton, 1989.

———. *An Outline of Psycho-Analysis.* New York: W. W. Norton, 1989.

———. "Autobiographical Study." In *The Freud Reader,* edited by Peter Gay, 3–41. New York: W. W. Norton, 1989.

——. *Civilization and Its Discontents*. New York: W. W. Norton, 1989.

——. *The Ego and the Id*. New York: W. W. Norton, 1989.

Fuchs, Barbara, and David J. Baker. "The Postcolonial Pasts." *Modern Language Quarterly* 65, no. 3 (2004): 329–340.

García, Cristina. "Translation as Restoration." In *Voice-Overs: Translation and Latin American Literature*, edited by Daniel Balderston and Marcy Schwartz, 45–48. Albany: State University of New York Press, 2002.

García Márquez, Gabriel. "The Desire to Translate." Translated by Daniel Balderston and Marcy Schwartz. In *Voice-Overs: Translation and Latin American Literature*, edited by Daniel Balderston and Marcy Schwartz, 23–25. Albany: State University of New York Press, 2002.

Gaspar de Alba, Alicia. "Introduction." *Velvet Barrios: Popular Culture & Chicana/o Sexualities*. New York: Palgrave MacMillan, 2003.

Gay, Peter, ed. *The Freud Reader*. New York: W. W. Norton, 1989.

Gellner, Ernest. *The Psychoanalytic Movement: The Cunning of Unreason*. Malden: Blackwell, 2003.

Genztler, Edwin. "Translation, Postructuralism, and Power." In *Translation and Power*, edited by Edwin Gentzler and Maria Tymoczko, 195–218. Amherst: University of Massachusetts Press, 2002.

Genztler, Edwin, and Maria Tymoczko. "Introduction." In *Translation and Power*, edited by Edwin Gentzler and Maria Tymoczko, xi–xxviii. Amherst: University of Massachusetts Press, 2002.

Ghosh, Bishnupriay. *When Borne Across: Literary Cosmopolitics in the Contemporary Indian Novel*. New Brunswick: Rutgers University Press, 2004.

Gigante, Denise. *Taste: A Literary History*. New Haven: Yale University Press, 2005.

Gikandi, Simon. "Globalization and the Claims of Postcoloniality." *South Atlantic Quarterly* 100, no. 3 (2001): 627–658.

Gilroy, Paul. "Analogues of Mourning, Mourning the Analog." In *Stars Don't Stand Still in the Sky: Music and Myth*. New York: Routledge, 1999.

Gitlin, Todd. "The Anti-Political Populism of Cultural Studies." In *Cultural Studies in Question*, edited by Marjorie Ferguson and Peter Golding, 25–38. London: Sage Publications, 1998.

Glascoe, Marion. *English Medieval Mystics: Games of Faith*. London: Longman Library, 1993.

Goldberg, Jonathan, and Cathy Davidson. "Engaging in the Humanities." In *Profession 2004*, 42–62. New York: MLA, 2004.

González, Marcial. "A Marxist Critique of Borderlands Postmodernism: Adorno's Negative Dialectics and Chicano Cultural Criticism." In *Left of the Color Line: Race, Radicalism, and Twentieth Century Literature of the United States*, edited by Bill V. Mullen and James Smethurst, 279–298. Chapel Hill: University of North Carolina Press, 2003.

Goodstein, Elizabeth S. *Experience without Qualities: Boredom and Modernity*. Stanford: Stanford University Press, 2005.

Gourgouris, Stathis. *Does Literature Think? Literature as Theory for an Antimythical Era*. Stanford: Stanford University Press, 2003.

Graybill, Lyn S. *Truth and Reconciliation in South Africa: Miracle or Model?* Boulder: Lynne Rienner, 2002.

Green, Jeffrey M. G. *Thinking Through Translation*. Athens: University of Georgia Press, 2001.

Grutman, Rainier. "Multilingualism and Translation." In *Routledge Encyclopedia of Translation Studies*, edited by Mona Baker, 157–60. New York: Routledge, 1998.

Grzegorczyk, Marzena. *Private Topographies: Space, Subjectivity, and Political Change in Modern Latin America*. New York: Palgrave Macmillan, 2005.

Guerra, Carlos. "Unofficial Conjunto Primer." In *Puro Conjunto: An Album in Words and Pictures*, 3–9. Austin: CMAS Books, 2001.

Gutiérrez-Jones, Carl. *Critical Race Narratives: A Study of Race, Rhetoric, and Injury*. New York: New York University Press, 2001.

Habell-Pallán, Michelle. *Loca Motion: Travels of Chicana and Latina Popular Culture*. New York: New York University Press, 2005.

Habell-Pallán, Michelle, and Mary Romero, eds. *Latino/a Popular Culture*. New York: New York University Press, 2002.

Hames-Garcia, Michael R. "Who Are Our Own People?: Challenges for a Theory of Social Identity." In *Reclaiming Identity: Realist Theory and the Predicament of Postmodernism*, edited by Paula M. L. Moya and Michael Hames-García, 102–131. Berkeley: University of California Press, 2000.

———. *Fugitive Thought: Prison Movements, Race, and the Meaning of Justice*. Minneapolis: University of Minnesota Press, 2004.

Hardt, Michael, and Antonio Negri. *Empire*. Cambridge: Harvard University Press, 2000.

———. "Globalization and Democracy." In *Implicating Empire: Globalization and Resistance in the 21st Century World Order*, edited by Stanley Arnowitz and Heather Gautner, 109–121. New York: Basic Books, 2003.

Harland, Richard. *Literary Theory from Plato to Barthes: An Introductory History*. New York: St. Martin's Press, 1999.

Hart, F. Elizabeth. "The Epistemology of Cognitive Literary Studies." *Philosophy and Literature* 25, no. 2 (2001): 314–334.

Hayles, Katherine. "Desiring Agency: Limiting Metaphors and Enabling Constraints in Dawkins and Deleuze/Guattari." *SubStance* 30, nos. 1 and 2 (2001): 144–159.

Hebdige, Dick. *Subculture: The Meaning of Style*. London: Routledge, 1979.

Heidegger, Martin. *Being and Time*. New York: Harper and Row, 1962.

Hernadi, Paul. "Why Is Literature?: A Coevolutionary Perspective on Imaginative Worldmaking." *Poetics Today* 23, no. 1 (2002): 22–42.

Hernandez, Arturo. *Peace in the Streets*. Salt Lake City: Northwest Publishers, 1995.

Hitchcock, Peter. *Dialogics of the Oppressed*. Minneapolis: University of Minnesota Press, 1993.

Hogan, Patrick Colm. *The Politics of Interpretation: Ideology, Professionalism, and the Study of Literature.* New York: Oxford University Press, 1990.

——. "Fictive Tales, Real Lives: Problems with Reading Law as Literature." In *Un-Disciplining Literature: Literature, Law, and Culture,* edited by Kostas Myrsiades and Linda Myrsiades, 271–290. New York: Peter Lang, 2000.

——. *Colonialism and Cultural Identity: Crises of Tradition in the Anglophone Literatures of India, Africa, and the Caribbean.* Albany: State University of New York Press, 2000.

——. *Cognitive Science, Literature, and the Arts: A Guide for Humanities.* New York: Routledge, 2003.

——. *The Mind and Its Stories: Narrative Universals and Human Emotion.* New York: Cambridge University Press, 2003.

——. "The Political and Intellectual Legacy of Edward Said: The Example of *Orientalism.*" *Journal of Commonwealth and Postcolonial Studies* 11, nos. 1–2 (2004): 1–29.

Holquist, Michael. "What Is the Ontological Status of Bilingualism?" In *Bilingual Games: Some Literary Investigations,* edited by Doris Sommer, 21–34. New York: Palgrave, 2003.

Holsinger, Bruce. *The Premodern Condition: Medievalism and the Making of Theory.* Chicago: University of Chicago Press, 2005.

Hopenhayn, Martín. *No Apocalypse, No Integration: Modernism and Postmodernism in Latin America.* Translated by Cynthia Margarita Tompkins and Elizabeth Rosa Horan. Durham: Duke University Press, 2001.

Horton, John. "Life, Literature and Ethical Theory: Martha Nussbaum on the Role of the Literary Imagination in Ethical Thought." In *Literature and the Political Imagination,* edited by John Horton and Andrea T. Baumeister, 70–97. New York: Routledge, 1996.

Horton, John, and Andrea T. Baumeister. "Literature, Philosophy and Political Theory." In *Literature and the Political Imagination,* edited by John Horton and Andrea T. Baumeister, 1–31. New York: Routledge, 1996.

Hutnyk, John. *Critique of Exotica: Music, Politics, and the Culture Industry.* London: Pluto Press, 2000.

Illing, Robert-Benjamin. "Humbled by History." *Scientific American* 14, no. 1 (2004): 86–93.

Jackson, Leonard. *The Dematerialisation of Karl Marx: Literature and Marxist Theory.* London: Longman, 1994.

Jameson, Fredric. "Third-World Literature in an Era of Multinational Capitalism." *Social Text* 15 (1986): 65–88.

Jaurretche, Colleen. *The Sensual Philosophy: Joyce and the Aesthetics of Mysticism.* Madison: University of Wisconsin Press, 1997.

Jenks, Chris. *Culture.* New York: Routledge, 1993.

Joffe, Josef. "The Perils of Soft Power: Why America's Cultural Influence Makes Enemies, Too." *New York Times Magazine,* May 14, 2006, 15–18.

Johnson, Gaye T. M. "A Sifting of Centuries: Afro-Chicano Interaction and Popular Musical Culture in California, 1960–2000." In *Decolonial Voices: Chicana and Chicano Cultural Studies in the 21st Century,* edited by Arturo Aldama and Naomi Quiñonez, 316–329. Bloomington: Indiana University Press, 2002.

Joughin, John J., and Simon Malpas. "New Aestheticism: An Introduction." In *The New Aestheticism,* edited by John J. Joughin and Simon Malpas, 1–19. Manchester: Manchester University Press, 2003.

Jrade, Cathy L. *Modernismo, Modernity, and the Development of Spanish American Literature.* Austin: University of Texas Press, 1998.

Kabir, Ananya Jahanara, and Deanne Williams. "Introduction: A Return to Wonder." In *Postcolonial Approaches to the European Middle Ages,* edited by Ananya Jahanara Kabir and Deanne Williams, 1–21. Cambridge: Cambridge University Press, 2005.

Kamala, N. "Translation and/in Gender." In *Translation Poetics and Practice,* edited by Anisur Rahman, 25–43. New Delhi: Creative Books, 2002.

Kapferer, Bruce. "Foundation and Empire (with apologies to Isaac Asimov): A Consideration of Hardt and Negri's *Empire.*" *Social Analysis* 46, no. 1 (2002): 167–181.

Kaplan, Caren, Norma Alarcón, and Minoo Moallem. "Introduction." In *Between Woman and Nation: Nationalism, Transnational Feminism, and the State,* edited by Caren Kaplan, Norma Alarcón, and Minoo Moallem. Durham: Duke University Press, 1999.

Katz, Adam. *Postmodernism and the Politics of 'Culture.'* Boulder: Westview Press, 2000.

Kellman, Steven, ed. "Preface." In *Switching Languages: Translingual Writers Reflect on Their Craft,* ix–xix. Lincoln: University of Nebraska Press, 2003.

Kernan, Alvin, ed. *What's Happened to the Humanities?* Princeton: Princeton University Press, 1997.

Kessler, Michael, and Christian Sheppard, eds. *Mystics: Presence and Aporia.* Chicago: University of Chicago Press, 2003.

Kochin, Michael S. "Postmetaphysical Literature: Reflections on J. M. Coetzee's *Disgrace.*" *Perspectives on Political Science* 33, no. 1 (2004): 4–9.

Korsmeyer, Carolyn. "Seeing, Believing, Touching, Truth." In *The Matrix and Philosophy,* 1–52. Chicago: Open Court, 2002.

Kossew, Sue. "The Politics of Shame and Redemption in J. M. Coetzee's *Disgrace.*" *Research in African Literatures* 34, no. 2 (2003): 155–162.

Kristeva, Julia. "Thinking in Dark Times." *Profession 2006,* 13–21.

Kun, Josh. "Against Easy Listening: Audiotopic Readings and Transnational Soundings." In *Everynight Life: Culture and Dance in Latin/o America,* edited by Celeste Fraser Delgado and José Esteban Muñoz, 288–309. Durham: Duke University Press, 1997.

———. "Rock's Reconquista." In *Rock over the Edge: Transformations in Popular Music Cultures,* edited by Roger Beebe, Denise Fulbrook, and Ben Saunders, 255–288. Durham: Duke University Press, 2002.

———. "The Sun Never Sets on MTV: Tijuana No! and the Border of Music Video." In *Latino/a Popular Culture*, edited by Michelle Habell-Pallán and Mary Romero, 102–116. New York: New York University Press, 2002.

Kundera, Milan. *The Art of the Novel*. New York: Grove Press, 1988.

Lacan, Jacques. *Écrits: A Selection*. Translated by Alan Sheridan. New York: W. W. Norton, 1977.

———. *On Feminine Sexuality, the Limits of Love and Knowledge: The Seminar of Jacques Lacan, Book XX Encore 1972-1973*. New York, W. W. Norton, 1998.

Lakoff, George, and Mark Turner. *More than Cool Reason: A Field Guide to Poetic Metaphor*. Chicago: University of Chicago Press, 1998.

Lang, Anthony F., and John Williams, eds. *Hannah Arendt and International Relations: Reading Across the Lines*. New York: Palgrave, 2005.

Laughlin, Charles A. *Contested Modernities in Chinese Literature*. New York: Palgrave, 2005.

Lavin, Enrique. "The Beats of Baja." *Village Voice* 46, no. 15 (2001): 71.

Lawrence, Matt. *Like a Splinter in Your Mind: The Philosophy Behind the Matrix Trilogy*. Oxford: Blackwell, 2004.

Lazarus, Neil. *Nationalism and Cultural Practice in the Postcolonial World*. Cambridge: Cambridge University Press, 1999.

Lazo, Rodrigo. *Writing to Cuba: Filibustering and Cuban Exiles in the United States*. Chapel Hill: University of North Carolina Press, 2005.

LeDoux, Joseph, Jacek Debiec, and Henry Moss, eds. *The Self: From Soul to Brain*. New York: Annals of the New York Academy of Sciences, 2003.

Leibniz, Gottfried Wilhelm. *Philosophical Essays*. Indianapolis: Hackett, 1989.

Levitin, Daniel J. *This is Your Brain on Music: The Science of a Human Obsession*. New York: Dutton, 2006.

Lila, Mark. *The Reckless Mind: Intellectuals in Politics*. New York: New York Review of Books, 2001.

Lindenberger, Herbert. *History in Literature*. New York: Columbia University Press, 1990.

Logothetis, Nikos K. "Vision: A Window on Consciousness." *Scientific American* 281, no. 5 (1999): 69–76.

Loomba, Ania, Suvir Kaul, Matti Bunzl, Antoinete Burton, and Jed Esty, eds. *Postcolonial Studies and Beyond*. Durham: Duke University Press, 2005.

Lotbinière-Harwood, Susanne de. *Re-belle et Infidèle/The Body Bilingual*. Toronto: Women's Press, 1991.

Love, Glen A. "Ecocriticism and Science: Toward Consilience?" *New Literary History* 30, no. 3 (1999): 561–576.

Loza, Steven. *Barrio Rhythms: Mexican American Music in Los Angeles*. Chicago: University of Illinois Press, 1993.

Ludwig, Sämi. *Pragmatist Realism: The Cognitive Paradigm in American Realist Texts*. Madison: University of Wisconsin Press, 2002.

McCarthy, Conor. "The Blinding Rhetoric of Rights." *Irish Times*, May 17, 2003, 62.

McGinn, Bernard, and Patricia Ferris McGinn, eds. *Early Christian Mystics: The Divine Vision of the Spiritual Masters.* New York: Crossroad Book, 2003.

McGowan, John. *Postmodernism and Its Critics.* Ithaca: Cornell University Press, 1991.

———. *Democracy's Children: Intellectuals and the Rise of Cultural Politics.* Ithaca: Cornell University Press, 2002.

McMahon, Darrin. *Enemies of the Enlightenment: The French Counter-Enlightenment and the Making of Modernity.* New York: Oxford University Press, 2001.

———. "From Happiness of Virtue to the Virtue of Happiness." *Daedalus* 133, no. 2 (2004): 5–18.

———. *Happiness: A History.* New York: Grove/Atlantic, 2006.

Malik, Kenan. *The Meaning of Race: Race, History, and Culture in Western Society.* New York: New York University Press, 1996.

Marcuse, Herbert. *One-Dimensional Man: Studies in the Ideology of Advanced Industrial Society.* Boston: Beacon Press, 1964.

Marez, Curtis. *Drug Wars: The Political Economy of Narcotics.* Minneapolis: University of Minnesota Press, 2004.

Marrouchi, Mustapha. "Counter-narratives, Recoveries, Refusals." In *Edward Said and the Work of the Critic: Speaking Truth to Power,* edited by Paul Bové, 187–228. Durham: Duke University Press, 2000.

Martin, Gerald "Translating García Márquez, or, The Impossible Dream." In *Voice-Overs: Translation and Latin American Literature,* edited by Daniel Balderston and Marcy Schwartz, 156–163. Albany: State University of New York Press, 2002.

Martinez, Tomás Eloy. "Trauma and Precision in Translation." In *Voice-Overs: Translation and Latin American Literature,* edited by Daniel Balderston and Marcy Schwartz, 61–63. Albany: State University of New York Press, 2002.

Marx, Karl. *The Communist Manifesto.* Harmondsworth, U.K.: Penguin, 1967.

———. *The Economic and Philosophic Manuscripts of 1844 and the Communist Manifesto.* New York: Prometheus Books, 1988.

Michaels, Walter Benn. "Diversity's False Solace." *New York Times Magazine,* April 11, 2004, 13.

Middleton, Richard. "Introduction." In *Reading Pop: Approaches to Textual Analysis in Popular Music,* 1–19. Oxford: Oxford University Press, 2000.

———. "Popular Music Analysis and Musicology: Bridging the Gap." In *Reading Pop: Approaches to Textual Analysis in Popular Music,* edited by Richard Middleton, 104–121. Oxford: Oxford University Press, 2000.

Mignolo, Walter D. *Local Histories/Global Designs: Coloniality, Subaltern Knowledges, and Border Thinking.* Princeton: Princeton University Press, 2000.

Mitchell, W. J. T. "Panic of the Visual." In *Edward Said and the Work of the Critic: Speaking Truth to Power,* edited by Paul Bové, 9–30. Durham: Duke University Press, 2000.

Mohanty, Satya. "The Epistemic Status of Cultural Identity: On *Beloved* and the Postcolonial Condition." *Cultural Critique* 24 (1993): 41–80.

Moll, Jorge, Roland Zahn, Ricardo de Oliveira-Souza, Frank Krueger, and Jordan Grafman. "The Neural Basis of Human Moral Cognition." *Nature* 6 (2005): 799–809.

Moya, Paula M. L. "Introduction: Reclaiming Identity." In *Reclaiming Identity: Realist Theory and the Predicament of Postmodernism,* edited by Paula M. L. Moya and Michael Hames-García, 1–28. Berkeley: University of California Press, 2000.

———. *Learning from Experience: Minority Identities, Multicultural Struggles.* Berkeley: University of California Press, 2002.

Mufti, Aamir R. "Global Comparativism." *Critical Inquiry* 31 (2005): 472–489.

Mukherjee, Sujit. "Publish or Perish." In *Translation Poetics and Practice,* edited by Anisur Rahman, 13–24. New Delhi: Creative Books, 2002.

Muñoz, José Esteban and Celeste Fraser Delgado, eds. *Everynight Life: Culture and Dance in Latin/o America.* Durham: Duke University Press, 1997.

Murphy, Gretchen. *Hemispheric Imaginings: The Monroe Doctrine and Narratives of U.S. Empire.* Durham: Duke University Press, 2005.

Myrsiades, Kostas, and Linda Myrsiades, eds. *Un-Disciplining Literature: Literature, Law, and Culture.* New York: Peter Lang, 2000.

Nabokov, Vladimir. "Problems of Translation: *Onegin* in English." *Partisan Review* 22, no. 4 (1955). Reprinted in *Theories of Translation: An Anthology of Essays from Dryden to Derrida,* edited by Rainer Schulte and John Biguenet, 127–143. Chicago: University of Chicago Press, 1992.

Nagappan, Ramu. *Suffering and South Asian Narratives.* Seattle: University of Washington Press, 2005.

Nara, Hiroshi, and Mari Noda. *Acts of Reading: Exploring Connections in Pedagogy of Japanese.* Honolulu: University of Hawaii Press, 2003.

Negrón-Muntaner, Frances. "Barbie's Hair: Selling Out Puerto Rican Identity in the Global Market." In *Latino/a Popular Culture,* edited by Michelle Habell-Pallán and Mary Romero, 38–57. New York: New York University Press, 2002.

Negus, Keith. *Popular Music in Theory: An Introduction.* Middletown: Wesleyan University Press, 1996.

New, Christopher. *Philosophy of Literature: An Introduction.* New York: Routledge, 1999.

Ngai, Sianne. *Ugly Feelings.* Cambridge: Harvard University Press, 2005.

Nietzsche, Friedrich. *On the Genealogy of Morals.* New York: Vintage Books, 1989.

———. *The Birth of Tragedy.* Oxford: Oxford University Press, 2000.

Nussbaum, Martha. *Poetic Justice: The Literary Imagination and Public Life.* Boston: Beacon, 1995.

Öhman, Arne. "Making Sense of Emotion: Evolution, Reason and the Brain." *Daedalus* (Summer 2006): 33–45.

Opitz, Andrea. "James Welch's *Fools Crow* and the Imagination of Precolonial Space: A Translator's Approach." *American Indian Quarterly* 24, no. 1 (2000): 126–142.

O'Rourke, James. *Sex, Lies and Autobiography: The Ethics of Confession.* Charlottesville: University of Virginia Press, 2006.

Palumbo-Liu, David. "The Morality of Form; or, What's 'Bad' About 'Bad Writing?'" In *Just Being Difficult? Academic Writing in the Public Arena,* edited by Jonathan Culler and Kevin Lamb, 171–180. Palo Alto: Stanford University Press, 2003.

Patton, Cindy. "Migratory Vices." In *Queer Diasporas,* edited by Cindy Patton and Benigno Sánchez-Eppler, 15–37. Durham, Duke University Press, 2000.

Patton, Cindy, and Benigno Sánchez-Eppler. "Introduction: With a Passport Out of Eden," In *Queer Diasporas,* edited by Cindy Patton and Benigno Sánchez-Eppler. Durham: Duke University Press, 2000.

Pavel, Thomas. "Fiction and Imitation." *Poetics Today* 21, no. 3 (2000): 521–541.

Phillips, Caryl. "The Insistence of Voices: An Interview with Caryl Phillips." *Ariel* 32, no. 2 (2001): 33–43.

Poddar, Prem. "Introduction: Violent Civilities." In *Translating Nations,* edited by Prem Poddar, 7–12. Oxford: Aarhus University Press, 2000.

Pollock, Sheldon, Homi K. Bhabha, Carol A. Breckenridge, and Dipesh Chakrabarty. "Cosmopolitanisms." *Public Culture* 12, no. 3 (2000): 577–589.

Poyner, Jane. "Truth and Reconciliation in J. M. Coetzee's *Disgrace.*" *Scrutiny 2: Issues in English Studies in South Africa* 5, no. 2 (2000): 67–77.

Pratt, Mary Louis. "The Anticolonial Past." *MLQ: Modern Language Quarterly* 65, no. 3 (2004): 443–456.

Pribram, Karl H. "A Century of Progress?" In *Neuroscience of the Mind on the Centennial of Freud's Project for a Scientific Psychology,* edited by Robert M. Bilder and F. Frank LeFever, Annals of the New York Academy of Sciences, volume 843, May 15, 1998, 11–19.

Priest, Dana. *The Mission: Waging War and Keeping Peace with America's Military.* New York: W. W. Norton, 2003.

Ramachandran, V. S. *A Brief Tour of Human Consciousness.* New York: PI Press, 2004.

Redfield, Peter. "Doctors, Borders, and Life in Crisis." *Cultural Anthropology* 20, no. 3 (2005): 328–361.

Reiss, Katherine. *Translation Criticism—The Potentials and Limitations.* Manchester: St. Jerome, 2000.

Reyna, José R. "Tejano Music as an Expression of Cultural Nationalism." In *Puro Conjunto: An Album in Words and Pictures,* 192–198. Austin: CMAS Books, 2001.

Reynolds, Simon. *Generation Ecstasy: Into the World of Techno and Rave Culture.* New York: Routledge, 1999.

Richardson, Elaine. *Hiphop Literacies.* New York: Routledge, 2006.

Rodríguez, Ana Patricia. "Encrucijadas: Rubén Blades at the Transnational Crossroads." In *Latino/a Popular Culture*, edited by Michelle Habell-Pallán and Mary Romero, 85–101. New York: New York University Press, 2002.

Rothberg, Robert I., and Dennis Thompson, eds. *Truth v. Justice: The Morality of Truth Commissions*. Princeton: Princeton University Press, 2000.

Russell, Bertrand. *Mortals and Others*. Volume 2: *American Essays, 1931–1935*. Edited by Harry Ruja. London: Routledge, 1998.

Rymer, R. *Genie: An Abused Child's Flight from Silence*. New York: Harper Collins, 1993.

Said, Edward. *Joseph Conrad and the Fiction of Autobiography*. Cambridge: Harvard University Press, 1966.

———. *Beginning: Intention and Method*. New York: Basic Books, 1975.

———. "Beginnings." Originally published in *Diacritics* 6, no. 3 (1976): 2–7. Reprinted in *Power, Politics, and Culture: Interviews with Edward W. Said*, edited by Gauri Viswanathan, 39–52. New York: Vintage, 2001.

———. "The Problem of Textuality: Two Exemplary Positions." *Critical Inquiry* 4, no. 4 (1978): 673–714.

———. *Orientalism*. New York: Vintage Books, 1979.

———. *The World, the Text, and the Critic*. Cambridge: Harvard University Press, 1983.

———. "Foucault and the Imagination of Power." In *Foucault: A Critical Reader*, edited by David Couzens Hoy, 149–155. Oxford: Blackwell, 1986.

———. *Representations of the Intellectual: The 1993 Reith Lectures*. New York: Pantheon Books, 1994.

———. *The Pen and the Sword: Conversations with David Baramian*. Monroe: Common Courage Press, 1994.

———. "Edward Said talks to Jacqueline Rose." In *Edward Said and the Work of the Critic: Speaking Truth to Power*, edited by Paul Bové, 9–30. Durham: Duke University Press, 2000.

———. "American Intellectual and Middle East Politics." Interview with Bruce Robbins. In *Power, Politics, and Culture: Interviews with Edward W. Said*, edited by Gauri Viswanathan, 323–342. New York: Vintage, 2001.

———. "Criticism and the Art of Politics." Interview with Jennifer Wicke and Michael Sprinker. In *Power, Politics, and Culture: Interviews with Edward W. Said*, edited by Gauri Viswanathan, 118–163. New York: Vintage, 2001.

———. "Culture and Imperialism." Interview with Joseph A. Buffigieg and Paul Bové. In *Power, Politics, and Culture: Interviews with Edward W. Said*, edited by Gauri Viswanathan, 183–207. New York: Vintage, 2001.

———. "An Exile's Exile." Interview with Matthew Stevenson. In *Power, Politics, and Culture: Interviews with Edward W. Said*, edited by Gauri Viswanathan, 313–322. New York: Vintage, 2001.

———. "The Intellectuals and the War." Interview with Barbara Harlow. In *Power, Politics, and Culture: Interviews with Edward W. Said*, edited by Gauri Viswanathan, 357–367. New York: Vintage, 2001.

———. "In the Shadows of the West." Interview with John Crary and Phil Mariani. In *Power, Politics, and Culture: Interviews with Edward W. Said,* edited by Gauri Viswanathan, 39–52. New York: Vintage, 2001.

———. "Orientalism and After." Interview with Anne Beezer and Peter Osborne. In *Power, Politics, and Culture: Interviews with Edward W. Said,* edited by Gauri Viswanathan, 208–232. New York: Vintage, 2001.

———. "Orientalism, Arab Intellectuals." Interview with Al Jahdid. In *Power, Politics, and Culture: Interviews with Edward W. Said,* edited by Gauri Viswanathan, 437–442. New York: Vintage, 2001.

———. "The Road Less Traveled." Interview with Nirmala Lakshman. In *Power, Politics, and Culture: Interviews with Edward W. Said,* edited by Gauri Viswanathan, 183–207. New York: Vintage, 2001.

———. "What the People in the U.S. Know About Islam Is a Stupid Cliché." Interview with Hasan Jafri. In *Power, Politics, and Culture: Interviews with Edward W. Said,* edited by Gauri Viswanathan, 368–384. New York: Vintage, 2001.

———. "Wild Orchids and Trotsky." Interview with Mark Edmundson. In *Power, Politics, and Culture: Interviews with Edward W. Said,* edited by Gauri Viswanathan, 164–182. New York: Vintage, 2001.

———. *Reflections on Exile and Other Essays.* Cambridge: Harvard University Press, 2002.

———. *Humanism and Democratic Criticism.* New York: Columbia University Press, 2004.

Saldaña-Portillo, María Josefina. *The Revolutionary Imagination in the Americas and the Age of Development.* Durham: Duke University Press, 2003.

Sandoval-Sánchez, Alberto. "Paul Simon's *The Capeman*: The Staging of Puerto Rican National Identity as Spectacle and Commodity on Broadway." In *Latino/a Popular Culture,* edited by Michelle Habell-Pallán and Mary Romero, 147–161. New York: New York University Press, 2002.

Sankey, Derek. "The Neuronal, Synaptic Self: Having Values and Making Choices." *Journal of Moral Education* 35, no. 2 (2006): 163–178.

Sartre, Jean-Paul. *Being and Nothingness.* New York: Washington Square Press, 1992.

Saunders, Frances Stonor. *Who Paid the Piper? The CIA and the Cultural Cold War.* New York: New Press, 1999.

Saussure, Ferdinand de. *Course in General Linguistics.* Edited by Charles Bally and Albert Reidlinger. Translated by Wade Baskin. New York: Philosophical Library, 1959.

Schaeffer, Jean-Marie. *Pourquoi la fiction?* Paris: Éditions du Seuil, 1999.

Schmitt, Carl. *The Theory of the Partisan: Commentary/Remark on the Concept of the Political.* Berlin: Duncker and Humboldt, 1963.

———. *Glossarium: Aufzeichnungen der Jahre 1947-1951.* Berlin: Duncker and Humboldt, 1991

———. *The Concept of the Political.* Chicago: University of Chicago Press, 1996.

Scholes, Robert. "Learning and Teaching." In *Profession* 2004, 118–127. New York: MLA, 2004.

——. *The Crafty Reader*. New Haven: Yale University Press, 2001.

Schwartz, Daniel. "A Humanistic Ethics of Reading." In *The Ethical Turn: A Reader in Ethics, Culture, and Literary Theory*, edited by Todd F. Davies and Kenneth Womack, 3–15. Charlottesville: University of Virginia Press, 2001.

Schuchardt, Mercer. "What is the Matrix?" In *Taking the Red Pill: Science, Philosophy and Religion in* The Matrix, edited by Glenn Yeffeth, 5–21. Dallas: BenBella Books, 2003.

Scott, David. *Conscripts of Modernity: The Tragedy of Colonial Enlightenment*. Durham: Duke University Press, 2005.

Searle, John. "Literary Theory and its Discontents." In *The Emperor Redressed: Critiquing Critical Theory*, edited by Dwight Eddins, 166–198. Tuscaloosa: University of Alabama Press, 1995.

Senghor, Léopold Sédar. "French, Language of Culture." In *Switching Languages: Translingual Writers Reflect on Their Craft*, edited by James Kellman, 35–41. Lincoln: University of Nebraska Press, 2003.

Serrano, Richard. *Against the Postcolonial: Francophone Writers and the Ends of the French Empire*. Lanham, MD: Lexington Books, 2005.

Shinn, Christopher A. "Fútbol Nation: U.S. Latinos and the Goal of a Homeland." In *Latino/a Popular Culture*, edited by Michelle Habell-Pallán and Mary Romero, 240–251. New York: New York University Press, 2002.

Shuker, Roy. *Understanding Popular Music*. New York: Routledge, 1994.

Simon, Sherry. *Gender in Translation: Cultural Identity and the Politics of Transmission*. New York: Routledge, 1996.

Simonelli, Thierry. "La magie de Lacan. Une récréation mathématique." In *Ethique et épistémologie autour du livre Impostures Intellectuelles de Sokal et Bricmont*, edited by Angèle Kremer Marietti, 227–241. Paris: L'Harmattan, 2001.

Sokal, Alan. "Transgressing the Boundaries: Toward a Transformative Hermeneutics of Quantum Gravity." *Social Text* 46–47 (1996): 217–252.

——. "A Physicist Experiments with Cultural Studies: A Confession." In *Quick Studies: The Best of Lingua Franca*, edited by Alexander Star, 3–9. New York: Farrar Straus and Giroux, 2002.

Sokol, Neal. "Translation and its Discontents." In *Ilan Stavans: Eight Conversations*, 78–98. Madison: University of Wisconsin Press, 2004.

Sommer, Doris. *Proceed with Caution When Engaged by Minority Writing in the Americas*. Cambridge: Harvard University Press, 1999.

——, ed. "Introduction." In *Bilingual Games: Some Literary Investigations*. New York: Palgrave, 2003.

——. *Bilingual Aesthetic: A New Sentimental Education*. Durham: Duke University Press, 2004.

Sosale, Sujatha. "Review of *Empire*." *Rhetoric and Public Affairs* 5, no. 4 (2002): 782–785.

Sperber, Dan. *Relevance: Communication and Cognition.* Oxford: Blackwell, 1995.

Spivak, Gayatri. "Poststructuralism, Marginality, Postcoloniality, and Value." In *Literary Theory Today,* edited by Peter Collier and Helga Geyer-Ryan, 219–244. Ithaca: Cornell University Press, 1990.

———. *Outside the Teaching Machine.* New York: Routledge, 1993.

———. *Death of a Discipline.* New York: Columbia University Press, 2003.

———. "The Politics of the Production of Knowledge." In *Just Being Difficult? Academic Writing in the Public Arena,* edited by Jonathan Culler and Kevin Lamb, 181–198. Stanford: Stanford University Press, 2003.

———. "Righting Wrongs." In *Human Rights, Human Wrongs: The Oxford Amnesty Lectures 2001,* edited by Nicholas Owen, 164–227. Oxford: Oxford University Press, 2003.

Spurgeon, Sara L. *Exploding the Western: Myths of Empire on the Postmodern Frontier.* College Station: Texas A&M University Press, 2005.

Stamenov, Maxim I., and Vittorio Gallese. "Mirror Neurons and the Evolution of Brain and Language." *Advances in Consciousness.* Volume 42. 2002.

Stavans, Ilan. "Beyond Translation: Borges and Faulkner." *Michigan Quarterly Review* 40, no. 4 (2001): 628–639.

Steiner, George. *Lessons of the Masters.* Cambridge: Harvard University Press, 2003.

Steen, Francis. "Introduction to Cognitive Cultural Studies." www.sscnet.ucla.edu/comm/steen/cogweb/Debate/Introduction.html

Sterne, Richard Clarke. "The Trial in *A Passage to India*: 'Justice' Under Colonial Conditions." In *Un-Disciplining Literature: Literature, Law, and Culture,* edited by Kostas Myrsiades and Linda Myrsiades, 206–218. New York: Peter Lang, 1999.

Stokes, Doug. *America's Other War: Terrorizing Colombia.* London: Zed Books, 2005.

Storey, Robert. *Mimesis and the Human Animal: On the Biogenetic Foundations of Literary Representation.* Evanston: Northwestern University Press, 1996.

Stratton, Florence. "Imperial Fictions: J. M. Coetzee's *Disgrace.*" *Ariel: A Review of International English Literature* 33, nos. 3–4 (2002): 83–104.

Sugiyama, Michelle Scalise. "Narrative Theory and Function: Why Evolution Matters." *Philosophy and Literature* 25, no. 2 (2001): 233–250.

Tagg, Philip. "Open Letter: 'Black Music,' 'Afro-American Music,' and 'European Music.'" *Popular Music* 8, no. 3 (1989): 285–298.

———. "Analyzing Popular Music: Theory, Method, Practice." In *Reading Pop: Approaches to Textual Analysis in Popular Music,* 71–103. Oxford: Oxford University Press, 2000.

Taylor, Timothy. *Strange Sounds: Music, Technology, and Culture.* New York: Routledge, 2001.

Tejada, Juan, and Avelardo Valdez. *Puro Conjunto: An Album in Words and Pictures.* Austin: CMAS Books, 2001.

Tenorio Trillo, Mauricio. "Essaying the History of National Images." In *After Span-*

ish Rule: Postcolonial Predicaments of the Americas, edited by Mark Thurner and Andrés Guerrero, 58–87. Durham: Duke University Press, 2003.

Tharu, Susi, and K. Lalita. *Women Writing in India.* New York: Feminist Press, 1991.

Thurner, Mark, and Andrés Guerrero. *After Spanish Rule: Postcolonial Predicaments of the Americas.* Durham: Duke University Press, 2003.

Tonme, Jean-Claude Shanda. "All Rock, No Action." *New York Times,* July 15, 2005, A21.

Trimble, Michael R. *The Soul in the Brain: The Cerebral Basis of Language, Art, and Belief.* Baltimore: The Johns Hopkins University Press, 2007.

Tsur, Reuven. "Some Cognitive Foundations of Cultural Programs." *Poetics Today* 23, no. 1 (2002): 63–89.

Turner, Mark. *The Literary Mind: The Origins of Thought and Language.* New York: Oxford University Press, 1996.

Tymoczko, Maria. "Post-colonial Writing and Literary Translation." In *Post-colonial Translation: Theory and Practice,* 19–40. New York: Routledge, 1999.

Tyrangiel, Josh. "The New Tijuana Brass." *New York Times* 157, no. 23 (June 11, 2001): 76–78.

Van Oort, Richard. "Cognitive Science and the Problem of Representation." *Poetics Today* 24, no. 2 (2003): 237–295.

Velasco, Juan. "Performing Multiple Identities, Guillermo Gómez-Peña and His 'Dangerous Border Crossings.'" In *Latino/a Popular Culture,* edited by Michelle Habell-Pallán and Mary Romero, 208-221. New York: New York University Press, 2002.

Venuti, Lawrence. *Rethinking Translation: Discourse, Subjectivity, Ideology.* New York: Routledge, 1992.

———. *The Translator's Invisibility: A History of Translation.* New York: Routledge, 1995.

———. *The Scandals of Translation.* New York: Routledge, 1998.

———. *The Translation Studies Reader.* New York: Routledge, 2004.

Vian, Boris. *L'ecume des jours.* Paris: Club Francais du Livre, 1965.

Vigil, James Diego. *Barrio Gang: Street Life and Identity in Southern California.* Austin: University of Texas Press, 1988.

———. *A Rainbow of Gangs: Street Cultures in the Mega-City.* Austin: University of Texas Press, 2002.

Viswanathan, Gauri. "Introduction." In *Power, Politics, and Culture: Interviews with Edward W. Said,* edited by Gauri Viswanathan, ix–xxi. New York: Vintage, 2001.

Wa Thiong'O, Ngugi. "Imperialism of Language: English, a Language for the World?" In *Switching Languages: Translingual Writers Reflect on Their Craft,* edited by James Kellman, 169–181. Lincoln: University of Nebraska Press, 2003.

———. "For Peace, Justice, and Culture: The Intellectual in the Twenty-First Century." *Profession* 2006, 33–39.

Wachowski, Andy, and Larry Wachowski. *The Matrix*. Los Angeles: Warner Studios, 1999.

Wade, Nicholas. *Before the Dawn: Recovering the Lost History of Our Ancestors*. New York: Penguin Press, 2006.

Wagner, Emma, and Andrew Chesterman. *Can Theory Help Translators? A Dialogue between the Ivory Tower and the Wordface*. Manchester: St. Jerome, 2002.

Wain, Martin. *Freud's Answer: The Social Origins of our Psychoanalytic Century*. Chicago: Ivan R. Dee, 1998.

Walker, Margaret Urban. "Moral Repair and Its Limits." In *The Ethical Turn: A Reader in Ethics, Culture, and Literary Theory*, edited by Todd F. Davies and Kenneth Womack, 110–127. Charlottesville: University of Virginia Press, 2001.

Webster, Bruce. "Fewer Noses Stuck in Books in America, Survey Finds." *New York Times*, July 8, 2004, B1–B4.

Weil, Simone. *La pesanteur et la grace*. Paris: Union generale d'editions, 1962.

Weiss, Timothy. *Translating Orients: Between Ideology and Utopia*. Toronto: University of Toronto Press, 2004.

West, Cornel. *Democracy Matters: Winning the Fight Against Imperialism*. New York: Penguin, 2004.

Wexler, Bruce E. *Brain and Culture: Neurobiology, Ideology, and Social Change*. Cambridge: MIT Press, 2006.

Whitfield, John. "Textual Selection: Can Reading the Classics through Charles Darwin's Spectacles Reawaken Literary Study?" *Nature* 439, no. 26 (2006): 388–389.

Williams, Gareth. *The Other Side of the Popular: Neoliberalism and Subalternity in Latin America*. Durham: Duke University Press, 2002.

Williams, Raymond. *Culture*. Cambridge, U.K.: Fontana Paperbacks, 1981.

———. *Keywords: A Vocabulary of Culture and Society*. London: Fontana, 1988.

Wolin, Richard. *The Seduction of Unreason*. Princeton: Princeton University Press, 2004.

Wood, Ellen Meiksins. "Unhappy Families: Global Capitalism in a World of Nation-states." *Monthly Review* 51, no. 3 (July-August 1999): 1–12.

———. "A Manifesto for Global Capital?" In *Debating Empire*, edited by Gopal Balakrishnan, 61–82. London: Verso, 2003.

Woolgar, Steve. "On the Alleged Distinction Between Discourse and Praxis." *Social Studies of Science* 16, no. 2 (1986): 309–317.

Wyszpolski, Bondo. "An Interview with Gregory Rabassa." *News for Brazil* 5, no. 97 (1994): 31.

Young, Robert. "The Linguistic Turn, Materialism and Race: Toward an Aesthetics of Crisis." *Callaloo* 24, no. 1 (2001): 334–345.

Zuckert, Catherine. "The Politics of Derridean Deconstruction." *Polity* 23, no. 3 (1991): 335–356.

Zunshine, Lisa. "Theory of Mind and Experimental Representations of Fictional Consciousness." *Narrative* 11, no. 3 (2003): 270–291.

INDEX

Hill, Joe, 68

Hindenburg, Paul von, 318n16

hip-hop. *See* rap/hip-hop

Hiraldo, Carlos, 312n2

Hirsch, E. D., 113

history: Constructivist theory of, 78; factors theory of, 301n15; Foucault's archeological history, 39–41, 284–285n13, 296n23; Hegel on, 56–57, 285n16; Nietzsche on, 37; Said on, 78–79, 82

History in Literature (Lindenberger), 113–116

History of Madness (Foucault), 34

History of Sexuality (Foucault), 35, 40–41, 285n14

History's Shadow (Conn), 292n2

Hitchcock, Peter, 127

Hitler, Adolf, 221–222, 295n17, 300n7, 318n16

Hobbes, Thomas, 217–218, 295n17, 318n14

Hobomok (Child), 292n2

Hogan, Patrick Colm: on author-as-reader, 241–242; on cognitive science, 262; on ethical excellence, 255; on fiction making, 323n15; on genres of literature, 249–251; on literature-as-law, 230; on memory and emotions, 244, 248–249, 262; on multiculturalists and curriculum, 91; on paradigm stories, 143, 242, 250–251, 322n9; on poetry, 252; and politics versus intellectual inquiry, 303n9; on romantic union, 250; on Said, 81–82, 293n5; on schemas, 243, 269; scholarship of generally, xi; on Theory of Mind, 321–322n5; on types of substructure within lexical item, 241

Holsinger, Bruce, 286n1

Homer, 139, 285n16

Hoover, J. Edgar, 317n12

Hopenhayn, Martín, 95, 103, 201–202, 208–210

Hopscotch (Cortázar), 325n2

Horton, John, 235, 253–255

house/techno, 311n11

How Novels Think (Armstrong), 281n11

How To Do Things with Words (Austin), 285n15

Hull, 187

Human Rights, Human Wrongs, 111

humanism, Derrida's critique of, 50–51, 55, 288n12, 291n24

Humanism and Democratic Criticism (Bové), 298n35

humanitarianism, 110–111, 188–189, 303n8

humanities: definition of, 266; and disciplinarity, 270–274; and interdisciplinarity, 265–270, 273, 274–277. *See also* humanities scholar/intellectuals; literature

humanities scholar/intellectuals: active push for equality by, 107–108; and class struggle, 118–119; of color, 109–110, 113, 116; criteria for university faculty, 275–276; as cultural workers, 111–112, 267–268; and culture wars of 1980s, 112–114, 115, 302n2; and current crisis in theory, 265–277; and democratic classroom, 268, 273, 324–325n2; and disciplinarity, 270–274; esoteric formulations of resistance by, 107, 279; function of teachers of literature, 270–277; and humanitarian relief, 110–111, 303n8; independent scholar/intellectuals, 119–120, 303n9; and intellectual freedom, 121–122; and interdisciplinarity, 265–270, 273, 274–277; and mandarins for capitalism, 111–112, 114–119; and obscure and difficult writing, 58–59; political

postcolonialism (*continued*)
on, 324n1; Spivak on postcolonial
as translated body, 304n5; Tenorio
Trillo on nationalism and, 199–200
Postethnic Narrative Criticism
(Aldama), 261
postmodern theory, 209–210
postpositivism, 217, 316n10
poststructuralism: and cultural studies,
178–179, 185; De la Campa on, 197;
in France, 178; and globalization,
195; Hopenhayn on, 208–209; and
Idealism, xiii; and Latin American
literature, 195, 197; and magical
realism, 313n4; Mignolo on, 195; and
postcolonialism, ix, 204; and postpositivism, 316n10; Woolgar on, 206;
and world-as-text theory, 206–207
Poulet, George, 76, 293n8
Pour quoi la fiction? (Schaeffer), 235
Powell, Colin, 116, 117
power: Bérubé on, 109; of bourgeoisie,
66; Foucault on, 39–40, 83, 295n14,
295n17; resistance and, 66; Said on,
82–84, 295n17, 298n34
Power, Politics, and Culture (Said),
75, 77, 78, 79, 80, 87, 292n3, 294n13,
297n25
pragmatic linguistics, 272
pragmatic pluralism, 268
Pragmatist Realism (Ludwig), 236
Pratt, Mary Louise, 94, 103
*The Prayers and Tears of Jacques Der-
rida* (Caputo), 287n10
prehistory. *See* Stone Age; Upper Paleolithic era
The Premodern Condition (Holsinger),
286n1
Pretty Vacant, 174
Pribram, Karl H., 283n5
Priest, Dana, 70
Princeton University, 109
The Prison Notebooks (Gramsci), 81

prisoners and prison intellectuals, 216,
217, 223, 231, 232, 315n7, 316nn11–12
Private Topographies (Grzegorczyk), 95
Proceed with Caution (Sommer),
192–194
Profession, 106, 265–267, 274, 275–276,
302n1
"Project for a Scientific Psychology"
(Freud), 20–21, 22
proletariat. *See* working class
Proust, Marcel, 247, 255, 260
Psyché (Derrida), 287n10
psychoanalysis: of Freud, 20–24, 30, 33,
282–283nn2–9; of Lacan, 29–33, 36
Public Culture, 109
Public Enemy, 309n3
publishing, 131–132, 145–146, 275
Puerto Rican Barbie doll, 168, 174–177
Puerto Rican hip-hop, 176

Queer Aztlán, 207
queer culture, 174, 309n3, 310n6
Quevedo, Francisco de, 284n12

Rabassa, Gregory, 124, 132, 134, 143
Rabelais, François, 101
racial/ethnic identity, 13–14, 16
A Rainbow of Gangs (Vigil), 169, 182–183
Rama, Angel, 198
Ramachandran, V. S., 5, 281n9
Ramón y Cajal, Santiago, 22, 283n6
rap/hip-hop, 147, 160, 176, 308–309n1
Rawls, John, 64
Reading Pop (Middleton), 161
Reagan, Ronald, 107, 114, 179, 302n2
reality principle, 21–22, 23, 33, 282n3
Rechy, John, 273–274
Reckless Minds (Lila), 318n16
Reclaiming Identity (Moya and Hames-
García), 316n10
Red Matters (Krupat), 292n2
Redfield, Peter, 110, 111
referent, 185